Seth's Broadway Diary

Volume 1

By
Seth Rudetsky

Dress Circle Publishing
New York

Dress Circle Publishing
Brisa Trinchero/Roberta Pereira
New York, New York
www.dresscirclepublishing.com

Introduction
October 22, 2014

Hello, Broadway lovers and/or people sifting through old books at a yard sale! I'm delighted you have my book, which is basically my very public diary. I feel like I should first tell you who I am, not only to give you some context for what you're reading, but also to fill my constantly anxiety-producing word count. My name is Seth Rudetsky and I grew up loving Broadway: listening to records every day, going to TKTS with my parents for tickets, performing in my school shows and taking scores out of the library and playing them on the piano. Even though I knew Broadway would be my career, I wound up getting a classical piano degree (!) from the Oberlin Conservatory and hoped to parlay that into playing in Broadway orchestras. Thankfully, it worked. I moved to New York and played for lots of shows like *Les Miz*, *Phantom* and *Ragtime*. I also did lots of sketch comedy and stand-up on the side. In 1997, I became a comedy writer on the *The Rosie O'Donnell Show* and got to write two opening numbers for her when she hosted the Tony Awards.

I really wanted to get back to performing onstage and wound up writing and starring in a one-person-show in 2003 called *Rhapsody in Seth,* which got me my first agent. I did a round of interviews to promote the show and one of them was on Sirius radio. Mike Peters, who ran the Broadway channel, heard my interview and hired me to host a daily Broadway music show which became *Seth's Big Fat Broadway.* Now, I divide my time between the radio show, writing books and shows (like my upcoming Broadway show *Disaster!*), doing *Seth's Broadway Chatterbox* and *Seth Speaks* where I interview Broadway stars each week, and touring the country with my show *Deconstructing Broadway* as well as doing concerts with Broadway ladies like Sutton Foster, Patti LuPone and Megan Mullally and posting them on my website, SethRudetsky.com.

Now, back to this book. It all began in 2007. Well, actually, it all began in 1994 when the Weisslers decided to revive *Grease!* starring Rosie O'Donnell and I played in the pit band off and on for years. Then, years later, another revival of *Grease* was planned, but this time the casting process was going to be done via TV. In January of 2007, NBC ran a weekly reality show called *You're The One That I Want* where the public voted on who would be the new Danny and Sandy. Because I'd already written the book *The Q Guide To Broadway* and my second book, *Broadway Nights,* was about to be published *and* I'd played the song "Summer Nights" around 1,000 times on Broadway, I was asked by Andrew Gans to write a weekly recap of the show for Playbill.com. It wound up being a really fun job and I loved putting my spin on the many mind-boggling aspects of that show (i.e. having Austin audition for Danny by singing and bustin' a move to "Ease On Down The Road").

Anyhoo, when the reality show went off the air, I was very pleased to receive an email from Andrew asking me to continue writing the column. But about what? Max Crumm and Laura Osnes were already chosen to star in *Grease*. Well, since basically everything I do is connected to Broadway (which I first fell in love with in 2nd grade when I saw the mid-'70s revival of *The Pajama Game*), I was given *carte blanche* to write about whatever the h*ll happened each week! So, this book is a weekly journal of my Broadway life; it's chock full of seeing Broadway shows like the closing night of *Rent* or the night Jeff Bowen was dragged off the stage during *[title of show]* or the night I saw *Spring Awakening* and helped Jonathan Groff and Lea Michele break (-ish) the law...plus, inside scoop on what it's like performing with tons of fantastic stars like Rosie Perez, Andrea McArdle and Betty Buckley as well as hi-larious stories about Patti LuPone, Raúl Esparza, Lea Michele, Chita Rivera, Norbert Leo Butz, Matthew Morrison, Sherie Rene Scott and *many* more, straight from their yaps! Note: as you read it, make sure you have your iTunes and Youtube.com browsers open at all times to watch/listen to the performances I reference.

I re-read all my columns before this book was published and I wanted to make some extra comments. So, every time you see this kind of writing, it's me in 2014 adding my two cents!

And, finally, after editing this book I realized I'm *constantly* talking about my weight. Let it be known I'm not morbidly obese...in the real world. But by Broadway standards, I should be wearing a muumuu that covers a pair of stretch pants featuring a pregnancy patch. Basically, Broadway folk live by different rules...and those rules don't include non-stop bowls of cereal at 11 PM.

All right, go read about Broadway!

- Seth Rudetsky

Betty, Charlotte, Shayna and *Carrie*!

April 3, 2007

There is a hole in my heart. A hole that can only be filled with a heavily padded two-hour reality series casting a Broadway show. There is an age-old question that our philosophers have been asking since the days of Socrates and/or the initial *Real World* episodes: How do you cope when your reality series goes off the air?

I've had to deal with the debilitating loss of *Pop Stars*, *Fight for Fame*, and *Showbiz Moms and Dads*, but ne'er has a reality show gotten so close to my true love: Broadway. And by "close," I mean throughout the run of *Grease: You're the One That I Want*, the word "Broadway" was spoken of up to a dozen times, but it was basically *American Idol* featuring two Ryan Seacrests.

All right, I'm going to move on emotionally. No more living in the reality show past. Instead I'm going to talk about my week, latest obsessions and recent gossip, AKA anything and everything Broadway!

Monday was a fantastic benefit produced by Amy Birnbaum and held at Joe's Pub for Family First Nights, an organization that brings inner-city kids to Broadway. How sad is it that some kids live in New York City and haven't ever been to a Broadway show? Think of that 15-year-old kid who, for some reason, never got to see *Metro, Chu Chem* or the two-month run of that Jackie Mason musical. What an incredible loss! The benefit featured Broadway folk rocking out to traditional Broadway songs. It was called *Scream Out, Louise* and, in reality, should have been titled *Riff Out, Louise*, but apparently that copyright is owned by *Brooklyn, the Musical*. I co-hosted with Scott Nevins, and it was a ton of fun even though his body fat is the same as mine but with the decimal point moved before the first number.

Tuesday, I flew to L.A. to interview/play for the amazing beltress Shayna Steele from *Hairspray*. We performed for a group of travel agents and stayed at the beautiful Hotel Bel-Air where I noticed that one of the salads in the restaurant was named after Nancy Reagan. Remembering back to the time she was in the White House, I decided to "just say no" to her namesake and instead ordered a delish lobster salad on brioche. And for all those people who've eaten meals with me, just know that I'm only vegetarian and Kosher when I can use it to make someone else feel bad.

Wednesday, I returned to New York and really started working on *Seth's Broadway 101*. That title is not only my goal weight, but also a show I'm putting together for The Actors Fund of America featuring a delicious singing and dancing ensemble, some of my favorite Broadway stars (because of my tastes, sopranos are limited to Laura Benanti and Kristin Chenoweth) and a full orchestra. And I mean full. At least 25!

Thursday was my *Chatterbox*, and I interviewed the beautiful and warm Charlotte d'Amboise. First of all, for all you people who think you have a cool accent and have always pronounced it "Dam-bwah," it's time to realize that the "s" is pronounced because her name ends in an "e." Please work on your French. Or in the spirit of the U.S. Senate in 2002, please work on your "freedom."

Of course, I obsessively talked about her experience in *Carrie*, and she confirmed what I had heard. Here's the background — The story of *Carrie* is so scary because it takes place in a typical high school in Anytown USA... sort of like *Grease*. Someone said that very sentence to the director, Terry Hands, and he agreed immediately... but the person telling the director didn't realize *Grease* is a homonym. So, instead of the set looking like a typical high school and the kids wearing clothes from a rack at the mall, the costumes and sets represented... Greece! Seriously! All white costumes, big white columns, etc. Yet, if you've ever heard any of the *Carrie* music, you'd know that it's a great score that was brilliantly sung by Betty Buckley, which brings me to the weekend. I got to hang with one of my favorite beltresses, Betty Buckley!

I went to Betty's hotel (she's doing a new show at Feinstein's at the Regency) to do a video interview with her. All I can say is, if I knew when I was in college that I would one day be hanging out with Betty in her hotel room, I would have fainted on the worn grooves of my *The Mystery of Edwin Drood* album. We gabbed up a storm, but the interview was only supposed to be 20 minutes, so a great story about her early chutzpah was edited out. Here it is.

Betty told me that she had tried out in New York for the lead in the London production of *Promises, Promises* and she clanked. She picked the song "Go While The Going Is Good," which has difficult rhythm changes that she messed up, *and* she didn't understand how to act the character (she was only 21). However, she knew she could do it if she worked on it. She was starring in *1776* at the time, where she had one big number in the first act and then didn't have to come back onstage until her bow. So, the night after the audition, she asked her dresser to take off her dress (which took 15 minutes because it had a million layers and little laces), and Betty ran to the theatre where *Promises, Promises* was playing in New York. She went to the stage door, found the stage manager and immediately burst into tears. She begged him to help her. He agreed to coach her on the character. Her agent pulled strings and got her a callback!

She went back in and this time felt she did *much* better. As she was walking out of the theatre where the callback was held (old school), the stage manager ran down the alley and told her to come back to do the whole thing again for the producer, David Merrick! She later found out that they wanted her to do it again, not so much for Merrick, but to see if her recent audition wasn't a fluke. She finished, went to her agent's office to say that it went well, and as she was walking to the elevator, the secretary ran down the hall to tell her that she got the part.

The moral is, if you believe you're right for something, work every angle you have to get a chance to prove it. And if all else fails, find a stage manager and burst into tears. He'll help you get the gig and/or an emergency prescription for anti-depressants.

My Sunday night was spent seeing the brilliant singer Marilyn Maye at the lovely Metropolitan Room. She has the nerve to be in her seventies and still sound *amazing*! *And* be hilarious! *Now in her mid-eighties and still got it!* On my way in, I ran into Christine Ebersole, who had gone to the early show. Christine stopped me and told me that she wants to come on my radio show. Wow! I had always wanted to interview her but thought she was too busy, so I had been getting ready to stalk her stage manager while crying hysterically. Phew!

Well, I'm off to start my week...

Monk, McArdle, Danieley and *The Ritz*
April 10, 2007

First of all, I totally forgot to tell you about Sunday *morning*. I did a little tiny reading of Terrence McNally's *The Ritz* at the Roundabout. And I mean we literally just read it. *The Ritz* is a 1970s play about a man on the run from the mob who hides out in a gay bathhouse. The Roundabout reading starred Kevin Chamberlin as the man on the run, Brooks Ashmanskas as the bathhouse slut and Rosie Perez as Googie Gomez, the Latin singer who can't sing. When I was first called to do it, I went from completely thrilled I'd have a funny role to terrified that I was being asked to read stage directions. We all know that job is thankless. Your lines consist of "Lights up" and "He exits" and "End of Act One." I knew that I would have tried to add subtext and been boycotted from reading Act Two.

Thankfully the director, Joe Mantello, got someone else for the stage directions and cast me in multiple roles. I don't want to overly impress you, but I ran the gamut from "patron" to "snobby patron" to "patron." I had up to and including five lines. But it was very cool to be asked to do it. I felt like a true theatre insider! Speaking of which, Michael Riedel mentioned me in his column about the *Grease* reality show and said I was the only theatre insider who was watching. I was actually very excited to be called a theatre insider in print! But I would like to say, for the record, there is at least one more.

Three weeks ago I got a frantic cell phone call from a one Mr. Jonathan Groff from *Spring Awakening*. He had neglected to TiVO that week's episode and seemed more devastated from that than from the aftermath of when his character whips Lea Michele with a switch. I had the episode still on my TV and quickly made him a VCR copy. *Talk about old school!* My point is, there were at least two theatre insiders watching the *Grease* show — three, if you count Kathleen Marshall.

Onto Monday. I went to my mom's house for the first Seder with James (my new boyfriend) and David Friedman. David is a brilliant composer/lyricist ("Help Is On the Way") and a raconteur extraordinaire. He told me a story of when he conducted a Broadway show, and the sound designer put the leading lady on a "limiter" — meaning that the sound level never got above a certain level during the Act One finale. During intermission she called the sound guy to her room and complained that she was belting her brains out, but never got the big sound she wanted. He said that he had put her on a limiter so she didn't overpower the chorus. She screamed, "I don't give a (bleep) about the (bleeping) chorus!"... and, unfortunately, didn't realize her body mic was still on. So her comment was broadcast to the dressing rooms of the very people she just claimed she didn't give a (bleep) about. I'm sure it was very comfortable on and offstage from then on.

Tuesday was the second Seder night, which I spent with my family, my boyfriend James, Paul Castree and his boyfriend (company manager Stephen Spadaro). Paul and I did *Forever Plaid* together and I'll never forget the one night during the song "Matilda" when he completely forgot the lyrics. Instead of "Matilda... come and sing along now, Matilda... help me sing this song now," he sang, "Matilda... sing it everybody (*Uh-oh!* He thought, *Must make the next section rhyme...*), Matilda... uh-duh, uh-duh, uh-dee!" It sounds crazy, but because he totally committed to it, it sort of worked.

On Wednesday, James and I saw a matinee of *Curtains*. I called Debra Monk that Monday to do my *Chatterbox* and she sounded *awful* and said she was really sick. I was expecting to see an understudy on Wednesday but instead I got Debra, slaying 'em in the aisles. As my friend Peter Flynn says, chalk it up to "Dr. Theatre." You can be sick as a dog, but once those stage lights hit ya, you're suddenly in perfect health! And then you collapse offstage. Brava!

I was totally obsessed with Patty Goble, who plays the no-talent movie star in *Curtains*, who has the lead in the musical within the musical. She's *hilarious*! That's the kind of show I would see over and over again just to see that first number where she stinks up the stage.

Wednesday night, James, Stephen and I saw the brilliant Betty Buckley at Feinstein's. Attention producers: Bring her back to Broadway... ASAP! After the show, we hung out in her Feinstein's suite, and she told us that when she first did *1776*, she didn't know anything about anything and, for some reason, thought she had to to wear dark make-up onstage. Also, even though Betty was a blonde, they had put her in a super-dark wig. Well, it was the first preview, and she was doing her first moment in the show, which is when her back is to the audience and she suddenly turns and her face appears in a window. Most of the rest of the cast were older men, and she is supposed to look youthful and fresh-faced and innocent. Well, she said that when she showed her face, the audience wasn't thinking "youthful" and "fresh-faced." Instead, they were thinking, "Gasp! *That's* what happened to Baby Jane!" Suffice it to say, the producers got her a lighter wig and fixed her makeup the next night to prevent any premature heart attacks in the audience.

Thursday was my *Chatterbox* with Jason Danieley. He and his wife are the couple with the most mispronounced names. For the record, his last name is pronounced like the name Daniel with an "ee" at the end. And her first name is pronounced Marin, not "Marion," and her last name is Mazzie, like May-Zee, not Ma-zzie. On a related note, I'm still miffed as to why ker-nel is spelled "colonel" and Shar-day is spelled "Sade," but that is irrelevant at this moment.

Jason talked about doing *The Full Monty* on Broadway and one particular devastating night. Normally, at the moment when the cast finally takes it all off, the audience is blinded by a giant *Full Monty* sign so they really can't see any "business." Well, the actors realized as the song went on that the computer had malfunctioned and the light cues were one ahead! So, instead of the blinding light cue that normally happens during the nudity, they realized they'd be disrobing in the full stage light cue for the bows. Jason remembers being mortified.

When I interviewed Patrick Wilson he, too, remembered the horrible moment when he realized he was going to be nude in full light. At the very moment before the final disrobe he uncomfortably locked eyes with a 12-year-old girl in the third row... and then was forced to demonstrate to her what the words "Full Monty" meant. Ah! First he was devastated and then enraged at her parents, thinking, "Why the H did they bring a 12-year-old girl to this show?"

Jason also talked about the brilliant performance of Kathleen Freeman and how the whole time she was doing the show, not only was she in her eighties, but she was going through radiation for lung cancer. He said that no one in the cast knew, they just thought that offstage she had less energy than onstage. I used to sub in the pit, and I can vouch that in every scene, she was *always* at full sass. I don't remember her ever missing a performance or laugh line. Talk about Dr. Theatre!

This weekend was dedicated to getting ready for my Actors Fund show, *Seth's Broadway 101*. I had the hilarious Charles Busch at my apartment as well as Andrea McArdle. Why has she never been the lead in *Mamma Mia!*? She'd sound amazing! She told me that all the original *Annie* orphans are having a 30-year reunion. Did you hear that? Thirty years! Mark your calendars: Winter 2037. 30-year reunion of *Spring Awakening*.

Andrea also said that "Maybe" had been put in a high key because Annie didn't wear a body mic, but she never understood how the littlest orphan could have her head in Annie's lap and been soothed to sleep by "Maybe far a-*waaaaaaay*" belted on a high D#.

I'm now starting my big week of rehearsals leading up to *Broadway 101* and hoping that the dancing I'm doing will counteract the delicious bowl of Waffle Crisps I'm eating. And yes, I'm busted, because it's so *not* Kosher for Passover... but c'mon, fellow Israelites, I'm stressed!

Broadway 101
April 18, 2007

Hey, everyone! Last Monday was the first rehearsal for *Seth's Broadway 101*. The show describes to the audience how Broadway works (what is a vocal arranger, orchestrator, swing, etc.) with live examples. At the first rehearsal, Devanand Janki, the choreographer, staged the dance segments. The first thing he did was the section about swings. If you don't know, swinging on Broadway is not the same thing as swinging in the movie *The Ice Storm*. ('70s key party? Anybody?) "To swing" means to understudy the ensemble. Usually one man for all the guys in the chorus and one woman for all the ladies. I wanted to show the audience how the swing has to be ready to go on at a moment's notice *and* how terrifying it is to go on for the first time. So in order to create theatre vérité, I made myself the swing. Have I ever swung before? No. Would they ever hire a swing whose leg extension is in the early double digits (39 degrees)? No. But I knew it would be exciting for the audience to see real fear and profuse sweating.

Anyhoo, Dev staged the number and apparently it's not good for your body to take dance class in college, take 20 years off, and then dance again full out. Let's just say, after that rehearsal I was only physically able to swing the role of Madame Armfeldt.

The more dances I learned, the more I realized how hard it is to be a gypsy on Broadway. I'm used to music directing and yelling at the cast to cut off on beat three-and-a-half. I didn't realize that you have no time to think about cutoffs when your lower body is doing one thing, your torso is doing another, your head is facing is one direction and you *still* have to think about minutiae like where your focus is (Dev was always yelling things like, "First look at the orchestra seats... then lift your eyes to the balcony"). There was no way I could sing and do all that, so after this week I must ask Ashlee Simpson to move over, because I am now the king of lip-synching. If all the body mics had cut out during the show except for mine, you'd have seen my mouth moving but heard only a stream of air coming out of my yap that was very similar to heavy breathing. How do people sing and dance at the same time? I couldn't even inflate my lungs. Hats off to gypsies everywhere!

Monday night, I saw the brilliant Kristine Zbornik's show at the Metropolitan Room. She is so unbelievably funny, yet is also able to belt Es. She brought down the house by just saying simply, "Antonio Banderas' cologne is sold *exclusively* at Walgreens." I'm also obsessed with her version of "Some People": "There I was in Mr. Orpheum's orifice... and he was saying to me, 'ARGH!!!!'" (followed by uncomfortable grunts).

Tuesday was more rehearsal and the day I found out how much I owed for taxes. Most jobs I have don't take out money, so I owe it all at the end of the year. My reaction was the kind you'd have after spending a day seeing a matinee of *Death of a Salesman*, an eight o'clock performance of *Marie Christine* and a special midnight showing of *'night, Mother*.

Wednesday, Raúl Esparza came by to work on his song, "Morning Glow." He told me that he thought Sondheim would love my *Broadway 101* show and that he would email him. First of all, I'm dying to know what his email is:
Goodthinggoing@aol.com?
Bring-in-bounce@verizon.net?
Also, who has ever said that in a sentence? "I think I'll email Sondheim." Okay, I think I'll

email Mozart.

Also, the previous Sunday, Patrick Pacheco wrote an article about the *Grease* reality show that ran in the LA *Times*. My friend Paul Castree was quoted, and I bragged to him that I had three paragraphs to his measly one. On Wednesday they reprinted it in *Newsday*. Paul still had his delicious paragraph, but they cut mine down a little. And by "a little," I mean to zero. Nary a trace. I've heard of instant karma, but never four-day-later karma. It was like karma mailed third-class.

Thursday, I hosted the *Chatterbox* with *Legally Blonde*'s Michael Rupert. I was obsessed when he told me that he did all these television shows when he was a kid like *My Three Sons* and *The Partridge Family*. It's so much cooler to have grown up in that time period. People my age can only brag about doing guest spots on *Silver Spoons* and *Alf*. He also said that when he auditioned to replace John Rubinstein in *Pippin*, Bob Fosse asked him to take off his shirt. Even though Michael said it was above board and solely because Pippin spends much of the show shirtless, to me it smacked of Coco in the movie *Fame* ("Tres jolie, Coco." Anybody?).

We also talked about him playing Marvin in *Falsettos*, and he told us about the myriad letters he got from kids who got the courage to come out because they saw the show. Or the glaring, uptight folk he'd see in the front row who'd be near tears by the end of the show. He also described how moved he was when he'd meet sickly looking men at the stage door who had flown to New York for an AIDS treatment. They'd always tell him how necessary it was for them to have seen the show. I remember seeing Falsettoland when it was Off-Broadway and loving it so much. Bill Finn and James Lapine wrote such real portrayals of gay people. So many times, gay characters in shows have one character trait: they are gay. And, P.S., that's not even a trait! It's like saying someone's character trait is the fact that they're white. Lapine and Finn made every character in *Falsettos* complex, like in real life. And the story is so incredibly moving. It's always embarrassing for me to be listening to "Unlikely Lovers" at the gym and be crying on the Stairmaster. I'm serious!

Friday, I met with Laura Benanti, and we had a long discussion about her wig for *The Wedding Singer*. She said she used her own hair when the show was out of town, but they wanted to make her look dowdier. She thinks someone was backstage washing windows, looked at the rag in their hands and said, "Hey! This can also be a wig!"

Friday was also the sitzprobe, meaning the first time the cast sang with the orchestra. We had a delicious 26-piece orchestra with a full string section. It was thrilling for us all to hear the *Gypsy* overture with all those instruments and so nice to see the musicians receive all that love from the cast. Friday was also the rehearsal for Manoel Felciano's section, and he warned me not to be shocked when I saw him. He has to gain 40 pounds for a Todd Solondz movie and has already gained 25. He said he's doing it by drinking ice cream shakes and not exercising. It was obviously a replica of my "diet" in junior high school, minus my signature supplement of Tastykakes.

Saturday and Sunday were a blur of run-throughs and me frantically going over dance steps. Suddenly it was Monday night.

We were sold out, and it was so nice for me to see the people in the cast who I admire so much getting a barrage of love from the audience. Pamela Myers sang "Another Hundred People" from *Company* just like she did in 1970 — in the original key! The audience demanded that she take a second bow. Andrea McArdle sang that last verse of "Tomorrow," and people freaked out. Before that I had talked about how devastated I was that I saw her replacement in *Annie* back in 1978, so after she sang, I whipped out my original Playbill (which had Laurie Beechman's autograph on the front!) and had Andrea finally sign it!

The whole time Raúl Esparza was singing, I saw a girl in the third row with her hands over face mouthing, "Oh My God!" The whole show was so thrilling to me.

Natascia Diaz did the section about quick changes. First she did a section from *Evita* where she goes from her small town to the cosmopolitan Buenos Aires and did a quick change, frumpy dress and long hair into tight skirt and short bob, when she changed cities. The whole thing was done in a matter of seconds while she was blocked from the audience by a bunch of dancers. She finished the number and then did the whole thing again. This time, however, she reversed the perspective so she was facing upstage and the audience was "backstage" so they could see everything. The crowd went crazy!

The whole thing ended with Norm Lewis singing "Lullaby of Broadway" with his signature velvet voice and the brilliant ensemble dancing up a storm.

I'm spending the rest of the week in an Epsom salt bath, and then this weekend I go to Palm Springs to play for Jennifer Hudson! I'll tell you all about that and my visit with my dad, who lives there, next week. Till then, take out your recordings of *March of the Falsettos* and *Falsettoland*, and cry up a storm!

Busch, Hudson and the Shaky Leg
April 24, 2007

Happy sixth anniversary to *The Producers* and farewell as well. Thursday was the sixth anniversary and Sunday was the closing.

I've been involved with *The Producers* since my birthday in 2001. First, a word about my birthday. It's on February 28. The same date that William Finn, Bernadette Peters, Kelly Bishop and Tommy Tune celebrate their birthdays. December birthday folk are always whining, "I never get a separate birthday or Christmas present. They're always combined." I hear ya, but let me simply say that it's just as annoying to share your birthday with four Tony Award-winners. Whenever theatre message boards print "today's birthdays," mine gets as much recognition as Sanjaya's will in a year. *Ooh! That's a dated reference!*

Anyhoo, on my birthday in 2001, I had brunch with Paul Castree, and I was complaining I had no money. Just then I got a call on my cell phone asking me to sub for *The Producers*! Oh yeah, a word about subbing. Subbing is like being an understudy in the pit. Every pit musician has around four subs, and it's very fun to do. And by "fun," I mean literally terrifying. When you sub, you first spend time learning the music you have to play at home and then you sit in the pit, watching the conductor so you know how it will look when you have to play. How many rehearsals do you get with the orchestra before you have to go on? None! Zero! You go from playing by yourself in your apartment to hearing "Ladies and gentlemen, the taking of photographs and the use of recording devices is strictly prohibited" with no transition. You're suddenly on Broadway. I think it's scarier than being an understudy. When you're an understudy and you go on for the first time, if you make mistakes, you simply correct them the next time you go on. When you're a sub, you *can't* make mistakes your first time because you don't even have the job yet. The first time you play is your audition, so if you're nervous and you clank it up, you're never asked back.

I'll never forget the first time I played *Kiss of the Spider Woman* with Chita Rivera. I was a nervous wreck! Ted Sperling was the conductor (he later won the Tony Award for orchestrating *Light in the Piazza...* one of the few Tony winners who doesn't upstage me on my birthday), and after a few songs he told me that a crazy vibrato was coming out of my synthesizer. Vibrato? Was my synth possessed by The Merm? Was she a poltergeist protesting the electronification of Broadway? I didn't know what was wrong, but it kept happening. Every note I played had vibrato. As the show progressed, a slew of technicians tried to fix the keyboard. Suddenly, during "Dear One," I realized that I was so nervous that my left leg had been shaking the whole time — on the volume pedal! The sound wave of vibrato was in direct correlation to the shaking of my gam. I gingerly lifted it off, and Ted suddenly looked my way and told me the vibrato had stopped. I shrugged my shoulders and chalked it up to a shoddy electrical connection, never 'fessing up that it all could have been prevented with a hefty dose of Valium.

Last Monday, I knew this was the final week of *The Producers* and assumed I had played it for the last time a while ago. While I was lamenting its loss (especially to my wallet), I interviewed John Treacy Egan for my radio show. On Broadway, he has played Franz Liebkind, Roger De Bris and was closing the show as Max Bialystock. What's encouraging for everyone struggling out there at horrible cattle calls is to know that John got cast from an open call. That's right, ye olde 16 bars. So haul out your cut-to-the-end versions of "Anthem" and "Ice Cream" —

it could get you a lead on Broadway! John also told me that one of his first roles was at a community theatre where he played Che and Christine Pedi was Evita. An Irish redheaded Che and a dark-haired, comedic Eva from Scarsdale. Hmm, maybe I *will* get to play Effie one day.

Back to subbing at *The Producers*. Even though I thought I had played it for the last time, I wound up being asked at the last minute to sub this week. Patrick Brady, the conductor, told me that I was the first sub to ever play the show on Broadway, and now, I was the last sub. As Justin Timberlake sings, "What goes around, comes around." As Christine Ebersole sings, "Around the world..." And as that guy in the '80s sang, "You spin me right round, baby, right round."

This weekend I flew to the West Coast to play for Jennifer Hudson. I spent the plane ride re-reading Charles Busch's moving yet hilarious *Whores of Lost Atlantis*. The book is a fictionalized version of how he started his theatre company, Theatre-in-Limbo, and how *Vampire Lesbians of Sodom* (called *Whores of Lost Atlantis* in the book) became an Off-Broadway smash. What's so inspirational about the book is, not only did he make *his* dreams come true, but he put all of his friends into the shows he wrote and made all of their dreams come true as well.

Busch performed "Bill" in my *Broadway 101* show last week, and I used him to prove that you don't need crazy high notes or an elaborate set to move an audience. He sang it with just a piano, some strings and a stool and the audience was riveted. You could hear a pin drop... or a leg shake. He showed everyone that you just need a connection to the words to draw an audience in. So many people told me that his rendition made them cry. And my Long Island mother told me that it made her "croy."

On Friday, I arrived in Palm Springs and met up with Jennifer, who was performing for a bunch of lawyers who were having their annual conference and hired her to belt up a storm. Ever since I started playing for her, she hasn't been allowed to sing "And I Am Telling You" in performance because the studio wanted to keep that special in the movie. But now that the whole Oscar season is over, she's finally allowed to do it! She sounded amazing, and the only disappointment I felt was not being able to do the whole fight scene leading up to it. I didn't get the impression though that she wanted me to sing the other roles of Jimmy, Curtis, Deena and Lorrell. Was she afraid of being out-riffed? You decide.

It's so fun accompanying Jennifer because she *always* sounds amazing. Totally full-voiced and nary a click track in sight! Also, the night we performed was the anniversary of her being kicked off *American Idol*, so it was extra poignant. She always does "Weekend in New England," which is the song that got her ixnayed, and if you ever hear her do it, you will feel ashamed that you didn't stay up all night voting for her when she was on *Idol*.

After the show, I drove to Los Angeles with my good friend Jack Plotnick. The drive became so tedious, and our conversation topics so scarce, that I was forced to sing all of "The Worst Pies in London" a cappella. Again, I say, if John Treacy Egan can do Che, why can't I do a Cockney charwoman?

Okay, this week I'm doing *Androcles and the Lion* for the Shaw Project and the Easter Bonnet Competition, and I'm seeing *Legally Blonde*. As one show closes, so another opens...

Shaw, Shindle and the Missing Glasses
May 1, 2007

First of all, Monday afternoon, I went to the East Side. Yes, that gets its own sentence because as a West Sider, it is a momentous occasion. For those of you who don't live in New York, it's akin to traveling from Paris to Leningrad and takes just as many train transfers. Also, it has streets and neighborhoods I've never heard of and have no idea the location of. I had to go to Gramercy Park South. Where in the world is that? I panicked and took a cab. I found out Gramercy Park South is actually East 16th Street. Why couldn't it be called that? I could have taken the R train to 14th Street and just walked. Who's going to pay me back the $14 for the cab? Who's responsible for that cryptic name? Do I bill the Robert Moses estate?

Well, the reason I trekked to that foreign land was because the sweet and talented David Staller asked me to be in *Project Shaw*. *Project Shaw* was founded by Staller, and the intention of it is to put on every single one of Shaw's works — sketches, one acts and full lengths. I played Androcles in *Androcles and the Lion*, which is about Christians being thrown to the lions. Since that's sometimes what it feels like for an actor on critics' nights, Staller decided to cast the show with critics to give them a taste of what actors go through. David decided that me being a deejay on Sirius made me critic-y enough to be in it. I played opposite Bruce Vilanch's lion, and I must say that for a role mostly full of stage directions ("the lion moans mournfully"), Bruce was hilarious! If they finally do revive *The Wiz*, have I got a lion for you... albeit, a white one.

I began the evening with the cockiness of "Bruce and I are the only professional actors on this stage," but by ten minutes in, I was in a fierce battle for laughs with Michael "comic genius" Musto and Michael "bring down the house" Riedel. The only thing that saved me was Musto only being featured in Act One and Riedel being unceremoniously eaten by a lion at the beginning of Act Two. Basically, I was surrounded by more laugh whores than you'd find at a Mario Cantone family reunion. Bravo, critics! And remember my shout outs to you when a Rudetsky extravaganza opens and you put pen to paper.

Tuesday was the Easter Bonnet Competition and *Legally Blonde*'s Laura Bell Bundy and I got to tell the audience who the judges were. Remember the old theatre adage "Never share the stage with children or animals"? Let me amend that to, "Never share the stage with a Chihuahua and a blonde in a pink bunny suit." I had to pull out all my shtick just to get anyone in the audience with a wandering eye to fix one of them on me. But the show was faboo as usual — the *[title of show]* folk (best show ever) and Chris Gattelli created the opening number, which was a hilarious stream of consciousness that had moments like Jeff Bowen considering whether they should have *Wicked* star Julia Murney belt out the opening number (cue Julia Murney on elevator in sexy gown rising to the stage, mic poised as she's about to sing) and then Hunter Bell remembering that she has eight shows a week and should probably save her voice (cue elevator with Julia Murney lowering under the stage while Julia angrily mouths "*Son of a...*").

Also, it was great to see Jo Anne Worley in the *Drowsy Chaperone* sketch. She featured her twirling pearl necklace bit, which has to be seen. She starred in my *On the Twentieth Century* concert for the Actors Fund and told my friend Charlie Schwartz that it's very important to "travel with your own props." What an old-school specific tip! Who even *has* their own props, let alone travels with them? I love it!

11

Thursday, I had Karen Ziemba on *Chatterbox*. She first talked about the '80s and her final audition to take over the role of Peggy Sawyer in *42nd Street*. She had to stand next to Jerry Orbach and was so nervous she'd be too tall that she wore rickety-rackety flats, but thankfully, he was a taller drink of water. She got the part and told us that Jerry was old-school and therefore never missed a performance. Attention members of various ensembles: aspire to be Jerry! She also talked about the first time she went on as Cassie in the national tour of *A Chorus Line*, and it was in an outdoor theatre. During the moment where she was yelling at Zach that she'd be proud to be a member of the chorus, she had been dancing so much that her body temperature was hotter than the air, so steam was rising off of her. The audience must have been like "Cassie must be right! After all, she is a wizard."

Friday, I saw *Legally Blonde*. First of all, shout out to Laura Bell Bundy for singing and dancing up a storm and doing it eight shows a week. I was winded from watching her by the "I want" song. Secondly, yay Orfeh! I was so obsessed with her in *Saturday Night Fever*. Whenever I played in that pit, I always turned my earphones way up whenever she was lending her signature riffs to "Jive Talking." Yes, I played keyboard for the song "Jive Talking." We all need rent money. Thirdly, so proud to see Jerry Mitchell graduate to directing. We used to create the production numbers on *The Rosie O'Donnell Show* years back and I was always miffed that, after assisting Michael Bennett *and* Jerome Robbins, he hadn't yet directed a Broadway show. Finally! And lastly, brava to Kate Shindle. Because of my obsession with high belting, she told me in advance that she hits some crazy notes in the show. I was psyched waiting for it and heard her belt some delicious E flats in Act Two. I was duly impressed, but I had heard her belt even higher before (an F) when she'd sing "See What I Wanna See" in various benefits. Suddenly, near the end of the song, she hit an E Flat, started sliding up and had the chutzpah to land on an A flat! And hold it! With vibrato! Unbelievable!

All right, this week I'm one of the judges in the *Mr. Broadway* pageant, and I'm then going to Albany for lobbying day! I love long car rides because I can blast all my favorite CDs — *Closer Than Ever, Ain't Misbehavin'* and *Evita* (with Patti! How dare you even ask!). *Remember traveling with a bunch of CDs? Remember CDs?*

See ya next week and peace out!

Whadda week! The last seven days had more beefcake in 'em than a *Naked Boys Singing* open call. Monday night was the first *Mr. Broadway* contest. It benefited the Ali Forney Center, which shelters homeless gay kids. Shockingly, in this day and age, many gay kids are forced to live on the streets because their families reject them. I was asked to be a judge alongside the six-packed Scott Nevins and the high G belting Nancy Opel.

Now, I love doing benefits, but this one had the essence of a probable stinker. A male beauty pageant? I smelled a drunken cat-calling audience. A talent segment? I had a vision of having to sit through everyone's audition song ("Anthem," "She Loves Me" and "Sara Lee"). A swimsuit competition? Hmm. I didn't have a bad feeling about that. In fact, that's what got me to the theatre. Anyhoo, Nancy, Scott and I waited backstage with trepidation, but from the moment the opening number started, we were severely pleasantly surprised. It was great! There were seven contestants: Mr. *Wicked*, Mr. *A Chorus Line*, Mr. *Mamma Mia!*, Mr. *Curtains*, Mr. *Hairspray*, Mr. *Tarzan*, and the title Nancy Opel thought was the most awkward one to have, Mr. *Mary Poppins*.

The talent segments were great. Mr. *Tarzan* said that his plan had been to break a world record in toe touches. He then found out that there isn't one in the Guinness Book, so if he simply did two, he'd be a record holder. But instead of a world record, he decided to beat his personal best and do more than 30, which is what he once did at the theatre. Throughout his whole explanation, Nancy Opel was looking nonplussed. She later admitted that she didn't know toe touches were Russian splits (jumping in the air in a split and touching your toes). She thought it literally meant bending down and touching your toes. She thought, "What the hell's the impressive part?" Anyhoo, Mr. *Tarzan* wound up doing 51 toe touches! I thought the next day *Tarzan* audiences might hear, "At this performance, the role usually played by Nick Sanchez will be played by somebody who can walk."

The most outrageous talent was Mr. *Mamma Mia!*'s (Frankie James Grande). His act consisted of him being Gollum from *Lord of the Rings* (with that crazy voice) as a contestant singing on the *Grease* reality show, *You're The One That I Want*. It was phenomenally daring because it could have bombed bigger than *The Blonde in the Thunderbird*, but the audience ate it up. As a matter of fact, he was the winner!

The interview segment was informative and funny and culminated with me asking Mr. *Chorus Line* what he would do if he was on for the role of Val and had to sing "Dance: Ten; Looks: Three." What would be the assets that he'd substitute for T and A? I ran to the piano and gave him an intro, and he launched into singing his greatest strength: "Jump spli-i-i-its!" He then demonstrated one. He jumped up, and micro-seconds later landed on the floor in a full 180 degree split. Incredibly impressive!

Then came swimsuits. As for the drunken cat-calls I had dreaded, they issued forth not from the audience, but from all three judges. Holy Moley! Mr. *Curtains* was wearing a sassy little number, and when he turned around, he was able to open the "curtains" and give everyone an eyeful! And Mr. *Chorus Line* wore a tiny suit that showed everyone you could put something extra large into something extra small.

At the beginning of the evening, we found out that when *Mr. Curtains* was a teenager, he had been thrown out of his house for being gay. But he then told us that not only has he reconciled with his Mom, but she now works at a shelter like the Ali Forney Center in Utah! Family seemed to be a big theme of the night. Tovah Feldshuh was a brilliant host and at one point told the audience that the two things you have to do as a parent is "love unconditionally and show up." She then gave a shout out to the various family members of the contestants in the audience. I was impressed that so many families came, but I know that I would have been mortified to be in front of my family, strutting my stuff in a dance belt masquerading as a bathing suit. Not because of the lurid sexiness, but because of the amount of love handle jokes I would have to endure at subsequent Thanksgivings. Being with my family is like being roasted at the Friars Club if they opened a branch in the Five Towns on Long Island.

Tuesday, I drove up to Albany with my boyfriend, James, to lobby for Gay Rights. Who knew you could speak directly to your representatives? What a great sense of power! And who knew my boyfriend had never heard my Actors Fund *Hair* CD? What a loss for him that I immediately rectified. Luckily the ride was long, so we were able to replay my favorite Shayna Steele riffs in "White Boys" and Julia Murney's amazing rendition of "Where Do I Go?" Where do I go, she asks? Straight to the lead in *Wicked*!

Wednesday was my monthly show at Cardinal Cooke Hospital. I've been volunteering for Lifebeat's Hearts and Voices for 15 years. We bring singers to people hospitalized with AIDS. It sounds depressing but it's actually so much fun. I'll never forget when I was working in the prison AIDS ward and one of the inmates/patients was obsessed with my friend's (the triple-threaded Naomi Naughton) rendition of "Nothing." He'd ask for it all the time. I finally got Priscilla Lopez to come in and sing it for him, and after the show I was talking to her about "Mr. Karp." She assured me that the whole song was real (except his name), and I asked how he died. Turns out, he killed himself! Wow. Was it left out of the song because it was too much of a downer? "Six months later I heard that Karp... had killed himself." Hmmm, I guess it also would have been too many eighth notes.

Over the weekend I saw *The Pirate Queen*, and brava to Stephanie J. Block for perilous ship climbing across scaffolds and perilous high belting across Ds and Es.

Sunday was my mom's birthday, and I threw her a surprise brunch with some of my friends. Stephen Spadaro (one of the Weissler company managers) got her a shirt that says "C'hai Maintenance." L'chaim! After the brunch, it was 2:30 and my mom wouldn't stop hocking me (Jewish expression for nagging) that we were going to be late to see *Talk Radio*, and she "hates being late for anything." I assured her that she was crazy and that we had more than enough time to get downtown. We got into a cab on 74th Street at 2:40 PM, and the traffic was suddenly horrific. By 3 PM were at 65th Street. So in a sense, we weren't late seeing *Talk Radio*. We simply never saw it. The good news is, she has a new story to add to her repertoire that includes her warning me to change trains at Jamaica when I take the Long Island Rail Road and me forgetting to do it one time, which landed me in the wrong station (that one's good for multiple "tsk-tsk-tsks" and head shaking from an elderly Jewish woman). Happy Birthday.

All right, I'm off to prepare for three Jennifer Hudson concerts this week. Let the belting begin!

Jennifer and Julia
May 15, 2007

This week was chock full of belting. First of all, on Monday, I played piano for Jennifer Hudson at the Metropolitan Museum of Art. It was a fundraiser for their costume collection. I got to the sound check early and a beautiful African-American woman asked me if I was going to see Jennifer later. I told her I would, and she asked me to say hello for her.

ME: Sure. What's your name?
HER: ...Naomi.
ME: (Naomi? As in supermodel Naomi? Ah! I can't remember her last name. Something with a C. Collins? Must clarify. Let me phrase question without using name) Um...aren't you famous for modeling?
HER: (Laughs.) Well, not that much anymore. (She leaves.)
SOUND MAN: Seth, you know that was Naomi Campbell, right?
ME: *That's* her last name!
SOUND MAN: (Glares)

Ooh! Just realized, I never gave the message. Jen, if you're reading this, Naomi says, "Hi." Wait. Is this my future? Intermediary between supermodel and Diva? Patti, if you're reading this, Iman says, "What up."

For a Met event the organizers asked Jennifer to sing "La Vie En Rose" because they were honoring somebody French. Now, while I think the song is pretty, it's not known for bringing down the house. Since it was the opener, I refused to let Jen do a mellow Piaf *fin*. Instead, I made up an arrangement for the ending. She sang it through, and then we did a tag:
(Slowly building) La vie en... (more) La Vie en... (Tremolo in piano) And-I-am-telling-you- (Fermata in the piano as she riffs à la "You're gonna lo-o-o-ove") La vie-e-e-e-e-e-e en- (Pause, then à la "me-eeee!") Ro-ose!!!!!

It made no sense, but got huge applause. Then she belted out two more songs ("Run to You" and "I Am Changing"), took her bow and exited. Well, the audience went *wild*! They demanded an encore. We hadn't planned one, but luckily, because I was too lazy to separate out what she was singing that night, I brought all of her music to the gig. She came back onstage and knew the audience would go crazy if she hauled out a certain song. Yes, she took center stage and belted a fierce "It's a Scandal, It's an Outrage" from *Oklahoma!* Anybody? No, actually I played three G octaves, and she launched into "And I Am Telling You." Brava!

Tuesday, I interviewed Stephanie J. Block and Alain Boublil for my Broadway show on Sirius. I spent a good part of the hour trying to pronounce the first and/or last name of Monsieur Boublil and essentially turned it into a combination of Eileen Brennan, Michael Bublé and Bebe Bensenheimer.

Stephanie is such a cool person who has been plagued by opening-night *nacht*mares. First, the night before she was supposed to open *Wicked* in Toronto, they were trying a new entrance for "No Good Deed" where she would fly in on a broom. It was a late-night rehearsal and, suddenly, one of the wires that was holding her up broke. The crew tried to get her down, but the computer kept overriding anything they did, so she was swinging around repeatedly above the stage, literally crashing into the light poles!

During *Pirate Queen* previews, everyone in the cast was spreading around a debilitating virus. She was able to avoid it until the critics came. She started the show on the big critics night, and ten minutes in had to have her understudy take over. Take this in, people: she was starring in a show and couldn't perform on a critics night! Do you know how sick you have to be to let yourself miss one of those nights? She was *devastated*. I was then obsessing with Alain about how much I love Frances Ruffelle as the original Eponine. He said that at the time of her audition, she was in *Starlight Express* in London, and they didn't think she'd be right. But when she walked in, she literally looked like those nineteenth-century illustrations of French waifs. And, I might add, she could belt an E ("I'm gonna scream, I'm gonna warn 'em here!") I remember interviewing Frances, and she told me that she was only 19 when she first did the show and didn't feel totally comfortable onstage. When they were staging her number, she didn't know what to do with her arms, so she folded them across her waist. Like a clichéd movie scene, everyone said, "That's it! Don't move!" That's right. The signature Eponine pose was really because of her uncomfortableness onstage. Brava, Mme. Ruffelle! Way to "take it from where you are"!

Wednesday, I went to Washington to play for Jennifer Hudson (again) at an event for the National Lupus Foundation. The event went long, and I wound up missing my train home. I took a flight the next morning that left at 6:50. Let me repeat that. My flight *left* at 6:50 AM. I haven't been up that early since high school drivers' ed. Not cool.

Thursday, I had Julia Murney on *Chatterbox*. I'm so proud she's starring in *Wicked*. I asked her about her sassy slide during "Defying Gravity" at the end when she goes, "No one's gonna bri-i-i-i-ing me down!" She claims it was because she was nervous belting the crazy high "me" out of nowhere, so she decided to slide up to it instead. Like I always say, out of fear of belted high notes comes brilliant phrasing. She also talked about her lucrative voice-over career. Particularly, the one time she needed some extra bucks, so she was the voice of a porn cable channel. She did one of her signature commercials, and let's just say I never realized what the first syllable of the month of October could rhyme with. We were trying to think of other dirty months that they could have used. I pitched "Janu-hairy."

Thursday night, I had one more Jennifer Hudson gig. It was for the Candie's Foundation, and before the show I was talking to Jennifer about how hard it must be to sing these big showstoppers for every live gig. She said it would actually be easier if she was doing it more often. When she toured with "American Idol," even though she was doing a show every night of the week, she didn't really have to worry about warming up. I knew what she meant. One would think that if you do 11 o'clock numbers all the time, you'd tire your voice out. But it's actually much better to be consistently doing them. I remembered doing my Actors Fund concert of *Dreamgirls* and how Lillias White always wanted to sing all the Effie songs full out during rehearsals so she'd get it into her body and not go into a state of shock on the night of the show. I still can't believe that Effie has to sing "And I Am Telling You" and follow it with "I Am Changing." Even though plot-wise it's many years between those songs, it's only around 25 minutes in real time.

That afternoon, my mom and I finally got to see *Talk Radio*. Christine Pedi is my co-host on Sirius radio and in *Talk Radio*, and she does a slew of the different voices who call Liev Schreiber.

Her acting and comic timing were both so great, and it was fun trying to figure out which characters she was voicing. It was also fun to see producer Jordan Roth in the audience taking his mother, producer Daryl Roth, and *her* mother to the show. Three generations of Roths. It was very "Gilmore Girls." *P.S. Years later, I was in the audience of MOTOWN with my Mom on Mother's Day and Jordan and Daryl were also there. Why are we being stalked by Broadway's top producers? And why won't they simply produce one of my shows?*

Okay, I have to gear up to read all the Broadway message boards about the Tony nominations *and* watch the finale of *America's Next Top Model*! Talk soon!

Talkin' Tony Noms
May 22, 2007

First of all, a problem with dating a guy who is raising a six-year-old daughter is that I have to have food for her in my apartment. Instead of munching on my fiber and flax seed-filled Uncle Sam's cereal, I'm about to eat a big fat bowl of Froot Loops because I bought her a jumbo size last Friday. You may ask, "Why buy a jumbo size when you know she's only staying over on the weekend?" and I may answer something couched in denial. But instead I shall admit: I bought it hoping she would eat a quarter of it and leave the rest for me. Here's the deal, I don't even like Froot Loops, but if it's sitting in my kitchen and there are pretty colors on the outside of the box, I'm in.

Oh, wait! Just remembered I did an emergency midnight run to Fairway last week and bought myself Cinnamon Toast Crunch. I'm gonna ixnay the Froot Loops (the spelling of "froot" is whimsical... and mandatory because you can't put the word "fruit" in the title of your food if it only consists of sugar, circles of starchiness and food coloring) and have a delicious bowl of CTC.

Oh yeah! That reminds me! Attention message boards: *please* stop referencing shows by their acronyms! Who started that madness? In my day, when we wanted a sassy nickname for *Phantom of the Opera* we shortened it *Phantom*, and *Fiddler on the Roof* has always been called *Fiddler* from Zero Mostel's original production through my high school's critically acclaimed production to the Topol revival in the late '80s. Who changed the rules? I'm not a World War Two trained code breaker who can figure out a panicked theatre board message entitled "New opera diva *fierce* in POTO" or "Why no Jews in FOTR?" I've spent way too much time staring at the screen of Talkin' Broadway mumbling "P... what starts with P? *Paint Your Wagon*?"

All right, let's talk Tony nominations. Yes, I woke up and watched them on NY1. Do you watch the nominations and fantasize what it would feel like to have your name called? Do you tape it, erase the sound and dub in your name? In all categories? If you do, can you tell me the technology you use because the only part I've mastered is taping it?

There were some glaring omissions. Where was Kristin Chenoweth's nomination? She was *so* funny in *The Apple Tree*, or should I say TAP?

It's kinda fun not having any total shoo-ins. Remember the year the Best Actress race was between Glenn Close and Rebecca Luker? I'm not saying that they were the front-runners, I'm saying they were the only two nominated! *And* Glenn hosted. It would have been pretty awkward if she had lost. What if she had left in tears? "Ladies and Gentlemen, for the remainder of the Tonys, the role of the host usually played by Glenn Close will be played by... Karen Mason."

Wednesday was a day of panic. I really wanted a Tony nominee for my Thursday *Chatterbox* but kept putting off calling anybody because I knew everybody'd be so busy. I decided to call *Legally Blonde*'s Laura Bell Bundy at 1:45 before the Wednesday matinee and had my whole schmooze pre-planned to leave on her cell phone. Well, instead of a message I got a high-pitched "Hello?" I was flummoxed and said, "Why are you answering the phone instead of getting into a fierce lace-front wig?!" Instead of hanging up, she graciously agreed to do the interview, and she was adorable. She has such a great personality and although we differ in age, let's just say May-December… of the following year, we both have reflux! I asked her why reflux seems to be so prevalent now, and she thinks it's because of Starbucks coffee. It *is* crazily strong. I have to pour a ton of half-and-half into my "tall half-caf" just to change it from black to black-ish.

Laura Bell also talked about doing the Off-Broadway musical *Ruthless* when she was a kid, and the bizarre fact that her understudies were Natalie Portman *and* Britney Spears. That's a *lot* of star power sitting backstage and being bitter. Laura Bell assured me that they were "super nice and not bitter," and I assured her that the Brooklyn Bridge *is* for sale. She also said that she turned down two pilots to do *Legally Blonde*, and I say brava! I love someone who puts Broadway above TV. It seems that so many people do Broadway just to get to TV. To do what, I ask? An amazing episode of *Two Guys, a Girl and a Pizza Place*?

This weekend I saw *Deuce* with my mother. The whole time I kept looking at Angela Lansbury thinking, "She used to sing 'Open a New Window' eight times a week. So cool!" It was pretty amazing to see her with Marian Seldes. There's a moment in the show where Michael Mulheren references them and says we won't see women like this again. It seemed like such an homage to their talent and history that I immediately started crying. And then tried to mask it because I knew my mother would be mad at me for not carrying around those portable Kleenex tissue packets.

OK, one more bowl of Cinnamon Toast Crunch. As the "hilarious" refrigerator magnet says, "My Diet Starts Tomorrow."

Straight Talk
May 29, 2007

Hi, everyone! There are two things I forgot to write about last week. First, I played an audition for my friend Andréa Burns, who's sassing it up in my new favorite show, *In the Heights*. She was trying out for the Jane Fonda part in the workshop of the new *9 to 5* musical. It's being directed by Joe Mantello and has music and lyrics by Dolly Parton. Well, Andréa and I were waiting in the Bernie Telsey lounge with all the other actors trying out for various commercials and the *Drowsy* tour when everyone started to look toward the elevator. I turned and suddenly saw that Southern sasstress, Dolly Parton! She walked across the lobby, and everyone was in a star-struck state of shock. I don't really remember what she was wearing, but I have a vision of a snakeskin one-piece. It was something amazing like that, and it closely framed her size zero figure. I couldn't believe she was going to be at the audition! I did harken back to the time I was staying home because I was sick in the early '90s and I asked my roommate, Tim Cross, to go out and rent me a movie. Well, instead of bringing me home a classic from the '40s I had never seen or a new release I had been salivating for (*The Crying Game*, *Single White Female*, etc...), he proudly brought me *Straight Talk*! Remember? That was the movie where a small-town woman, played by Dolly, becomes a radio therapist by giving the people "straight talk" instead of supposed psycho babble. It is *so* not my style. Suffice it to say, it lasted ten minutes in my VCR. Has anyone *ever* sat through that entire movie?

But I decided to forgive her that atrocity and walked into the audition room willing to make peace. Apparently so was she, because her friendliness was mind boggling! She was all a-twitter because Andréa had brought her own accompanist (me). She said something to the effect of "Sakes alive!" or "I'll be a horny toad!" Andréa sang and as soon as she finished, Dolly full out applauded. Literally applauded! It was so down home and friendly. I left Andréa in there to do her scene and felt so good walking out that I strongly considered putting "Straight Talk" on my Netflix queue. That feeling lasted the entire elevator ride down to the first floor of Telsey Casting and was quickly replaced by a hankering for an iced latte.

Update: bad news for Andréa, she did not get the Jane Fonda part, but good news for her, *In the Heights* is moving to Broadway! And although Stephanie J. Block didn't get a Tony nomination for *Pirate Queen*, she did get the Jane Fonda part in the workshop. Brava!

Secondly, I forgot to mention the baby shower I went to for Jessie Stone and Chris Fitzgerald. I've known Jessie since right before we did the '94 revival of *Grease!* (I started as a piano sub), and it was so weird for me to see her eight months pregnant. Rizzo's the one whose preggers, not Frenchie. Jessie used to make me laugh so hard when she'd tell me the story about going to a Broadway audition in her early twenties, but by accident using her very first résumé that had only high school credits. The auditioners were like, "Wow, I see you've played Mama Rose... interesting."

The whole party was hosted by Andrea Martin, who has one of the most gorgeous Manhattan apartments that she got in the '70s and still costs like $10 a month because, as people always say to my chagrin, "Nobody wanted to live on (insert Central Park West, Columbus Avenue, the West 70s, etc.) back then."

One of Jessie's friends came up to me and told me she's the one that called me months ago on my cell phone. She explained that she listens to me on Sirius radio a lot and heard me ask what the meaning was when Evita sang "Although she's dressed up to the nines, at sixes and sevens with you." She knew the answer because it's a British expression and her sister studied in England. She got my cell number from a friend and called me, but I was on the subway, so it kept cutting off and then she'd call me back or vice versa. This went on an awkward amount of times until we both gave up. Anyway, she never identified herself on the phone, only saying that she was a friend of Sam Pancake. Turns out, she's *Gilmore Girls* star Lauren Graham! She was mortified to tell me about her stalker-ish phone call, but Jessie forced her. She's really funny and we somehow started discussing pronunciation, and she said that "err" as in "to err is human" is pronounced "uhr," as in purr. She told me about arguing for the proper pronunciation when "err" was in a *Gilmore Girls* script, which essentially ended with the line being cut. Lauren said that she obsesses over minutiae like that and once had a boyfriend yell that he hated when she "*conden*scended" to him. She faced an incredible moral quandary about whether to correct him or not. The whole thing sounded like a real life version of Maltby and Shire's "Crossword Puzzle." Loni Ackerman? Anybody?

Anyhoo, this week featured a big birthday party for Kelli O'Donnell (Rosie's wife) that I played for. Kelli requested her favorite singers, and they all showed up to belt up a storm. It was held at the fabulous Ars Nova, and the show opened with Julia Murney singing "Raise the Roof." How dare she do eight shows a week and still be able to belt Ds on her night off! One of my favorite singers, Darius de Haas, did "I Am Changing," and even though he had just flown in from Japan, he sounded *amazing*. The highlight of the evening was Norm Lewis and Audra McDonald singing "Wheels of a Dream." *Foreshadowing them both starring in PORGY AND BESS?* Audra was also on her night off and used the sound of the audience applause to mask her warming up. My boyfriend was standing right next to her and said every time the audience clapped, he heard "Mee-ah, Mee-ah, Mee-ah." Norm had the nerve to hold the D right before the "And he will ride" and take it up to an A. Is there anything he can't do? The most gorgeous baritone in the world, yet high As as well?

Speaking of Audra, I saw *110 in the Shade* and loved it! She is so likeable onstage and adds so much humor to something that could be played very drab and depressingly. As I watched her I thought, "I am watching a musical theatre star in the prime of her career. How cool!" I thought about that and wondered if she'd be on Broadway in 20 years. Then I looked to the left of her and saw John Cullum, who's been performing on Broadway since the 1960s! Forty years on Broadway! I'm gonna have him on my radio show soon, and I can't wait to grill him about Barbara Harris, Madeline Kahn and Judy Kaye.

Writing about Audra reminds me of buried babies (*Ragtime*, scene two anybody?) so therefore I'm reminded that I saw *Coram Boy*. It was so exciting, original and thrilling! My question is, why would a show like that have to put up a closing notice so soon? My next question is, what did the woman next to me have in a plastic bag that she had to retrieve several times during the show? I had a mini-breakdown. When they search your bag upon entering the theatre, they should confiscate weapons, recording devices and all plastic bags. Unfortunately, that means my mother will never be able to come to the theatre again. Everything she carries is in multiple plastic bags. She'll literally put a bottled water in a plastic bag... and then put that plastic bag in a bigger plastic bag. Not joking! It's like one of those Russian dolls.

All right, I'm off to give *Straight Talk* another chance. Talk to you in ten minutes.

The Setup
June 4, 2007

Happy June! June is one of my favorite months because even though I graduated from high school way back when Molly Ringwald was the new, big thing (*Sixteen Candles*? Anybody? *Fresh Horses*? Nobody?), every June 1, I still feel the joy I felt knowing it was the last month of the school year.

This week began with the culmination of a bizarre experience. Back in January, I answered an email from a friend who told me about an audition for a TV host. I was in a rage because it was being held on the East Side (Is there any easy way to get there besides using the Helipad on 34th Street?), but I went anyway. I knew it was a swanky audition because it was held at an Au Bon Pain. As I always say, why rent a studio and have a monitor when you can easily find an empty table in the back of a chain restaurant? Tara Rubin, you could be saving a mint of money by staking out a corner at Hot and Crusty.

I met the lady "auditioning" me and looked for the camera that would put me on tape. I instead saw two businessmen, a homeless person and the fixin's bar with half and half, whole, two percent *and* skim milk. The auditioner was very friendly and said that the show would have a different host talking about his or her favorite part of New York. I told her I was most familiar with the theatre district and the Upper West Side, and she then told me that the hosts had to be pop culture savvy and she therefore needed to ask me some questions. She asked me ten questions, and I answered three correctly. Suffice it to say, I did not know that Ted Turner founded the Goodwill Games, amongst many other things. But she liked my personality and said that she'd tell them I aced all the questions, and I would probably get the gig.

I got a call a few days later offering me the show and, actor style, told them to call my agent. They told me that because it's a new show, they weren't going through agents. Huh? What was the show, I asked. They told me that it's new so they can't really talk about it. Again, *huh*? Why so many secrets? Why was I suddenly in an episode of *24* — one that would eventually get the show canceled because it's not even that interesting. Nothing made sense, but because of my natural actor whore-ishness and a desperation to add something new to my reel, I accepted the job. A week later I showed up on the corner of Columbus and 74th to meet the producer, Donna. She told me that the show car would pick me up, take me to Don't Tell Mama on 46th street, and I'd film an episode talking about my favorite midtown spots (AKA Amy's Bread). Donna kept making cell-phone calls to the other producers and finally said that the car was stuck in traffic and I should take a cab. She gave me $20 and said that the crew would meet me there. I got in the cab, gave the address of Mama's and was suddenly accosted by non-stop blinking lights on the roof of the inside of the cab.

Yes, I was on an episode of the Discovery Channel's *Cash Cab*. The whole thing about hosting a show about New York was one big, fat setup! I had never seen the show and found out that it consists of a cab driver asking me questions as he drives me to my destination, and every correct answer would win me money! He said that if I got three wrong, I had to leave the cab. Well, I freaked out because I remembered the auditioner asking me questions and me getting three out of ten right. I didn't want to be kicked out of a cab on 54th Street and Ninth Avenue! What would I do in that neighborhood? Go to Mee Noodle Shop? Well, suffice it to say, I knew the answers to all the questions except the last one (Q: What is the Urban Dictionary's definition of the computer term NSFW? A: Not Safe For Work.), and I won $300! The point is, if you audition for something that seems fishy, then get the gig and it seems fishier, you should take the gig and you could win money! Or wind up in a snuff film. *P.S. To this day, people are constantly tweeting me and saying they saw me on CASH CAB. My episode repeats all the time! P.P.S No residuals.*

Thursday, I interviewed Rupert Holmes on *Chatterbox*. What a talent! He's done everything. First of all, he wrote music for *The Partridge Family*. I always thought that they were the cool version of *The Brady Bunch* until Ricky came along and ruined it all. And Holmes wrote the flip side of "Daddy, Don't You Walk So Fast." Do you remember that childhood downer? The only thing sadder than that was the book *Bridge to Terabithia,* which is essentially the children's version of *The Year of Magical Thinking*.

Rupert said that he was writing and singing on his own albums when he got a phone call. "Hello, this is Barbra Streisand, and I'd like you to write some songs for my upcoming movie *A Star Is Born*." He responded with that old chestnut, "That's the *worst* Barbra Streisand imitation I've ever heard." Instead of hanging up, she got back at him by giving herself that horrible '70s perm. Well, maybe that wasn't to get him back, but let's all acknowledge that it was a national tragedy.

Regardless, he wrote her that sassy song "Queen Bee" and "Everything," which was a big high school girl audition song before "Out Here On my Own" stole its thunder. Rupert also conducted Barbra on her *Lazy Afternoon* record and for some songs that were never released. He actually conducted that fabulous clip of her singing "Make Our Garden Grow" where she holds the last note for a crazy length of time. He said he remembered thinking that he was gonna run out of orchestral music, but he didn't want to be the one responsible for cutting off La Streisand, so he did a massive *ritard* and it was thrilling! Look for it on YouTube and watch!

We talked about *Drood* and Betty Buckley's unbelievable high E at the end of "The Writing on the Wall." He said that the song was supposed to end on a B, but when they did the workshop performance, the adrenaline got to her and she went up to an E. Everyone was obsessed, and it was immediately added to the show. Get that CD and listen because Betty gives one of the best Broadway performances ever. Rupert not only wrote the book music and lyrics to *Drood*, but he orchestrated the whole show as well! At that time, the Imperial Theatre had an orchestra minimum of 27 musicians. Get back to that CD and listen to how fabulous the orchestra sounds! *Drood* also had a brava cast. Not only the fabulous leads, but Rob Marshall, Judy Kuhn and Donna Murphy in the chorus! Holmes said that whatever role Donna went on for, she was voted the murderer. She was electrifying in any role she played. When Betty left, Rupert begged the producers not to give to the role to some TV personality, but to the person who would give the best performance. They asked who he meant, and Donna Murphy got her first Broadway leading role!

FYI, I've received many letters from *Straight Talk* fans. Apparently, the movie is amazing. Hmm... I don't retract what I say (even though I love Dolly), but I appreciate your passion and think we may just have different tastes. On that note, I suggest you rent Ashley and Mary-Kate Olsen's *New York Minute*. I think you'll love it.

Years of Cullum

June 12, 2007

Let's first talk about the week leading up to the Tony Awards! Tuesday, I interviewed John Cullum for my Sirius radio show. What a career! He was in the *original Camelot* as Sir Dinadan! Then he was the matinee Don Quixote in *Man of La Mancha* when Richard Kiley wanted to do only six shows a week. I asked him about starring in *On the Twentieth Century* with Madeline Kahn. One day, Madeline missed a rehearsal and asked how her understudy, Judy Kaye, did. John said that she knew all the lines. Madeline missed another rehearsal and asked again how Judy did. John said that she knew all the songs. Madeline missed a third rehearsal and this time when she asked John about Judy, he simply warned her, "Don't miss any more," AKA Judy's got it goin' on. Suffice it to say, Judy was brilliant and took over the role after Madeline left very early in the run. Also, speaking of the Tony Awards, when Judy Kaye became the star of the show, her small role of the maid was taken over by... Christine Ebersole! I love learning about understudies who later become stars. I think about those audience members in the '70s who were like "I'm outraged! I bought tickets to *Grease* to see Jeff Conaway — *not* his understudy Richard Gere!"

Wednesday, I put together a Broadway review for a benefit of the Jed Foundation, which helps prevent suicide of college-age kids. I had Kristine Zbornik sing the parody she wrote about the subway to the tune of "People": "People... piled on top of people... are the nastiest people in the world..." My favorite is the part is "With one person... taking up two spaces..." I'm so happy for Kris because she told me that she just got cast in the new Harvey Fierstein/John Bucchino musical, *A Catered Affair*. Brava!

Thursday, I interviewed Orfeh and her husband Andy Karl at *Chatterbox*. Best line of the *Chatterbox?* I asked Orfeh what she did at the High School of Performing Arts. She answered, "My major was drama." Andy added, "It still is."

Anyhoo, they both met doing *Saturday Night Fever* and Andy said that when he gave Orfeh an engagement ring, she threw it at him. I was ready for her to refute the story, but she concurred. She said that after the show one night, they ordered in Chinese/Cuban food, and he hid the ring in a take-out container. Orfeh said that she hates surprises because she's a control freak and had no inkling that he was going to propose. When she saw the ring box buried inside the rice, it was so shocking to her that she threw it like it was burning her hand. He then got down on one knee (with full turn-out, I'm sure, because he's a fierce dancer) and proposed. The whole courtship to marriage was just six months. *They've been together since 2000 and they still are today! Brava whirlwind romances!*

Tony night was fun as always, and my favorite win was Julie White for *The Little Dog Laughed*. She was so unbelievably funny in that show. I interviewed her on *Chatterbox*, and she was a riot. She told me about meeting her husband for the first time. It was at a barbeque. He was in his twenties, and after they had been chatting up a storm, he finally asked her, "How old are you? Like 35?" She said, "I said yes. Because I was 39, which is 'like 35'!"

Brava and congrats to all the winners!

The Game of Celebrity
June 18, 2007

I'm writing this column after celebrating Father's Day with my boyfriend, James, and his six-year-old daughter, Juli. First I took them out to brunch. And by "brunch," I mean dinner since it took two hours to get our meal. But it didn't matter because it was delish, and we got French toast on the side. Yum. Then we went bowling at Chelsea Piers, which was super fun. Juli essentially got the same score I did because she used bumpers in the lane. Have you seen them? They're literally walls that come up to prevent a child from having the bowling ball go in the gutter! When did bumpers come into existence? I never had that option at my signature bowling birthday parties circa '76, '77 and '78. I did, however, have a birthday cake with a fruit filling every year, even though I hate fruit in my desserts. I'm still angry I didn't just have delicious yellow cake with chocolate icing. But that's an angry confrontation I've yet to have with my mother (but plan on having one day when I'm in my mid-50s à la Barbra and Lauren Bacall, "Mirror Has Two Faces"-style).

Okay, on to Broadway. And by "Broadway," I mean Off-Broadway. I spent Monday at the York Theatre Company doing *NEO* (which stands for New, Emerging, Outstanding). It's a yearly fundraising event for The York that features the work of NEO (see acronym explained) composing teams. I was asked to sing a funny song by Benj Pasek and Justin Paul *years before their Tony nomination for A CHRISTMAS STORY!* about a guy who is PO'd at his ex-boyfriend. It's called "In Short," and most verses end with a version of the lyric "In short... I hope you die." The audience *ate up* the bitterness. It was hosted by the talented composer Bobby Lopez (*Avenue Q*) *And by AVENUE Q I also mean BOOK OF MORMON, FROZEN and basically anything else that allows him to live in a golden palace* and the hi-larious and hi-belting Ann Harada. The last time I heard from Ann was when she sent me an email lauding my book *The Q Guide to Broadway*, yet begging me to let her copy edit my next one because her former proofreader sensibilities were up in arms from reading it. I wasn't offended at all because there are some *crazy* mistakes in the book, including a section on Rush Tickets that refers to them as "Tush" tickets.

So many great people performed, including the amazing Lynne Wintersteller. I have always been obsessed with her voice on the *Closer Than Ever* CD ("Life Story" is gorgeous), but until I did a reading with her last year, I never knew that she's also fun-nee. Where is her Broadway starring vehicle? I was saying backstage that there should be more shows for women over 40. Is there only *Mamma Mia!* and *Menopause, The Musical*? Why is that all there is? And why must they only start with the letter M?

I hung out backstage with post-Elphaba Ana Gasteyer. We have had some hilarious times together. Once, for my birthday, I thought it would be nice to have a low-key party and spend the night with my close friends playing my fave game, Celebrity. I wanted around 15 people at my Celebrity party, and I was miffed by Ana acting odd during the phone call when I invited her.

A week later, I called to confirm whether she was coming or not and to tell her the version of Celebrity that I play. There was an awkward pause, then the question, "Celebrity is a game?"

"Yes," I answered, finally realizing the weirdness from the last phone call. She literally thought I was having a birthday party and inviting only my "celebrity" friends! How shallow did she think I was! "Hi, Myron. I have known you since high school and I'd love to invite you to my party, but your lack of famous-ness prevents me. However, I left an open letter on the *Spring Awakening* message board inviting any cast members to come. Mm-hm. No understudies. I'm sure they understand. After all, it's a 'Celebrity' party."

Another time, Ana and I were talking on the phone and she sounded down. I asked what was up, and she told me that her dad had just died. I screamed, "Oh, no! How terrible!" She explained that she was especially upset because her cabaret act was the next day (!) and she was having trouble memorizing her words. Huh? Priorities, anybody? That seemed a little too show-biz obsessed... even for me. I assumed that maybe her dad had been sick for a while, and that's why she was able to move quickly from the death of a parent into the realm of difficulty of memorizing a Juice Newton medley. Finally, after some more strange comments from her and talk about getting a dog, I realized I had heard her totally wrong. She didn't say her dad died. She said her *cat* died! I was mortified. I finally told her what I thought she had said and admitted the silent judgments I was feeling about her as she lamented the difficulty of committing "Almost Over You" to memory. She was so annoyed because she had been silently praising me the whole conversation thinking, "Finally! Out of all my friends, Seth has had the only appropriate reaction to this news." (See: "Oh, no! How terrible!") P.S. She would never do a Juice Newton medley. That was added for comic effect. More P.S., how could *anyone* do a Juice Newton medley? What happens after "Break it to Me Gently"?

Thursday, I interviewed theatre legend Jonathan Tunick. He has orchestrated so many classic Broadway shows my head almost fell off. I asked him to describe what an orchestrator does. I thought he'd say that an orchestrator takes what the composer has written (usually for piano) and divides it up between the instruments of the orchestra. He did say that, but then he said that a good analogy is lighting. "If the music is the set, the orchestration is the lighting. It colors it, it gives it texture, it gives it shading, and it can express the unspoken... the subtext. It can tell you what the character is not saying but rather feeling or... maybe even unaware of." Well said!

He also talked about the sitzprobe, which is the rehearsal where the actors sing with the orchestra for the first time. To go from singing with a rehearsal piano to a full orchestra is one of the most thrilling moments for any company of a musical. I then realized the sitzprobes he's been to. These were the *first times* these songs were heard with an orchestra: *Follies* ("Dorothy... there'll be two violins playing as you sing the last line of "Losing My Mind"); *Company* ("Vocal minority. The brass plays along with you in "Tick Tock" when you go "Dot Dot Dot Dow!"); *Promises, Promises* ("Burt... what's a Turkey Lurkey? And Donna... doesn't your neck hurt doing that?"); not to mention *A Little Night Music, Merrily We Roll Along* and *A Chorus Line*. There were many orchestrators on *A Chorus Line* because everybody was busy that season, and it was a downtown show that no one thought would ever move uptown! Jonathan said he's not 100% sure, but he thinks he did the Opening, "At The Ballet" and "Nothing."

To have been at those sitzprobes and heard all those classics — I want to have some of his memory cells implanted into my brain as soon as that operation is foolproof.

Saturday, I went back to The York to see the Musicals in Mufti series because they were doing *It's a Bird... It's a Plane... It's Superman*. My old buddy Stuart Ross, who directed and wrote

Forever Plaid, directed and milked much comedy out of the great cast, led by Cheyenne Jackson. Can I just say, I'm still devastated that Cheyenne wasn't nominated for a Tony Award for *All Shook Up*? He has *such* a fantastic voice and is a great comedian. I thought good-looking people aren't supposed to be funny. What happened to "Because I was so odd looking, I learned to make people laugh in order to get by"? It's not supposed to be, "I'm great looking *and* hilarious... and I have a cool first name."

Saturday night, I went to see one of the most talented people I know, Jeff Roberson as Varla Jean Merman. If you haven't seen Varla, get thee to *YouTube*. My favorite number is the "Schoolhouse Rock" parody ("A Noun's a Person, Place or Thing"). The 3rd verse is about a friend of hers who meets a French producer who promises to put her in a film, but she is never heard from again. The chorus goes:

"Oh, any person you can know/*Like a desperate girl, or a seedy Frenchman/*
And anyplace that you can go-/*Like a bar, or the bank of the Seine/*
And anything that you can show-/ *Like fake credentials, or a snuff film/*
You know they're nouns..."

Finally, I want to tell you what Rupert Holmes is most proud of. I interviewed him on Sirius, and he said that his biggest fear is forgetting to turn off his cell phone and having it go off during a show. He said he figured out the perfect ring, so he won't be devastated if it happens. I racked my brain trying to think what it was. Applause, I asked? He told me that wouldn't work. What if it went off during a quiet scene? Then what? He held up his phone and played me the ring that won't get him busted. This is it: *cough cough.* Seriously! He literally recorded a cough! He said that light coughing is the one noise you can expect to hear in any audience, be it comedy, drama, musical, etc. Also, it's his actual cough, so if someone looks over, he can just do it live for theatrical vérité. Isn't that brilliant?

Okay, everyone. Happy post-Father's Day, and go listen to a stunning Tunick orchestration and figure out the characters' subtext. And if someone coughs, answer the phone!

Sittin' Playin' Piano — With Andrea McArdle
June 26, 2007

Andrea McArdle sings "Maybe." David Hyde Pierce muses about *Spamalot.* Alysha Umphress astounds — and not just because of her name. Anyhoo, the week began with *Annie* rehearsal. Here's the deal. A few years ago, I had Andrea McArdle at the *Chatterbox*. Usually, at the end of the show, I ask my guest to sing something. Well, I've heard Andrea sing "Tomorrow" live before, but I'd never heard her sing "Maybe." Why had I never heard her sing it? Well, when I was growing up, my mother was notorious for getting me tickets for all the shows I wanted to see... *right* after the original cast had left. Why see Andrea McArdle when you can see her replacement? Why see Patti LuPone in *Evita* when you can see the replacement's matinee cover? Didn't my mother understand that I listened to those albums every day of my childhood and I wanted to hear Patti belt the "I'm their Savior!" modulation in "Rainbow High" and Andrea vibrato the last syllable on "together for*ever*" in "I Don't Need Anything But You"? But, alas, it was not to be. The only cool replacements I saw during my childhood Broadway forays were in *Pippin.* Priscilla Lopez as Fastrada and Betty Buckley as Catherine. But unfortunately I was six, so I fell asleep right after "...leave your fields to flower."

Anyway, I asked Andrea to sing "Maybe" at the end of the *Chatterbox* and she said she hadn't sung it since she did her last performance as Annie 25 years before. I looked at her with a "your point being?" expression and started playing the vamp. Of course, she sounded amazing. It made me realize that I wanted, nay, *needed* to hear her sing the whole score. I thought, why not do a special version of the show with her as Annie? I pitched the idea to Gregg Kaminsky from the Rosie Family cruise, and it's actually gonna happen the last night on the boat! I got Harvey Evans to play Daddy Warbucks and Rosie to be Miss Hannigan. Who says you can't go home again? I'll finally heal those wounds from March 1978 and forgive Andrea for leaving the show.

So, this week I started work on *Annie*, and Andrea and I got together to go over keys. It was so thrilling to play the melody of "It's the Hard Knock life for us, it's the hard knock life for us" and hear her sing "'stead of treated!" She's still got it!

Thursday, I had David Hyde Pierce at the *Chatterbox*. He's hilarious. But after every funny comment, total blank face-ness. He's dryer than whatever Texan town Audra and John Cullum live in. He said he grew up obsessed with Monty Python and it was super weird doing the first reading of *Spamalot* because he was doing Eric Idle next to Eric Idle. He knew the show could be a blockbuster, but was nervous about his big number. He thought it would either be hilarious or get the show boycotted by B'nai B'rith. He remembers singing the phrase "you won't succeed on Broadway..." and then nervously singing "...if you don't have any Jews." The line got a big fat laugh, and David knew the show was gonna be a hit.

Friday night, I went to a show called the After Party at The Laurie Beechman Theater. I heard a sasstress I hadn't heard before: Alysha Umphress. I want to give her a shout out, but since I can't pronounce her first *or* last name, I will give her a "write out." She sang "Where Are the Simple Joys of Maidenhood" and worked it! The arrangement was in a jazz style, and she put in *the* coolest riffs. Not the kind of riffs that make you turn off *American Idol*; the kind that, if Julie Andrews had employed them, the show would have run longer than the original 875 performances (thank you *IBDB*). *Alysha came to Broadway in AMERICAN IDIOT and recently played the Bette Midler role in the out-of-town production of BEACHES. Werk!* I was there to play for Christine Pedi who's doing a new show at The Metropolitan Room. She was trying out her version of "And I Am Telling You" as sung by people like Joan Rivers, Bernadette Peters and Little Edie ("oh no, there's no way I'm living without you, Mother Dear...").

All right, next week I have Tony Award-winner Debra Monk at the *Chatterbox* and I see the all-Asian production of *Falsettoland!*

Putting on *The Ritz*
July 3, 2007

Okay, I've been holding out on you. I sort of got big news a while ago, but I kept waiting for complete confirmation before writing about it. And by complete confirmation, I mean a signed contract. Remember a few weeks ago when I wrote about doing a one-day reading of *The Ritz* at Roundabout? Well, a little while after that, Joe Mantello called me and said that the *The Ritz* was going to happen in the fall, and he wanted me to be in it! I'm thrilled because it will be my Broadway debut (above the pit)! In the reading I had such pivotal roles as Patron and Snooty Patron. When Joe called, I had no idea which of the myriad one-line roles I was being offered. Well, I was thrilled when I got my contract and it not only read "as cast" (meaning whatever little roles come up in rehearsal), but it also had me down as Snooty Patron! I was so excited to see the word "snooty" before patron. That's one step above just plain Patron!

So, this week I was meeting with Joe outside his rehearsal for *9 to 5*, and the talented/cute Marc Kudisch walked by. He asked what I was up to, and I told him that Joe just cast me in *The Ritz*. I downplayed it and said I essentially had very few lines and I was playing tiny roles like Snooty Patron... even though I was secretly proud of snagging that part. Joe piped up and said apologetically, "Actually, I think someone else is playing Snooty Patron." Ow. My role just lost an adjective. I looked devastated but then told Joe I'm happy with any part since this is my Broadway debut. He stopped looking guilty and said, "Exactly! What are you complaining about, Meryl!" He got me.

Anyhoo, during the reading we did, I coveted the role that Brooks Ashmanskas is playing and asked my agent if I could be the understudy, assuming the powers that be would say a quick and decisive yes. Instead, they said a quick and decisive, "You'll have to audition." So, last week I went in and read for Joe, big-time casting director Jim Carnahan and the playwright himself, Terrence McNally! It was a triptych of honchos. I like auditioning, but don't you hate the moment right after you finish your audition? After I read, I have to use so much control to not obsessively repeat, "Did I get it? Did I? Did I?" I can't stand pretending I'm comfortable walking out of the room not knowing how I did. Note to all casting directors: my jaunty exit punctuated with a convivial "Great seeing you! Have an excellent day!" is a *total farce*. Inside I'm *desperate* for any and all information. The good news is, once I know whether I got it or not, I'm pretty much fine. My friend Paul Castree has a rule that you're allowed to be devastated for 24 hours if you don't book something, but after that you have to move on. So, I don't lament lost roles, it's the waiting that's brutal for me! Thankfully, I only had to wait one day for my agent to call and say I *am* understudying Brooks! I'm so crazily excited!

Here's what else happened this week. I interviewed the great Debra Monk, who is currently starring in *Curtains,* at the *Chatterbox*. Firstly, she talked about how green she was doing her first play in college. She got cast on a whim and knew *nothing* about theatre. She showed up, and the director said he wanted to start with the opening scene. He told her to say the first line at the window, start making toast after the phone rang and finish her tea on the last line. She did the scene that way, and the next day when she showed up, he said he wanted to run it. Well, this time she started the first line at the door, finished her tea right away and never made toast. He asked why she wasn't doing what they decided the day before, and she was completely confused. She had no idea she was supposed to do the same thing every time! She did the show and loved it and then discovered that people make a living acting. It was so foreign to the way she grew up because she said that her family was blue collar, and everyone hated their job — she had no idea you could earn a living doing what you loved. When she finally moved to New York, she couldn't get work or an agent, so she and her friends wrote an act about a rockabilly band and decided to run it once a week at the Westside Arts Theater. It was the '80s, and that part of town literally had groups of rats running around the sidewalk, mixing it up with the prostitutes. The show was slated for 11 PM at night, so they begged their friends to come and comped their admission, except for making them buy one drink. The show got great word of mouth, and they finally got a little blurb written about them in the Post.

Suddenly, 11 producers wanted to buy the rights! The show became *Pump Boys and Dinettes* and moved Off-Broadway and then to Broadway! It was then nominated for a Tony Award opposite *Joseph, Nine* and *Dreamgirls*! Monk remembers being backstage at the Tonys right after Jennifer Holliday blew the roof off the theatre with "And I Am Telling You… " She said the audience went *crazy* from the *Dreamgirls* number. The curtain opened, and then "there we were. The whitest show ever." It was a letdown for everyone… onstage and off.

The real devastating part was that after writing a Tony-nominated Broadway show *and* starring in it, she still couldn't get an agent! After the show closed, she had such trouble landing work that she took a gig in the Midwest doing *Pump Boys* in a mall! A part of the stage led to the loading dock, and one day a UPS man actually came onstage and asked someone to sign for a delivery…and Deb did. Maybe now he can sell it on eBay?

The great part is that she heard that The Louisville Rep was having auditions for their season, and she flew herself there and asked to audition. They kept saying that she had to be submitted by an agent, but she begged and said that she flew there on her own dime and just wanted a chance. She auditioned, got a part, and while she was in Kentucky, she finally got a New York agent who she's still with today. I love that she took her career into her own hands and wasn't afraid of begging.

Sunday night, I went to Caroline's Comedy Club to see my old buddy, Linda Smith, whom I used to be a writer with on *The Rosie O'Donnell Show*. Her stand up is hi-larious. She said she loves the beach but can't deal with the sand, so she wants to stay in her apartment and pretend she's at the beach. "First, I'll gather up a couple of radios and put them all on different stations, then I'll invite over a really loud family with kids and make 'em sit right next to me… and then I'll just sit in front of a fan and try to light cigarettes."

OK, I saw the all-Asian version of William Finn's brilliant *Falsettoland* and, as I predicted, I literally cried from start to finish. I went twice this week because I love it so much and, of course, in the middle of my weeping, my mother leaned over and (loudly) asked if I had allergies. I was in a rage that she didn't pick up on the fact I was crying, 'til I realized that I was pre-crying. That's when you know a show so well, you cry way too early because you know the devastating things that are gonna happen later on. For instance, the second time I saw *Ragtime*, I broke down in tears as soon as Audra walked onstage. Hence, my mother assumed it was hay fever that made me do non-stop nose blowing during the hilarious "Baseball Game" song. It was very well directed by Alan Muraoka, and the cast was top notch. I think the show should perpetually be playing in New York. The characters are so rich. There's no hero, no perfect person. All the characters are flawed, and that's what makes them real. And the story is so beautiful. It's about what love really is. Not, "Oh, you're great looking and nice, I love you," but true love like 13-year-old Jason deciding to have his Bar Mitzvah in Whizzer's hospital room because he loves his father and he loves Whizzer.

This coming week starts intense rehearsals for The Rosie Cruise… and then we sail next Saturday.

I want to close by writing about Thommie Walsh, the original Bobby from *A Chorus Line,* who passed away two weeks ago. I met Thommie when he worked on a show I did with Kristine Zbornik and Varla Jean Merman called "Holiday Hams." Thommie staged the songs but spent much time answering my obsessive questions about his Broadway career… especially his first Broadway show, *Seesaw*. Thommie was in the original version that was playing in Detroit (on its way to Broadway) when the director was fired and Michael Bennett was brought in to fix the show. Michael, in his direct way, ixnayed most of the ensemble by walking around backstage and telling them they were fired right before they went onstage! Thommie said he would be backstage stretching, see Michael coming, and literally hide behind a costume rack to avoid being canned! He needn't have hidden because Michael loved him as a performer. He kept him in the show and, of course, a few years later, cast him as Bobby in *A Chorus Line*. He then went on to do brilliant work on the other side of the stage with *The Best Little Whorehouse in Texas, My One and Only* and one of my absolute favorite shows, *A Day in Hollywood/A Night in the Ukraine*. Thommie was hilarious and multi-talented and will always be remembered as a part of Broadway history ("If Troy Donahue could be a movie star… then I could be a movie star…").

Xanadu's Holy Rollers and More
July 10, 2007

Let me give you pre-cruise updates. Last Monday, I hauled it downtown to the Metropolitan Room and saw Christine Pedi do her new show, *Great Dames*.

She did a great version of "A Spoonful of Sugar" which she did all sexed up... a phrase I never thought I'd use to describe that song. And she closed with her brilliant rendition of "And I Am Telling You" sung as Bernadette, Little Edie, Joan Rivers, etc. that I described last week. She was recording the show for an upcoming CD and got crazy cheering throughout, but the accolade I was the most excited about telling her was that, during the performance, my boyfriend leaned over to me and whispered, "She's got a *great* body." It's exactly what I'd love an audience to be whispering whenever I perform. But if it had the same pronoun it would sort of be devastating.

Tuesday, I interviewed *Xanadu*'s Tony Roberts at Sirius. What a career! His first big break literally was just that. When Robert Redford took off two weeks from *Barefoot in the Park*, they decided to put on his understudy, and Tony got a two-week gig as *his* understudy. Right before the two weeks began, the replacement was playing baseball in the Broadway Show League and broke his leg! Tony went on for the full two weeks, and when Redford left, he became the replacement!

Tony also starred in *How Now, Dow Jones* (check out *Bluegobo.com* for fab footage). That show had a short run because Equity went on strike and when the strike was over, David Merrick decided to punish the cast by closing the show. It sort of gives you a comeback to say to those people who complain about the lack of Broadway shows with one producer. Tony was also one of the stars of *Annie Hall*, which is one of my all time favorite movies. He has a great part, but said it could have been much bigger. When he shot the movie, he had a beard and when the shoot was over, he couldn't wait to shave it off. The next day Woody Allen called and said that he had all these new scenes he wanted to film with Tony. Oh no! There was no time to wait for Tony's beard to grow back so the scenes were never filmed. How depressing is that? Don't they have fake beards in Hollywood? Insert closeted gay actor joke here.

Thursday, I had Victoria Clark on the *Chatterbox*. You need to find a copy of her *Piazza* performance on *The Tony Awards* ASAP! She talked all about what it's like being on the Tonys. You do eight shows during the week, but you're also spending time at Radio City doing camera blocking. Morning of the Tonys, she had to wake up at 7 AM so she could rehearse again at Radio City in full costume. Then, out of her costume, went to the theatre to do the show back in costume again. Finished the matinee, got into her glam gown for the red carpet. Got to Radio city and put back on her costume again. When she was backstage, she was reviewing the new speech Craig Lucas had written her to start the number. It set up who and where her character was. Well, as Adam Guettel was making his speech in front of the curtain accepting his Tony, literally seconds before she got onstage, a stagehand told her that her body mic wasn't working and handed her a handheld mic that was twice the size of Bob Barker's. What about her handheld props? How could she carry a mic and her gloves, pocketbook and guidebook? She shoved them all into her other hand and went into a full anxiety attack/shut down. Kelli O'Hara must have noticed it across the stage, even though Radio City is the size of a football field, because Vicki heard Kelli yell, "It'll be OK! Don't worry!" Well, that relaxed her enough to walk out onstage and start her newly memorized speech into her microphone while walking forward towards a moving camera and also looking at the stagehand to the side of the camera who was making enormous hand motions. She thinks he was telling her that her body mic was still broken. This went on 'til the last moment of the speech where he gave her a big "A-OK" sign and took the microphone away, and she immediately started singing. You have to watch it to see her panicked walking, shifting eyes and last minute mic trade off. Terrifying/hilarious! Of course, the number sounded beautiful... and the hat trick at the end worked!

James' birthday was Friday night and we went to see *Xanadu* and loved it. Chris Ashley directed all the comic moments so cleanly and Doug Carter Beane filled the script with his usual comedy sass. Speaking of which, I ran into him outside the theatre and asked why he had the nerve not to want Julie White for the lead in *Little Dog Laughed* (as per her Tony acceptance speech). He said it was because the role was completely different when he wrote it. The character was blank-faced and incredibly cold. She came in to the audition with her high energy and warmth and was completely wrong, but he loved her comedy so much, he totally re-wrote the role for her. So, he said, she was *amazing* in the part but he *still* doesn't want her for the role the way it was originally written!

The *Xanadu* cast is so talented, it's mind-boggling. Comedy stars Jackie Hoffman and Mary Testa have tons of great line readings and their version of "funking out" on "Evil Woman" is a big, fat brava. All the backup muses sing up a storm, and the two leads are brilliant. Kerry Butler is so funny and sounds phenomenal. It takes so much skill to be comically imitating someone (Olivia Newton-John) while still giving full-out high soprano yet belting up a storm. I can't believe she sings eight shows a week, yet after the show she told me, "actually, this show is really vocally easy for me." Huh? It's every part of the female range!! So, what would be difficult for her to sing? Coalhouse Walker? And Cheyenne Jackson is perfect as Sonny. As usual, gorgeous and hilarious. And, like Kerry, vocally brilliant. After the show, I complimented his incredible flexible riffs, and he said he added an extra one for me because he knew I was in the audience! Can that be considered a form of flirting? Let's just say yes.

OK, now it's Monday morning on the cruise, and I have to run to the breakfast buffet. My mother just called me in a panic and said it closes in a half-hour! Out of my way at the Waffle Bar!

The Rosie Cruise, Part I
July 17, 2007

I'm back from the Rosie cruise, and I'm too scared to weigh myself. My friend Tim said that we were doing Body for Life-style dieting on the cruise (six small meals a day), but changing the modifier from "small" to "mammoth." There was one dinner where I fully acted out during dessert and had two Tiramisus and some chocolate cake. Of course, after 11, I went to the late night buffet just to meet my friends, thinking there was no way I would eat, but there was a crepe bar. I'm talking fresh-off-the-grill crepes. Of course, I had to have one... but then I noticed the "make your own sundae" bar. Ever since I saw a commercial for "Zips" when I was a kid (anybody remember?), I've been obsessed with making my own sundae. Suffice it to say, I made my own sundae as well as confirming my future outfits would include drawstring pants. But enough about my eating disorder, bring on the cruise details.

Saturday: Got onto the ship early (you're not supposed to call it a boat... it's like calling an "Original Cast Recording" a "Soundtrack") and started rehearsal for that night's show, "Rosie's Broadway Belters." The opening number had great lyrics by Michael Lee Scott sung to "Magic to Do": "We've got cruisin' to do... just for you/We've got tons of events each day/ Where the seas are serene." Rosie: "And no split screen!" That was a sassy reference by Michael Lee to Rosie's last day on "The View" where she and Elisabeth Hasselbeck duked it out. When Rosie sang that line, the ensemble held up a pic of Elisabeth. I guess it was immature on my part, but I suggested we add a mustache to the photo. Of course, someone in the audience took a photo and it wound up in US Magazine. Where's my commission?

Since a lot of couples get married on the boat, I thought it would be fun to do a marriage song with a twist. Hence, Jimmy Smagula and my boyfriend, James, sang "Old Fashioned Wedding." It sounds great with two guys, and I changed the key so both James and Jimmy had to belt B flats! When Rosie introduced the number, she talked about Jimmy being in the audience of her TV show years ago, saying he wanted to be on Broadway, and since then he's been in three! Or, as Rosie said, nine. Oy! She exaggerates more than my Mom!

The show closed with three singers doing an audience sing-along of "You Light Up My Life." After a few measures, Capathia Jenkins stormed onstage and said we couldn't end the show that way. She launched into the brassy "(Let a Big Black Lady) Stop the Show" from Martin Short's *Fame Becomes Me*. I'm obsessed with the lyric "Now if Julie Andrews had a black maid in that play, well then *My Fair Lady* would still be running today." Hilarious! The brilliant team of Marc Shaiman/Scott Whitman wrote it, and, P.S., I just hung up the phone with Marc, who told me that the workshop for their new musical, *Catch Me If You Can*, begins rehearsals this week starring Nathan Lane, Christian Borle and Tom Wopat. *Only one stayed with the show!* He managed to give me the information while also berating me for being so out of the loop. Kudos for double tasking.

Sunday: Egg White omelet for breakfast, counteracted by a "side" of oatmeal with a cup of brown sugar. Mmmm. That afternoon I did a *Chatterbox* interview with Andrea McArdle. Amazing. First of all, I hope you know that she wasn't cast as Annie originally. She was Pepper, the tough orphan, and the girl they had as Annie was adorable and sweet. When they started previews at Goodspeed, the creators realized that Annie wasn't adorable and sweet, she was sassy and street smart. Andrea was bumped up to the title role and played it on Broadway and in London where Molly, the youngest orphan, was Catherine Zeta-Jones! And Daddy Warbucks was Michael Douglas! All right, the Daddy Warbucks part was a lie, but not particularly far-fetched.

I demanded that she talk about my favorite TV movie *Rainbow* (the young Judy Garland story), and she said that she had a terrible time filming it. Jackie Cooper directed it and did things like tell her to look at the wall, which she would do. Then he'd say "Okay, we got the shot." She literally has certain close ups where she's supposed to be feeling something deep, and the feeling is actually "hmm... pretty wall."

I asked her about college, and she said that she got into NYU, but got offered *Jerry's Girls*, so she left. She regrets it, but if she hadn't done that tour, we wouldn't have the fabulous recording of her doing "Wherever He Ain't" and "Look What Happened to Mabel." Listen to it when you can. She holds the last "Ma" of "Mabel" straight tone and then adds vibrato. Perfect.

Carol Channing was on that tour and heard Andrea complaining about always having to sing "Tomorrow" or, as Andrea called it, "The T Song." Carol sternly told her that although Leslie Uggams (who was the other lead) is a great singer, she doesn't have a signature song, so Andrea better appreciate how lucky she is that she does. Carol has a point, but I'd be curious to know if she's ever seen Leslie's "rendition" of "June is Bustin' Out All Over" on *YouTube* because she certainly makes it her own. *Go to my website and look up the video I did with Leslie where she explains it all!*

Anyhoo, Andrea also said that Carol would get wigs on 14th Street and ask Andrea to cut them for her ("to look like Madonna"), and Carol would love Andrea's shoes and frequently buy the same ones for herself... but in a size 10. Size 10? You know what they say, big feet, big... um, range? And by "range," I mean scanning the entire bass clef. Also, Andrea was always miffed that in every publicity shot, for some reason Carol looked younger than springtime and Andrea looked like ye olde hag. Carol's advice? Always wear something nautical. Looking around the ship's lovely Spinaker lounge, I realized that Andrea's story was informative *and* timely. Wait a minute... didn't Barbra always wear a sailor top in all her photos in the '60s? She had the nerve to steal Carol's look *and* film role!

Andrea talked about playing Fantine on Broadway in *Les Miz* and having to come back as a boy on the barricade in Act Two. She said that at one performance, she was eating a giant bag of M&Ms backstage and put them in her pocket before she got on the barricade. Her character got shot, and because she had friends in the audience, she did an incredibly dramatic death that involved flailing her body upside down on the barricade. Of course, clackety clacking out of her pocket came pouring multi-colored M&Ms. The good news for my musician peeps was that because the stage was raked, the orchestra suddenly got a ton of M&Ms raining down on them, which no doubt provided some much-needed carbs to get through the last half hour of the show. That was one of the many times she was written up to Equity. Another time, she found something called "circus" backstage. Was it a perfume? She didn't know. She put it on the orphans pillows. Turns out, it was amyl nitrate or "poppers. " She put the pep in Pepper that night!

Sunday night, my good friend Jason Little, who won best actor in Minneapolis for playing Hedwig, belted out some songs from *Hedwig*. My favorite part was at the beginning of "Tear Me

Down" where Hedwig normally name-drops the city he's in (When I first saw Jason do the show in the Midwest, it was "Don't you know me Twin Cities?"). On the boat, Jason hilariously used the literal nautical location of where we were to start the song. He strutted out and shouted, "Don't you know me Greenwich Mean Time Starboard naut 38?" Amazingly awkward.

After his songs, Jason got a standing O, and we all rushed down to see Sandra Bernhard. I've always been a fan of hers ever since *Without You I'm Nothing*. And I had the privilege of telling her, that morning while waiting to get my signature hot cereal with the abundance of brown sugar, her show was great. She began with "And I Am Telling You" (seriously!) and did a whole riff on Angelina Jolie. My favorite part was when she commented on Angelina constantly carrying her kids everywhere ("Has Maddox *ever* walked on the ground?").

All right, I've been writing forever, and I'm only up to the first full day on the cruise, so I have to continue this tomorrow. I'm off to rehearse for the NYCLU benefit I'm doing tonight at The Skirball Center, and I've got to find something nautical to wear.

The Rosie Cruise, Part II
July 20, 2007

This is part two of my Rosie cruise experience. I'm typing slowly because I'm lacking energy. My body now demands a steady influx of bread/sugar/deep-fried products and it refuses to fully function unless I attend at least one buffet a day. My boyfriend and I went to Trader Joe's and stocked up on "healthy food" now that we're back on dry land, and I've spent the last few days trying to explain to my stomach that smorgasbords are for special occasions and do not normally occur six times a day. By the way, I got an email from my friend Amy Corn saying, "I read your last column. Did you really eat that much for dessert?" Short answer: "yes"; long answer: "...and it was delicious."

Anyhoo, we're now on (last) Monday, the third day of the cruise. We docked in Cape Canaveral and many people went off to Disneyworld. I made that mistake on the first cruise and opted out this time. It's a long, hot bus ride and then a long, hot day so I opted to relax on the boat, i.e. eat non-stop.

Tuesday, we docked in a Dutch oven, I mean, Key West. With the ozone layer almost gone, a two-block walk gave new meaning to the expression "sun kissed." I could feel my collagen evaporating and deciding ne'er to renew itself.

That night, four of my friends (Richard Roland, Michael Klimzak, Tim Cross and JD Daw) performed a bunch of songs from *Forever Plaid*. That show is literally perfect. The James Raitt harmonies are so beautiful and creative and Stuart Ross wrote such clear-cut characters that make each character distinct within a few lines. And even though we just did a small version of it, everyone kept commenting on how much heart there was in the show. The only problem was that all of us hadn't done it for years. And I mean *years*. So, not only did everyone have to re-learn the harmonies, but the four Plaids who are supposed to be clean-cut young guys cut down in their prime were well into their sixties. I'm exaggerating, but let's just say I'm glad it was a large venue.

Wednesday, we docked on a private Island that the Norwegian Cruise Line owns. James, his friend Cheryl and I went snorkeling, and I was having fun till they both pointed out a barracuda. I didn't know if you're supposed to remain immobile so they'll leave you alone or if you're supposed to get the hell out of the area. I opted for the "get the hell out" route, but I was wearing a mask, a life vest and flippers, so I moved as fast as a glacier. Luckily, the barracuda ignored my attention-getting splashing and I relaxed until James spotted a stingray. That was it for me and I hightailed it to the beach and a virgin Piña Colada.

That evening, Euan Morton did a fabulous concert. He has 1,000 megawatts of stage presence and a glorious voice. I always think he sounds like the male Karen Carpenter. He sang the haunting "Stranger in this World" from *Taboo* and the beautiful "Hallelujah." He also ripped his shirt off at the end of the show, which made it clear to me that he and I were eating in different places on the boat... with different sized portions. Rosie has an organization called Rosie's Broadway Kids that teaches inner city kids musical theatre lessons and Euan offered to sing any kid on the boat to sleep if the parent would make a $50 donation to the charity! How cool was that?

Thursday featured *Sibling Revelry*, which consists of sisters Liz and Ann Hampton Callaway and their sassy music director, Alex Rybeck (who also celebrated his birthday on the ship!). Ann and Liz sound great together and are both so funny. At one point Ann was doing patter but was hilariously upstaged by Liz walking up and down the aisle hawking her CDs. Then Ann "accidentally" discovered her 15 MAC Awards onstage. Liz countered that by sauntering to the stage to reminisce about her Tony Award. "Nomination," Ann quickly added. Brava bitchery!

Finally, Friday arrived. I'm talking *Annie*. Even though Steve Marzullo was the music director, he let me conduct the opening trumpet solo in the Overture. Then I came forward and told my story about my obsession as a child with what I call "The Red Album." I told them how I never got over having to see Andrea McArdle's replacement when I saw *Annie* on Broadway. That sadness was compounded by watching the show and realizing I could never be in it because all the orphans were girls. But in the middle of Act One, I noticed that there were two newsboys in the "NYC" number and I was suddenly thrilled because there were boys in *Annie*. Yay! I *could* be in the show I was obsessed with! I then realized that the newsboys were actually girl orphans dressed up as boys. That's right, I told the ship audience, I was fooled by a couple of 11-year-old "drag kings." I said that most everyone I knew who was my age had dreamed of being an orphan in *Annie* and wished they had seen Andrea play the title role. "Tonight," I said triumphantly, "through the magic of R Family Vacations, those dreams will come true."

I set the opening scene (an orphanage in December), and all the girl orphans ran out because Molly (Sarah Uriarte Berry) had a bad dream about missing her parents. I ran offstage, donned an orphan smock, and ran on shouting "Oh, my goodness, oh, my goodness..." Yes! I was Tessie, the "oh, my goodness" orphan!

It was so fun doing "Hard Knock Life"... for me. The other girls had a breakdown because we kept it in the original key. Andrea said that Charles Strouse found out how high little kids could belt "Hard Knock" and then, since they're angry, took it up a half step so the song would make all the orphans sound strained. Well, if little kids had trouble hitting the high notes, imagine adult ladies. Suffice it to say, the words "nodes" and "vocal damage" were bandied about. Along with, "I'm gonna kill Seth." The end of the song, though, was fun for everyone because the director (Dev Janki) had us pretend to throw our bucket of water at the audience, and instead of splashing everyone, out came multi-colored confetti. Cool!

Andrea was amazing as Annie. First of all, she was totally believable as an 11-year-old orphan. She has the same spunky sass that made her a star back in '77. Rosie and I were backstage plotzing during "Tomorrow," and at the end of the tumultuous applause, someone in the audience screamed out a heartfelt "Thank you!"

I introduced "NYC" by saying that the original "Star-to-be" solo was the late, great Laurie Beechman, but Andrea played the role in the TV movie. "So, Andrea played Annie on Broadway and the Star-to-be in the film. Too bad she can't do both roles tonight. *Pause*. Or can she!?!?!!" I exited and "NYC" began as usual, but in the middle, the crowd circled around Andrea as Annie, and when they opened up again, she had done a quick change and become the Star-to-be! The only problem was, for some reason, we could only find one suitcase for her, so it made no sense when she sang "...three bucks, two bags, one me." I'm just curious why we couldn't find another suitcase *on a cruise ship*!?! Didn't anybody pack? Who cares, Andrea found her D flat on "...to-ni-i-i-i-i-i-ight! The Y..."

Rosie was a brava as Miss Hannigan. Hilarious and on her gig, musically! I went up to her suite earlier in the week to teach her the "Easy Street" harmony (her suite was on the top deck of the boat and had eight bedrooms and two outdoor hot tubs!), and she nailed it during the show! I knew she could do it because she was able to sing three-part harmony backing up Megan Mullally on "Freddy My Love" when we did *Grease!* Of course, according to Megan, Rosie was *also* able to make dinner plans with her friends in the audience while she was dancing "Born To Hand Jive" by mouthing "Meet me at Orso at 11." Seriously.

The most fun was when I got to do "You're Never Fully Dressed Without a Smile." If you haven't seen the original staging, get thee to *YouTube* and watch the Tony telecast. Peter Gennaro's choreography is brilliant because it's not technical for kids, but it's totally character appropriate and has built-in audience applause moments. At the very end of our "Smile," we were joined by kids on the ship that had been practicing the dance all week. I felt so happy to dance with them... and incredibly upstaged.

I announced to the audience that Harvey Evans was playing Daddy Warbucks and told them his amazing history (15 Broadway shows, including *Follies* and playing Tulsa in the original *Gypsy!*) and then, to show the audience that he still "had it," we put a dance break in the middle of "I Don't Need Anything But You." He and Andrea did a challenge tap and they both had clean-as-a-whistle sounds... even on the pull-backs!

At the end of the show, tons of kids from the ship came up and sang "New Deal For Christmas." Bobby Pearce did a brilliant job with costumes, culminating with Andrea coming out in the middle of the song in an exact replica of the Annie red dress. She looked amazing! She did, however, draw the line at wearing the red fright wig.

Right before we left the stage, Andrea started a reprise of "Tomorrow." At the end, everyone onstage was singing along during "You're always a d-a-a-a-ay... a-a-a-a-a-a," and then I cut everyone off so Andrea could end by herself with "-w-a-a-a-a-a-a-a-a-a-y!"

After the show so many people came up to me and admitted they had the same *Annie* orphan fantasy and asked me if I was freaking out onstage. I have to say I was mostly very concerned with hosting it and getting my steps right... except during "Maybe." All the orphans were on the stage, and Andrea was comforting Molly by singing "Maybe far a-w-a-a-a-a-a-y... or maybe real nearby," and I suddenly thought that this is what the original orphans experienced. Sitting on the stage, facing out towards the audience and looking at Andrea, center stage, singing. I thought about how, as a kid, I would always look at the cast album photo of the orphans in their beds with Andrea in the middle and how I was now, literally, in that picture. When I realized that it was something I always wished for, never thought could happen, and was actually happening, I started crying. Who wouldn't?

All in all, the Rosie cruise was thrilling and life changing —like it always is!

Another Hundred People

July 24, 2007

First of all, when did it become the third week of July? It seems like only yesterday I was obsessing about *America's Next Top Model* cycle six. How did we suddenly get to the final episode of Kathy Griffin's *My Life on the D-List*? Also, on a side note, when did a TV "season" become five episodes? Remember *The Mary Tyler Moore Show*? Twenty-four episodes? Kathy Griffin began season three a minute ago, and now this week is the season finale! That's like starting *Gypsy* with "Let Me Entertain You" and immediately segueing to "Rose's Turn." The only positive aspect would be skipping "Little Lamb." I know it's a beautiful song, and it sets up the Louise character, but suffice it to say that when I would listen to that album as a child, I couldn't lift that needle fast enough.

This week began with the NYCLU benefit that I emceed and music-directed at the lovely Skirball Center. It opened with the brilliant Tony Kushner reading a piece that I demanded he get published in the New Yorker. I'm sure he was like, "I kind of have a Pulitzer… I don't need to get my piece in 'Shouts and Murmurs.'" Fair enough.

Jesse Tyler Ferguson was, as usual, so funny. He accompanied himself on the guitar and began his piece by saying, "I'm not a very good guitar player." He followed that statement with "I am, however, an amazing singer." So dry! Then he said there would be a part of the song where he'd ask for applause as if he just held a long and impressive note. Sure enough, halfway through the song, even though he had only sung a middle C, and held it the length of an eighth note, he demanded applause… and got it! Brava on the manipulation!

LaChanze came to rehearsal and wanted to sing "Another Hundred People." Unfortunately, she couldn't remember what key she sang it in. I name-droppedly told her that she sang it in B major in the '95 *Company* revival, just so I could show off my Broadway knowledge. She was impressed that I remembered (the reaction I wanted), and I called Michael Lavine, who has every score ever, and he offered to fax it to me. Then I realized that I've been playing that song since high school in C major, and if I tried to play that Sondheim hand twister in another key, I could make seafood risotto with the amount of clams that would be spewing out of the piano. I scurried over to LaChanze and changed my braggart "you sang it in B major" statement to "you'd sound amazing in C major." Thank goodness LaChanze is the nicest person ever and she obligingly belted the whole thing up a half step. Phew!

The coolest part of the whole evening was at the after party. During my stand-up segment, I talked about the pen pal I had as an 11-year-old. Instead of writing her a letter, I, not surprisingly, decided to make her a 45-minute tape of me singing and playing the piano. Of course, when I finished, I thought, "I've gotta keep this. It's *way* too good to send!" After I told that story to the crowd, I played the section of the tape where I sing "Tomorrow," featuring unflattering riffs, an unasked-for blue note and certain notes not less than a quarter tone and up to a half step flat. When I talked about my pen pal, I mentioned that I had connected with her through the magazine everyone my age was obsessed with, *Dynamite!*. I always hear the audience murmur agreement when I do that part. Then I hold up one of my many issues (Monday, I chose the issue with Sarah Jessica Parker's TV show, *Square Pegs*, on the cover), and I always hear gasps. Well, cut to after the show, a young man approached and told me that his father created *Dynamite!* Holy (fill in the blank)! He also said that his Mom created *Bananas*, which was the magazine you were supposed to graduate to when you got to high school, but I kept up my *Dynamite!* subscription well into my menopause. He also told me that his parents always listen to me on Sirius! I couldn't believe it! It definitely wasn't a "bummer." (Remember that section of the magazine? "Don't you hate when you wake up early for school... and it's Saturday!" Hilarious! ...when you're nine.) I asked what his parents did now. Turns out his mom is in children's book publishing and his Dad is a writer of children's books.

ME: Oh, really? What's his name?
SON: R.L. Stine.
ME: (Passed out with dollar signs floating around my head.)

Tuesday, I interviewed Lee Wilkof on my Sirius radio show. He was the original Seymour in *Little Shop of Horrors* and told me that periodically he would come back and play Seymour for a limited time or rehearse with the new Audreys. He remembers one rehearsal with an Audrey that he thinks may have been a standby or an understudy. Regardless, he definitely remembers that she was the sexiest Audrey he had ever worked with. He told me that when he got to kiss her, he practically had a breakdown... and he worked with a lot of Audreys. Turns out, that sexpot understudy/standby was... Donna Murphy! And, quite frankly, she's still got it!

Friday night, I went to see Broadway legend Betty Buckley at the Blue Note in the West Village. Right before the 10:30 PM show, I scrambled to get her a birthday present, but the stores near the Blue Note that were open only sold a wide variety of bongs. Not cool. James and I loved the show, and she sang one of our favorites, "Come On, Come On," sounding exactly like she did in her Carnegie Hall concert from more than ten years ago.

After the show, we went to her dressing room and she told me that she recently had an audition for a M. Night Shyamalan film. She was asked to film herself and send it to the casting director. She and her assistant, Cathy, drove from her Texas ranch to Fort Worth, a city an hour away, to get a camera that was compatible with a Mac. They then drove back to her ranch, filmed her audition, and Cathy went to transfer the film so she could make FedEx by five o'clock. Annoyingly, it *wasn't* compatible with the Mac! She frantically called the store, and they told her to bring it in and they would transfer it. Cathy drove back to the store, and when she got there, the store said that they wouldn't do it. Ah! She only had an hour 'til she had to FedEx it! She called Betty, who was riding one of her horses (!), and Betty told her, "Wrap the camera in bubble wrap and mail the whole thing!" And that's what she did. Betty got a callback and flew up to N.Y. When she walked in, M. Night was laughing and busted her for mailing an entire camera. The great news, is, Betty got the film role! I'm so excited there's going to be belting in an M. Night Shyamalan movie. "I see de-a-a-a-a-ad (high E) people!" *Betty isn't the only Tony Award-winner in the film. There's also Victoria Clark!*

Okay, this week is *110 in the Shade* again and then *Gypsy*. Note to self: "Little Lamb" is a vital song in the score and should not be spent rifling through the Playbill.

Gypsy, *The Ritz* and P-Town
July 31, 2007

Greetings from Provincetown, or as it's also called, P-town (tip o' the hat to *Urinetown*?). Last Sunday night, I saw *Frost/Nixon* and sat right behind Charles Busch's director Carl Andress in the upper right box seats. We felt like a combination of Glenn Close from *Les Liaisons Dangereuses*, Raoul from *Phantom* and the "Let's go flying" guest star from *Will Rogers Follies*.

After seeing *Frost/Nixon*, all I dream about is living back in the '70s. I don't even smoke, but all I want to do is book a flight on TWA or Pan Am and light up a Newport. The performance was an Actors Fund Special Performance and if you don't know, it's an added ninth show where all the ticket money goes to the Actors Fund of America. It's on a dark night for most shows, so the audience is filled with Broadway performers. They're always so exciting because, even though they take place in the middle of a run, having all those Gypsies in the audience gives the actors so much energy that it's like seeing an Opening Night performance.

Monday night, I played piano in the pit of *Phantom* and had one of my signature debacles. During "The Music of the Night," I was counting the measures I had to rest until I played, and suddenly the bass player in front of me turned around and scared me because she was wearing a crazy mask that covered three quarters of her face. Musicians are often trying to lighten up the repetition of playing in a pit by doing something "wacky," so I assumed she was trying to parallel the Phantom's mask with her own "hilarious" version. I sort of laughed and was still counting measures and noticed that she refused to turn back around and kept saying something unintelligible. I sort of indicated that I got her Phantom mask reference by covering my face with my hand and pointing to her mask. Still, she continued playing while facing me. Finally, I looked beyond her and saw the conductor also looking at me. I suddenly realized that we were at the bridge of the song and I hadn't yet played note one. I later found out that the bass player was wearing the mask because she doesn't want to breathe in the Phantom fog that flows down from the stage. Turns out, I had miscounted and missed my first cue. She had turned around to try to get me to play. Unfortunately, because she was wearing a mask, I couldn't hear what she was saying, which was essentially, "*PLAY!*" So the whole time I was supposed to be playing my beautiful piano arpeggios, the conductor was watching me stare at the bass player and imitate the Phantom's mask by putting my hand over my face. *I did a video about this that's become one of my so-called classics! Watch it on SethTV.com!*

Wednesday, I saw *Gypsy*. First of all, it was phenomenal to hear that delicious overture with a full Broadway orchestra! Nowadays, the overture is when people read their *Playbill*s and chat up their neighbors. But because it was an actual full orchestra and not four synthesizers with a drummer, the audience was riveted. The difference in sound changes the whole attitude of the crowd. I actually saw a harp player! I thought they had been outlawed from Broadway in '97.

I have to talk about Laura Benanti as Louise; she's so brilliant that she made "Little Lamb" fantastic! As I've written before, I've always been so bored during that song, but while she sang (beautifully), she showed the loneliness and vulnerability of her character so beautifully it was devastating. Plus, her comedy was *brilliant*. The splitting headache she indicates getting in Act Two when Mama Rose hauls out yet another "I had a dream" literally made me LOL. Speaking of laughs, Marilyn Caskey as Electra! She took the stripper that has the least material to work with, honed in on one lyric ("I'm electrifying and I ain't even trying") and hilariously based her whole character on "not even trying." Is she on Valium? In a coma? Post-lobotomy? It's a brilliant comic turn.

And of course, there's Patti. First of all, the voice. She's been starring on Broadway since the '70s, and she still sounds *the same*! Is there a larynx aging in an attic somewhere? I watched her during the bows and thought that she is truly a gift to Broadway. Oftentimes I get depressed that I wasn't alive to see Angela in *Mame* or Barbra in *Funny Girl*, but I was so thankful on Wednesday that I've been able to see Patti through the years. Why isn't she in a musical every year!?!?!! If she's gonna do another play like *The Old Neighborhood* again, they'd better add some belting. The nicest thing was that during Patti's solo bow, the whole cast stood in the wings applauding her. Usually, the cast rushes back to their dressing rooms to get their wigs/costumes off, so the fact that they wanted to give Patti riotous applause says a lot for her and the company.

Now, a *The Ritz* update. I not only have a (little) part in the show, but I'm also putting together the number that Rosie Perez is performing in the show as Googie Gomez. The super-talented Chris Gattelli is choreographing the show *Pre-Tony Award for NEWSIES!*, and he and I have been creating the number for the past week. Friday, we presented it to Joe Mantello and Rosie Perez in my apartment. Rosie was adorable. She was mortified that she was late, but I totally understood because she did something that everyone does at least once. She wanted to go to 72nd Street but by accident took the A train, which goes from 59th to 125th Street! It's so shocking when that happens. You're so close to your destination, and suddenly you're in Albany.

I was nervous presenting the stuff to Rosie, but she was super nice and laughed right away. If you don't know the plot, Googie is a minimally talented songstress who is performing in a gay bathhouse to further her non-existent Broadway career. Chris and I tried to make a medley of the most inappropriate material possible, and while I don't want to give anything away, suffice it to say that there's a section featuring her singing "Sabbath Prayer" from *Fiddler*!

I'm writing this all in my charming Provincetown one-bedroom apartment, feeling an actual breeze from the bay. James and I drove up on Saturday with Maggie, my lab mix, in the back seat. His daughter Juli is in Texas with her Gran and arrives Tuesday. Sunday was the R Family Cruise sponsored "Broadway Brunch" where the high-belting Farah Alvin sang "Meadowlark." I first met Farah when she joined the *Grease!* revival to understudy Jan. I was teaching her the backup to "Freddy My Love" and noticed she had incredible vocal placement. I casually asked her if she knew *Evita* and when she said that she did, I immediately launched into the vamp for "A New Argentina" and forced her to sing "He supports you..." on non-stop E's. After that delicious diversion, I was forced to go back to plunking out the notes to "so-o-o blue..."

Sunday night, we all went to see *Varla Jean Merman Loves a Foreign Tongue*. Varla is really Jeffery Roberson and he always puts together an amazing evening. The show celebrates foreign cultures and has my kind of chestnuts like Varla bragging that "I've performed in 15 foreign countries... and I've done shows in three of them." She also proudly demonstrates that she's learned how to say "this sore is not contagious" in ten different languages.

All right, time to enjoy "Family Week." And by enjoy, I mean having Cape Cod Ice Cream, fish and chips and clam chowder. At this rate, I should comfortably fit in during "Bear Week."

Luxury Problems
August 6, 2007

Have you heard the expression "luxury problem"? Like the quandary Jerry Herman was in in eight times a week during the mid-'60s: "Hmm... should I see the first act of my smash musical *Hello, Dolly!* and then catch the second act of my smash musical *Mame*? Or vice versa?" That was me and my boyfriend all last week. We went up to Provincetown to do some shows for "Family Week" because it was run by the R Family Vacations people (who do the Rosie cruise). Essentially, we're both in the worst moods now because our vacation wasn't perfect. So, I know that's a luxury problem, but please allow me to vent. Firstly, we went to a restaurant that lured us in with a man standing in front of it holding a menu. I looked at it and decided that I wanted the delish lobster salad and thought the prices were A-OK. James and I sat down and (a) they then informed me that they no longer make lobster salad and (b) when we both opened our menu, we noticed that someone had meticulously put liquid paper on every price and raised it a dollar. But I guess the one menu they managed to miss was the one the man was holding outside. I'm sure that was just a coincidence.

Then James got food poisoning from said restaurant and had to start using the bathroom as often as a typical *Christmas Carol* at Madison Square Garden daily show schedule (believe me, that's a ton of times a day). Also, since I was doing my own show, the theatre gave me a great one-bedroom apartment. "Great," except for the fact that most of P-town has that Massachusetts attitude of, "Why would anyone possibly want air conditioning? This state was founded on hard work and deprivation. Sweating all night long is a badge of courage. Pass the chowdah." The whole first night was brutal. I tossed and turned because I felt like I was starring in Farah Fawcett-Majors' first dramatic turn ("The Burning Bed." Anybody?).

So, finally, the second night I had a complete breakdown from the heat *and* feeling bad for James with his upset stomach. And I couldn't believe how extra hot the apartment was. The weird thing was that every time I went to the window to get some air, I felt even hotter. Could it be *that* hot outside? Finally, I bent down near the window pane to see why it was so boiling in that area, and my hand touched a scalding hot radiator. That's right, James' six-year-old daughter Juli had tried to put on the overhead light hours before and, by accident, turned the heat on — to 80 degrees! That was it for all of us. I grabbed everybody and booked us a room at "Christopher's by the Bay," which is a great guest house. The only thing we cared about was that it had *air conditioning*. We all traipsed over there at 11 PM and, even though I was getting free housing from the theatre, I paid for the next three nights because I don't enjoy vacationing in a Dutch oven.

Anyhoo, while in P-town we all went to see that divine drag artist, Edie. Edie is really Christopher Kenny, a fiercely tall, beautiful ex-ballet dancer with whom I've done tons of benefits with and who was in the *Threepenny Opera* revival last year. Edie is a very sweet, adorable character, and the show went over great with the guys and gals in the audience *and* the many children in attendance. By the way, not only did six-year-old Juli love Edie, but so did ten-year-old Maggie... my dog. Before the show, we were all eating outside and ran into Lea DeLaria. She mentioned that Edie's show was starting. I said I didn't have time to take Maggie home. She told us that she plays the same theatre and it's dog-friendly. I didn't really believe her, but the next thing I know, Lea walked us in, and Maggie planted herself in the aisle... *and* she loved it. I always knew she had a campy sense of humor.

Also, here's a pronunciation lesson that should be taught in "Survey of Theatre" classes across the country. It's LAY-uh Salonga and LEE-uh DeLaria. James and I were sitting outside and heard some pretentious guy say to his circle, "Let me introduce you all to my good friend, Lay-uh DeLaria." That's like saying, "Let me introduce you to my good friend *Wise Guys*." It's *Bounce*, people! *Bounce! Actually, when it finally opened in New York, it was ROAD SHOW. Yowza!*

All right, here's the part where the vacation plummeted. James, Juli and I went to "George's Pizza" and bought some pizza. As we were sitting at the table eating, I got up to get Juli a cup of water.

MAN BEHIND COUNTER: We only sell bottles of water.
ME: Oh... I just want a paper cup of water.
MAN BEHIND COUNTER: We don't do that.
ME: Plastic bottles are bad for the environment.
MAN BEHIND COUNTER: You can buy a paper cup... for $1.75. That's the price of a bottle of water.
ME: (Defiantly) Fine.
MAN BEHIND COUNTER: (Takes cup of water, puts ice in it, turns on faucet, fills it. Takes $1.75 from me.)

I was totally going to lead a *Ragtime*/"He wanted to say"/Emma Goldman-style protest of the restaurant... but it was way too hot to picket. So I just told the story to everybody I could, making me sound either like a folk hero or that crazy person on line at Fairway that you avoid by staring straight ahead.

Anyhoo, I did my *Deconstructing* show at the Provincetown Theater (which, by the way, is a really nice space), and it went great. The terrifying thing about P-town is that people don't buy tickets for shows essentially until "places." So the whole day I was devastated because Juli decided to have a play date that night instead of coming to my show, and I thought that meant I lost half my audience. But thankfully, at the last minute, I wound up having a great house.

We finally fled P-town after James had a fight with a toy store because they wouldn't let Juli use the employee bathroom (I stared straight ahead, Fairway-style) and decided to drive down the Cape to visit my old college friend, Liz Higgins. Liz and I were piano majors at Oberlin, and she now lives in Boston. I always use her as an example when I talk to Broadway synth players about "checking your patch." The different sounds synths play (organ, electric piano, sound effects) are called "patches," and you change them by hitting a switch... either on the synth or with a foot pedal. But sometimes, the switch doesn't work or it skips two sounds ahead, so you should always check to see what patch you're on before you play. Liz was playing *A Christmas Carol* in Boston and during a love scene, she was supposed to play two soft chimes. Unfortunately, she had it on the "scary ghost" patch. So, instead of the lovers hearing the sound of a distant church bell (ding... ding), they literally heard "who-o-o-o... who-o-o-o-o" with signature old man ghost vibrato.

While I was at the Cape, I heard that the Actor's Playhouse is closing. I'm devastated because that's where I did my one-man-show, *Rhapsody in Seth*, and I loved that theatre. I'm thrilled though because there was an article in Backstage about actors that performed there who moved on to greater prominence, and it included my name next to James Earl Jones' and Robert DeNiro's! Do you think that they also emailed the article to their parents like I did?

So, we all had a great time with Liz and, as we drove home, I thought that the vacation would end on an up note. Then in the car Juli said, "There's a bug on Maggie." I thought, "Oh! Juli's so cute! She's concerned because a fly landed on Maggie." I turned to look where she was pointing and saw a blatant tick on the inside of Maggie's ear! We pulled over, bought tweezers and James pulled it off. I thought to myself, "Why should I be panicked that it had Lyme disease… just because the last place we went to a rest stop was in Lyme, Connecticut?!?!" Ah! Why don't they at least change the name of that town? Who wants to make a pit stop in Hepatitis, Rhode Island?

We finally got home, and I calmed myself down by realizing that everything I was upset about was a luxury problem. I walked into my apartment, ready to do some new video blogs and discovered that I left my brand new laptop at Liz's house on the Cape… and she had left for Boston. Let me end with this old chestnut: I need a vacation from my vacation. And a new laptop.

Kerry, Anthony and Sideburns
August 14, 2007

First of all, my hair. Joe Mantello wants us all to grow our hair out until rehearsals begin for *The Ritz*. We're going to have our hair cut into '70s styles, so the more hair we have to work with, the better. It feels bizarre to have crazily long sideburns. I don't know if I look like a Village Person or a Yeshiva student.

This week I did an interview for my Sirius radio show with the ultra nice and brilliantly talented Kerry Butler. Back in the day, Kerry and I performed in a kids' nightclub called "Youngstars" when we were super young (she was super *super* young). At the end of the show, all the kids in the show got to wear the T-shirt of the Broadway show they were in at the time, so there'd be kids doing the finale in T-shirts that said *Annie, Peter Pan, Evita*... even *I Remember Mama* (!). Kerry and I, however, had never done a Broadway show and we're *still* devastated that our T-shirts were blanker than Sofia Coppola's face throughout *Godfather: Part III*.

There are so many *Annie* audition devastations out there, but Kerry's tops the list. She actually has two that need to be told. First, she auditioned to be a replacement orphan on Broadway and actually got to the final callbacks! She was in Catholic Elementary School, and her principal made a loudspeaker announcement on the day of her last audition asking the students to pray for her. One student named Joey Mazzarino heard the announcement while he was sitting in class and thought, "Pray that someone gets a part in a show? That's ridiculous!" He refused... and Kerry got cut. She was devastated years later when Joey revealed to her that he boycotted helping her out with a little prayer... especially since she wound up marrying him! No wonder she didn't take his last name.

The real doozy of a story happened a little later. She went to the audition for the *Annie* movie and, again, got to the final callbacks! That night there were a few messages on her family's answering machine. Could one of them be "the" message? Her mom pushed play, and suddenly they heard what they had been waiting for: "This is a message telling you that you've been cast in the *Annie* movie. Congratulations!" Kerry remembers jumping up and down screaming. But then wait! There was another message: "Um... that last message was a mistake. Sorry."

Can you believe that!? She got to have ten seconds of joy followed by an eternity of heartache. I was plunged into a depression when I heard that story... and then more so when she told me that she didn't save the messages. How much fun would that be to actually hear? I'm sure that Kerry *was* devastated that she didn't get cast until she actually saw the movie — she then probably had a feeling similar to the "devastated" passengers who couldn't book a ticket on the initial voyage of the Titanic.

Kerry's done so many shows it's mind-boggling. We talked about her playing Belle in *Beauty and the Beast*, and I asked her what happens if the contraption that helps the Beast do his transformation back into the Prince doesn't work. Due to the non-disclosure agreement she signed that said all she's ever allowed to reveal about the special effects in the show is that they're "Disney Magic" (oy!), she clammed up... except to tell me that on opening night in Toronto, it malfunctioned. The orchestra, however, still played all that transformation music, so the Beast (Chuck Wagner) did what's required when it malfunctions: he filled the time by doing a *modern interpretive dance*. Seriously! Kerry was filled with hilarity/mortified at the awkwardness… but then *doubly* mortified when the Isadora Duncan transformation ended and the audience applauded! Canada, have you no shame?

I told her how fierce I thought her roller skating is in *Xanadu* and she told me she's notoriously uncoordinated. She was Penny Pingleton in *Hairspray* and revealed that, after the Tony Awards, Marissa Jaret Winokur told her that she TiVo'd the Tonys and watched their performance of "You Can't Stop the Beat," and she loved how crazily klutzy Kerry looked. Kerry was horrified to admit that "You Can't Stop the Beat" was the one number in the show where she thought she was making Penny look like an amazing dancer. She thought Penny's journey in the show was from klutz to cool and culminated in her amazing dancing during the finale. Ouch. That may have been her *sub*text during the number, but her actual text was clankstress.

In terms of the roller skating in *Xanadu*, she flat out told the director (Chris Ashley) that she wouldn't be able to act 'til the end of the rehearsal period. So much of her comedy is physical, and she said that she needed to spend her rehearsal time becoming comfortable with what her body was doing on those '80s skates. She told me that she'd come home from rehearsal almost every day and cry. Thank goodness Chris let her mark the first three weeks of rehearsal because I saw the show, and her skating is roller-disco perfect and her performance is hysterical.

On Thursday, Anthony Rapp came to the *Chatterbox*, fresh off the heels of his triumphant return to *Rent*. I asked him about all those *Rent*-heads out there and if there was any inappropriateness. He said that the only indecent proposals he ever got in fan mail were when he was on Broadway playing Charlie Brown. Disgusting? You decide. Actually, I will. *Yes.*

Of course, we had to talk about his teen film hit *Adventures in Babysitting*. He screen tested for it, but the producers felt that, due to the success of the Molly Ringwald teen films, his blond hair would remind audiences too much of Anthony Michael Hall. So he screen tested a *second* time, and this time they dyed his hair red… with permanent dye! If he hadn't gotten the film, I'm sure watching the red hair color grow out wouldn't be a devastating daily reminder of the film he didn't book.

I asked him how cool the premiere was and how popular he became in his high school because he was one of the stars of a Hollywood feature film. He told me that (a) nobody in his school cared, (b) there was no premiere and (c) he went to see it in his local Cineplex and had to buy his ticket. Ow, ow and yowtch.

This week I'm excited to see some Fringe shows (especially the laugh-out-loud Kelly Kinsella's *Life Under Broadway*, which I saw last year at Ars Nova and loved) and also slightly terrified to have my costume fitting for *The Ritz* at William Ivey Long's studio. I finally have to put on that revealing towel. Did they have love handles in the '70s?

A Robe, Please, for the *Ritz*
August 21, 2007

Let me get my costume ordeal, I mean "fitting," out of the way.

Since *The Ritz* takes place in a 1970s bathhouse, I've been preparing myself for a skimpy costume. And by "preparing," I mean binge eating. Two weeks ago, I got the call for the fitting, and even though the costumes are by William Ivey Long, the fittings were at a sassy place in the garment district run by a lovely woman named Jennifer Love. I asked her how many people meet her and make references to a.) Jennifer Love Hewitt and b.) Jennifer Convertibles. She said often to "a" and never to "b." What? Jennifer Convertible Sofas were a staple of my childhood commercial watching alongside ads for the game Mousetrap and Gnip Gnop. Anybody?

So, even though I was joking around, I was also preparing myself for the depression of being squeezed into a towel and parading about. I was, however, not prepared for the pleasant surprise of seeing a long, white bathrobe hanging on the costume rack. Ah! I thought, I'd feel comfortable wearing that on Broadway. I could show a little chest and, if the audience is lucky, a little gam.

Unfortunately, my fantasy was short-lived because I was suddenly asked to try on a pair of underwear. "To wear under the bathrobe?" I asked. Oh, these costume people are such purists, I thought. Even though my underwear wouldn't be seen, they wanted to make sure I had on a nice, tight pair. I was informed that the underwear *might* be worn under the bathrobe, or it might simply be worn. By itself. With nothing else. Isn't that against Equity rules? Subjecting an actor to love handle viewing by a general audience? I slowly stripped off my clothes à la Coco from *Fame* and put on said underwear. The "good" news is that I could fit all of my fat over the top and sides of the underwear. Excellent. Surely this is the worst part, I thought. Then, *Flash!* That's right. Photos had to be taken front, side and back(fat), so that final decisions could be made on who in the cast should wear a towel, a bathrobe or just underwear. At least that's what I was told, but I know that those photos are going to be shown the next time there's a William Ivey Long dinner party. They'll be passed down a long line of costumers from a chortling Bob Crowley to a guffawing Willa Kim. *P.S. Now as I read this I think I was probably ten pounds less than then I am now. I wanna see those pics!*

This week I also had the pleasure of interviewing the two comic cut-ups from *Xanadu*, Mary Testa and Jackie Hoffman, at the *Chatterbox*. They're laugh riots singularly, but together they are a melting pot of hilarity. Mary talked about working with Bill Finn on the early Marvin Trilogy and walking home from Bill's apartment late at night. She and Alison Fraser would walk closely together because the West 80s in those days were not so safe. Around 1 AM, they passed by a hotel residence and an elderly man was having trouble working the door. Mary wanted to help, but Alison warned her about the rough element in the neighborhood. Mary told Alison to calm down. It was a very old man! What could happen? She approached gingerly and helped the man with the door. Ah. Good deed done. She then asked if he wanted anything else. "Yeah," he growled, "Gimme some P----!" They both ran away screaming!

Jackie talked about her first audition in New York. She went to an open call for *Merrily We Roll Along*, and the casting director looked at her photo and said, "I don't think so, Jackie." Mary immediately said that should be the title of Jackie's next show at Joe's Pub. Brava.

Then Mary talked about being the swing for *Barnum*. She had to cover all the ensemble women, and they all did circus tricks. She wasn't nervous going on for any of them, except for Sophie Schwaab (who later went on to play Rosabella in *The Most Happy Fella* revival). Sophie was a world champion twirler and, suffice it to say, Mary was not. She was assured she would never go on. Of course, one day, Mary arrived at the theatre and was told she was on for Sophie. A hush fell over the theatre. Firstly, she had to wear a pink unitard. Please don't get any ideas, William Ivey Long. Secondly, she noticed that the backstage area was extra crowded. Why? Because word got out and crews from other shows flocked to the theatre to see what was gonna happen on that stage! It was like when the Christians were thrown to the lions. Mary said that the big number was "Come Follow the Band," and normally Sophie was in front, leading a parade and doing trick after trick. Twirling three batons with one hand, throwing them up in the air, doing a cartwheel and catching them all, etc. Well, Mary knew she had to do something. She couldn't just stand there and sing, so she just twirled one baton at a time, threw it in the air and would then watch it land in some random spot across the stage. But she made it look like an amazing trick, by pointing with a flourish to wherever it landed. As in, "I didn't catch it on purpose, instead, look how far I can throw it stage right!"

Jackie talked about being offered the final *Hairspray* reading (she played the female character track: Prudy, the jailer, the gym teacher, etc...). She loved the reading so much, but felt she'd never get it on Broadway because her career refrain had been "I don't think so, Jackie." She finished doing the reading and, on her way out, told Marc Shaiman that she hoped Lea DeLaria had a great time playing it on Broadway. He assured her that she'd play it on Broadway and, I *do* think so, Jackie, she did!

Broadway was a little terrifying to her, though. She was so used to doing Off-Broadway that she called one of her friends freaking out when she heard that she would be wigged.
"I don't know how to put on a wig," she cried.
"There are people there who do it for you, Jackie," her friend explained.
"*Every time*?!?!?" she sobbed.

I asked Mary what it was like being Liza Minnelli's understudy in *The Rink*. She said that the first time she went on was on a two-show day, July 4th, because Liza checked herself into The Betty Ford Clinic after the matinee. That made Jackie quip, "Hey, what are you doing between shows? *Rehab*!"

Mary played the show for two weeks while they rehearsed Stockard Channing to take over the role. Stockard then took over... and it played an additional two weeks. Ouch. Mary said that Chita Rivera is very in the moment when she performs, but likes to have everything she does pre-planned and almost choreographed. Mary is the opposite. She likes to change things up. Finally, one day, Mary did something different, and it caused Chita to change the way she had always done a particular line.

"Aha!" Mary said teasingly to Chita after the show. "I got you!"
"You did," Chita said, admitting to changing a moment in the show. "And it didn't work!"
Busted! They had different acting styles, but still, Mary said that Chita was phenomenal to work with.

This week, I also had an audition for *Spamalot*. I had to learn "You Won't Succeed on Broadway," which is fun-nee, and they also told me to bring my own music just in case. I got to the audition five minutes before it began and realized I didn't have my regular audition song. I did what every New York actor does when he needs music ASAP: I placed an emergency call to Michael Lavine. He has everything ever composed, and he'll send it anywhere. Within one minute, he was faxing my old chestnut to Chelsea Studios. He's amazing.

A little while ago when I was in P-town, I was doing a show for Family Week and realized I didn't have the music that Marya Grandy (*Les Miz*) was singing. Michael was driving in from Williamstown, but told me that if he rushed home and went up to his apartment before returning his rental car, he'd be able to fax it to me in 45 minutes, I'd have the stage manager get it and Marya would be able to sing it as the 11 o'clock number. He got it done, and Marya brought down the house. I don't know if we should focus on the praise he deserves for keeping Broadway music alive, or the derision I deserve for being so mind-bogglingly irresponsible twice in ten days.

And finally, I saw the recent Broadway revival of *Grease.* I wrote a weekly blog about the reality show earlier this year, so I sat and watched it with a fond heart. It's also the show I played piano for the longest on Broadway, so I watched it with a lot of eye-rolling and "if I never hear this song again..." But let me say, it was so fun to see the winners, Max and Laura, live! Sort of like a musical theatre version of *Broadway Danny Rose*. And I was super impressed with the voices of Daniel Everidge (who played Roger) and Lindsay Mendez (who played Jan). *Lindsay has since become a star! She later originated in DOGFIGHT and also played Elphaba in WICKED!* They interpolated some sassy high notes in "Mooning" that made me totally look forward to getting the CD in the fall. And brava Jenny Powers as Rizzo. I worked with her last summer at the Perry Mansfield New Works festival in Colorado, and I was busting her for always playing nerdy soprano roles. She told me that's not really her, and boy was she right. She looks so gorgeous in the role and her acting and singing are delish. And I know my Rizzos! In my *Grease!* days, I saw Jody Watley, Debby Boone, Rosie O'Donnell, Maureen McCormick, Tracy Nelson, Sheena Easton and Brooke Shields. Oh, yeah, and MacKenzie Phillips, Joely Fisher and Linda Blair. You know, I do a lot of joking in this column, but I ain't joking now. Those women all played Rizzo. Don't get me started on the Vince Fontaines I've seen. OK, you did. Cousin Brucie, Joe Piscopo, Donny Most, Mickey Dolenz, gymnast Dominique Dawes. Oh, wait. She was Patty Simcox. Ow, my head hurts.

OK, that's it for now. I have to go to bed. Rehearsals for *The Ritz* begin tomorrow! Note to self: buy highlighter/look over script/schedule lipo.

Kevin, Donna and a Unitard
August 28, 2007

First, a clarification. The show I'm doing is called *The Ritz*. Like the cracker. The reason I'm clarifying the name is because I've been congratulated on being cast in *The Rink*. Three times! Hopefully, people think I'm the young sassy Liza Minnelli role and not the older Chita Rivera track.

Anyhoo, rehearsals began last Monday. It's very exciting starring in my first Broadway play. And by "starring," I mean that on the morning we were scheduled to start dissecting the script, our illustrious director Joe Mantello walked into rehearsal, looked at me and asked, "What are you doing here?" Now that I'm an actor, I guess I can use that moment for a sense memory of "mortification." Yes, people, I showed up by mistake. Apparently, my two lines did not need dissecting. We all laughed... one of us only on the outside.

I actually have been doing non-stop laughing at rehearsal. Turns out, Joe Mantello is so much fun. I first figured that because he was such a bigwig, he would be distant and unfriendly (father issues, anyone?), but instead he's like your best friend at theatre camp. We all spend breaks huddled around a laptop while he shows us his favorite *YouTube* videos. (Please watch the amazing entrance at the beginning of Tandi Iman Dupree's drag act — unbelievable!)

On Tuesday, I got a call from my agent telling me that I had a callback for a commercial. Yes, it was for a department store I never heard of; yes, only on cable; and yes, it was never to run in any big cities, but I wanted it! I asked when it filmed and turns out it was during the three days I was supposed to go on a vacation, so *The Ritz* wasn't planning on scheduling me at rehearsal! I could do it! Excellent. All I had to do was go in and nail that callback. The first annoying part was that, since the role was a piano player in a department store, they told us to wear a tux (to the first audition and the callback). I guess that if we came in wearing a regular outfit, it would be impossible to imagine what we looked like dressed up. Who says TV people have no imagination? Yay! It's fun hauling around a big, hot tuxedo on a subway in August.

The next stressful part was that if I got the commercial, I'd have to leave Thursday night for L.A. and miss the *Chatterbox*. The callback was on a Tuesday, early afternoon, so I assumed I'd know by the end of the day. No. Now, you know when you go to a commercial callback, you're agreeing to be put "on hold," and you have to keep yourself available on the shoot days until you're told that you're released. Since I'd have to fly to the West Coast on Thursday night, I knew they would make a decision by Wednesday morning.

No.

It was now Wednesday afternoon, and I didn't know whether to book my *Chatterbox* or not, because I didn't want to have some Broadway star agree and then have to ixnay them to film a rickety-rackety cable commercial. My agent called the commercial people and told them my predicament. They said they understood and would notify us as soon as possible. Well, suddenly it's Wednesday at 6 PM, and I'm *still* on hold for Thursday night through Sunday. Since my agency would be closed overnight, I wouldn't know till Thursday morning. Dare I book someone that last minute? I finally placed an emergency phone call to Kevin Chamberlin late Wednesday night, and he said he'd do the *Chatterbox* and wouldn't care if I canceled.

Speaking of Kevin, he was such a fun guest. He's one of the few actors who has done *Chatterbox* three times! He talked about his first Broadway musical, which was also my first Broadway show as a piano sub. It was Lincoln Center's short-lived *My Favorite Year*, which I renamed *My Favorite Week*. I only got to play it three times, but it was a great piano part. Kevin said that he was so excited to be in it and could not wait for his parents to see him on Broadway. Unfortunately, on opening night he was a little too excited and forgot to put on his suspenders during the big "Manhattan" dance number. He literally spent the whole number knowing his parents were watching him dance with one hand while holding up his pants with the other. He also said that Lainie Kazan had so many electronic appliances in her dressing room that she blew the lights in the hallway of dressing rooms! I wanted to know what she had plugged in, and he speculated multiple curling irons and The Fry Daddy.

He then talked about doing *Abe Lincoln in Illinois*. Y-A-W-N! Doesn't that title imply the most boring show in the world? "Abe Lincoln" = I'm drowsy. "In Illinois" = and I'm out. It had an enormous cast, and he only appeared at 8:15 and then again at 11:15. He said that, on some nights, he would do his first scene then hop on the subway at Lincoln Center and go down to the Village and hang. One night, his friend had a show at the Duplex on Christopher Street at 9 PM, and Kevin was able to do his first scene, take the subway from Lincoln Center to the Village, see his friend's act, congratulate him after, and easily make it back for his last scene. I asked if he was nervous about the subway breaking down, and he said he could have walked and made it back in time.

He played Horton in *Seussical* and said he loved it when Rosie O'Donnell played The Cat in the Hat. She would take questions from the audience, and one night a little kid asked how long Horton the Elephant's trunk was. Rosie told him, "He says it's seven feet, but actually, it's really five."

I also asked Kevin about the brilliant *Dirty Blonde* in which he starred with the writer Claudia Shear. He did a lot of Mae West research and told us one hilarious story about how quick she was. One night Mae was walking through a casino in Vegas, and a guy called out from the craps table, "Hey, Mae! I'll lay ya ten to one!" She, without missing a beat, replied, "It's an odd time, but I'll be there." Brava!!!!

Speaking of *Dirty Blonde*, that's where *The Ritz* began. Kevin said that one day after the show, Joe Mantello approached him and said that he wanted to do *The Ritz* with him and Rosie Perez. Kevin said he was totally interested, and Joe got on it. And it only took seven years to happen. I guess I better plant the seed now for Joe to direct me in *The Gin Game*.

At Sirius, I interviewed Donna Murphy. She's so fun and, FYI, her hair looked amazing. I must find out what deep conditioner she uses. She talked about her first Broadway disappointment. *Hair* was revived in the late '70s, and Donna auditioned because one of the understudies was leaving. They said they loved her, and she'd be hearing from them. Well, she was at NYU, and this was before cell phones. And, apparently, before room phones. She gave them the number to her dorm and waited anxiously for their call. She said she harassed the guy who ran the phone constantly to see if they called. They never did, and she was *devastated*. It wasn't until way later when she told someone the story that she found out that *Hair* closed right after her audition!

Her first Broadway show was *They're Playing Our Song*, and for her audition she sang that classic song "This World" from *The Me Nobody Knows*. Anybody? Actually, I know it because my sister did that show when she was in high school. There's nothing like seeing a 99% Jewish high school sing songs of kids in the 'hood. I recall a lot of "torn" jeans and boys wearing base.

We talked about her playing Fosca in the *Passion* workshop and how she worked all the time to create the character. It was great for the audience, but she said her husband was like "Honey, it's a reading. I don't want to have breakfast with Fosca. She's a downer!"

I brought up her absences in *Wonderful Town* because I wasn't sure if everyone knew what really happened. She said that she was backstage right before "One Hundred Easy Ways," and she coughed to clear her throat and wound up hemorrhaging a vocal cord! Her doctor said that she'd need *months* off from singing, but she didn't want to quit the show. She had waited so long to do it since she first did it at Encores! Finally, another doctor said that if she had a week of silence, she could heal it, so she didn't speak for a week and went back. Of course, it was preview time, so there were non-stop early morning publicity events, the recording, and finally opening night. Sadly, because her chord wasn't totally healed, it got damaged again.

She said that this went on repeatedly: she'd come back to do the show, but the damage never got a chance to heal. For some reason, she made a deal with the producers to not discuss what was going on in public until way after the show closed! I still don't understand why, but unfortunately it led to a lot of dishy talk about her. She said she didn't care if people thought that she totally lost her voice, but she was devastated that they thought she didn't care about her fellow cast members or the audience. And the horrible part was that she wasn't allowed to reveal what was going on! Anyhoo, she's fine now and has a delish part in the new film, *The Nanny Diaries*. *And, years later, her great part in TANGLED!*

Okay, I'm off to bed early 'cause tomorrow is more rehearsal. The "good" news, I not only wear a skimpy towel, but Joe Mantello informed me that Act Two will feature me in a unitard. Why?! What's happening? Am I being Punk'd? I do *not* look attractive in a unitard. I'm the only person who's going to have his debut on Broadway and immediately follow it with his boyfriend breaking up with him. Here I come, Equity *Match.com*.

Xanadu and *Zanna, Don't!*
September 4, 2007

This week I finally started rehearsing my part in *The Ritz*. If you're like my mother, you're thinking, "Why do you need to rehearse for two lines?" (direct quote, 8/25/07). But besides my two sentences, I have a variety of things to do throughout the show, so, stop being mean, Mom, et al.

First of all, Monday was our full cast "meet and greet." We had our official Equity meeting where we took a vote about whether lunch should be an hour or an hour and a half. Why? Who needs that much time? Is that for people who want to rehearse in the morning then quickly pop over to the Hamptons for a seafood salad? Is there any evidence of a company *ever* voting for an hour-and-a-half lunch? Is it a holdover from when the company of the original *Romeo and Juliet* needed time to saddle up their horses and ride over to Bristol for the lunch special? Was there even Equity in Shakespearean days? Ye olde Equiteye?

Then we walked around and investigated our dressing room assignments. For those who have been chomping at the bit, yes, I am sharing a dressing room with former porn star Ryan Idol. I'm sure I won't feel inadequate on every level.

The most amazing thing is that we're actually rehearsing on the set! *The Ritz* is a farce, and if we tried to rehearse it in a studio, it would just be all of us trying to stay within the lines of a floor covered in different colored tape that somehow represented a multitude of doors and three different levels. Every two minutes would be the stage manager interrupting with "Rosie, the yellow tape is the second floor and the green is the top level, so stay on the blue," or "Brooks, you just walked through a wall."

Anyhoo, our sassy director, Joe Mantello, pleaded his case, and Scott Pask, our fabulous set designer, built an amazing multi-leveled set that we're having the best time gallivanting on!

The cast is super nice, and everyone shares the same anxiety about having to wear a towel onstage. Except for, it seems, Ryan Idol, who donned his towel for all of Saturday's rehearsal. Suffice it to say, there was much distraction amongst certain male members of the cast, and I briefly had no memory of what my two lines were.

Speaking of distraction, this week I had a *Chatterbox* with *Xanadu*'s Cheyenne Jackson. He was born in Idaho and after he graduated high school, he decided he needed to move to the big city. He therefore hightailed it to New York City. Oh, I'm sorry. I mean, he moved to Spokane, Washington because it had *two* gay bars.

He eventually moved to Seattle and did a show with Marc Kudisch where he was Marc's understudy. Marc told him that if he ever moved to New York, he would set up a meeting with his agent. Cheyenne moved, and Marc's agent signed him! His first audition was for *Thoroughly Modern Millie*. He said it was his best audition ever because he didn't know what was at stake. No one knew who he was, so there was no expectation in any way. He got called back and had to tap, which he doesn't do. So, he just "sold it" upper-body wise and promised Rob Ashford (the choreographer) that if he got the part, he'd learn how to tap. They brought him in for a final audition on the stage of the Marquis where *Millie* was playing. After he sang and read again, director Michael Mayer walked up to him with the creative staff and said, "Well, this is a story for *Broadway.com*. A small-town boy moves to New York, has his first audition and books the job. Cheyenne, you're coming to Broadway!" (Note to Michael Mayer, I guess it's also a story for *Playbill.com*.) Cheyenne started crying, and they all hugged. Then, as Cheyenne was leaving the theatre, he ran into Kudisch backstage. Kudisch was playing Trevor Graydon and didn't even know Cheyenne was auditioning.

> KUDISCH: Cheyenne! What are you doing here?
> CHEYENNE: (Crying) I'm your new understudy!
> KUDISCH: (Crying)
> ME WRITING THIS: (Crying)

Cheyenne also said that, even though he loved doing the workshop of *Xanadu*, he didn't want to do it on Broadway because it would conflict with a film he wanted to do and because Jane Krakowski wasn't doing it. She played Clio/Kira opposite him in the workshop, and he couldn't imagine anyone else playing the part. He was devastated saying no, but he also told his partner that he felt it would come back to him. So he wound up filming his next movie and then, a *week* before the Broadway opening, director Chris Ashley called him late at night and told him that James Carpinello broke his leg, and they were supposed to open in a week. Cheyenne still didn't feel comfortable doing it with another Kira, so he went to see it. He saw Kerry Butler and thought she was totally different from Jane, but amazing! He immediately said yes and relearned the part and all the changes that had been made since the workshop. He ran through the show on Thursday because he was supposed to start the next day, but after the run-through, the creative staff asked him if would go on that night because they knew that the Friday audience would be full of internet posters, and they wanted to give him a performance that wouldn't be immediately followed by CarpinelloLover45 posting "Just Back from *Xanadu...*" on *AllThatDish.com*.

Right now, I am writing this from beautiful Salem, CT. Dev Janki —the award-winning director-choreographer of the brilliant *Zanna, Don't* — has a family-owned house that he rents every summer that can literally sleep 30 people. It's not a mansion — it's more like bungalows, and he's been having these retreats for his friends since 2001.

Going to Dev's is always the highlight of my summer... and the highlight of my dog's year. Maggie runs around non-stop, and when she gets back to NY, she sleeps for two days straight. The best part is that it's always teeming with musical theatre people, and every meal is rife with hilarious stories about onstage antics. I was obsessed with James Hadley's story about Debra Monk's understudy in *Thou Shalt Not*. They were having an understudy rehearsal, and the stage manager literally said, "Let's take it from the stroke." The Debra Monk character has a major stroke during the show that cues a dance number.

It's kind of embarrassing to pretend to have a stroke onstage, so the understudy said her line with little conviction and then muttered, "...And... then I have a stroke." Suddenly, CUT!

MUSIC DIRECTOR: I need the actual full stroke. You need to say, "Ooh, ooh... ah," ...twist your mouth to the left... and then the music comes in.

The understudy looked mortified that she had to do it again. She said her line once more, but this time added a lackluster "Ooh, ooh, ah..." Suddenly, as her mouth was contorting, CUT!

MUSIC DIRECTOR: I need it louder!

Of course, by now, the ensemble offstage was laughing hysterically. The understudy finally did her complete stroke/became paralyzed, and the ensemble entered and circled her while trying to contain their laughter. They spun her around in her wheelchair, and when her back was to the audience, she came out of her paralysis just long enough to give her fellow cast members the finger.

Let me sign off by saying Happy Labor Day, everyone!

More Luxury Problems
September 11, 2007

Okay, remember when I talked about having "luxury problems" a few weeks ago? Well, apparently I'm still sitting in the lap of luxury. In mid-July, I auditioned for a film starring Cameron Diaz and Ashton Kutcher. Cut to a few days ago when I found out that I got the part! My first feature film! And it's my signature line limit: two! Plus, I'd be playing those lines opposite Ashton Kutcher, which could easily have led to an impromptu make-out session. Yes, I know he's married, but can't I harass him sexually and then claim I was "punking" him? Regardless, the question is moot because the movie films on a Tuesday and Wednesday during previews, and the powers that be won't let me take off those shows.

My mother tried to help me plead my case: "Why won't they let you take off? You have such a small part!" Truthfully, I don't even know how I could do a contemporary movie with my crazy '70s hairstyle. A girl named Camille, who only knows me from my Sirius radio show, came to my *Chatterbox* this week, and when I walked in, her mom told me that she exclaimed, "He looks like John Travolta!" I don't think she meant *Pulp Fiction* John, I think she meant Tony Manero John. Hmm... maybe I could get a gig if they do a sequel to *Stayin' Alive* (*Barely Alive: Still Kickin'*?).

Anyhoo, I'm writing this column from my Studio 54 dressing room. We are in the middle of "10 out of 12" rehearsals, meaning we have to keep 12 hours free and work for 10 of those hours. It's essentially X-treme Tech. There's that old chestnut that goes, "If Hitler were alive today, I would make him be in a musical during its out-of-town tryout." I will amend that to say that he should be in the middle of tech rehearsal for said musical. People, it's brutal! We have an opening scene that consists of around 15 lines. We teched that mother for *hours*! Caroline Aaron, who plays Vivian, told me that beginnings and ends of acts take forever to tech. She did *The Sisters Rosensweig* and said that Act One ended with one of the sisters opening up a present and saying a line. It took *one whole day* of tech to do it!

The beginning of *The Ritz* is the one scene that's not in a bathhouse. It's an Italian deathbed scene, and Joe Mantello put me in it as one of the mourners. I play the hunky Italian Stallion in a pair of tight jeans. Oh, I'm sorry, I mean I play an Italian *grandmother* in a shapeless black dress and veil! That's right. I'm debuting on Broadway in old lady drag. And my religious Jewish mother will be so proud to hear me say my first lines on Broadway: "Hail Mary, full of Grace..." Just in time for Rosh Hashanah.

One of the reasons we had to tech it for so long is getting me on and off stage in my *Whatever Happened to Baby Jane?* wheelchair. I think I've now been relegated to a walker. I want the kind that Jackie Hoffman talks about in her hilarious comedy act: "One day," she admits, "I accepted a delivery for my elderly neighbor because she was out and about. It was a walker attached to a commode. I was mind boggled. If this lady needs a walker attached to a commode, how was she able to be 'out and about'?"

The sound cues by our celebrated sound designer Tony Meola are so cool! Every cue is a delicious '70s classic: "Love to Love Ya, Baby," "Macho Man" and my favorite, "Mama Told Me Not To Come," where the amazing Scott Pask bathhouse set is revealed and all the guys flock on. I feel like I'm in a musical whenever we run it, it's so fun! I'm wearing an amazing '70s pantsuit with a belt, and when I walked by Joe Mantello, he greeted me with "Hey, Sally Jesse." Then, I had to get into my next costume. I saw what looked like a hand towel, and suddenly realized that the white swatch of fabric was the towel I was supposed to wear around my waist! The other boys in the cast have waists that begin with a "2" (28, 29, etc.). I haven't been in the 20s since I was in my teens. I was horrified, but finally decided to bite the bullet and put it on. Though skimpy, it got around my middle. David Turner is in the cast, and we spend the whole time backstage gabbing and laughing. I showed him my "costume" and asked him, "Do you think I can get away with this? With my fatness?" He said that that was a horribly phrased question, because if he says yes, he's essentially saying that my fatness is sufficiently masked, and if he says no, it means that my fatness does not allow me to "get away with it." True 'dat. My dresser turned me around and assured me that I looked good, and then Brooks Ashmanskas walked by and complimented my upper body. Hmm, I thought... maybe all that working out paid off! I felt a surge of confidence as I came onstage and walked around the bathhouse strewn with Adonises in skimpy towels: Why was I so scared? I still got it!

I arrived the next day, and my dresser told me that it's "been requested" that I wear a bathrobe. I guess I do still got it: and by "it," I mean a slew of love handles. Whatever! I have the "character" track. I decided to own the bathrobe and "make it my own." I tucked one side of the bathrobe in my belt, which gives me an amazing slit down the side. I showed it to William Ivey Long, and we both decided it looks like the dress Lucille Ball wore when she made a special appearance at the Oscars. Anybody?

Speaking of David Turner, he had a five-minute break to go to the bathroom, which was ruined by Ryan Idol walking in and using the next urinal. Suddenly, David's bodily function was unable to function. Suffice it to say, his bladder was suddenly more shy than Carol Burnett was during *Once Upon a Mattress*.

By the way, with all my complaining about my two lines, I've literally said both wrong in rehearsal. Instead of "Careful, Googie," I said, "Watch it, Googie," and instead of "We're busy," I said, "We're resting." Maybe I need to downsize to one line.

This week my friend Jack Plotnick is visiting me. He's here to do an East Coast version of his amazing acting workshops. First of all, if you can ever attend one of his classes, hie thee! Secondly, if you have an audition coming up, get to his website (*jackplotnick.com*) and read his section about affirmations. All you have to do is release your need — like "I release my need to impress" or "I release my need to be funny." It sounds kinda stupid and new age-y, but it really works! I released my need to have six-pack abs, and now look at me! They're nowhere to be seen.

This week I interviewed Broadway's hottest couple, Jenny Powers and Matt Cavenaugh. Jenny is playing Rizzo in *Grease*, a role she first played in high school. Wouldn't it be great if we could all play our high school roles on Broadway? I'm still waiting for the next revival of *Fiddler on the Roof*, so I can show the world my Rabbi. Anyhoo, she fessed up that she was a pageant girl on the advice of Kate Shindle (Miss America '98 and currently in *Legally Blonde*). I kept dishing that line that pageant girls give: "It's not a beauty pageant, it's a scholarship contest." Really? I didn't have to sign up for my student loan in a bikini. Regardless, Jenny's pageant wins did actually wind up paying for her last two years at Northwestern. When she moved to NYC, she was asked to audition for the oldest sister in *Little Women*, but she didn't want to be pigeon-holed as the pretty soprano ingénue, so she said no. They then offered her the part. It was like a live-action version of the "God why don't you love me, oh you do, I'll see you later Blues." Essentially, "We'll deign to give you an audition. Wait, you don't want the part? Then it's yours!"

She said Maureen McGovern, who played Marmee, was wonderful. Maureen would fly to different places in the world to do concerts on her day off, come back to the show on three hours sleep and still sound *amazing*. Maureen has had a lot of ups and downs in her career. After her first big single ("There's Got to Be a Morning After") won the Oscar, she couldn't get work and had to work as a secretary! Can you imagine? When I interviewed her, I asked, jokingly, if she disguised herself as "Maureen Schwartz." She said I was right! She knew she couldn't say her real name because it would be too weird so she would answer the phone with "Glenda Schwartz, can I help you?" Turns out, I'm psychic! But only about things that can't possibly help me.

Matt talked about doing *Urban Cowboy* and told me that even though he doesn't read reviews, he knew what they said because the day after it opened, he would walk in a room, and suddenly people would make a distinctive lack of eye contact. The show was going to close right after it opened, and at the last performance, the cast came onstage because they were going to end with some songs that were cut out of town. Suddenly, the producer came onstage and announced that she was gonna keep it open! Ah! Whose blood pressure can take such ups and downs? The show wound up staying open another month giving many audiences the chance to see Matt's complete lack of body fat.

Okay, kids. Friday is the first *Ritz* preview! Can't wait! And Happy (Jewish) New Year!

Broadway Nights and Days
September 17, 2007

I just made my Broadway debut, and yet I feel strangely empty. Just kidding, it was *amazing*! Okay, here's what led up to it. Remember how I said we were in "10 out of 12" rehearsals? Where you keep 12 hours free, and you're in rehearsals for 10 of those hours? Well, the only thing that was getting me through those rehearsals was knowing that there were only going to be two of them. Guess what? We had five of them!! We added those extra hours because the woman who played Kevin Chamberlin's wife was replaced at the last minute. Even though it was hard on the cast to find one of our company members gone, Brooks Ashmanskas cheered us up when he told us about the phone call he got from Martin Short, who was in a vacation house with Marc Shaiman and Scott Whitman. Martin left Brooks a message saying, "We heard that one of the female cast members was being replaced, and we're all worried *sick* about you." Hilarious.

Let me just say that tech rehearsals are *brutal*. Now, I know it's obnoxious to be complaining about being in a Broadway show. It's like when I was single, and couples would lament to me that "it takes so much work to be in a relationship." Zip it! You have a boyfriend. Keep your trap shut. So, even though I know I'm annoying, allow me to tell you what a tech is like. You start a scene, full of adrenaline — the first word of the first line is uttered, and you immediately hear the stage manager say, "Hold, please." Then, you sit for ten minutes onstage while something is adjusted. Lights? Sound? Who knows? You're just told not to move.

Or you finish a scene, excited to take a break (and to get out of your old lady drag, in my case), and as you're leaving, you hear "Okay, we're going back, people." Over and over. And over. It's like Sartre's *No Exit* with an Equity break every hour and a half. The only fun part is chatting onstage while the lights/sound/whatever is being adjusted. Ashlie Atkinson, who plays Vivian, told us about a fellow student who went with her to acting school. During the final showcase, he was supposed to chop up a chicken during his scene. On the day of his performance, he decided to use a *cleaver.* I pretty much knew where the story was going once I heard that key word. So, yes, you guessed it, in the middle of the scene he literally cut off the tops of two fingers... *and* tried to keep going!! Thankfully, he finally stopped the scene, fled to a hospital and got them sewn back on. Then, Jeffrey Thomas and I started obsessing about that reality show where women audition to become *The Starlet*. Faye Dunaway was the head judge, and we couldn't remember what her tag line was when she kicked off a contestant. We knew it had the line reading of "You're fired" but with a theatrical bent. All I thought of was "You are *not* off book" or "'Places' has *not* been called," but Jeffrey finally Googled it and told me it was "Don't call us, we'll call you." Why is that any better?

While we were teching, I was still doing other stuff in my "free" time. I did my Sirius radio show every day and had Andréa Burns (who just finished recording her first CD, *A Deeper Shade of Red*) come in and co-host with me. She's the standby for Rosie Perez, and the timing of *The Ritz* schedule is perfect because, in the spring, she starts *In the Heights* on Broadway. Andréa and I were reminiscing about the failed auditions I coached her for. She went in for the Tommy Tune production of *Grease* way back when, and I suggested she sing that old pop tune "See You in September." I helped her come up with some moves and told her that at the end of the song, she should give a sad, little wave. Well, she sang it for Tommy Tune, hit the last note and gave a tiny, forlorn wave. Tommy looked at her... and gave the exact same wave back. How brilliant/devastating to dismiss someone by stealing their choreography!

Remember how last week I did a stage cross in a towel during Act One and was told to wear a bathrobe ASAP? Well, this week we were staging the very last moment of the show, and our sassy director Joe Mantello told me to exit my room in a towel and walk stage left. "Aha!" I thought. "I'll be robed for Act One, but the Act Two audience will finally see all the work I've been doing in the gym. I still got it!" We started the scene, I crossed in my towel, and as I approached the wings, I heard the frantic running of feet. The *second* I walked off the stage, a panting costume assistant informed me that William Ivey Long wanted to remind me to always wear a robe. OK, already, I get it!

So, finally tech was over, and it was time for the first preview. Let me give you a list of the debacles that ensued — essentially all caused by me. First, I want to explain that it's difficult to do a show where you're offstage for long periods and then have to randomly enter the stage. I like the kinda show where you come on and stay on. That being said, during the first preview, I did my first scene as the old Italian Grandmother, then I did the first cross where I enter the bathhouse in my amazing '70s outfit, and then I retired to my dressing room to wait for my first act scene where I actually have a little dialogue. While I was downstairs staring in my dressing room mirror, I heard a line onstage that sounded familiar and realized it sounded familiar because I usually hear it from the stage! That's right. I flat out missed one of my entrances. The good news is, no one noticed. Actually, the *bad* news is no one noticed. Ouch. Does the song "Mr. Cellophane" mean anything to you?

Secondly, I complained to my dresser because my dance belt was way too tight. All of our clothes are washed between shows, and I told him that someone must have shrunk it. Well, I'm devastated to admit this in print, but I will; after 15 minutes of complaining, I realized that I put it on *backwards*. Do you know what a dance belt looks like? The back has a single, thin strap. A thin, cutting strap. That strap was literally over my front and, let me just say, I'm not surprised that it hurt. Or that I can no longer have children.

Thirdly, the Studio 54 theatre has very little wing space, and during the opening scene, my friend Jeffrey has to wheel on a bed. He was constantly warned by the tech crew to watch the scrim. The scrim tears easily and is incredibly expensive. Every time we ran the scene, the crew would tell him to be super careful and not be "that guy," as in "that guy" who tore the scrim. Poor Jeffrey, I thought, the pressure on him is *enormous.* Well, during the Sunday matinee, I was leaving the stage and carrying my walker with the bottom facing straight out from me to expedite my exit. I veered slightly to the right and got my walker caught on something. Hmm, I thought, "What's tangled around my walker?" Yes, people. I was "that guy." I tore the scrim, and the devastation you feel when that happens is second only to a dance belt cutting into your bladder.

The best news is that the audiences have been amazing all weekend. It's so fun to hear laughs throughout the show instead of "Hold, please."

This week is also special because my first novel, *Broadway Nights*, just got shipped out from the printers!

Well, I'm off to the gym, everyone. Peace out and enjoy that delicious crisp weather!

Brian, Lea and *Bubbles*
September 24, 2007

I just finished the second week of previews for *The Ritz*. It's so fun! I have a little feature that's at the end of Act Two, so it gives me something to look forward to during the whole show, besides acting out with food. I'm the king of eating a healthy Zone Bar before the show, and then by intermission scavenging in the wig room for Twix Bars.

Off Topic (as they say on the message boards): I got an email that I was so proud of deciphering. Some man asked me about a song I played on Sirius. He said, "It was about a guy who didn't want to get married, but his friends said it was okay, and there was something about a chair." I got a splitting headache 'til I realized he meant "Being Alive" ("*Someone to sit in my chair...*"). Why are those the only references he remembered? How about the words "Being Alive," which are repeated a *thousand* times!!

Speaking of Sirius, I interviewed Brian d'Arcy James, and I busted him on the pretentious three names, but he said he had to add the d'Arcy because there was another Brian James in Equity. Hmm... it's one thing to add a middle name, but a middle name *with* an apostrophe? That's pushing it. Actually, he said he first tried to just use an initial, but since his middle name is spelled d'Arcy, it was Brian d. James and even he knew that only e.e. cummings could get away with that.

We talked about *Harmony*, the musical by Barry Manilow and Bruce Sussman. Brian had the lead, and I was the vocal arranger. You may be shocked to know that I do vocal arrangements, but I think you'll be more shocked to know Brian's character name was Rabbi. I guess Alfred Molina wasn't available. We both thought the show has a *ton* of potential — great story and score. It's about an actual close harmony group called The Comedian Harmonists from 1930s who were German but internationally known at the time. They were disbanded by the Nazis because there were Jewish members in the group, and they faded into obscurity. I first worked on it at the La Jolla Playhouse back in '97, and it finally came here a few years later to get ready for a Broadway production. We rehearsed up a storm and were preparing to leave for our out-of-town tryout in Philadelphia. The *day before* the whole cast was leaving, we were told it was all canceled. The producer didn't really have the money he said he did and, essentially, that was that. The show was totally blocked, ready to go, and, suddenly, everything was off! The cool thing is, the guys who were cast as the Harmonists got to perform with Barry in his concerts across the U.S., and they're on his DVD doing two songs from the show.

At the *Chatterbox*, I had Lea Michele, another name I had to bust. I've never heard a more obvious first and middle name since Ann-Margret. I asked her if her last name was Fleishberger or Schwartzbaum, and she 'fessed up it was tres Jewish. I don't know why people don't keep their real last names. Rudetsky is beautiful. Anybody? Nobody.

Lea said she got into theatre because, when she was eight, her friend was auditioning for Young Cosette in *Les Miz* and needed Lea's parents to take her to the city from Jersey. Since Lea was there, she auditioned, too... and got it. I was mind-boggled that her friend didn't realize this whole scenario was doomed from the start. The same thing happened when Vicki Clark brought Ted Sperling to play for her *Sunday in the Park* audition in the '80s, and he was offered a pit pianist job and she was ixnayed. Didn't they know it was right out of the opening scene of *Fame* when Leroy "helps out" his friend auditioning for the Performing Arts High School? Keep those Leroys away from your auditions or pay the consequences: a scene with you cursing while walking down the stairs.

Lea got to play Young Cosette, Young Eponine and understudy Gavroche. I wish I got to do drag as an eight-year-old. Also, what happens when one of the little girls goes on for Gavroche? After the barricade shoot-out scene, does someone discover Gavroche's body and scream, "Sacré bleu! He's a she!" Billy Tipton style? (Does anyone remember him/her? The trumpeter who was married with kids but was really a woman? Too obscure?)

Anyhoo, after *Les Miz*, Lea got *Ragtime*, which began out of town in Toronto. She played the daughter of the immigrant played by the talented Peter Friedman. I asked her how annoying it was to be silent the whole show except for saying "My father speaks for both of us." She said she didn't mind. Then, I confronted her and asked that if her father spoke for both of them, how come she sings up a storm in the opening number. She said that she never thought of that. Maybe her father speaks for both of them, but she belts by herself.

She started working on *Spring Awakening* when she was 14! Before you think the show has been being developed for 20 years, let me remind you it wasn't like when *we* were 14 (when Alf was big) — it was only a couple of years ago. The cool thing is, she's been playing the role ever since the beginning of the formation of the show. The uncool thing is, she's had to audition for each incarnation of the show! Before the Off-Broadway production, she was getting emails from her "friends" saying they were trying out for her role! She called the director (Michael Mayer) and told him that she still looked young enough and that she wanted to come in and audition... and, of course, she got it. I asked her about bearing her breast onstage, and she said that when the show was Off-Broadway, she got a handwritten note in her dressing room from Michael Mayer saying, "I think you should show your breast at the end of the act." Hello? Where's the build up? Where's the: "Tell me if you're comfortable with this"... "I know this may be shocking"... "Not since Janet Jackson," etc... She said she ran into Jonathan Groff backstage before the show, and I asked if he was carrying a photocopy of the same note with the word "breast" scratched out and replaced with "butt."

Last weekend was my boyfriend's daughter's birthday. Juli turned seven, so we took her to *Gazillion Bubble Show*. If you haven't seen it, it's essentially a woman named Ana Yang onstage doing all these amazing things with bubbles and lights. I wouldn't say her character had much of a "journey," but it was totally super cool to watch. She chose some kid audience volunteers to come onstage, and Juli kept being not picked. I could tell Juli was disappointed, but I was thinking that it's important that she learn how to deal with that feeling. Then, Ana asked for an adult couple to come onstage, and when James and I weren't picked, I realized that it's important for *me* to learn how to deal with that feeling. I was in a rage, but it subsided after the show when we all took a picture inside a bubble.

All right, I'm off to do a photo shoot with the cast and Terrence McNally for *Genre* magazine! Peace out!

Ritz, Rent and Worley
October 1, 2007

What to wear to *The Ritz* opening night party? I want to get a real '70s outfit to keep it apropos, but from where? I guess I could raid my old closet in my mom's house, but all the clothes I wore in the '70s won't work now. Not because I was a kid back then and the clothes won't fit my adult body... au contraire, I was sporting a waist similar to the one I have now. The words "pants" and "husky" went hand-in-hand for me back then. I just don't think any of my old clothes were hip enough to make a splash today. Although, I remember one pair of pants I had in fourth grade... on each leg was a lion and underneath, it said, "Your den or mine?" My question is: why was a nine-year-old wearing such a suggestive outfit, Mother? *Pretty Baby*? Teri Shields? Anybody?

I saw *Rent* this week and Adam Pascal and Anthony Rapp were great. Typical me, I spent a chunk of the show obsessing over the fact that Anthony is in full winter gear for most of the show. Did he have a fit during tech rehearsals? "Hello! I'm performing on a stage under 1,000 lights! Why are you making me wear a scarf? And why must it be wool?" Doesn't he long to do the finale in just a bikini? Revival of *Good Vibrations*? Anybody?

Adam Pascal's voice is so amazing as per usual. It always has that signature rasp, but then he'll shockingly go up to a crazy high note with no effort. He played Freddie in the Actors Fund concert of *Chess* I put together, and quite frankly, *my* face was more strained while I was conducting than his was while hitting high Cs.

My only complaint about *Rent* was that there were some moments where the band sounded louder than the singers. It made me recall that classic Carol Channing story. Apparently, after she saw *Rent*, she came backstage and "complimented" the cast by saying (read this with the Carol Channing accent/enormous smile), "I didn't understand a word you said, but the *energy*...!"

On Thursday, I interviewed Jo Anne Worley at the *Chatterbox*. She told me that she grew up on a farm in the Midwest but made extra money working as a waitress at a truck stop. She said she never told anyone she wanted to go into performing. She was engaged at 17 and told everyone she wanted to be a nurse. Cut to — she took her truck stop money, hightailed it to Nyack, NY, to work as an apprentice in summer stock, and told her fiancé she'd be back right after the summer. Essentially, he's still waiting.

She talked about her first professional foray into singing, which was playing the role of Katisha in *The Mikado*. She said she got a great laugh because, while the Mikado was singing, she would take out a tomato, put a ton of salt on it, bite into it and then offer it to the audience. Apparently, it was also her first foray into upstaging. Brava!

She made her Broadway debut in a revue of Billie Barnes novelty songs and Walter Kerr of New York Times went *crazy* for her. He spent two paragraphs describing the mouth contortions she did while parodying an opera singer. Unfortunately, the show lasted a weekend. But then she got to be the standby for Carol Channing when *Hello, Dolly!* was doing its out-of-town tryout (but never went on).

She was very excited when she was in L.A. and got an audition for a TV show, but she didn't have a way to get there because she didn't drive. Her friend also had an audition and said, "Why don't we go together? I'll drive!" It's a good thing she got a lift because the show was *Laugh-In*! Jo Anne got it and her friend didn't. How many times do I have to warn my readers that the whole "come along with me to my audition" always leads to the *Fame* Leroy opening scene?!

Jo Anne then talked about her foray back onto Broadway in the late '80s. She said the producer of *Prince of Central Park* called her and said that they wanted her to replace the leading lady and was she available? Was she?! Yes! Well, not really... she was doing *Mame* in Los Angeles, but this was Broadway calling! They'd have to let her go, right?

N-O.

The producer said she signed a contract and had to finish out the run. Jo Anne said that she was friends with Angela Lansbury and she would ask her to finish out the run instead. The producer said, "I advertised Jo Anne Worley, and that's who will be playing Mame." AH!

She finished out her run in L.A., rushed to N.Y. and learned the part in four days. Interestingly, the length of time it took for her to learn the part is the same amount of days the show ran. It's that old equation we had in freshman year algebra: Length of rehearsal = Run of show = Flop.

And, finally, the old-school Broadway sasstress Alice Playten came to see *The Ritz* this week. She is so cool. She was a replacement Baby Louise in *Gypsy* opposite the Merm as well as the original Bet in *Oliver!* and Ermengarde in *Hello, Dolly!* Get thee to *Bluegobo.com* ASAP, and check out her Ed Sullivan clip from *Henry, Sweet Henry*. Watch the part where she asks the audience to donate money into her hat. She checks inside the hat, sees that there's nothing and gives the most amazing face ever! Also, check out the ensemble. Baayork Lee, Pia Zadora (!), and coming in for the last section of the song and standing in the back row, Priscilla Lopez! *Alice passed away a few years later. A great talent missed by many.*

Okay, one more week before opening! Peace out!

Adam Pascal, Prop Drops and Stokes
October 9, 2007

I dropped my prop. That's not a euphemism. I have a feature in Act Two of *The Ritz* and as I exited, I dropped my prop. For the rest of the show, I couldn't stop obsessing about it. Especially, because I knew critics were in the house. Nowadays, critics come during the last couple of shows before Opening Night. I wasn't sure that there would be critics there that night, until I was talking to someone on the creative staff who flat-out told me... without me asking! Note to staff member: keep your trap shut about things like that. Although, note to myself: keep my trap shut as well. I told my friend David Turner that our mutual friend Paul Castree was in the audience and he told me that, in the future, I should zip it. He said that he spent the whole show thinking: "Hmm... I wonder if Paul will like the way I always read this line. Well, I guess we'll never know since I can't re-create what I normally do because I'm thinking about Paul's reaction."

Well, I had the same problem after I dropped my prop. The next scene is where I have my signature line "Careful, Googie." I was onstage obsessing about why I dropped my prop, if I broke it, if the audience now hated me, if the critic would mention that the show would have been a hit were it not for the butterfingers of a one "Seth Rudetsky," etc... when I heard silence onstage. Oh, no! That's me! I quickly spat out "Careful, Googie!" but was now obsessing that the review headline would be "Quick paced farce becomes slow paced dirge due to Rudetsky's slowness on the uptake." My friend Jack Plotnick says that actors are like Jacob Marley after they make a mistake. Instead of letting it go and moving on, they add it to the chain of shame they wear. True 'dat. *We actually wound up getting a pretty good review from the NY TIMES, fueling my expectation of a long Broadway run. I'm still waiting.*

My friend Aaron, who's hilarious, came to *The Ritz* over the weekend. He sassed me with a text message right before the show.

ME: Watch for me in the opening scene. I'm the old, hunched over biddy in black with a walker.
HIM: So, you won't be wearing a costume?

Brava! Oh, yeah... speaking of which: in the last scene in the show, there're a bunch of us onstage in a crowd, and at one point we're supposed to be happy about something Kevin Chamberlin does. Well, usually we all applaud, and I ad lib a word or two. Cut to last week when, for some reason, no one in the crowd audibly applauded, so all you heard was my exposed vocal ad lib. In the middle of the scene, in total silence, the audience heard me shout out a loud, nasal, *Brava!* to Kevin Chamberlin. I was mortified.

I got to interview Adam Pascal on Sirius this week. I asked him about what Broadway shows he saw growing up, and he told me that he saw *Les Miz* but didn't remember much of it... because he was such a little kid. He was mortified when I told him that it opened on Broadway in 1986 when he was a teenager. Hmm... maybe he saw the original French production. *Quelqu'on? Personne.*

I asked Adam if my favorite song in *Rent* was his: "La Vie Boheme." He said a decided "no." I was shocked, outraged and more than a little put off (not really, I just wanted to see what it was like writing that). Anyhoo, he said that "La Vie Boheme" has always made no sense to him from an acting perspective. He asked me how come his character, who hasn't left his apartment in months, is suddenly laughing, singing and shaking his butt in a restaurant. Hmm… I guess that is the definition of zero to 60: from house-bound to on-table butt-shaking. He said he's finally given up trying to justify it and just does it. As an audience member I say, yes, it makes no sense, but it sure is fun to watch. So dance, monkey, dance!

He talked about doing *Aida* and how terrifying it was when the set broke. At the end of the show, he and Heather Headley were inside a "tomb" that was lifted pretty high above the stage. Suddenly it fell three feet… then it fell all the way to the stage! He and Heather tumbled out, and someone from the show literally yelled, "Is there a doctor in the house?" Adam said he remembers looking up as a confident man bounded up to the stage saying, "I'm a dermatologist." Whoever yelled for the doctor should have been more specific. He and Heather were rushed to the hospital, and Adam remembers that one of the orderlies gave Heather his number. So I guess it all worked out.

I also got to interview Brian Stokes Mitchell at the *Chatterbox*. He calls himself the "luckiest man in show business." His first minute in L.A. he got *Roots: The Next Generation*. Then, while doing a play in Los Angeles, the producers of *Trapper John: MD* were in the audience, and that's pretty much how he got that part. Although his luck ran out during his first foray onto Broadway. First, he did the short-lived *Mail*, and then he did *Oh, Kay!* which was David Merrick's last show. He said that Merrick had a stroke before *Oh, Kay!* began rehearsals, but he was still very present at rehearsals. Stokes remembers singing a song onstage with Tamara Tunie and hearing Merrick yelling in the audience. Of course, he and Tamara thought it was something about them but, turns out, Merrick was raging because he noticed that one of the drapes on the set had a wrinkle. Merrick closed the show temporarily because he was going through a divorce, and if the show was closed for seven weeks, his wife wouldn't get any cut of the box office. Merrick then re-opened the show, but Stokes bowed out after he heard his new co-star was Rae Dawn Chong who, let's just say, was not musical theatre royalty.

Stokes and I met when I was the rehearsal pianist for *Kiss of the Spider Woman*, and he took over for the lead role of Valentin. He said that he learned how to lead a company from Chita Rivera, who knew *everybody's* name at the theater. Speaking of names, I asked him about "Stokes." When I met him, he was Brian Mitchell… what up? He said that during *Ragtime* he began to research names and how certain names had power. The best is a one syllable beginning and last (like Tom Cruise). He felt that the scan of Brian Mitchell was clanky and was going to change it to something totally different… but then decided that all he had to do was add his middle name. I was fascinated 'til he said that Seth Rudetsky was a good name. All I can say is, try making a collect phone call with that clunker. *P.S. My editor just told me this reference was too old for most people to remember. YAY! It's fun feeling like Hume Cronyn. P.P.S. An even more dated reference.*

The most exciting news is: this Thursday is opening night!!!! Next week I'll give you all the scoop… Peace out!

Opening Night
October 15, 2007

Opening night was *so much fun*!

But first, the days before. On Monday, my boyfriend got a babysitter. That was so exciting! We were actually able to make plans at night. Normally, we're like the opposite of vampires. We're only out during the day. Anyhoo, we hightailed over to Ted Sperling's gorgeous apartment for my first foray into one of his signature game nights. He has the ground floor of a brownstone with a beautiful garden in the back. I decided that this would serve as the beginning of many, many trips to his city oasis. Of course, he immediately informed me that he's moving. Well, at least I got to see it once. *P.S. It had such an effect on me and James that our next three apartments had backyard gardens!*

Anyhoo, there were a ton of people whom I did not know, some I recognized, and some I did many low-paying readings with. The gorgeous Kelli O'Hara, soon-to-be Nellie Forbush in Lincoln Center's *South Pacific,* was there with her new hubby, Gregg Naughton. I was also thrilled to see the multi-talented Jeff Blumenkrantz, whom I first met while I was still in college doing a New York internship back in the late-mid-'80s! Also, I hung out with cutie pie Steven Pasquale, whom I heard is rumored to play Lt. Cable. *But didn't because he was doing RESCUE ME on TV and they wouldn't allow him to do a Broadway show at the same time.*

Everyone came to play "running charades." That's where you have three teams of people (or in this case, three teams consisting of various Tony nominees/winners/egregiously overlooked), and each team is in a different room. Apparently, this game is only for people on a white contract who can afford more than a studio. There is one person with ten titles (movies, songs, plays, books, etc.) who is centrally located, and every time a team gets a right answer, they run back and get the next clue. Whatever team gets all ten first, wins. My favorite mistake was when David Turner gave the title *Dobie Gillis*, which was an old TV show. The Kelli O'Hara team was stumped on it for the whole time period. We later found out it was because the clue giver had never heard of it and mistakenly told the group: A) it was a song and B) it was one word. It's one thing not to know what it is, but why commit to something it's not *and* not take to take the time to read both words?

Tuesday, at Sirius radio, I interviewed one of my favorite Broadway composers, Stephen Schwartz. He said that when he first started out, he wanted to write Broadway music that had the essence of Joni Mitchell, Laura Nyro, The Mamas and the Papas, James Taylor and various other late '60s, early '70s singer/songwriters. He created a meld of all of them combined with his own sass. And he writes his own lyrics! I don't think that he gets enough credit for coming up with a new sound for Broadway. He paved the way for William Finn, Andrew Lippa, Jason Robert Brown and Tom Kitt to name a few. Stephen had the nerve to have *Godspell*, *Pippin* and *The Magic Show* all come to Broadway while he was in his twenties. So young! He said he was thrown when he went from *Godspell* to *Pippin* because *Godspell* was Off-Broadway and so informally put together. The cast would improvise harmony, and when it sounded good, they would keep it. When he walked into rehearsals for *Pippin*, he was shocked that the cast wanted the harmony written out! But he did write it out, and now listen to the amazing backup for

"Morning Glow" or the beautiful harmony in the finale. My favorite part is when Ben Vereen and Leland Palmer sing "Think about the beauty... in one perfect flame." Gorgeous!

He was very concerned with trying to sell his cast albums as crossover pop albums, and that's why he decided to cut the opening number off the *Godspell* album. I guess he thought that people who liked pop music didn't want their albums to begin "Wherefore, O men of Athens..." He also said that he took out a lot of the brass parts in the *Pippin* orchestration on the album so it didn't sound too Broadway. That's also why "Magic to Do" does the signature pop "repeat and fade" at the end. And why Irene Ryan adds all those crazy riffs during "No Time At All." Anybody? Nobody.

I saw *Pippin* when I was a little kid and one of the few things I remember is that the lyrics to "No Time at All" came down on a scroll for the audience to sing with. Stephen said that he loved folk groups growing up, especially The Weavers, and they always had a sing-a-long so he decided that when he did a Broadway show, he'd have one, too. Stephen also confirmed the crazy David Merrick story that happened during *The Baker's Wife*. Producer Merrick had the nerve to hate "Meadowlark," but everyone else wanted it to stay in the show. He finally figured out the one way the song wouldn't be performed: he snuck into the pit after a Wednesday matinee and stole the music so the orchestra couldn't play it that night! Brava, cuckoo bird!

Stephen got the idea to do *Wicked* because he was in Hawaii with John Bucchino, who was playing a Womyn's Music Festival. They were in a boat and Holly Near was describing a book she was reading by Gregory Maguire, which happened to be *Wicked*. Stephen immediately thought that it was "so him" and soon asked his lawyers to get the rights. It took a year to finally get them but the show never got the rights from *The Wizard of Oz* movie. That's why they can only mention things in the original *Oz* books, but not the movie. They couldn't say "Toto," so one day Kristin improvised "Dodo," and they kept it. They also can't say "ruby slippers," so it's become the tripping-off-the-tongue "jeweled shoes." Stephen did put some Harold Arlen tips of the hat in the score. The "Unlimited... my future is unlimited" motif that Elphaba sings is actually the same notes in "Somewhere over the Rainbow." Sing it and you'll see...it's so cool!

He's always been completely obsessed with Irving Berlin's signature two-songs-that-sound-different-but-actually-go-together ("I hear singing and there's no one there" vs. "You don't need analyzing"). That's why he's put one of those type songs in most of his shows: "All for the Best," "Two's Company" and, I didn't realize 'til he told me, "Loathing." The verse "What is this feeling, so sudden and new" goes with "Loathing... unadulterated loathing." He said the trick is to make them sound like they would never go together. Bravo!

All right, let's discuss *The Ritz* opening night. In case you're wondering if the hype about a Broadway opening is accurate, let me tell you that it is! It was literally like my birthday. I had a million cards all over my dressing table: from the cast, creative staff, friends, etc. Tons of flowers, candy and some incredible gifts. My two favorites were: Andréa Burns, who covers Rosie Perez, took a picture of me backstage in my full '70s costume. She blew it up and put it in an engraved frame that said, "Congratulations, Seth! Broadway debut, October 11th, 2007!" It's such an amazing present! Also, remember when I said that I told Jeffrey Thomas about my favorite episode of the TV show *Fame*? It's the one where the secret service guy tells Carol Mayo Jenkins that the President isn't coming to the show and she "doesn't know what to say." And then she replies with a raised eyebrow: "There's only one thing to say... Places, everybody.

Places." Jeffrey literally tracked her down and got her to send an 8x10 signed with "There's only one thing to say… Places, everybody. Places"! I went into shock!

The ironic part about the actual performance on opening night is that it is the one night where there are never any critics (they all come before opening). However, in this case, it was the only show where I was really nervous! Who cares about critics when all of the Broadway elite is in the audience? Jon Robin Baitz, Nathan Lane, Kathleen Marshall, Walter Bobbie, Marian Seldes, Raúl Esparza, Michael Mayer, Jessica Stone, Rob Ashford, Dick Scanlan, Harriet Harris, etc. And, to boot, my big feature in Act Two is me singing an earnest "Magic to Do" from *Pippin* and Stephen Schwartz was there! I was having a panic attack before I went on but did my *JackPlotnick.com* affirmation ("I release my need to impress") and had a great time. Stephen gave us the rights to the song if he could get tix to opening, but when he saw me at the cast party, he told he was taking back the rights. He, thankfully, was joking, and my unitard-clad moment lives on eight shows a week!

The one sad part is that the weather prevented my mom and sister from coming. They live on Long Island, and the trains stopped working because of the rain and the tornado watch! My mom was so sad she was missing it, but she had seen the show already, so essentially all she was missing was hanging out with a ton of Broadway celebrities and an amazing party. In other words, her sadness was valid.

I saw some reviews and thankfully, no one mentioned my dropped umbrella. However, one was much worse. It said the bathhouse patrons were a mix of boys with washboard abs and trolls in towels. What the-? I don't have washboard abs so, by process of elimination, I'm devastated.

OK, everyone. I'm off tonight and then Tuesday, I'm back in *The Ritz*! Can't wait to troll around in that towel!

Autobiographies, Understudies and Betty!
October 22, 2007

Ouch! This was the week of accidents, injuries and regurgitation! Details to follow. First a chronological rundown of the week.

Monday night, I did *Celebrity Autobiography* with some amazing co-stars including Tony Roberts, Mary Testa, Jackie Hoffman (all from *Xanadu*), Karen Ziemba (doing an amazing Elizabeth Taylor), Richard Kind (whose child goes to the same school as my boyfriend's) and my good friend Jack Plotnick. It's the show where we read autobiographies verbatim. Elizabeth Taylor's written dialogue keeps randomly harkening back to the fact that she's Jewish, so when the section of the book came when Elizabeth runs into Eddie Fisher years after their divorce, Karen Ziemba was hilarious reading the part where Elizabeth politely nods to him at Sardi's and says (with a 1940s accent), "Mazel Tov."

I loved reading the part of Star Jones' book where she differentiates between Star, who's the Diva, and her real name "Starlette," who's underneath it all. "Take away the wigs, the eyelashes and my *fabulous* clothes, and you'll find me at White Castle... *feasting* on a half dozen of those greasy, square burgers!"

Jack was so good at subtly busting Nancy Reagan's horrible treatment of daughter Patti Reagan. When Patti was a toddler, she wouldn't swallow her string beans, so the pediatrician advised Nancy to leave Patti in her high chair until she swallowed it all. Jack raised an eyebrow and slowly continued: "*An hour and a half later*, they were still in her mouth..."

The show was a little intimidating to perform because *Saturday Night Live* producer Lorne Michaels was there, sitting with Alec Baldwin. My boyfriend, James, said that he's sure the show convinced Alec *not* to write an autobiography.

The show got out early enough for me, James and Jack to hightail it to Carnegie Hall and see the second act of Brian Stokes Mitchell's concert for the Actors Fund. There was so much Broadway in the audience! We were seated behind Tyler Maynard (from *Altar Boyz*) and Sarah Gettelfinger (from *Dirty Rotten Scoundrels*) and in front of Betty Buckley. Stokes sounded great, as usual, and the big orchestra was delicious, too. The last song was "Grateful" by John Bucchino, and it was sung right after Stokes described how the Actors Fund helps *everyone* in the entertainment field, not just actors. After the show, I complimented the director, Richard Jay-Alexander, on the cool idea of bringing up the house lights during the song. It really drove home the point that we're all in it together, and the Actors Fund couldn't exist without the audience to donate. Richard said that the concert was going long, and if it went into overtime, it would cost thousands of dollars. So, actually the house lights came on in the middle of the number to make sure people knew that they had around one minute to vacate. Out of necessity spawns brilliance!

The Ritz is now officially open so here come the injuries. At the end of the show, there's a chase scene. A couple of nights ago, I was running through the audience and as I was running up the stairs to the stage, I fell on all fours. First of all, right before that scene, Rosie Perez introduces me as a contestant in the talent contest named Sheldon Farenthold and I do a little number. Even though I'm introduced by name, there's no dialogue in the show where I'm actually called Sheldon. Well, right as I fell, Brooks Ashmanskas yells out, "Watch it, Sheldon!" Then as I'm on the ground I hear, "Sheldon, are you OK? Sheldon!" Both lines were said less out of concern for my well-being as they were just for the comedy of actually addressing me as Sheldon.

Anyhoo, I got up and felt fine. Cut to that night, my leg hurt so much it literally kept waking me up. I then arrived at the theatre to see my understudy learning my number! I assured him that there was *no way* I wouldn't be going on. I saw *All About Eve*! And I did *Applause* in summer stock.

I actually wasn't that outraged he was trying to learn my number because it was understudy rehearsal. Now that the show is open, the covers have officially begun to learn their roles. I cover Brooks Ashmanskas and learned his lines during previews in case I had to go on, but we just started officially rehearsing. Our great stage manager, Tripp, told us that, because the run only goes through Dec. 8, there's a good chance we'll never go on, but we have to be ready just in case. We finished rehearsal on Friday and were about three quarters through learning the blocking for Act Two. I got to the theatre for the Saturday matinee and saw that one of our leading men, Terry Riordan, had injured his back and Billy Magnussen, his 22-year-old-just-got-his-Equity-card understudy, was on! It was shocking! *A few years later, Billy got nominated for a Tony Award for VANYA AND SONYA AND MASHA AND SPIKE and played Rapunzel's Prince in the INTO THE WOODS film!* It just goes to show how sudden it is when it happens. I assumed there'd be days of an actor complaining that he wasn't feeling well, a warning from the stage manager that it wasn't looking good, and finally an understudy told that he was on. Instead it was a terrifying, last-minute shocker. One afternoon, Billy and I are in street clothes going through our blocking, the next minute he's in full costume about to make his Broadway debut in a leading role!

The good news is, he was on his gig! He got through everything without a hitch and was on for three shows! We all hope that Terry gets better, but the whole thing definitely added some excitement to the weekend shows.

I interviewed Betty Buckley this week, and she was so much fun! First of all, her "new" CD, *Betty Buckley 1967*, is out! It's a recording she made with a jazz trio when she was a teenager that she sent to her boyfriend and a NY agent. They played some of it on her Bravo special, and Phil Birsh, Richard Jay-Alexander and Andrew Gans from Playbill Records convinced her to release it. She sounds amazing. She said that she's learned something from listening to it all these years later. Nowadays, when she does a CD, she's constantly re-recording phrases and/or punching in notes she doesn't like, but all the songs on *Betty Buckley 1967* were done in one take. She wants to recapture some of that "singing for the sake of singing" and not the over-thinking/trying-to-make-perfect version of performing she sometimes does nowadays. She wants the spontaneity and joy of her early youth, not the arduous perfection-seeking so many artists fall into.

Betty talked about wanting to be in the original *Pippin* on Broadway because she had been obsessed with Bob Fosse ever since she was 12. Her agent told her the *Pippin* people weren't interested in her. Jill Clayburgh got the part and when she left, the *Pippin* people wrote Betty and said they were interested in her auditioning for the original but were told that she left the business! What!?! She finally found out that her agent steered her away from the audition because he also represented Jill Clayburgh and knew he could get more money for Jill because she had done a film. Hmph! "Not interested" indeed! She fired her agent and wound up getting the part of Catherine and staying in the show for a year and a half. "Why so long?" I asked. "To pay for my acting classes… and my therapy." Brava honesty!

Ironically, I was just made dance captain of *The Ritz* and told my boyfriend that the extra cash would cover *my* therapy! Too much info? Um… physical therapy?

I asked Betty how she went from playing the step mom on *Eight is Enough* to starring in *Cats*. She said that when *Cats* was announced, a lot of women wanted to sing "Memory." Rumor has it Cher was vying for the part! Anyhoo, at that point, Betty had hit it big with *1776* in the late '60s but still didn't really have a signature role/song like many of her contemporaries. She went in for many *Cats* auditions, and at her final callback, she asked the director, Trevor Nunn, to come to the stage so she could say something. She told him that there were indeed other women who could sing the part as well as her… but there weren't any women who could sing it better… *and* it was her turn! She knew that could either backfire or pay off, and thankfully it was the latter! However, once she started rehearsals, it was a nightmare. Trevor wanted to make the other dancers really think of her as the rejected cat, Grizabella, so he didn't let her sing for the cast during the first weeks of rehearsals. Instead, he made her do dance rehearsals with the cast, knowing that she was not at their level. She remembers doing horrifying *chainé* turns across the floor but not being allowed to sing "Memory." It was à la Jerome Robbins separating the Sharks and the Jets during *West Side Story* rehearsals to keep them adversaries. I'm sure the desired result is achieved, but at what cost? Can't you just say to the cast, "Act like you don't like Grizabella," instead of making a belter do turns to the left?

Betty said her only job assignment in *Cats* was to "stop the show." Does the word "pressure" mean anything to you? "Your only job is to achieve world peace." Of course, she couldn't do it at first. She'd sing "Memory" and get tepid applause. Ouch. One day she said she saw a homeless woman walk by her apartment on 79th Street, who was dressed crazily with streaked lipstick, yet walked with a fashion-plate attitude. Betty realized that was the key! She had been playing Grizabella as pathetic and self-pitying, but she instead decided to play it like she had something beautiful to share. She began applying this attitude towards the end of previews, and feels she finally got the hang of the role after a while. Sadly it was after critics came, but thankfully she got it in time to win the Tony Award. It *was* her turn!

OK, this Thursday's *Chatterbox* is with the legend Chita Rivera! Olé!

Chita, Chamberlin and "Chad"
October 29, 2007

This week started out with a benefit for Theatreworks USA (which does touring children's theatre) at The Rainbow Room. It was a swanky fundraiser that Kevin Chamberlin hosted and where director Michael Mayer was honored. Years ago, Michael directed *Hansel and Gretel* for them... and now he's a Tony Award-winner! Michael said that when he was first an actor, he used to try out for Theatreworks, and "in keeping with their tradition for excellence, I never got a callback." Hi-lar! John Gallagher, Jr. made a great speech about Michael where he talked about getting his audition for *Spring Awakening* and being so excited when he heard it was gonna be directed by Michael... even though he had never seen one of his shows. John then told the audience what a great director Michael was... admitting that the only Michael Mayer-directed show he's now seen is *Spring Awakening*. By the way, John never considered himself a musical theater singer. He was shocked when he got a callback for *Spring Awakening*. He told me that when he showed up at Lincoln Center (where the callbacks were), he saw a ton of singer-types, which put him into a panic, so he fled! He called his agents to tell them forget it, and they convinced him that he had to go back. Cut to — he got the part and won the Tony! I wonder if there've been other people who've left auditions before they were seen, who, if they stayed, would have won a Tony.

This reminds me of my good friend Paul Castree. He had an audition for *Ragtime* when it was coming to Broadway and, even though he was mainly a singer, he had to go to a dance call. Graciela Daniele was teaching the combination, and it involved some classical ballet steps. Paul had definitely danced in shows, but only jazz. He had *no* ballet training and decided he should leave. As he was leaving, the casting director told him to stay because the artistic staff liked him. Paul was flattered but knew he would look super-awkward doing a ballet combination. The casting director told him that everyone's dancing could be at a different level and to stay and just do his best. Paul went back, and as he was learning the combo, he saw a guy in front of him who looked *awful*. He thought, "Oh, no! That's what I look like! I can't take the humiliation!" and he ran past the casting director and out of the audition. Months later he went to see the show on Broadway and (a) he loved it so much that he was devastated he wasn't in it, and (b) the guy who looked awful *was* cast! Paul was so mad at himself for not staying. The moral is, let *them* decide if you're right for the show! You never know what they're looking for!

The gala ended with me and Kevin Chamberlin singing a really cute duet by Joe Iconis called "Plants Make Wonderful Pets" from the show *The Plant That Ate Dirty Socks. Joe later went on to write tons of stuff for NBC's SMASH!* It was so fun singing with Kevin. I felt like Roger Bart in *Triumph of Love*. Or Anthony Blair Hall in *Seussical* (later replaced by Aaron Carter). Anybody? Nobody.

Thursday, I had Broadway legend Chita Rivera at the *Chatterbox*. I told her it was the 50th anniversary of *West Side Story*. "Why didn't anyone tell *me*?" she asked. "I've been living the life of a 35-year-old woman!" And she ain't joking. She looks amazing. I was talking to a stagehand who was touring a show and the green room windows showed the bottom of people's legs, à la Laverne and Shirley's apartment. All the stagehands were standing around and cruising the bottom halves of the women who were walking by. They saw a pair of legs walk by that made them all start shouting dirty things, and in walked Chita, age 65, attached to said gams! And she's still got 'em!

West Side opened in 1957 and I told her how odd it was to me that day-to-day Broadway was the same 50 years ago. "You know," I said, "half-hour call, understudy rehearsal, eight shows a week — " and she interrupted with, "And we actually *did* eight shows a week." Ouch. She has a point. When I did *Grease!* in '94, there literally was a big congratulatory note on the callboard when there was a performance with no understudies on. Seriously.

Then we got into *West Side Story*. I complimented her on belting the D on "...and put *that* in!" in "America" and contrasted it with Tatiana Troyanos' version on the operatic recording in the '80s. Let's just say if Tatiana's tones were a mode of transportation, they would be a *covered* wagon.

I asked about the rumor that "America" used to have the male dancers in it. Chita said that Peter Gennaro (Jerome Robbins' assistant) did the Latin dances, and he first choreographed "America" with the Sharks. They presented it to Robbins, and the next day, the men were out. Chita liked it better that way because there was a sassy power to having all women. I was talking about the choreography at the end of the number and she started telling me about a bump she had on her forehead back then that she couldn't explain. Turns out, when she would leap and touch her foot to the back of her head, she was actually bringing her foot so far forward, it was hitting her forehead! Who has that kind of stretch?

As for the *West Side Story* movie, after she accepted that she lost the role of Anita, she said that she didn't mind seeing Rita sing her song or dance her dances. But it was torture for her to watch her wear the purple dress. That was *her* dress! She was taught how to use the under-colors. You let the audience think it's just a purple dress and then once in a while, give 'em a flash so they think, "Did I just see some colors underneath that skirt?"

We then segued to *Bye Bye Birdie*. The creative team was interested in her for the role of Rosie but she had heard the show was terrible! She didn't want to appear rude, so she told her agent that she would listen to the score, be polite and then her agent would say, "We'll think about it." This way her agent could deliver the bad news later that Chita wasn't available. Well, as soon as Chita heard the first act, she jumped and said, "I *have* to do this musical!" So much for the plan. By the way, so many great Chita stories are in the brilliant book *Supporting Player* by Richard Seff. He was the actual agent (as well as agent to Ethel Merman and Rex Harrison, and the man who introduced Kander to Ebb, etc...). It's an *amazing* read!

She also told us that Paul Lynde was hilarious. Mean sometimes, but hilarious. He played Mr. MacAfee and originally only had 13 lines. "But then Gower put that kid in front of him [the son, Randolph MacAfee], and the ad-libs started flowing! Lee Adams just started adding them to the script!" She loved working with Dick Van Dyke so much and they just did an Actors Fund benefit out in L.A. They performed the song "Rosie," and Chita got tears in her eyes talking about how she told him how lucky they are to have done what they love to do... and to still be doing it so many years later. On that note, she said that when she and Shirley MacLaine did a benefit together recently, they began by looking at each other across the stage and screaming with glee, "We're alive!!!!"

She mentioned doing some choreography with her back to the audience and, when I balked at a star turning upstage, she said that was an incredibly powerful position. She would come up the elevator at the beginning of "All That Jazz" in *Chicago* with her back to the house and then slowly turn around. She said she remembers doing it one night and when she turned, two guys in the front row freaked out yelling, "Oh, my God! That's Chita Rivera!"

Now, let's counter Chita's years of brilliance with a little of my less-than-professionalism. One night at *The Ritz* last week, Patrick Kerr walked by me onstage and whispered "You're in the audience." Huh? I had to remain onstage for a while in a group scene so I couldn't question him, but then Brooks Ashmanskas whispered, "You're in the first row." There were a bunch of cute guys in the center front seats, but I couldn't figure out who was supposed to be me. The dark-haired muscle guy? The geeky, but super-hot hunk? How flattering! Then Brooks softly said, "Front row, house right, last seat." I looked past the cute Chelsea boys and let my eyes settle on an older white-haired woman, dressed completely in black with orthopedic shoes, AKA the opening outfit I wear as the aging Italian Grandmother. She captured my look so completely we could have toured in *Side Show*. I was at first mortified and then thought it was hilarious and did my signature turn-upstage-to-laugh routine. And, if my stage manager is reading this, I did that new move because my *character* thought of something very funny at that moment. I guess "Sheldon" thinks that seeing a man threatened by a mob hit man with a gun is a laugh riot. Note to self: Investigate how many times you need to be written up to Equity before you can be fired.

Finally, on Sunday night, my boyfriend, James, and his seven-year-old daughter, Juli, and I saw *The Drowsy Chaperone*. Bob Saget is the new Man in Chair and he was great! During the first scene he talks about the plot of *The Drowsy Chaperone* and mentions a "gay wedding." Juli looked at us excited and said, "Gay wedding!" Then Bob Saget explained what "gay" meant in the '20s. Later on, during the song where Janet sings "I Put a Monkey on a Pedestal," Juli asked me what a pedestal was. I told James that I love that she doesn't know what a pedestal is, but she knows what a gay wedding is. We're raising her with an open mind!

Okay, this week is a salon for Broadway Cares/Equity Fights AIDS and I'm also going with Juli's class to the Bronx Zoo. Peace out!

You There in the Front Row
November 7, 2007

Whew! I'm exhausted from running the marathon. Actually, the first part of that sentence is correct, but there's no factual basis for the second part. I was just too embarrassed to write that I have the nerve to be exhausted when we've all been given the gift of a Daylight Savings Time extra hour. I do have the right to be a little tired. My boyfriend, James, had to go to Houston so I've been taking care of Juli. Though, essentially, she's in school 'til 3 PM, then she has afterschool programs 'til 6 when the babysitter picks her up, and by the time I'm home from the show, she's asleep. So, Hollywood-celebrity-style, my version of "taking care of her" is not 24 hours of parenting, but 45 minutes in the morning when I get her ready for school.

Actually, I love getting her ready in the morning because all she wants to do is sleep in and only be woken up for something fun. So, I've found the best way to get her awake is to fully lip-synch something sassy. We both get what we want: She gets a show to wake up to, and I get to play Effie. On Friday, I did the *Dreamgirls* fight scene that happens right before "And I Am Telling You," and she was rapt! Thursday, I was blasting Neil Sedaka (whom I love!), and she asked if that was a boy or a girl. I told her that Neil is a great male singer with an amazingly high voice. Another Neil song came on and I said, "I love his voice!" She whirled around and said, in shock, "*That's* a boy?!?!" I guess she bought it for "Calendar Girl," but "Laughter in the Rain" was pushing it.

Last Monday, I performed in a salon for BC/EFA. That's right, a salon. No, I didn't travel back in time, I went to a very swanky apartment building located on Central Park South and took the elevator to the 26th floor. The apartment was loaned to BC/EFA, and people paid cash to hang out in the gorgeous living room with a full terrace overlooking the park and see a performance every ten minutes. It was so fun! Joy Behar was there and hilarious as usual. She commented on the Bush twins being named Jenna and Barbara, as in "J and B." Paul Shaffer played and sang and told us that he got his green card when Stephen Schwartz invited him from Canada to be the pianist for Broadway's *The Magic Show*! Who knew? Chris Sieber was the host and said he's getting ready to do *Shrek* where he's gonna play the character that's super short. I wondered how they're going to create the illusion, and he said he's doing it old school: He's going to walk on his knees! It's nice to know that technology hasn't replaced the technique I perfected in seventh grade when I would entertain my friends imitating that woman from *Poltergeist* ("Go into the light... there is peace in the light!").

I chatted up Norm Lewis, my favorite male Broadway singer. He's shirtless as King Triton in *The Little Mermaid*, so he had to get his body back into the shape it was when he did *Wild Party* on Broadway, AKA woof! He looks great! Also, I'm kvelling because he said he's halfway through his first CD. Finally! I've always said that he should have one of those Andrea Bocelli/Josh Groban careers. When I play the recording of him singing "We Live on Borrowed Time" by David Friedman on my Sirius radio show, I am always deluged with letters... more than for any other artist. I'm so excited because his CD will be a trip down memory lane for me. We first met when I cast him (non-Equity) in a production of *Joseph...* at the Candlewood Playhouse. His audition song was from *Hello, Dolly!...* and it was one sung by Dolly. Yes, he did "Before the Parade Passes By," and he was amazing! He told me it's going on the CD. Brava! Hopefully, he won't begin it with her monologue ("Ephram... lemme go"). *OMG! Get his CD! He sounds amazing!*

I also saw the gorgeous Sara Gettelfinger who made me laugh so hard a while ago. We were seeing a Broadway show together, and we were both outraged at one of the actors holding notes way too long. The song was supposed to be casual and chatty, yet all we heard were whole notes, vocal placement and vibrato. Sara said that his subtext was: "Time out from the show everyone. Just so you all know… I have an *amazing* voice." Sara gets a brava on nailing it!

Tuesday, I interviewed the brilliant composer/lyricist Maury Yeston for my Sirius radio show. First of all, I was shocked that he went to Yeshiva! Who knew he was Jewish? I guess "Maury" should have been a tip-off, but the Yeston threw me. He said that his grandparents' last name was Yes, and they emigrated through England. The English knew that they would get whiplash from constantly swerving their heads every time someone said "Yes," so they added an English suffix (i.e. Wellington, Harrington etc.).

He was a Professor at Yale, and some of his students are now part of what's called "The Yale Mafia": David Loud (who left Yale mid-term to be in *Merrily We Roll Along*), Scott Frankel (composer of *Grey Gardens*) and Ted Sperling (Tony Award-winner for orchestrating *The Light in the Piazza*).

In the beginning of the '80s, Maury had written a musical version of one of his favorite Fellini movies *8 1/2* and, because he added music, he upped the number in the title to *Nine*. He did a reading at Yale but didn't have the rights to the film. Someone who saw it loved it and thought Fellini should give Maury the rights, so she wrote Fellini a letter. That "someone" was Katharine Hepburn! I love that she had his address (Fellini, Villa #5, Italy).

Maury won an award that gave him money to do it Off-Broadway and someone who knew Tommy Tune gave Tommy a copy of the show. Tommy called Maury and said that he should give back the award money. "What?" said Maury, *The Simpsons*-style. Tommy felt the show shouldn't play Off-Broadway, but should go right to Broadway!

During auditions, Maury said that all the women had such a European look/attitude, but all the guys had an "I just got back from dinner theatre in Indiana" look. They couldn't find any men who had the right look for the show (besides the lead, Raul Julia). Tommy asked Maury if he could write out all the male roles except for the lead, and Maury loved the idea! First of all, it made Raul seem much more like a powerful movie director because he was the only man on that stage, and secondly, Maury loved the vocal stuff he could do with so many women. That's how he decided to have them all sing the overture. I asked about the song "A Call From the Vatican" where one of Guido's girlfriends says very suggestive things on the phone. Maury said that people think that he invented phone sex! Hmm… I've never had phone sex where the person on the other end hits a high C. Then again, Beverly Sills never returned my calls.

After *Nine* won the Tony Award for Best Musical, a producer suggested that Maury do a musical version of *The Phantom of the Opera*. He did and it was headed for Broadway… Then there was a little announcement in the paper saying that Andrew Lloyd Webber was considering doing a musical about *The Phantom*. Maury said that even though it wasn't definite, just a possibility, *all* the funding dried up immediately. People knew that Lloyd Webber's show would be a hit in London (if it happened) and then come to Broadway. *P.S. Where it's now the longest-running show.* So, Maury's show lives on regionally and in Europe but ne'er

Broadway.

Tommy Tune called him in the late '80s and said that *Grand Hotel* (a musical composed by Wright/Forrest, who wrote *Kismet*) had opened in Boston, and the review said, "They might have saved *My One and Only*, but they can't save this one." Tommy asked Maury to come and help. Maury went out to eat with Wright and Forrest and said that he was mortified to be there because he knew that it was every composer's nightmare. Turns out, Wright and Forrest couldn't have been more gracious and said that they wanted him to help because they knew the show could close and wouldn't dream of putting all these people out of work. They just wanted credit given for whatever song they wrote and vice versa. Maury realized that Wright/Forrest wrote a very old-school linear show, and Tommy was doing a non-linear/no-set show that needed a different type of music. Maury wrote an opening number (there wasn't one when the show started in Boston!) and many other songs, and *Grand Hotel* wound up being nominated for many Tony Awards (including Best Musical and Score). It also wound up running for more than 1,000 performances. Take that, Boston critic! Unfortunately, it also gave us that commercial where we found out that woman's husband "worked in the area." Anybody remember that?

I brought up the brilliant performance by David Carroll, who played the Baron. I was so blown away by his performance and was so frustrated that he didn't sing the Baron on the CD. Turns out, Wright/Forrest were holding out on allowing a CD because they wanted a recording of the show they originally wrote, and not the Broadway version (!). So, it took a long time for them to come around and agree to a CD with a combo of Forrest/Wright and Yeston music. Well, by that point, David Carroll was very sick with AIDS, but the powers-that-be were going to record him singing to just a piano track and then add the orchestra later. David apparently was much sicker than anyone thought because he arrived at the studio, told everyone he needed to go to the bathroom and, sadly, died while he was in there. The beautiful part is that there's an added track at the end of the CD, which is David singing "Love Can't Happen" during his cabaret act at Steve McGraw's. The ending of that song is one of the most thrilling moments I remember experiencing in the theatre. He got to the end of the song and sang, "When love comes, you'll know..." on an E flat. I remember thinking, "Surely, he's not going to go any higher," and then he sang "And... I... kno-o-o-o-o-ow!" on an A flat, and I almost fell out of my seat. It was unbelievable. And even though he had to physically climb all around the set because his character was also a thief, he said that hitting that last note was the hardest thing he ever had to do onstage. You must listen to it and hear that man's voice!

This week, during a performance of *The Ritz*, shockingly, I started laughing onstage yet again. But this time, I will not take the blame for it! I blame All Hallows Eve. Two guys showed up to see *The Ritz* and thought that it was a Broadway tradition to dress up in the audience. It isn't. They were the *only* ones in costume and they were dressed as bacon and eggs. Yes, one was bacon and one was eggs. They looked adorable, but they were sitting in the front row! How can I pretend to be scared of Carmine Vespucci brandishing a gun when I see a delicious breakfast order inches away? And it was even more bizarre because they weren't commenting on their costumes... they were just sitting there watching the show. An enormous fried egg and a side of bacon with *Playbills* in their laps. Normally, at the end of Act One, Rosie Perez shakes hands with someone in the front row, and during intermission we told her that we loved that she shook the hands of the bacon. She was shocked when we told her that he was bacon. She assumed he was a Rabbi! Hilariously, she thought the strips were his tallis. I politely informed her that there's a *big* difference between a Rabbi and bacon.

I'm very excited that my book *Broadway Nights* has been released and, of course, I keep obsessively checking my Amazon reviews. They've been great... every customer reviewer gave me five stars! *Until...* I checked last night and saw that I got two stars (!) from a woman who flat out admitted to just skimming it! I was devastated! It pulled my whole ranking down. I decided to investigate and see what other books she's reviewed. Suffice it to say, she gave five stars to a book about Chronic Fatigue Syndrome because she's had it for 15 years... and she's also 82! An 82-year-old with chronic fatigue? "I'm elderly and so, so fatigued... but I'll use what little strength I have to pull down Seth Rudetsky's ranking. Did it. Zzzzzzz."

All right, I'm excited because this is a Joe's Pub week. I'm going Monday night to see the sweet-voiced and hilarious Andréa Burns (*In the Heights*) celebrate her newly released CD (*A Darker Shade of Red*), and then next Sunday, I'm seeing another Diva whose hair is a lighter shade of red: Miss Coco. If you don't know who that is, rent the film *Girls Will Be Girls*. She's hysterical! Oh, and if you come to the show, please don't wear your breakfast.

Burns, Jenkins, Shindle and the Strike
November 12, 2007

Oy! The strike! *Referring, of course, to the strike that closed all Broadway shows for a few weeks!* It's so bizarre that I'm in one of the few shows running. It's not like I chose to do *The Ritz* because I knew it would be immune from the strike, it just worked out that way because Roundabout Theatre Company is under a different contract. I'm hoping by the time you read this, all the Broadway shows will be back on. Actually, why don't I add more to that wish: I hope all the Broadway shows will be back on, including some that have closed. That's right. Not only the current *Rent, Hairspray* and *Drowsy Chaperone*, I want to see *Evita* with Patti LuPone and *Drood* with Betty Buckley ASAP. Local One, that's what you need to focus on while negotiating.

This week began with a benefit for *Only Make Believe*, a great organization founded by Dena Hammerstein (Jamie's widow) that brings theatre to hospitalized children. It was great to see Julia Murney again, fresh off of *Wicked*. She sang "Life of the Party" from *Wild Party*, which was Idina Menzel's song in the final version of the show, but was Julia's song at one point. Most people associate "Raise the Roof" with Julia's character, but when I first saw it, Idina's character sang it and she was played by Sara Ramirez. That show had more swapping than the movie "The Ice Storm." Capathia Jenkins sang "(Let a Big, Black Lady) Stop the Show" from *Martin Short: Fame Becomes Me*. If you haven't downloaded that song from iTunes, stop reading now and get thee! It is so hilarious, and she sounds *amazing*! She hits an amazing F sharp (with vibrato) and holds it forever! No wonder she almost got Effie in the film. She told me that when she went in for her screen test, they had her do the entire fight scene into "And I Am Telling You." And not lip-synched, totally live. She said that she gave it *all* she had, and when she finished, she was completely exhausted. Then Bill Condon (the director) came over to her and congratulated her. Following that with "Okay, we're gonna take it again from the top and this time try to blah, blah, blah." Again!?! Long story short: Jennifer Hudson won the Oscar.

At the benefit, Capathia's backup was sung by the hilarious Jill Abramovitz, Mary Ann Hu (who just got the Bloody Mary understudy in *South Pacific*!) and Jason Michael Snow. I recently sent him a congratulatory text message because I saw his name on *The Little Mermaid* cast list. He sadly informed me that I was mixing him up with Jason (no middle name) Snow. He's Jason *Michael* Snow. Ouch. There are two Snows on Broadway? Wait, what about Jessica Snow Wilson? How does she feel about all of this? And what if she got married to Jason? Would she be Jessica Snow Snow? And didn't this kind of humor go out in the '70s?

Anyhoo, right after the benefit, I hightailed it to see Andréa Burns' CD release show. Her new CD *A Deeper Shade of Red* just came out, and it's fabulous! *And* her act was amazing! She did a long version of "I Feel Pretty" interspersed with stories about all the different times she's played Maria. From when she was first 15 years old (she sang the first verse sprightly and joyous) to years later when she was perhaps too long in the tooth (done à la Karen Morrow) to mere months after giving birth (sung through exhausted tears). She ended it by saying she'd play the role into her eighties and then proceeded to sing it Stritch-style (AKA throatily spoken: "I feel pretty... A-a-a-and entrancing").

The next day, I interviewed Andréa on my Sirius radio show. She talked about being a sophomore at NYU and, for fun, going to an audition for the European tour of *West Side Story* just to experience a real New York audition. They needed a Shark girl who could understudy Maria. The girls all had to learn a section from "America," which also happened to be the exact section she had learned in her Performing Arts High School in Miami. She completely knew it but that didn't stop her from pretending to slowly learn it and then being able to suddenly nail it. She got through the dance call, and they asked her to sing. She washed off all her Anita make-up, wore a simple top and sang the high C at the end of the "Tonight Quintet." They told her that the tour left in three days for Berlin and they wanted her to be on it. Suffice it to say, her parents were not pleased that her tuition that semester was for naught. But Andréa felt she had no choice. She'd be performing all over Europe with a full orchestra and tons of dancers that worked with Jerome Robbins — including Nicole Fosse. As a matter of fact, Nicole said that her mom would be visiting at the end of November and wanted to cook for the cast. So Andréa spent Thanksgiving eating a turkey cooked by Gwen Verdon!

The sad part was that she was told the woman playing Maria never missed, so there was no way she'd *ever* go on for the role. And therefore, they gave her no rehearsal for the role. And, of course, she had to go on for Maria right at the beginning of the run, with only a few hours' notice and no rehearsal. Haven't people learned their lesson after Shirley MacLaine was told that Carol Haney "never missed" *and* the world was told that the Titanic would never sink? Stop making absolute statements!

Later on, she took over the role of Maria and developed a major crush on her Tony… and wound up marrying him! She's been married to the brilliant (now director) Peter Flynn for ten years, and they have an adorable three-year-old son, Hudson.

Andréa then told me about her first big New York break. When she came back to New York, she ran into someone she went to musical theatre summer camp with (French Woods). P.S. French Woods is the name of the camp, not someone's drag name. *P.P.S. Juli now goes there. It's the most amazing place ever!* Anyhoo, her friend was getting a show produced featuring his music, and he asked her to come over to sing through stuff, just so he could hear it out loud. Turns out, he thought she sounded amazing doing his songs, and he (and director Daisy Prince) put her in the show. Her friend was, of course, Jason Robert Brown, and the show was *Songs for a New World*. The hilarious part is that Billy Porter couldn't do the recording because he was under contract with another label, so they had to take Billy out of the already photographed cover photo and stretch and manipulate everyone else's photo to take up the lost space. It's crazy. Look at the cover of the CD, and you'll see "Andréa" sitting on a stool. And by "Andréa," I mean Andréa through a funhouse mirror manipulated by the 1.0 version of Photoshop.

Right now she's the standby for Rosie Perez in *The Ritz*, and in the spring she'll open on Broadway in *In the Heights*. The last time she covered a role was when she was the Belle understudy in *Beauty and the Beast*, and she prides herself on not being one of the many utensils in the ensemble but "the" broom. There was only one, and she was *it*. The devastating story is that she was asked to play Belle for ten performances so Kerry Butler could go on vacation. What's devastating? Well, her whole family came up from Florida, but she didn't want them to see her first show, so they all bought tickets for the following night. During "Be Our Guest" her heel got caught in one of the tracks on the stage that are used to bring scenery on and off. She fell and knew that something was wrong with her foot. She found out later that she broke it! She got up but didn't know how she was going to finish the number. Suddenly, her hands were grabbed by Lumiere, so he could spin her around. The late, great Patrick Quinn was playing Lumiere, and Andréa started whispering to him, "Don't spin me! I hurt myself!" Unfortunately, he couldn't hear her and assumed she was telling him how excited she was that she was on, so he gave her an extra-vigorous spin! Yay! I'm sure the children loved seeing Belle being spun while her face registered blinding pain. Later on, Patrick was mortified, and he and Andréa always laughed about it. After she was put down, she staggered to the center of the stage to start the signature "Be Our Guest" kick line. Could she do it? She thought, "Well, I am the lead in this number, right in the center. It would sorta make sense if everyone kicks but me." But the trouper in her came out, and she did the full can-can high kicks with a broken foot. She got offstage, said she was injured, and within two seconds her wig and costume was pulled off and she was rushed to the ER. Her mother had decided to come after all because, "I'm not going to have my daughter playing a lead on Broadway while I'm at dinner!" No one knew where her mom was sitting in the audience but they found her quickly. How? They made the announcement "The role of Belle will no longer be played by Andréa Burns" and they looked for the woman who jumped out of her seat! The other headache was that Andréa was getting married in a few weeks. She healed well enough to be able to walk down the aisle without her cast…very carefully. After the wedding, Vicki Clark (who had no idea about the foot) told her, "That was the best walking down the aisle I've seen. I've never seen someone comfortable enough to just take their time."

Andréa's gotten great reviews for her CD, and I think the break-out song is gonna be "BTW, Write Back" by *In the Heights* composer/star Lin-Manuel Miranda. It's about a devoted musical theatre fan who keeps writing to the *myspace* page of her favorite Broadway star. AKA me at age 12 if *myspace* and/or the internet existed back then. Or, quite frankly, computers. *P.S. Remember myspace? That faded out quicker than my decision to cut out sugar.*

At Andréa's show I ran into Ted Sperling, who's getting ready to music direct the Lincoln Center revival of *South Pacific*. I am always devastated to see revivals because usually they shrink the orchestra and it sounds like a synthesizer face-off. But he told me the revival is gonna have the same number of instruments as the original production in the 1940s! Brava!

Friday, I did an interview with *Legally Blonde*'s Kate Shindle for a bunch of theatergoers from the Carolinas. Kate was crowned Miss America 1998 and I first asked her about the beginning of the pageant when all 50 girls are onstage and it's suddenly whittled down to 15. I assumed that the girls know who's being ixnayed, but she said that they don't know until that moment. Unfortunately, the losing girls have to come back throughout the pageant and perform back-up, and Kate said we should watch closely because there are always a couple of girls missing 'cause they're too traumatized/raccoon-eyed to continue. The cool thing about her winning is that Kate's platform was AIDS education, and she toured all over the country talking about it. She said she would visit schools in the Midwest and Deep South where they would normally never discuss such things, but because she was Miss America, they would let her come to the school and educate the kids. Brava!

Jerry Stiller and Anne Meara saw the Saturday matinee of *The Ritz*, which was super cool. First, because I love them both, and secondly because Jerry was the original gangster, Carmine Vespucci, in the Broadway and film version of *The Ritz*. After the show, they met the cast, and our current Carmine, Lenny Venito, got to meet Jerry. Jerry told us that, during the original run of the show, someone broke into the dressing room of the theatre and stole the mink coat and gun that's featured heavily in Act Two. Jerry ran to the stage manager freaking out because the second act couldn't happen without those props. The stage manager said he'd handle it and left Jerry there. Ten minutes later, he came back with a gun and a coat. "Where'd you get them?" asked Jerry. The stage manager explained, "I got the gun from a cop outside, and I got the mink from a lady in the fourteenth row!"

OK, everyone. Here's hoping that by the time this column comes back next week, Broadway will be back to business!

Max, Laura and Hilarity at *The Ritz*
November 20, 2007

What? The strike is still on? Didn't I specifically ask Local One and the producers to end it? Oy! It's definitely been a hardship on audience members and everyone involved, but the most devastating thing about the strike is that it took place during BC/EFA's audience appeal fundraising period. They lose $40,000 a *day*! And that money is counted on by AIDS organizations all over the world... soup kitchens, hospices, etc. If you get a chance, go to *BCEFA.org* and buy something from their holiday catalogue.

This week I interviewed Max Crumm and Laura Osnes, who won the *You're the One That I Want* competition and are now playing Danny and Sandy in *Grease*. I started my career on *Playbill.com* writing about their TV show, which makes me feel a special connection to them, plus I played piano for the last *Grease!* revival, so I also feel a little like the Sheila to their Maggie. (AKA, jaded hag to their starry-eyed naiveté).

Laura grew up in the Midwest and worked as an understudy in *Aladdin*, which was playing at the Minneapolis Children's Theater. One day, the two leads were doing the scene where they're supposed to back into each other and they wound up completely colliding. They had to be taken to the hospital (they really got injured... including the Aladdin completely chipping his tooth), and Laura and the other understudy got to go on. She was so excited because it was a two-show day... and then was outraged when the leads wound up going on that night! How dare they be so professional? But the sparks between the two understudies flew... and now they're married!

She got cast as Sandy in *Grease* at a Minnesota dinner theater and had to take a weekend off to audition for *You're the One That I Want*. Max was in California at the time and thought it could be fun to audition for the TV show. He wasn't sure if he would or not, but happened to wake up at 6 AM on the morning of the audition, so he figured that since he was up, he would go.

I talked with them about the ludicrous moment when all the contestants were forced to stand and sing in unison, and supposedly based on that performance, producer David Ian would make cuts. How stupid did the TV show producers think we were!? Why would the final decision be made based on how they all sounded singing a cappella? The cuts were obviously made beforehand, and the producers thought it would be a creative way to do them. Laura said that they triple checked that everyone was in their right position before they started because David Ian walked around (wearing a stern expression) and carrying a clipboard that obviously had all the cut people's position on it, and they wanted to make sure he wouldn't cut the wrong person. She also said that if you watched it, it lasts an arduous 7 minutes on the TV show, but it actually lasted 1,000 times *longer* when they were filming it.

We discussed that final episode, and Max busted the people on the chat boards who said that Austin didn't care about his mother because he didn't hug her right after he lost. He actually ran past her to do a quick change because he and Ashley were devastatingly forced to be in the ensemble while Max and Laura sang the finale as Danny and Sandy. Can you imagine? "Barbra Streisand, you've lost the Tony Award to Carol Channing. Now, take off that gown, put on a frock and dance back-up for 'Before the Parade Passes By.'"

This week also had some hilarity at *The Ritz*. Brooks Ashmanskas has a line near the end of Act Two where he pretends to be the Private Eye whose name is Brick. "It's me, Bunny! Brick!" Well, the line he said before that got a really big laugh, and it sort of threw him. Unfortunately, it threw him enough for him to then say, "It's me, Bunny! *Brooks*!" It was an amazing moment to watch because as soon as he said, "Brooks," he realized what he did, and all the color drained from his face. After I said my next line, "Careful, Googie!" I started whispering "Careful, Rosie." I always try to maintain a mix of 90% professionalism, 10% acting out.

Even though BC/EFA is losing a tremendous amount of money due to the strike, the good news is that *The Ritz* is working super hard to fundraise due to the amazing leadership of our stage manager, Tripp Phillips. Tripp was the stage manager for the *Jersey Boys* national tour last year — that was the first national tour to actually win the Easter Bonnet fundraising over all the Broadway shows! Brava! Anyhoo, many nights we not only collect money in buckets, sell autographed posters/programs and the *Carols for a Cure* CD, but we also auction items. Young hunk Justin Clynes and ex-porn star Ryan Idol have been auctioning off their towels (seriously! Once for $700!), and the dedicated Rosie Perez also auctions off her earrings. One night, someone actually said they'd pay $2,000 for her bra! She literally wriggled out of it onstage, autographed and forked it over!

I was collecting after the show one night and a woman approached me and commented that the time period being shown onstage was not consistent with today. "I mean," she shook her head, "the bag the leading man carries says *Pan Am*." I looked at her, confused. "Well," I said, "it takes place in the '70s." Pause. "Oh… I didn't know that." What? The stage is filled with '70s pantsuits, afros and disco music. The whole bows are choreographed to Donna Summer's "Last Dance." Maybe we should be more presentational and have a character stand center stage and say, "I love living in the 1970s. One day it will be 2007, but not for many more years."

My sister came in from Virginia to see *The Ritz*, and she was telling the woman next to her that I was in the show. The woman looked in the program and asked, "So… he plays Us?" Nancy was confused until she looked down and saw my credit in the Playbill (Sheldon Farnethold, u/s Chris). She politely explained the u/s means understudy. My questions are: 1. Why is u/s the only "character" she focused on when there are two proper names surrounding it? 2. Who spells "us" with a slash in the middle? 3. How can I play a pronoun?

Saturday night, James and I went to see Chita Rivera's late-night show at Feinstein's. Apparently we also traveled back in time because she looked and sounded faboo. The good news for theatre fans is that she does some of her classic songs including "Kiss of the Spider Woman," "A Boy Like That" and (for you *Rink* fans) "Chief Cook and Bottle Washer"! I have to say though that the most thrilling moment for me was watching her do "All That Jazz." I was obsessed with *Chicago* as a child. It was the first show that I knew by heart and then saw on Broadway. She was such an important part of what made me love Broadway, and to see her so brilliantly do the song I saw her do 31 years ago had me full-out crying in the audience.

Speaking of which, Sunday night, I had my book release party/show/Actors Fund benefit for my new novel *Broadway Nights*. I read scenes with the brilliant cast of *[title of show]*, the hilarious Mary Testa and the comic genius Andrea Martin. I literally had to stop myself from crying because I grew up obsessively watching SCTV every Friday night, and to be standing onstage reading a scene with my comedy idol was such a dream come true. Heidi Blickenstaff sang the song "A Way Back to Then" from [title of show], which is about recapturing the joy and hope you had as a kid obsessed with theatre and the song references little-girl-Heidi listening to Andrea McArdle on the record player. Well, Andrea was one of the performers at my book event, so Heidi got to sing it in front of her which was obviously so moving to Heidi. Then, after the chapter in my book where the lead character sees *Annie* and decides to ixnay opera and become Broadway obsessed, Andrea McArdle got up to sing. She thought she was gonna do "Everybody Says Don't" but realized she wasn't when I started playing the vamp to "Maybe." Sorry! I needed to make Heidi's dream come true and it was amazing to watch Heidi weeping while Andrea sang.

This week, James, Juli, James' mom and I are going over to my mom's house for Thanksgiving. I've already asked William Ivey Long if he can upgrade my *Ritz* robe to an extra-fat. Bring on the stuffing!

"Vicki/Victoria" and Rosie's Costume Malfunction
November 27, 2007

Happy post-Thanksgiving! Who acted out with food? I did! I went to my Mom's house with James, his mother, Juli, and my sister, Beth, and friend Tim Cross. First of all, we made the wise choice of renting a car to go out there, so instead of a half-hour train ride, we had an hour-and-a-half car ride. That damn parade ruined everything... including my love of Broadway (more on that later). After we ate, we saw *Enchanted*. My favorite part was the fact they put all of the Disney princesses in cameo roles. Jodi Benson (Ariel) was Patrick Dempsey's secretary, Paige O'Hara (Belle) was a soap actress and Judy Kuhn (Pocahontas) was a harried mother. I love when they do things like that... like giving Chita Rivera a cameo in *Chicago* and John Waters a feature in *Hairspray*. Perhaps when they make the movie of *The Ritz*, I can strut across the screen and... oh, they made it already? Thirty years ago? Well... (said *Bewitched* Samantha Stevens-style).

I interviewed the talented Tony Award-winner Victoria Clark (*The Light in the Piazza*) for my Sirius radio show. First of all, in real life she goes by Vicki and apparently a lot of folks don't realize that it's short for Victoria. She teaches voice, and she said that students have come over for their first lesson, looked at her face, looked at the Tony Award sitting on her piano and said, "Hmm... I know your name is Vicki Clark, but you happen to look a lot like an actress named Victoria Clark. Weird." Hello!? The face is the same, the Tony Award is the same and the first syllable of the first name and the last name are the same, but that's simply not enough for people to assume the obvious. Let me reverse the expression to "When you *don't* assume, you make an a**out of you and Victoria."

She talked about understudying Faith Prince in *Guys and Dolls* and how she was called for a special rehearsal because she wasn't hitting Nathan Detroit's face exactly right with her handkerchief during "Sue Me." She snuck her parents into the rehearsal because she knew they would not believe the minutiae one has to worry about as an understudy if they didn't see it.

She was also the understudy for 11 parts in *Sunday in the Park with George*, and there was another understudy who was competitive and literally tried to sabotage her during an understudy run-thru. They were standing backstage, and suddenly the understudy told Vicki that it was their cue. Vicki said that it wasn't her entrance yet, and the other understudy hissed, "*Yes, it is*!" and pushed her onstage! It was very *Showgirls*... without a staircase and/or horrifying lap dance.

She actually didn't want the role of Smitty in *How to Succeed*... because she had just given birth a month before and was getting two hours of sleep a night. Of course, she got the gig, and the show had such a nice long run that her son was able to come see it! Unfortunately, it also ran long enough for him to learn how to talk. He was sitting in a box seat with his dad, and when Vicki began a scene with Matthew Broderick, she suddenly heard "Hi, Mommy!" The audience started laughing, but Vicki tried to stay in character. The scene continued, and so did another "Hi-i-i-i-i, Mommy!" Finally, she heard the sound of a muffled "Hi, Mommy" as her son was obviously taken out of the box seats and spoken to sternly by his dad. The scene finished, her son came back and Vicki exited out the big double doors onstage. As she was walking out she heard, "Bye-e-e-e-e, Mommy." That's what I call a shout-out!

We talked about her vocal technique, and she said that she never had a vocal problem throughout the whole run of *The Light in the Piazza*. Unfortunately, the show was so emotionally debilitating that she was having tons of physical problems, but the voice never gave out. I complimented her on the consistency of her accent. So many times I've heard actors have an accent when they do dialogue but then totally drop it when they sing (see: *Jim Nabors' Greatest Hits*). I love how in "Dividing Day" she sings, "Dashing as the day we met, only there is something..." and pronounces the word "only" "own-ly" like a Southern belle. She said that the mother of one of her son's elementary school friends is from the South and Vicki had her record the entire script and lyrics into a tape recorder (three times!) so Vicki could copy her.

One of the reasons she had a hard time getting cast in *Piazza* is because people only knew her as a comic actress and they didn't think she could do a dramatic part. She struggled to prove she could do drama and now she literally has casting agents nervously asking her agent if she can do comedy. Yay! It's fun having a whole body of work yet only being remembered for your last job.

On another note, my radio show on Sirius is called *Seth's Big Fat Broadway* and after *The Ritz* one night, I heard an audience member approach one of the other cast members and ask where I was. He pointed to me and the audience person was mind-boggled. "That's him? Then why is his show called 'Seth's *Big, Fat,* Broadway'?" What's the confusion? It's called *Seth's Big, Fat Broadway* not "*I* am big and fat *on* Broadway." Although, I do admit I am always complaining about my weight on the air. When I was on *Law & Order: CI*, a woman with a hilariously thick Southern accent called the Sirius message center and left me this message: "Seth, I saw you on *Law & Order*... and you looked totally different than what I thought. From the way you talk, I thought you'd look like the lead from 'La Cage aux Folles'... the French version. Let me describe him: He's fat, he's got a big butt... he whistles, he whoops... and he's *adorable*. But you! (here's where it got crazy)... you look like *Hugh Jackman*!" I guess anyone you expected to whistle, whoop and have a big butt and then doesn't immediately looks like Hugh Jackman.

This week there was a theft at *The Ritz*! At the end of Act One, Rosie Perez (as Googie Gomez) does a big medley that's supposed to be a mess. At the end, she does a high kick, "accidentally" kicks off her shoe, then angrily throws it offstage. Well, the shoe didn't quite make it offstage and sat all the way stage right for the rest of the number. As Act One ended, there was a blackout for a couple of seconds, and when the lights came up, the shoe was gone! It was very *Murder, She Wrote*... without a murder and/or four-time Tony Award-winner.

Coincidentally, one of the original *Ritz* cast members (who played a bathhouse patron) came to the show and was chatting with me as I collected for BC/EFA. He said that Rita Moreno would kick her shoe into the actual audience, yet it was never stolen. He finally asked her how she always got it back, and she told him that she wrote something on the inside of the shoe: "There is a seven-foot tall Puerto Rican who will attack you as you exit if you don't return this shoe."

He was shocked to be seeing a show in Studio 54 because he used to come here when it was the famous disco. He said that in those days the bathroom had all these colognes you could apply, and it was useful when people were using the stalls to take drugs. If someone was hogging the stall too long, you'd take one of the colognes and start spraying over the top of the stall so they'd flee. I guess you could tell that someone was a heavy drug user if they reeked of Halston Z-14.

Back to Googie's number. Right near the end, there's an amazing quick change, where Rosie disappears behind a curtain and goes from a turquoise pantsuit to a purple sassy dress in literally four seconds. Unfortunately, it didn't quite work Tuesday night, and she wound up in half the dress and half the pantsuit. All of us patrons watch the show from the box seats, and it was impossible to keep a straight face. She looked like a moth that hadn't quite come out of its cocoon.

Back to the Thanksgiving Day Parade. I generally dislike the Broadway performances because I hate watching lip-synching. The whole point of Broadway is the fact that it's live, so it's always a downer to me to watch a song that I like turned into an Ashlee Simpson concert. And can we also discuss commercialism under the guise of children's entertainment? "Look! There's a giant balloon of Snoopy (OK, that makes sense)... And the Hamburglar (hmm... pushing it)... And North Fork Bank (what the...?)."

Here's a question: what do M&Ms mean to you? Broadway! They do? For some reason, Jonathan Groff and Lea Michele stood on top of an M&M float and sang "Give My Regards to Broadway." I ran into Jonathan on 49th Street the night before and he told me that it was gonna be a sort of rock version of the song. I guess by "rock version," he meant a version that retained the lyrics of the song but dispensed with that pesky melody/rhythm and any original chord changes. However, I will say that they both sounded amazing! There was a fabulous high note that I had to rewind twice! And I loved *Xanadu*. Could Kerry Butler or Cheyenne Jackson possibly sound/look any better? Short answer: no.

We ended the week with a fabulous birthday party for Kevin Chamberlin where Rosie Perez's friend baked a delicious *tres leches* cake. The translation of "tres leches" is "Do not eat this if you have to wear a revealing towel eight times a week." Sadly, I did and I do. I guess that's why it's now called *Seth's Big Fat Ritz.*

A Momentous Week
December 3, 2007

Monday night, I saw back-to-back shows. Franc D'Ambrosio (the longest running Phantom) was at the Thalia Theater (in Symphony Space), and he sang up a storm. Three-quarters through the first act, he decided he needed a sip of water and someone brought it onstage for him. After he drank a little, he said it was the first time that he's ever had water onstage. What? His show is an hour-and-a-half long, and it's mostly singing! How can he sing so much and never need to wet ye olde whistle? *P.S. Shoshana Bean has since told me she thinks it's a badge of courage to do an entire show without ever drinking water. Why? Who's judging these people? A camel?*

Anyhoo, I immediately hightailed it with my boyfriend to see the wonderful Victoria (Vicki) Clark. A) she looked gorgeous, and B) she sounded it. She sang all the songs from her new CD (*Fifteen Seconds of Grace*) with an 11-piece-band. She said that everyone thought she would just use a piano/bass and drums, but she wanted it to sound like her album, so she got all her musicians to haul it to the beautiful Samuel Kaplan Penthouse. It felt like such a New York night; we were surrounded by such a stunning view with NY celebs left and right and were inches away from such a glorious singer. The title song from her CD is beautiful/devastating to me. Then, for her encore, she did "Fable," and as soon as it began, my boyfriend had to pull me back because I was leaning all the way down my aisle trying to see if Kelli O'Hara would start crying at the beginning of the song or at the end. There was also something so sweet about seeing Ted Sperling play for Vicki because they went to college together and here they are, years later, both at the top of their careers, still working together as old friends.

On Tuesday, I got to interview *Little Mermaid* star Sherie Rene Scott for my radio show on Sirius. I asked her about the Rene, and she said she had to add it when she joined SAG because there was another Sherie Scott, but not in Equity. But then it got annoying having two professional names, so she kept the Rene. She grew up in Kansas and knew when she was very young that she wanted to be in New York. When the show *Tommy* was first performed, it played at La Jolla Playhouse. When it transferred to Broadway, they kept the whole cast and only replaced the girl who played Sally Simpson. Sherie got the gig. Even though she was thrilled to make her Broadway debut, she said that it was incredibly difficult to walk into a rehearsal with a cast who all knew each other and was mourning the loss of a beloved cast member... and you were the person replacing that cast member. Fortunately, by the end of the day, they accepted her and she l-o-v-e-d that cast. That's where she met Norm Lewis, and now they're both in *The Little Mermaid*. She said that her agent called her last year and said that they wanted to see her for *Mermaid*. Sherie said that she had been firm with her agent and told her that she was sick of going in for roles that she was too old for. She informed him that she was a little long in the tooth and didn't look good enough in a bikini to play Ariel, and her agent said, "Stop before you go any further. It's for the sea witch." Sherie was mortified and wondered why she hadn't learned her lesson because, a year before that embarrassing phone call, her agent called and said she had an audition for the Broadway version of *Mary Poppins*. Sherie said, "I know you don't want to hear this, but I don't think I'm age appropriate to play Mary Poppins," and yet again her agent cut her off and said, "Don't go any further... it's for Mrs. Banks."

Sherie said that she went through three months of auditions for *The Little Mermaid* (*not* the title role). She said that, fortunately, it wasn't the kind of audition that she hated... where you go to a rehearsal room and sing for ten people behind a table. It was the kind where you go to someone's apartment and sing around their piano. How civilized! She said that her character has three songs and the show has ten new songs! I can't wait to see it!

Thursday, I interviewed Bernie Telsey, casting director extraordinaire, at the *Chatterbox*. Turns out, he began as an actor! He was Matthew Broderick's understudy in *Brighton Beach Memoirs*... out of town. He was replacing an understudy who got a TV show. It was explained that if the TV show wasn't picked up, the guy would come back and Bernie would be ixnayed. And that's what happened. Wah. Sad Face. COL (*Crying Out Loud*). So Bernie never got to understudy it on Broadway.

I asked Bernie about casting *Rent*. He said when he got the demo tape of the show (with songs sung by Jonathan Larson), he asked the NY Theater Workshop if they'd consider not doing it! Before you think he has no taste whatsoever, let me just say that everyone I've interviewed who was in that original cast said that the demo sounded horrible because, even though Larson was a genius writer, his singing on the demo was decidedly not up to snuff. Taye Diggs was the first person they cast in the show (coming right from Lincoln Center's *Carousel*) and the hard role to cast was turning out to be Roger. Bernie finally had one of his people comb the Village Voice for those ads where people offer rock 'n roll voice lessons. They then asked the teachers to send in any of their students who were interested. Bernie said that, the next day, the lobby was filled with a mélange of kooky looking people... and Adam Pascal (who was sent by Idina Menzel). They prayed he could sing... and he was amazing (even though he couldn't perform with his eyes open... rock star style). Thank goodness everyone loved him and Adam got the gig.

I told Bernie that so many actors think that they "blew" an audition and asked him what he considers to be a bad audition. Bernie said it's when an actor isn't prepared — when they don't understand what the role is or don't know their material. Obviously, one sometimes gets material at the last minute, and you can't know it well, but you still have to be on your gig. I informed him that actors are not fond of casting directors because we think that casting directors are keeping us out of auditions, but he said that he'll usually always bring someone in if the agent or actor is passionate about being seen. He actually hopes that every actor that comes in gets the part which, FYI, is a nice thing to know when you're feeling nervous walking in the room. He then ended the show by showing a video of himself from his acting days playing a nasty gossip columnist on *The Guiding Light* and a hilarious commercial he did where he played a priest. I vaguely remembered seeing it. He was nervous that the food he was eating was so delicious, it was sinful. The tag line was "So delicious, it has to be a sin." All I can say is, a Jew from Long Island playing a priest? *That* had to be a sin.

All right, onto the big show. Around a week ago, I got a call from Jeffrey Seller telling me that when the strike ended, there was gonna be a big celebration. He asked for some song suggestions that said Broadway and/or Xmas, and we talked about "There's No Business Like Show Business" and "We Need A Little Christmas." I begged him not to do one of those events where everyone stands onstage and sings in unison. "Get some amazing stars," I pleaded. "Like Bernadette or Angela Lansbury." He said that Bernadette was a great idea, but Angela wouldn't happen because she lived in L.A. A few days later, he called back to tell me that Bernadette said yes, and I remembered that Angela had just seen *The Ritz* and was therefore in NYC. I told him that, he called her, and she said yes! He then asked me if I would conduct the orchestra! Of course, I said yes and asked how many strings would be in the pit. Jeffrey didn't know what theatre we were using, and he finally got back to me and said it would be at the Marriott Marquis, and they didn't use any strings in that pit. I said that we *had* to have them... and he totally agreed! Phew! I would have hated to go on strike during the end-of-the-strike celebration.

The first amazing thing was that I got to have a private rehearsal with Angela Lansbury. She didn't have any handlers with her, no assistants... just her. And, of course, my boyfriend begged to be there. She first thought that the song should be one step down... but after singing it through, she said that we should try it in the original key... and she sounded great! It was like hearing the record I listened to obsessively... but live and right next to me! I asked her if she ever thought of doing an act (can you imagine the stories she has?), and she said that she can only sing as a character, not as herself. I began to fantasize about her coming back to Broadway in a musical. Can you imagine how thrilling that would be? She's still got it! *And it happened a few years later with A LITTLE NIGHT MUSIC!*

This all happened last minute (late Thursday afternoon for a Friday show), and the people in The Producing Office literally worked 'til three in the morning getting everything together. I showed up Friday, and there were a ton of Broadway people on the *Drowsy Chaperone* set, and I had the delicious orchestra in the pit. I went onstage to teach the two songs because there were new lyrics by *Avenue Q*'s co-lyricist/composer, Bobby Lopez. The end of "There's No Business Like Show Business" was a brava: "But now we're back in business and we're feelin' good/'Cause Broadway's doing what Broadway should/If only we could say the same for Hollywood!/Let's go on with the show!" *Remember? The Writer's Guild was on strike at the time.*

Bob Martin hosted the show as the character Man in Chair from *The Drowsy Chaperone*. He talked about how hard the strike was on him. "I mean, how many times can a single middle-aged man see *How the Grinch Stole Christmas*? Once. Once is the answer. And even then, the ushers keep a pretty close eye on you." Then he moved toward the refrigerator and asked the audience, "Can I offer you a soda? Or as they say in Canada, 'Can I offer you a soda?'" There's actually not much difference between us and our pacifist neighbors to the North. Well... I guess the pacifism." He had trouble opening the fridge and asked for help... and out walked two stagehands. The audience loved it, and then they all opened the fridge and Bernadette Peters walked out... looking in her early thirties. Has she aged since *Mack and Mabel*? She sang the beginning of "Show Business" (sounding amazing... including at the 10 AM sound check). Bob Martin said he loved it... but was hoping for "Anything You can Do"... but since they're from the same album, he was okay with it. Then Bernadette opened up the fridge and someone representing (almost) every Broadway show paraded out... in full costume. It was a spectacular image that should be re-created somewhere... Tony Awards anyone? By the way, Bernadette brought her own conductor, Marvin Laird, to conduct her solo section of "Show Business," and I asked Marvin how long he'd been working with her. Turns out he met her on *Gypsy* — not the one she did in 2003 — the one in the early '60s! Bernadette was the Agnes understudy. That's a *long* working relationship. Brava to both of them. Marvin wrote the hilarious musical *Ruthless*, which gave Britney Spears her Equity card (she was Laura Bell Bundy's understudy), and he also wrote for Siegfried and Roy in Vegas! He told me that the first time he went over to their house, they were swimming in a pool with a bunch of tigers. I thought he meant that the tigers were roaming around the pool area, but he said that the tigers were swimming in the pool with them!

Everyone sang "Show Business," and then Bob heard another knock. He was annoyed and it wound up being his neighbor… Bob Saget, also dressed as Man in Chair. Saget said that he heard music coming from the apartment and wanted to borrow Bob Martin's record of *Gypsy*. Bob Martin said, "You just can't go to somebody's apartment and ask for their recording of *Gypsy*… without specifying which one! Merman? Tyne Daly? Angela Lansbury? I also have a bootleg of Linda Lavin." Bob Saget asked for the Lansbury one, and Bob Martin got the album out of his bookshelf. The album he was holding was obviously not *Gypsy* because no one had thought to put the real record on the set, so Bob adlibbed "I keep it in a Dean Martin Album cover" and shuffled Bob Saget out.

Then, another knock… and in walked Angela Lansbury, which garnered an immediate, spontaneous standing ovation. C'mon people! *Anyone Can Whistle*, *Mame*, *Dear World*, *Gypsy*, *Sweeney Todd*… history! She led everyone singing "We Need a Little Christmas," and I couldn't believe the seat I had. I mean, it wasn't a seat, but when you're conducting a show, you're so close to the actors onstage it's like being in a special front row. It was *thrilling*! I'm so glad that it's been preserved on video online, and we've been playing it non-stop on Sirius.

Well, the end of the strike sadly happens to coincide with the end of the run of *The Ritz*. I'll write next week… after my final performance. Wah. COL.

And so it ends. _The Ritz_ played its final performance on Sunday, Dec. 9. Thank goodness it was a great show that day. My number in the second act went great! OK… here come some details.

I never wanted to be totally clear about certain aspects of the show so I wouldn't ruin it for people coming to see it, but now I can describe some stuff to you all. First of all, in Act Two there's a talent show at The Ritz bathhouse and my character, Sheldon Farenthold, was a contestant. In the script it says that Sheldon sings a burlesque song while popping balloons attached to his body. Our hilarious director Joe Mantello decided to change it to be very _au courant_. Since the play takes place in the mid-'70s, _Pippin_ would have been a Broadway hit at the time. As soon as I got cast, Joe said he wanted me to sing "Magic to Do" and have all these white gloved hands somehow around me. (The original Fosse choreography had Ben Vereen surrounded by all the people wearing white gloves, and because of the cool lighting, all you could see was Ben and the floating gloves.) I thought that William Ivey Long would construct some black apparatus I'd wear with gloves coming out of it à la Carol Burnett wearing the curtains in that _Gone With the Wind_ sketch. Instead, at rehearsal our assistant choreographer, Michael Lee Scott, suggested that they put white gloves at the end of the skeleton of umbrellas. The umbrellas with white-gloved hands were constructed, and when I opened them up in front of everyone, it looked hilarious! Chris Gattelli choreographed me spinning them and doing some _Liza with a Z_ choreography, and Jules Fisher and Peggy Eisenhauer lit me amazingly… which makes sense since Jules did the original _Pippin_!

I made Sheldon vocally unstable and decided to hit the high note ("Join us… _Co-o-o-ome_ and waste an hour or two") in a horrible mix while changing the vowel from "come" to "coom" like singers do when they need help "placing" a note. After running it though, I thought that the number needed one more joke and Jason, the assistant stage manager, and I came up with having a reveal of two white gloves placed on the butt of my black unitard, à la Barbra Streisand in _The Owl and the Pussycat_. It worked! I have to say that the number was always so much fun to do… especially because all I had to do was open up the umbrellas to get a laugh. Prop humor can be deliciously easy (see Jo Anne Worley).

The other thing I didn't write that much about in the column was the Googie Gomez medley. Chris, Joe and I put it together, and it was a conglomeration of Broadway hits done completely inappropriately. While we were in my apartment, Chris said he wanted to do the "39 Lashes" from _Jesus Christ Superstar_, and I had said that I wanted to do "Sabbath Prayer" from _Fiddler on the Roof_. I suddenly said, "Why don't we combine them?" and I played the funky "Heaven on their Minds" vamp from _Superstar_ while singing "Sabbath Prayer" above it. Then Chris and I decided that the back-up boys would punctuate the song by whipping Rosie.

ROSIE: "May the Lord protect and defend you."
BOYS: (whip) One!
ROSIE: "May he always shield you from pain."
BOYS: (whip) Two!

It seemed so bizarre and too much our specific sense of humor that we thought for sure it would get cut, but, turns out, it went over amazingly every night! There was one section that was cut early on because the number was too long, but I must admit that I miss it. At one point, the boys touched Rosie suggestively and she said, "No touching the merchandise! You gotta pay cash for that! That's right... it's *cash for the merchandise, cash for the button hooks...*, etc."

That is correct! We did a funky version of "Rock Island" from *The Music Man*! And... it was cut.

The most stressful/successful story is that Joe wanted the medley to begin with something grand and regal. We finally came up with "Bali Ha'i." Unfortunately, we wound up being denied the rights at the last minute! I wasn't upset, because I totally understood why. *South Pacific* is about to open at Lincoln Center, and I think they felt that it would be weird for an audience to watch that beautiful song in their production but have a part of their brain remember Googie Gomez mangling it. But the problem was that we kept thinking we were gonna get the rights and didn't find out that we definitely didn't have them until two days before the first preview! Well, that was the same night that Rosie got her end of Act One wig. It was a red perm, and she was joking around during tech singing, "The sun'll come out... tomorrow." Joe ran up to me and said, "What if Googie opens the medley with a solemn 'The sun'll come out... mañana!'" We tried it out on the cast, and it got an enormous laugh... much bigger than the one for "Bali Ha'i!" It was one of those situations where a barrier actually made things turn out for the better. But there was one more problem. *The Ritz* was supposed to happen in 1975. Joe asked me when *Annie* was on Broadway. I told him that it opened in 1977. He turned to the cast and mock announced, "The show now takes place in 1977!" But then someone in the cast suggested that perhaps Googie saw a workshop of *Annie*, and that's where she got the song. Problem solved.

OK, let's go back to the beginning of the week. I did a benefit called *Gimme a Break* for The Transport Group theatre company. It's a show where each person tells of their first break and then performs something related to it. Anne L. Nathan was so funny talking about being a young character actress. While she was in high school, she played 'em all. The Grandmother in *Pippin*, Mama Rose in *Gypsy* and the role that every young girl dreams of: Fraulein Schneider in *Cabaret*. However, she told us that her first break was getting the role of Bloody Mary, the wizened sage, in *South Pacific*. "What was impressive is that I just turned 13." Agreed! She then proudly said, "I will now sing the song that I used to book Bloody Mary." I was obsessed with her using the verb "book" for a school show. Brava! (And brava for her version of "Don't Rain on my Parade." She's still got it!)

Danny Burstein talked about one of his first gigs when he met Tony Randall. Danny told Tony that he wanted to teach one day and Tony said, "What would you say is the most important thing to teach about acting?" Danny said, "Reacting." Tony said, "Ah... it is listening!" Danny said that listening is part of reacting and Tony said, "Don't contradict me you a**hole!!" This was not said angrily... it was said with a dry Tony Randall line reading. He then said, "It takes *ten years* to learn how to listen correctly." Uh-oh. I better start soon! Tony said that he was thinking of starting an acting company in New York, and Danny told him that he'd love to do it if it ever happened. Years later, Tony called Danny and invited him to be in his National Actors Theatre, and that was his Broadway debut!

The whole benefit honored Michael Patrick King who was the executive producer/director of *Sex and the City* (he's now directing the movie) and *The Comeback* (with which I am obsessed!). Michael talked about theatre people versus television/film people and how there is so much financial reward in TV/film. He said that theatre people's rewards are always emotional and spiritual (as opposed to financial) and, unfortunately, they turn that against themselves and feel that they're doing something wrong. I really loved hearing that. Why do some people consider an actor more successful for having a role on a headache-y sitcom as opposed to doing a brilliant show for low buckage? I remembered turning down an audition for a TV show that I probably would have gotten last year so I could do *Torch Song Trilogy* at the Gallery Players in Brooklyn and get paid in train fare... but I don't regret it! It was amazing for me!

This week at the *Chatterbox* I interviewed the incomparable Rosie Perez. She was hysterical! What a storyteller... and what a life! She grew up in Brooklyn and always wanted to be the next Jacques Cousteau (who knew?). She was studying biology in college, but because her sassy dancing in clubs was seen by certain people, she started getting hired to choreograph major hip-hop stars. One night, she was at a club and saw Spike Lee having a "big butt" contest onstage. She was so annoyed, she got onstage and started making fun of it, and the club owners went to throw her out! Spike intervened and said it was meant to be that they met and told her to call him to be in his next film! She had only done one play at her Catholic school and never thought of being an actress, but she showed up to audition for the casting person, who immediately asked her if she had a monologue. Huh? She certainly didn't. The casting person told her to make one up about the character. Rosie asked for a description. "Well," the casting person said, "she's a poor Puerto Rican, on welfare, with kids and — " "OK!" Rosie cut her off because she didn't need to hear any more, she knew exactly who that was. Rosie started talking as the character, basing her on her aunt... but was so nervous that she started crying. Uh-oh! She thought fast and feigned that it was part of her monologue, holding her imaginary baby closer... telling him it would be all right. She got the part in *White Men Can't Jump*, filmed it and went back to working as a choreographer. People were annoyed that she was late sometimes for rehearsals, so the record company got her a driver. An intern named Sean. Sean Combs! Yes, Puff Daddy! He was her driver, and he'd always tell her to watch out because he was going places. Apparently to the Royale Theatre to star in *A Raisin in the Sun*.

Rosie then got a job choreographing the fly girls for the TV show *In Living Color*. She wanted to cast Jennifer Lopez, but Marlon Wayans wanted another girl who was then fired two weeks later. Marlon still said no to Jennifer, so Rosie put her job on the line and insisted he give her the gig because she knew that, even though Jennifer wasn't a great dancer, she had incredible star quality. She was right! (Although... *Gigli*? Anybody?)

Rosie really wanted a role in *Fearless* but couldn't get an audition (even though she had done two films at that point!). Her agents said that her only option was to go to an open call, so she did. She remembers that her number was 83. She was waiting so long that she drank too much coffee, and as soon as she walked in the room with the director, she got "Montezuma's revenge." She asked where the bathroom was and found out that it was right in the room... separated with only swinging French doors. She was mortified. "I ran the water, I sang... I did everything I could to create some noise." She was so devastated that she started crying. Finally, she got herself together, walked out and the director, Peter Weir, said, "Ah! *Now* you look perfect!" She hadn't done anything but cry and have an incredibly upset stomach, but the casting director looked at her as if to say, "Go along with it," and Rosie thanked Peter for noticing how she changed her look. The role was of a Catholic woman whose baby is killed in a plane crash. He asked Rosie to pray and say the "Our Father," so she said it like you do if you've done it your whole life in Catholic School… incredibly fast. After the audition, her agent called her and said, "I don't know what you did, but the director loved you!" She found out that she was the only auditioner who prayed like a real person. Everyone else prayed like they were in a movie. Rosie got the gig… *and* an Oscar nomination. This is yet *another* example of someone feeling that they're right for a role and not giving up 'til they get it! Brava, Señorita Perez!

OK… back to *The Ritz*. I've been thinking about what I will miss. I loved showing up and seeing my friends in the dressing room. We had so many stupid running jokes that made me laugh. I helped out with the various musical sections and Jeffrey Thomas, who played the "snooty patron," always accused me of trying to sabotage him when I gave him advice about how to sing the song he sang in the onstage talent contest. He first started calling me "Sabotina," then changed it "SaboTina Yothers." *Family Ties*? Anybody?

Also, there's something so nice about doing something during the day and suddenly thinking, "Wow! In so-and-so hours, I'll be on Broadway!" It was a delicious constant in my life and something to always look forward to. *And* I'll miss the bizarre rituals. Rosie asked me to remind her that she had to unstrap her shoe in the middle of the medley so it would fly off when she kicked. So, right at the end of scene one, we'd see each other in back of the bathhouse set and I'd say a rhyme to help her remember: (pointing to myself) "I'm a Jew, (pointing to her strap) don't forget your shoe." This turned into me just pointing to her strap saying "shoe" and her pointing to me saying "Jew." Then, after a month, we graduated to just pointing at each other without saying anything. And finally, the last eight weeks it became a contest to see who would point first. I'd sneak around the corner of the set before my first entrance and find her getting her wig adjusted with her finger already pointing at me. The only times I won were when she was distracted by talking to Lucas Near-Verbrugghe or when I once did my quick change super fast and got to the back of the bathhouse before her. It sounds moronic, but it became an important part of my night!

Ah, well… I'm sad to see the show go, but so happy I got to make my Broadway acting debut in such a great company of actors doing such an incredibly fun show. I'll always remember the image of the company bows on the last show. While we were dancing our curtain call to Donna Summer's "Last Dance," Kevin Chamberlin turned around, and there were tears streaming down his face. If a veteran like that can be devastated, so can I!

OK… this week I'm psyched to see the Actors Fund performance of *Mary Poppins* and my friend Anika Larsen *Now a Tony nominee for BEAUTIFUL* starring in her new theatre company's (JARADOA) production of *Serenade*. Hopefully, that will get my mind off the closing so I don't spend each night in my apartment putting on my unitard while trying to recreate what has ended… and, quite frankly, considering the way I looked in said unitard, what never should have been!

Matt, *Mary* and a Brady

December 17, 2007

I just spent my first week post-*Ritz*. I was prepared to be completely devastated, but I haven't been. I think it's because I've been super busy since the show closed... or because I've pushed down all my feelings and will have a complete breakdown 30 years from now, *Prince of Tides*-style. OK, so here're all the fun things I did this week to escape my feelings. Monday night, I played piano for the amazing Andréa Burns at the GLBT Center in the Village. It was a part of an evening where they thanked all the Center's major donors. P.S. I love The Center. They have great programs for parents/kids, great lectures, help for teens grappling with their sexuality and a variety of fun clubs. Although, I'll never forget the time I decided to join a book club at The Center many years ago. I got to the meeting early and noticed there were already some people there, but I was too shy to speak. I walked around the room, gazing at some of the photos on the wall while everyone was catching up with each other. Obviously, everyone in this book club knew each other well because they were talking about some personal stuff. Finally, I meandered over to the group and sat down because it was around two minutes before the book club was about to begin. Suddenly, I felt someone grabbing my right hand... then my left. What the-?

"God, grant me the serenity to accept the things I cannot change..."

That's right! I got to the book club so early, I had actually crashed an Al-Anon meeting! I was mortified that people thought I showed up for the last seven minutes of a 12-step meeting, and that I spent it walking around the room, casually looking at pictures while people were sharing their innermost feelings.

Tuesday, I interviewed the *cute* Matthew Morrison for Sirius. He told me that when he was a teen, he spent a few years in a gang. I was horrified/about to call for security until he told me some more details like (a) he's from Orange County and (b) they spent their time spraying graffiti and breakdancing. Gang? They sound about as scary as the kids in the musical *Big*.

He went to NYU for a while, and while he was there, got cast in a fake boy band that was featured on Letterman. Their name was "Fresh Step" (as in the kitty litter), and they supposedly sang the theme song to the movie *Talk to the Hand*. The sad part is, people thought they were real. Although, is O-Town much different? The choreographer was A.C. Ciulla, who was doing *Footloose*. Matt auditioned and got his first Broadway show. He then got cast in the ensemble of *Hairspray* as an understudy for the role of Link. James Carpinello was playing the role but wound up getting a film job, so Matt was offered the part for the Seattle tryout. They told him that there was no guarantee he would do it on Broadway. I asked him if knowing that he was being evaluated the whole time he was in Seattle stressed him out, and he told me that it actually gave him incentive to work super-hard. He did a great job in Seattle and, combined with Marissa Jaret Winokur pushing for him to continue to play opposite her, he got the gig on Broadway... and an Outer Critics nomination!

The next Broadway show he was asked to audition for was *The Light in the Piazza*, and he said a resounding N-O. He heard that score and decided that it was way too operatic for him... plus the role was for an Italian, and he has blond hair! They kept coming back to him asking him to audition, and he kept telling them to "peace out." Finally, he decided to give it a try. I asked what the audition was like, and he said he had to sing in Italian and he also remembers Bart Sher, the director, asking him to run around the room like a young guy in love. Thank goodness I've never had an audition like that. It would consist of me muttering that my doctor told me not to run because of my knees and then awkwardly taking the orthotics out of my shoes. Of course, he got the role of Fabrizio but told me that he wasn't expecting a Tony nomination. He only wound up getting the Outer Critics nomination during *Hairspray*, so he didn't want to get his hopes up again. On the morning of the Tony Award nomination announcement, he woke up to watch NY1, trying not to expect anything, and heard *Spamalot*'s Michael McGrath's name. He knew the nominations were in alphabetical order and told his roommate that he didn't get nominated. Then he realized that McGrath is not after Morrison (it's hard to think alphabetically at 8:20 AM) and decided to rewind the TV. Sure enough, he got nominated! He happened to be talking to his roommate right when his name was called. Attention upcoming nominees: the rule is when watching to see if you're nominated for a Tony, keep your trap shut 'til your category is completely over. Or else you'll have to ride the roller coaster of depression to elation mixed with humiliation for not knowing the alphabet.

After *Piazza*, Matt went out to L.A. In the summer, Lincoln Center called and asked if Matt was interested in playing Cable in the upcoming revival of *South Pacific*, but he told them that he wanted to focus on TV/film work (he had recently done *Dan in Real Life*). Months passed, and Lincoln Center called again to gauge his interest, and Matt was still in LA... but the writers' strike was happening. AKA get me my old dressing room at the Vivian Beaumont ASAP... I'm in!

I know that Matt did a lot of dancing in *Footloose* and *Hairspray*, and I asked him if he missed it... and turns out, he does! He said he's dying to do a role where he can sing, act *and* dance! I was so happy to hear that. Whenever I talk to people who started as dancers, they're always like Catherine Zeta-Jones ("I've hung up my dancing shoes"). Hmm... maybe Matt can end "Younger Than Springtime" in a full split. *I think Matt *may* have gone to LA after this interview to pursue TV. I hope it works out for him!*

Thursday, I got to interview Barry Williams at the *Chatterbox*. I immediately launched into a "why, when, how" about the *Brady Bunch Variety Hour*. He said that Sid and Marty Kroft (*Sigmund and the Sea Monsters*? Witchiepoo? Anybody?) wanted to do a *Donny and Marie* show with a pool instead of an ice skating rink. Well, I can say that they achieved the pool part. Barry said that they told him since he and Florence Henderson were the only ones who could actually sing and dance, they would be heavily featured. It didn't quite turn out that way, which you'd know if you've seen one of the two DVDs available. Unfortunately, there's also Tony Randall reading (in rhythm) a poem by Dame Edith Sitwell. Said poem is read over a score by 20th-century composer William Walton. Maureen McCormick sings a pathos-ridden "If I Could Save Time in a Bottle," and there's also a funky version of "Tangerine" sung by Ann B. Davis and Rip Taylor dressed as giant ducks. And much, much horribly more. Around a year before the variety hour, Florence Henderson called Barry and told him that she heard that they were looking for a Pippin for the national tour. He flew to New York and saw the show and was blown away. He grew up in California and the only musicals he saw were very old school, so he was shocked and delighted at how hot the sex scenes were in *Pippin*. He said that he auditioned with the song "Corner of the Sky" and had learned the little bit of choreography that happened during the chorus. On "Rivers belong where they can ramble," you're supposed to move your hands like a winding river, and during "eagles belong where they can fly," Pippin spreads his arms like a soaring bird. After he sang, Barry said that Fosse came down the aisle and gave him the best direction he ever got. Fosse approached him wearing his signature black shirt with the sleeves rolled up and a cigarette dangling from his lips and said, "Nice job, kid, but you're giving me a Cessna. Give me a 747." Barry got the gig, loved doing it, but left the show because he got what was supposed to be a great job offer. That job was *The Brady Bunch Variety Hour*.

This week I also went to see the Actors Fund performance of *Mary Poppins*. First of all, the set is amazing... but that didn't stop me from refusing to clap along with the audience when the house was revealed. Here's my rule: I refuse to clap for anything that can't acknowledge my applause. FYI, I thought Ashley Brown was fantastic. She was super funny and sounded great. She literally ended one song on a crazy high D! I'm estimating that was the note because the only way I could test it was by trying to sing it quietly in my seat (I have a crazy high falsetto), and usually, if I can hit it, it's a C. if I can squeak it it's a C sharp, and it's a D if it causes Mariah Carey-style vocal damage. Ashley also did some sassy dancing throughout the show. It was so great to see a leading lady act, sing and dance. Hmm... perhaps that's the role Matthew Morrison has been waiting for.

Finally, Saturday night, I did *lots* of holiday parties. First James, Juli and I ran down to Don't Tell Mama to meet my L.A. friends Steve Rabiner and Marco Pennette. I first met Marco when I was playing for *The Jerry Lewis Telethon* for his friend Tia Riebling, who was playing Rizzo in the '94 revival of *Grease!* He had just created the show *Caroline in the City*, and a little while later he wound up hiring me to write a song for David Hyde Pierce who played an IRS employee who dreams of being on Broadway and finally lands an auditions for *Cats*. Sample lyric: "I help small businesses to clean up their debts, but in my mind I'm doing double pirouttes!"

Then James, Juli and I dashed up to the West 60s to go to the holiday party of my old comedy partner, Maria Bostick. We did a show in the mid-'90s called *Dial M for Marjorie* that I fantasize about doing again one day. One of my favorite sections was when she's auditioning for the musical version of *Lolita* called *Oh, Lo*.

AUDITIONER: OK, right off the bat, let me ask you some questions. They're just formalities. Are you willing to go out of town?
MARJORIE: (*desperately positive*) Yes, I am.
AUDITIONER: Can you operate a tractor trailer?
MARJORIE: (*Same line reading*) Yes, I can.

Then, we got Juli a babysitter and hightailed it to Brooklyn to visit my agent, Richard Fisher. We got off the train with Chris Sieber and his partner, Kevin Burrows. Chris just finished a seven-week workshop of *Shrek*. Seven-week workshop? Isn't that an oxymoron? That's like a three-hour first act! Ooh, speaking of *Les Miz*, I've got to see it again before it closes because I'm obsessed with Judy Kuhn.

Anyhoo, after Brooklyn, we hightailed it all the way up to the Columbia area to visit our friends Michael Klimzak and Phil Fabry who are in town only briefly because they've just started working at a brand-new musical theatre school in Korea. Michael is one of the funniest people I know and on his résumé's special skills section, he used to list "imitating my mother."

OK, this week is the always-exciting Gypsy of the Year Competition, and then we all head down to Texas for a week. Yes, I'm going to Texas. I'm sure I won't stick out like a Jewish sore thumb. I'll write next week's column from Houston, y'all!

The Gypsy in Their Souls
December 25, 2007

Howdy y'all. That's right, howdy y'all. Does that sound natural? I thought not. I'm writing to you from Houston, Texas, where my boyfriend, his daughter and I are visiting his mom, sister, sister's boyfriend and cousin. There's plenty to write about from down here, but first let's begin in New York.

Last Monday and Tuesday was the Gypsy of the Year Competition. After fundraising for six weeks, Broadway shows put on a variety show (where one wins a "Best in Show" award), *and* there are awards for the Broadway, off-Broadway and national tours that raised the most money for BC/EFA. The most amazing part of this year's production was that the opening number was a salute to *West Side Story* to celebrate its 50th anniversary. The number began with current-day gypsies playing Jets and dancing the opening. Suddenly, the original Bernardo entered, and the audience went wild. He crossed the stage as the Jets watched his every move and right before he exited… he pulled out a switchblade. He's still got it! Then the original Riff (Mickey Calin) came out and sang, "When You're a Jet." He was amazing! And still so great looking! I kept thinking he was about to get off the rhythm of the music but turns out he was doing sassy back phrasing. Make it your own, Riff! He was suddenly joined by a slew of original *West Side* gypsies, and they finished the number together. I got to watch them rehearse Monday afternoon right before the show, and when the original Jets entered, and I saw all that history on the stage, I immediately started crying. Broken only by Christine Pedi sitting in back of me, tapping me on the shoulder and whispering, "Is that Harvey Evans?" Note to Christine: When you see someone's shoulders shaking from emotion, do not ask for Broadway gypsy clarification.

Anyhoo, Carol Lawrence then came on to sing "I Feel Pretty" with some current gypsy ladies. I'm obsessed with the fact that dance training never goes away. Carol Lawrence is in her seventies, but she did ballet moves across the stage with such grace. After "I Feel Pretty," Chita Rivera stormed the stage and launched into "A Boy Like That." When she sang "One of your own kind, stick to your own ki-i-i-ind," she added her signature vibrato, and the audience literally applauded! James and Juli saw it with me and later on James told her what a momentous event she had witnessed. She's only seven and I realized it would have been like me seeing a 50-year-reunion of the original *Show Boat*. All right, let's be honest age-wise; the original *Mikado*.

The whole number ended with everyone singing the "Tonight" quintet and, yet again, tears streamed down my face as I thought that these were the people who actually sang this song eight times a week. And they were *still* selling it to the balcony, old-school!

I wrote the Gypsy of the Year sketch for *The Ritz*, and it was essentially a lesson for the young gypsies on Broadway. The other cast members and I acted out signature Gypsy lore that has been around forever. The kind of stories that have been passed along for so many years, no one even knows if they're true, but they're classics nonetheless. We acted out *Wait Until Dark*, where the leading lady plays a blind woman being pursued by a murderer. During the final scene, he stalks her in her apartment, she turns off all the lights, opens up a kitchen drawer, pulls out a knife and stabs him. The Gypsy lore is that during one performance, no one had pre-set her knife, so the drawer was empty. Since she was supposed to be blind, she couldn't really run around the kitchen looking for a knife, but she had to kill the murderer or the play wouldn't end! She was panicking and opened the nearby fridge, hoping for something she could kill him with. Unfortunately, the only thing there was a bowl. She had no option but to take it out and scream "Poison Jello" as she wiped the fake contents on the murderer's face. End of scene... and career.

The biggest laugh happened during our *West Side Story* segment. In the show, after Tony is killed, Maria confronts the Sharks and the Jets while brandishing a gun. "How many bullets are left in this gun, Chino? Enough for you? You? All of you?" Well, one night, a Maria brandished her gun as usual. "How many bullets are left in this gun, Chino? Enough for you?" And the gun went off. There was an awkward silence until Chino realized the audience saw/heard what happened, and he had to act like he was shot. He looked around at the other cast members who didn't know what to do, and finally he realized he had to die. He slowly crumbled to the ground as Maria looked uncomfortable. So, now there was Tony's body on the ground, killed by Chino, and Chino's body next to him. Killed by Maria. The show ended with the gangs carrying off Tony's body as usual, but nobody knew what to do with Chino's. Finally, everyone just stepped over him and left him there.

At the end of Gypsy of the Year, *The Ritz* won the award for raising the most money of any play: $139,514! Then we found out that our sketch tied for first runner-up! We tied with *Xanadu*, who combined with *Stomp* (calling themselves *Stompadu*) and did a phenomenal a cappella song led by Annie Golden and put together by Marty Thomas. I was so thrilled we got two awards! I was backstage with Jeffrey Thomas from *The Ritz* and told him that I've done a lot of Gypsy sketches but never won. By the third time I said how excited I was to win, he reminded me that we actually came in as the runner up. *And* that we tied. Hmph. Jeffrey has a way with a stick pin. Then we went out to Starbucks with my friend Tim Cross. I checked my messages, and my agent told me to call her about *Lend Me a Tenor* for which I had auditioned the day before. I told Tim and Jeffrey that I must have gotten a callback. I called my agent, and she told me that I was cast! I hung up and told Tim and Jeffrey that I got the gig. Tim looked at me sadly and said, "No callback? I'm sorry." Hilarious!

I told my agent I'm taking the part. The good news is, it's a brand new theatre. The bad news is, it's in Northport, Long Island. The good news is, it's Patti LuPone's hometown. The bad news is, it's an hour-and-a-half commute. But it's a great director (BT McNichol), a funny part (the bellhop), and I'll get insurance weeks! And comic genius Michele Ragusa is in it, too! I'm so excited! I start rehearsals Jan. 2. It's so fun to be on vacation and have a job to look forward to! Speaking of vacation, let's go to the Texas part of my week.

James, Juli and I flew down on Wednesday, and the next day we drove to Dallas to visit James' grandma. We left Juli with James' mom and drove to Ft. Worth to hang out with Betty Buckley. For those of you who don't know, around five years ago, Betty sold her Upper West Side apartment and bought an enormous ranch back where she grew up. I've been inspired by her move and have decided to leave the comforts of the West 70s and move back to my hometown on Long Island where I can enjoy the local mall, a non-stop stream of my mother's "helpful" advice and various taunts from local teenagers. Just kidding.

Anyhoo, Betty (or Betty Lynn as she's known by her friends) met us for dinner with her mom, whose name is Betty *Bob*! We had delicious Tex-Mex at a restaurant that Betty has been going to since she was a girl. Betty Lynn said that her mom used to be a singer, but stopped 50 years ago (she's now in her eighties!). At a recent concert, she surprised her mom by bringing her onstage to sing "It Had to Be You." Her mother was a nervous wreck, but Betty had all the lyrics printed and laid out, and worked out the key with her band beforehand. Her mom begged Betty to begin the song, and soon Betty Bob joined in. Her mom said that she didn't want the audience to be bored, so she realized she had to "give it a little something." Betty Lynn said that Betty Bob suddenly started pulsating her shoulder to the rhythm and the crowd loved it. I wish I had been there!

Then we all went to see the film of *Sweeney Todd*. I liked that they kept so many songs from the show in the movie and I'm so thankful that movie musicals are being made again, but I was annoyed to read Sondheim's quote to the *Times* that he prefers actors to singers. Why doesn't he prefer people who can do *both*? I don't understand why there is still the notion that you can either have an actor or a singer. There seems to be a pervading attitude that if you do a musical and sing badly, it's because you're a great actor. Isn't it just called you have a thin voice? Have we all forgotten Bernadette Peters, Patti LuPone, Angela Lansbury, Betty Buckley? Are they not wonderful actors *and* singers?

Speaking of Betty, James and I then drove (with her leading the way in her new Prius) to Betty's ranch. She now not only does her concert and theatre work, but she competes as a horse cutter. Seriously! She rides a horse in a stadium with a bunch of cattle and tries to separate one cow from the herd. She showed us pictures of herself in the competition, and her face is so full of concentration, it's amazing. You only have two and a half minutes and your goal is to separate up to three cows. She's been doing phenomenally well and said that the prize she won in her last competition paid for her new horse! She introduced us to her two horses, Scat Cat and Wild Bill. She offered us a chance to ride and when I found out it wouldn't be like the birthday party donkeys I remembered from my youth, I politely declined. Of course, James fell in love with Scat Cat and now wants a horse. I said "perhaps later, dear," my signature condescending husband answer. We slept in Betty's fabulous guest house and bid her *adieu*. She was on her way to a riding lesson, and we were headed back to Houston. For those of you that are nervous she's given up performing, rest assured she has plenty of concerts coming up and she has a great role in the upcoming M. Night Shyamalan film.

All right, I'm gearing up for a Texan Christmas. A holiday I don't celebrate in a state I'm scared to enter. Have a great holiday, everyone, and I'll write next week from the Big Apple instead of the Lone Star state!

The Old Year Passes
December 31, 2007

Last week began in Texas with the second half of my visit to James' family. I have a total block against driving, and even though I have a license, I haven't driven in almost ten years. Literally, the last time I remember being behind the wheel was when I was working on *The Rosie O'Donnell Show*, and we were spending sweeps month in L.A. That was the beginning of '98. So, of course, whenever James and I go anywhere, I make him drive... even the six-hour trip to Provincetown. He can't understand why I have such a fear of driving and is constantly asking me to give it a try. So, finally, on the way from Betty Buckley's ranch near Dallas/Ft. Worth to Houston, he convinced me to give it a try. The traffic was so light that it seemed like a perfect place to re-enter the driving world.

We pulled off the road to get food, and he told me that he'd drive me to the entrance of the highway, and then I could take over. I tentatively pulled onto the right lane of the highway and kept going. It was nerve-wracking, but I was doing it! He had been driving for three hours already since we left Dallas and we had two more to go before Houston. James was so appreciative of me giving him a much-needed break from driving. Suddenly, after twenty minutes he abruptly yelled "What the-!" I managed to not crash the car and asked him what was going on. Turns out he had just seen a sign that said "TO DALLAS." That's right... I was going back the way we came! It was actually his fault because he brought me to the wrong entrance, and he apologized, but I refused to keep driving because my anxiety was now back to sky-high. So, because he now had to double back, my version of "giving him a break from driving" was in actuality giving him another 40 minutes of driving. My work was done. *P.S. It's now 6 years later... still haven't driven!*

He could never fathom where my fear of driving came from... until later that day. I called my Mom and started to tell her the story. As soon as I said, "James wanted me to drive a little today," she interrupted with "*Please* don't! It's *so* dangerous!" I assumed she thought I was driving for hours on a busy six-lane highway, so I offered a "But there was no traffic" and was met with a "*Please* don't!" Then I followed with, "I only for drove for 20 minutes," and got an "It's *very* dangerous!" Essentially whatever came out of my mouth was cut off with a stream of pleading, fear and foreboding. And the anxiety source material was found.

I spent Christmas with James' family and received so many gifts from them that James and I literally were asked to pay extra money when we were boarding the plane because our suitcases weighed so much! We were too cheap, so we transferred tons of stuff into our carry-on bags and we now share a delicious bout of sciatica.

Anyhoo, back in New York, I got to interview nine-time Tony Award-winner Tommy Tune for my Sirius radio show. He told me that the first day he arrived in New York from Texas, he auditioned for a Broadway show (*Irma La Douce*) and got it! I told him that it was very Betty Buckley (the first day she arrived, also from Texas, she booked *1776*). I recalled that I arrived from Texas the day before and only had lower back pain to show for it. During the '60s, he went from show to show and in the process met Michael Bennett who choreographed him in *A Joyful Noise*. That was the beginning of a long friendship/working relationship, and, according to the Bennett biographies, rivalry.

Tommy got cast as Ambrose in the *Hello, Dolly!* movie, and I immediately asked him for a Barbra story. Here it is: during the scene where he elopes with Ermengarde, he had to climb up a ladder with Barbra. Before they shot the scene, director Gene Kelly told him, "Hold on to Barbra as tight as you can… do *not* let her fall!" Barbra arrived on the set dressed in her enormous period dress, hat and gloves, Gene yelled "Action," and they began ascending the ladder. Tommy had his hands gripped around Barbra as tight as he could and suddenly she began yelling. He gripped harder, and she suddenly screamed "Cut!! CUT!!" Turns out, he wasn't gripping her fingers, he was gripping her signature Streisand fingernails! Production stopped, and she was rushed to her trailer. She finally came back, and Tommy ran up to her and apologized and asked how her nails were. She paused. She spoke. "They're damaged."

He went to Europe in the early '70s and was subletting from Michael Bennett, who was out of town in Detroit. Tommy said he arrived from the airport and when he walked into Michael's apartment, the phone was ringing. This was before answering machines, so he picked up to take a message. It was Michael. "Don't unpack. I'm doctoring a show and I need you. Fly to Detroit now." Tommy flew there and got to the theatre to watch *Seesaw*, a show about an unlucky-in-love dancer. He asked Michael why he was doing a show that seemed so hopeless, but Michael said he thought that it could be saved. Michael fired Lainie Kazan who was playing the lead (she didn't look like a dancer) and put Michele Lee in the role, rehearsing her during the day while Lainie played it at night. I'm sure it wasn't awkward at all when Michele and Lainie would pass each other in the hotel they *both stayed at*! Then he put Tommy in the role of Michele Lee's best friend… and Tommy was devastated to be replacing someone whose wedding he attended *and* whose sister played Ermengarde opposite him in the *Hello, Dolly!* movie! Michael Bennett was ruthless when it came to people's feelings sometimes. But he knew how to fix a show… and give people complexes for years.

Anyway, Tommy took the role and was nominated for a Tony! I asked how he felt when he was nominated, and he said that it was bizarre because all he ever wanted to do was dance in the chorus. He loved doing that so much, he never thought he'd do anything else. Tommy talked about Tony night and said that it was a bittersweet experience for him. At the time, he was dating Michael Stuart (the original Greg from *A Chorus Line*), but the powers that be told him that he had to have a girl as his date at the Tonys. He was shocked because he was playing a gay character in *Seesaw*! Actually, he said during the interview that he was playing the *first* gay character in a musical, and I corrected him by saying that Duane in *Applause* was the first… and he one-upped me by telling me that he was originally offered the role. Busted!

Anyhoo, he decided to ignore what they told him and bring his boyfriend to the Tonys. Well, because of that, when the camera filmed each nominee in the audience before the award was given, they went to a photo of him instead! I was shocked and asked how the TV audience would even know that it was his boyfriend, and he said everyone sat boy, girl, boy, girl. He wound up winning the Tony, but the memory of that night has always been tinged with sadness, and Tommy said that for everyone who thinks gay rights hasn't come far, just remember how it used to be! *Cut to Marc Shaiman and Scott Wittman smooching it up in 2004!*

In the mid-'70s, Tommy started on the path towards being a director, and that meant making some tough decisions like turning down the original *Annie*. His agent felt that if he accepted being choreographer of *Annie*, he'd never graduate to being director. Tommy said that

Michael Bennett was always frustrated during the years he spent just choreographing because he knew he could direct, and Tommy didn't want that to happen to him. He waited it out and was offered a chance to be choreographer of *The Best Little Whorehouse in Texas* and asked Peter Masterson if he could co-direct (à la Michael co-directing *Follies*). Peter said yes, and that changed Tommy's career… and, he said, his bank account!

I asked him about that brilliant number he created for Michael Jeter in *Grand Hotel*. He said that they couldn't find someone to play the role of Kringelein and Tommy remembered seeing Michael play The Dormouse opposite Meryl Streep in the Public Theater's *Alice in Wonderland*. He tracked him down and found out that Michael was working as a secretary in a law firm. Tommy brought him in and at the audition Michael Jeter told everybody that he didn't sing. Tommy wanted to know if that meant that he had never sung, or if he was literally tone deaf, so he had Michael match different pitches… which he was able to do. Tommy sat with him onstage, held his hands, and asked him to sing something really simple. He remembers Michael's hands shaking terribly as he sang, but he got through it. Of course, his acting in the audition scenes was brilliant and he was cast. But Tommy forgot to ask him to dance. He said he likes to see how everyone can dance at an audition, just in case it's needed somewhere.

Well, one day during rehearsals, Michael was holding himself on the bar (drinking bar, not ballet) and making his body do these crazy Raggedy Andy/spineless/no-bones-in-his-body moves. Tommy saw it, loved it and made it the basis for "We'll Take a Glass Together." You all need to go to *Bluegobo.com* ASAP and watch it… it's literally what I put on every time I want to love Broadway. The two moments I love are when the bar is pulled away right near the end… you can hardly see it, but it's thrilling… and then the very last button when Michael jumps in Brent Barrett's arms… so satisfying!

I feel that Tommy is one of the all-time great directors because he can take a show that isn't working and make it a hit (like *My One and Only* and *Grand Hotel*). That's the skill that made Michael Bennett, Gower Champion and Jerome Robbins such brilliant directors. Tommy told me that the most important person needed to fix a show is the librettist. I had always thought it was the songwriters, but he explained that many flop shows had brilliant scores, and I realized he's right! (See: *Merrily We Roll Along* and *Rags*). Shout out to librettists!

I begged Tommy to come back to Broadway, and he said he had gotten really depressed because so many of his friends (especially Michael Bennett) died of AIDS. He felt he had no one to talk to and bounce ideas off of. He fled to Vegas for a few years to do *F/X* (where he won entertainer of the year). The thing he loved about Vegas is that "you get to do ten shows a week. On Broadway, you only get to do eight a week." *Get* to do? I explained that many people put in their contract that they'll only do six a week! He patiently explained that his father was a farmer and used to tell him that if he didn't go to bed dog tired at the end of the day, he didn't work hard enough. Hmm… was his father related to Chita? Same work ethic.

The good news is, he's back from Vegas and he just started an online art gallery with beautiful pictures that are c-h-e-a-p (some are as low as $20!). He feels that people need to have affordable art. Get thee to *TommyTuneGallery.com* and here's hoping we'll see his work again on Broadway!

The rest of the week was dedicated to seeing shows I've been wanting to see but couldn't because I was doing *The Ritz*. So, first James and I saw *The 25th Annual Putnam County Spelling Bee*. It was hilarious! The new cast was fantastic, and my friend Jennifer Simard was *brilliant* as Rona Lisa. If you've never seen the show, you may not know that they bring up three audience members and make them participate in the Bee. I'm obsessed with the comments that Rona Lisa and the vice-principal make about them. After the show, Jen told me that many of the comments are made up on the spot! One guy was dressed in a button-down sweater and loose corduroy pants and, when he approached the mic, Jen gave his background information: "Fred Lackey likes to intimidate the other contestants by dressing as their Dad." She followed it with "Fred Lackey is sick of being considered everybody's lackey and is changing his name to Sting." When Fred was asked to spell a word and started running out of time, she warned him with "Five seconds, Sting."

I was also obsessed with how she'd say a funny line and then start writing something on the pad on her desk. I told her I loved the total lack of acknowledging she just said a funny line and she told me that was based on the Bea Arthur school of saying a laugh line; you say the line and then immediately occupy yourself with something during the laugh. I remembered that backstage at *The Ritz*, the other actors and I would talk about Bea's signature picking lint off of her sweater after she'd land a zinger on *The Golden Girls*.

Friday night, James and I went downtown to see *Gone Missing* and I thought the acting was so great! The whole show is culled from real people talking about things they've lost. One woman's answering machine message about an expensive high-heeled shoe she lost at PS 122 was so hilariously annoying: "I've notified the head of PS 122, the director, the music director, the house manager, and *no one* is calling me back. I have a photo of the shoe that I'm gonna email to you so you can make a flyer… and I'm also attaching a map highlighting the places I want the flyer hung up." Seriously! I was obsessed with her controlling-ness! Also, as I was watching the show, I realized that I knew one of the cast members, Lexy Fridell (we did a show together where I got my Equity card), and I thought she was *excellent*... especially as the woman talking about losing her necklace down the drain of her shower. Then I checked the program and found out that she was actually an understudy! BRAVA!

Saturday, we saw our second Bill Finn show of the week — *Make Me a Song*. Everyone in the cast sang great (shout out to my friend Sally Wilfert and her gorgeous mix!), and Darren Cohen burned up the keyboard. And after hearing four lines of "Unlikely Lovers," I, as usual, had tears streaming down my face. Bring back *Falsettoland*!

Then we ran up to Lincoln Center to see *The Glorious Ones*. It was so fun for me to see Marc Kudisch in a fabulous lead role. We first worked together in Kansas City back in the early '90s where I music directed *Forever Plaid* and he played Smudge. He's such a great character actor and truly knows how to act a song. I find that some actors don't act while holding a note, but he's so good at filling it with subtext. Also, everyone knows that Natalie Belcon, from the original *Avenue Q*, is funny but her costume as Gary Coleman wasn't very sexy. Finally, New York can now see she's a beautiful woman! With a high belt! Thank you to the music of Flaherty and Ahrens and that fabulous push-up bra!

Finally, on Sunday afternoon, we went to brunch with my Mom at Marseille (delish!) and saw the matinee of *Die Mommie Die!* Charles Busch is so brilliant. I would so love for him to go back to what he did when he first started out and write and star in a different show each week. He is so mind-bogglingly funny, but you never feel that he's just going for the laugh. He perfectly blends imitating the grande dames of film with keeping everything he's doing rooted in reality. And, as you watch, you always want to be best friends with the women he plays. After the show, Charles made a sweet speech thanking us for being such a great crowd. He said that they had some bizarre audiences during the strike because they got the run-off from *How the Grinch Stole Christmas*. He recalled one evening playing the show to a group of 200 high school marching band members! He then muttered "...strange bedfellows." Hi-lar!

OK... I'm saying farewell! This week I start rehearsals for *Lend Me a Tenor*. As we would say in sixth grade to provoke gales of laughter, "see you next year!"

Judy, Judy, Judy... and Julia
January 7, 2008

Happy New Year! I'm writing this from rehearsal for *Lend Me a Tenor*.

That's right, my role is big enough to give me ample down time to write... and by "big," I mean "small." I actually love my role. I play the bellhop and I come on every once in a while and annoy everybody. I'm sort of the Gladys Kravitz of the show. The theatre is the newly built John W. Engeman Theater in Northport, but thankfully, we're rehearsing in New York.

When I graduated from high school, I thought I was done with Long Island, but it keeps calling to me. And I mean literally calling. Last week, I wrote about how my mother has given me a terrible complex about my driving, and that's why I haven't driven in years. She called me the second she read it (New Year's Eve) and I assumed that by seeing in print how her lack of confidence in my driving has debilitated me for years, she would be apologizing. This was the conversation:

MOTHER: Hi. I saw that you wrote about how you've been scared to drive for all these years...
ME: (Preparing to magnanimously accept her apology) Yes...?
MOTHER: Let me just say... YOU ARE A MENACE TO OTHER DRIVERS! *That* was what I was trying to say!

Why is that any better!?!?!

Speaking of New Year's Eve, I spent it at my apartment with James and my friends Tim Cross (from college), Stephen Spadaro (one of the company managers of *Chicago*) and Paul Castree (his boyfriend, recently of *Young Frankenstein*). We planned on having a game night but wound up watching tons of videos first. We watched two of my favorites: "We'll Raise a Glass Together" from *Grand Hotel* (mentioned in last week's column) and Karen Morrow's "I Had A Ball" from *The Ed Sullivan Show*. Brilliant!

Right before midnight, my friends asked me to put on the television for the countdown, and my TV was on some station that was showing *When Harry Met Sally*. It was the scene where Meg Ryan fakes the orgasm and I insisted on watching Rob Reiner's mother say, "I'll have what she's having," which unfortunately happened at midnight and 30 seconds. In other words, we missed the countdown so I could watch a laugh line from a 21-year-old movie I've seen 1,000 times. I guess it was worth ruining my party.

On New Year's Day, James, Juli and I went to Julia Murney's parents' apartment to have pancakes. It sounds random, but it's been a Murney tradition for almost 20 years. Julia invites tons of her friends, who invite all of their friends and the apartment winds up looking like the Equity Lounge. Julia wears an apron and asks how many pancakes you want and then ladles 'em out... with a big plate of bacon that the non-vegetarians wolf down (not me). I hung out with married couple Barbara Walsh and Jack Cummings (who runs The Transport Group). Barbara always looks amazing and I asked her the signature "What have you been up to?" question. She told me she just filmed a great commercial. I asked if her type was "young Mom." She then informed me it was promoting a medicine for menopause. And that's why I'm not a casting director. It sounds like a hilarious commercial... she gets a hot flash and throws herself into an ice machine!

I then chatted with Nancy Anderson, who told me that she was helping Celeste Holm clean her closets. First of all, that last sentence gets an "only in New York" tag. Secondly, if you don't know, Celeste Holm was Bette Davis' best friend in the film *All About Eve* as well as the original Ado Annie. Not the recent one with Patrick Wilson, I'm talking the version seen by FDR. Nancy told me that there was one bag filled with clothing swatches and she decided to look all the way to the bottom of the bag. It was filled with Celeste's diaries from the late 1920s! They had writing in those days!? And apparently, Celeste remembers every person mentioned in those pages. I'm dying to know if there's any amazing theatre stories like: "Went to an open call for a new show called *Porgy and Bess*. Got typed out."

This week I interviewed Judy Kuhn at the *Chatterbox*. She told us that her first big Broadway audition was for *The Mystery of Edwin Drood* and the final callback was for *all* the creative staff: producer Joe Papp, composer Rupert Holmes, director Wilford Leach, Graciela Daniele (choreographer) and her assistant, Rob Marshall. She was asked to sing a song that ends with the character of Edwin Drood angrily leaving the theatre. The director told her to sing it and then storm out like it would happen in the show. Judy started singing and told me that she spent the whole time thinking, "Did he mean for me to *literally* storm out of the room?" Finally, she thought that she should go for it full out, so she hit the last note, glared at the creative staff, grabbed her stuff, stormed out of the room and slammed the door. She then realized that the lobby was filled with other actors waiting for their callback. She murmured that she wasn't really angry and then started to wonder what she should do next. Was that the end of her audition? Should she open the door and go back in? Hmm... She waited for an awkward period of time. Then Robbie Marshall stuck his head out of the door and thanked her. Uh-oh. Sometimes the ol' "Thank you" is the kiss of death, but turns out, she got it! Phew. That gig demonstrates her brilliant voice - she understudied the high soprano part of Rosa Bud *and* the Betty Buckley belt of Edwin Drood! Unbelievable.

On the third preview, she got a call at three o'clock in the afternoon telling her that she was on for Rosa Bud. It was so early in the run that no one had ever rehearsed her. Nonetheless, they quickly went through everything with her and she got through everything she needed to do. Or so she thought. At the very end, all the characters hold signs with numbers on them, and the audience votes for who they think the murderer was. Whoever is chosen as the murderer has a special song they have to sing with lyrics that explain why and how they did it. After the voting, Judy headed offstage to do a quick costume change and prepared to run back onstage to watch Cleo Lane sing a song and then watch the murderer sing his or her song. As she was coming offstage, the stage manager pointed at her and said, "It's you." She laughed. She had spent the afternoon reviewing the regular role of Rosa Bud... not the extra song she'd only have to sing if she was voted murderer. He pointed again, "It's *you*!" Before she could scream, "I don't know the lyrics!" she was being put into her last costume and was suddenly onstage. All through Cleo Lane's song, she was trying frantically to remember the lyrics. And the extra song she had to sing ended on a crazy coloratura note. I asked her how it went, and she said she has no memory of performing it. That's what the brain does after trauma: it never happened.

She left *Drood* because she got cast as Bella in *Rags* starring Teresa Stratas. She said Teresa was an unbelievably great artist. One day they were rehearsing her song "Blame it on the Summer Night," and Teresa was resting her voice. Judy said that even though Teresa performed the song in barely a whisper, the whole cast was riveted. That's how emotionally connected she was to the material. *Rags* had lots of problems… one of which was that the director was fired a few weeks before the show opened on Broadway… and was never replaced!

Unfortunately, it opened on a Thursday and closed three days later. The cast decided to have a march from TKTS to the theatre to protest the closing of the show. As Judy told us, "We were so naïve." I asked her what she thought the march would achieve. She laughed and said she probably assumed "millions would join us!" I said that I would have joined (if I hadn't been in college) because the score to *Rags* is fan-effing-tastic. As a matter of fact, it got a Best Score and Best Musical Tony nomination! And thus begins another amazing story. Judy got the role of Cosette in the original *Les Miz* right after *Rags* closed… and was nominated for her first Tony Award. She was going to sing "One Day More" with the *Les Miz* cast on the Tonys, and Teresa Stratas was going to sing from *Rags*. Well, right before the telecast, Teresa dropped out, and they asked Judy to sing the *Rags* title song. That would mean that she'd sing as Bella in the *Rags* number and Cosette in the *Les Miz* one! The title song from *Rags* is a brilliant number, but much longer than the time it was allotted for the Tony telecast. They kept trying different cuts in the song to make it fit and still be effective. Finally, they came up with the final version, and Judy learned it with the new funky cuts. She was thankful that her award category was first because she wanted that stress over with. Frances Ruffelle, who played Eponine in *Les Miz*, won and Judy now only had to worry about her two numbers. The people who ran the show told her that a PA would come get her from her seat and bring her backstage with plenty of time. The first commercial break came, and no one got her. Second one, still no one. She was incredibly stressed because she had no idea where she went in the lineup. Finally, even though she had been told to wait in the audience, she decided to go backstage. As soon as she got there they screamed, "Where were you? You're on next!" They threw her wig and costume on and, minutes later, pushed her onstage to sing. She started the song, hoping to remember all the new cuts. As she was singing, she heard the orchestra start playing the wrong section. She then thought, "Wait a minute. The orchestra is on tape… *I'm* in the wrong section!" Yes, she had started to sing the bridge instead of the tag of the verse. Dick Latessa, who was playing her father, was a pro and went right along with her. Finally, the bridge started and she repeated what she just sang. The funny part is, I've seen the video of that performance many, many times and never noticed she had made a mistake until *years* later. She's so committed throughout and so is Dick Latessa!

Judy finished the number, and let me say that the last three notes of the song are so unbelievably thrilling that I've worn out my original tape from rewinding it so much. Judy ran offstage and started asking people in panic, "Did you hear what I did? Was it noticeable?" Then, suddenly, her wig and costume were being taken off, she was put into a totally new look and was back onstage in 19th-century France! And, of course, stress or not, she sounded amazing in the *Les Miz* number, too!

We also talked about the brilliant triptych of stars in *Chess*. It was her, David Carroll and Philip Casnoff. They all sound so great on the CD, it's crazy! She thinks the show failed because it was about the mistrust between The East and The West and, right before it opened, The Cold War ended. Hmph. Another thing I can blame Ronald Reagan for! Judy thinks the show would work better today because there's an us vs. them type feeling going on now in the U.S. I also think it could work because the score is fabulous and very ambitious! I did a concert version for the Actors Fund a few years ago with Josh Groban, Adam Pascal, Julia Murney and Sutton Foster, and let me say that trying to figure out how to conduct the meter changes at the beginning of "One Night in Bangkok" required a slide ruler and AP calculus.

Judy just closed in *Les Miz*, playing Fantine, who is Cosette's mother. The only weird moment for her was in the last scene when she'd be singing as Fantine, and she'd see Cosette by the bed. Not since *Chinatown*'s "She's my mother, she's my sister."

All right, people. By the end of this week I'll be in tech for *Lend Me a Tenor*, and then we open! What happened to the delicious days of six weeks of rehearsal, three months out of town and then two months of previews. Do the words LORT mean anything to you? Have a great week!

A *Tenor*, a Soprano and a *Mermaid*
January 15, 2008

I began rehearsals last week for *Lend Me a Tenor*, so naturally I'm already in tech. Huh?!?!

I feel like I'm in one-week summer stock again (where you rehearse and perform a different show each week), but the difference is, when I did one-week stock, I was the music director in the pit and had the luxury of reading music. Now, I'm one of the poor actors onstage desperately trying to remember my lines, blocking and which facial expression I'm using out of my signature mugs.

On Thursday, I interviewed Christine Ebersole at the *Chatterbox*. We started the show with Scott Frankel (composer of *Grey Gardens*) at the piano. Yes, I usually play for the guests, but I wanted Christine to sing "Around the World," and the piano part is tendonitis-inducing. Scott told me that it's based on Chopin's "Revolutionary Étude," which is a tip o' the hat to Little Edie's first song in Act Two, "The Revolutionary Costume of the Day." Of course, Christine sounded amazing on it and it was thrilling for me to be on the side of the stage as she sang it and to watch her face, which is so open and seems to have such an enormous well of emotion underneath it. I asked Christine how she first learned of the *Grey Gardens* documentary and she said that she had free time while living in L.A. and rented five DVDs. *Grey Gardens* was the first and only one she wound up watching. She said she was so riveted that the friend she was living with would essentially slide food into the room through a slot à la prison. A few months later, in December, her agent called and said that she was offered a Terrence McNally play at Sundance to workshop, but she told him that she couldn't possibly uproot her life during the holiday season and go to Sundance, even though it was for the fabulous Terrence McNally. Her agent called back and told her he knew she'd say no, but *another* show wanted her for Sundance... *Grey Gardens*. She forgot all about the holidays and said YES! A little while later she was at Sundance creating Little Edie while avoiding Terrence McNally.

Christine moved from the Midwest to go to acting school and, after she graduated, she started waitressing. This was in the mid '70s and, at the time, Christine Andreas was playing the maid in *Angel Street* on Broadway (the play that's the basis for *Gaslight*). Suddenly, she got the role of Eliza in the *My Fair Lady* revival. Christine Ebersole auditioned to replace Christine Andreas, got the gig and told us that she waltzed into her waitressing gig saying "Ta, ta! I'm going to Broadway! See ya around!" *Angel Street* closed unceremoniously and three weeks later Christine was at the restaurant, begging for her job back.

In the late '70s, she auditioned to replace Judy Kaye's original role as the maid in *On the Twentieth Century* because Judy took over the Madeline Kahn role. Christine said that there were a ton of women waiting to audition along with her. She walked in, sang, and Hal Prince ran to the stage and said, "Kid, can you learn the part in four days?" She said, "Sure!" and he hired her. She felt terrible leaving the audition area and walking through the slew of women waiting to get in and audition because she knew there wasn't a job available anymore! She played the maid and understudied Judy Kaye. Christine told us that she went on for the lead around eight times but her voice wasn't yet up to snuff. She would see conductor Paul Gemignani raising his eyebrows in the pit trying to get her pitch up to the high notes. But, she notes, even though she was a bit of a vocal clunkstress, she got all her laughs. Brava! Actually, half a brava. Bra.

After *Twentieth Century*, she got an audition for the role of Laurie in the *Oklahoma!* revival. Everyone thought of her as a soprano because of her role in *Twentieth Century*, but she really wanted to be Ado Annie, AKA get the laughs. She asked if they would consider her for that role instead — she auditioned and got it! That cast was stupendous. Laurence Guittard was Curly, Harry Groener was Will Parker, Martin Vidnovic was Jud, and the lady who unintentionally gave Christine her first break, Christine Andreas, played Laurie!

Christine did the show for around a year and right after she gave her notice, she was asked to audition to replace the woman playing Guinevere opposite Richard Burton in a big tour of *Camelot*. At her audition, she was suddenly joined onstage by... Richard Burton! She said it was one of those moments where she was shaking hands and politely saying, "Nice to meet you," while inside she was screaming, "It's Richard BURTO-O-O-O-O-ON!!!!!!!!!!!!"

À la *On the Twentieth Century*, she had to learn the part in less than a week, but instead of it being the role of the maid (and then understudying a lead), it was the actual leading lady with tons of dialogue and songs. She did her final performance of *Oklahoma!* on a Sunday matinee and then flew up to Canada on Monday. She was looking forward to finally getting to do her one run-through on Thursday night, but unfortunately Richard Burton came up to her before and said in his signature accent, "These lights are killing me. You don't mind if I skip the run-through, do you?" That's right, her only time doing the whole show from start to finish with her co-star would be opening night! And because the woman she replaced was short and she's tall, the first time she got to wear her costumes was *also* opening night. She told us that in the middle of "The Lusty Month of May," she suddenly heard a devil voice in one ear saying, "You have *absolutely no idea* what you're supposed to do next, do you? Mwa-ha-ha-ha-ha-ha!" In the other ear she heard, "Be here now. Be here now." Both voices fought it out and obviously the good voice won because, at the exact last second that Christine had to sing something, the correct words came out.

She remembers most of 1981 as a blur because she had three major things happen that are on the high-stress list: she got divorced, she moved *and* she got a new job (*Saturday Night Live*). All in one week!!!!! People thought she got *SNL* because she was related to producer Dick Ebersol, but she is not. Note the difference in last name spelling.

In the speech she made when she won the Tony Award for *Grey Gardens*, she remarked that she was told in L.A. her career was over. I asked for elaboration on that devastating comment. She recounted that, in the late '90s, she asked her agent why she wasn't getting any auditions, and he laughed condescendingly and simply said, "Christine, you're 45." Three neutral words that, when said with excitement, can add joy to a birthday party, but when said with derision can make you want to quit the business... and life.

A little while after that, she was driving to see a producer who, ten years earlier, had handed her a script and asked her to star on a TV show with Rosie O'Donnell. Only now she wasn't being handed anything. She was auditioning for him for a part on *Ally McBeal*... that had six lines. She got it, but was shocked when she was in the courtroom scene, and Lucy Liu said to the judge, while pointing at Christine, "Why can't I say anything? You let that old lady speak." The whole cast then laughed because Christine did that ol' gag of looking over her shoulder to see the old lady Lucy was referring to. But Because Christine hadn't read anything in the script but her own part, she really thought Lucy was pointing at someone else. She wasn't. Then

Christine looked at the cast and saw how skinny they were. Then she looked at the stand-ins and saw they were skinnier!

Christine went to her dressing room and looked in the mirror. She started pulling up her cheeks to see how she'd look with a face-lift. Suddenly she thought, "I am defining myself through things that I have no control over: my age and how my body looks." But she knew that she still had her talent, and if anything, it had gotten even better. She looked at herself again and thought, "I gotta get outta here!" She decided to hightail it back to NY... and two years later won the Tony Award for *42nd Street*! And now she has *another* Tony Award to add to her collection!

Finally, let me just say that my mother had yet another traumatic audition. If you don't know, a few years ago, my agent met my mom and decided that she'd be great for commercials. Also, if you don't know, she's 75 years old and has no (zero) acting experience. Yet she's managed to parlay that combination into numerous auditions that always end in disaster(s). P.S. Please don't think that she's the victim of the disasters. On the contrary. Most of the problems at the auditions stem from her stubbornness and hubris. She proudly told me that she refused to say DQ instead of Dairy Queen at a recent audition because "no one my age would call it DQ." And at a deodorant audition last month, she was asked to pretend to drive on a parkway but instead of having her hands on the steering wheel and watching the road, she spent the whole time checking and re-checking the side-view mirror. When the director cut her off and exasperatedly asked her what she was doing, she explained "I have friends who don't drive as well as I do and they always do that before entering a parkway." He asked her to just get on the parkway and wave on the car in back of her. She got on the parkway, but thought it would be funny, instead of doing what the director said, to do a Queen Elizabeth wave to the car behind her. Apparently, from her lack of a callback, it wasn't.

And don't forget! I'm soon doing a reading/signing of my novel *Broadway Nights* with Christine Ebersole, Cheyenne Jackson, Kristine Zbornik, Denis O'Hare and Andrea McArdle. And next week I'll be able to tell you about the opening of *Lend Me a Tenor*! Uh-oh. I'd better learn my lines.

Broadway Nights and a West End Star

January 21, 2008

Shh! I'm sitting backstage at The John W. Engeman Theater.

It's about to be "places" (or "beginners" as they call it in London... or shall I say, as they call it "across the pond" for full pretentiousness). I'm sitting in my bellhop outfit, and I just finished warming up. That's right, I do a vocal warm-up every night because my first entrance consists of me barging into a hotel room and singing part of an aria from *Figaro*. It ends on a high A and even though I'm not belting it, I got so nervous during the final dress rehearsals that my A came out sounding like a dry wind in the Sahara — replete with sand particles. Anyhoo, I've found that if I run it onstage before half hour, it comes out fine. Also, it's *a cappella*, so I think I was starting the first pitch too high in some of the run-throughs and wound up belting Idina's last note in "Defying Gravity." Now I use a pitch pipe right before I go on so I have the note in my head.

This whole week has been *exhausting*! On Monday I traveled to Long Island to rehearse in the afternoon for *Lend Me a Tenor* and then left halfway through rehearsals to take a train back to the city to go to the Lincoln Center Barnes & Noble for a reading/signing of my novel, *Broadway Nights*. The great news is the reading was *packed*, and I'd love to think it was because I have such a loyal fan base/household name recognition, but I have a sneaking suspicion it was because I had a slew of Broadway folk performing with me. Speaking of which, when I first sent out an invite to my email list, I advertised that Cheyenne Jackson would be playing the part of my best friend. Ten minutes later I got an email from a guy who meant to forward it his friend, but pushed "reply" instead. It said, "Hey! Do you want to see Seth at Barnes and Noble? Do you think Cheyenne will show up?" I sent back a sassy reply saying, "I got your email by accident... and *yes*, Cheyenne is showing!!" Cut to Sunday, Cheyenne emailed me saying that he suddenly has to do a publicity event for *Xanadu* that he can't get out of and it conflicts with the reading. I begged and pleaded with him to work it out somehow. He was devastated that he was letting me down, but I explained that it wasn't about letting me down; it was because my reply to that email was so sassy and certain. Why did I have to be as brazen as the architect of the "unsinkable" Titanic? Well, Cheyenne was able to arrange a car to take him from the event to Barnes & Noble, so he *did* show up! I asked if the email writer was in the audience and got severe silence in response. Maybe the email should have read, "Do you want to see Seth at Barnes and Noble? Do you think *I* will show up?"

Anyhoo, the event went *great*! I read the lead character, Stephen, who's a piano sub on Broadway, desperate to conduct his first Broadway show. Kristine Zbornik (about to be in *A Catered Affair*) played my psycho governess, Mrs. Remick. Kristine and I worked together in the '90s doing a weekly variety show we put together called *Saturdays at Rose's Turn*. She does a character named Anita Lomax, who's an aging alcoholic singer, and my favorite sketch we'd do featured Anita raging about her latest audition.

SETH: How'd your *Sunset Boulevard* audition go?
ANITA: It stank! They had their minds made up *way* before I fell in the orchestra pit. (Laughs derisively.) It's all prejudice, you know. I mean, think about it; a man's graying at the temples, he's sexy, right? I drink a case of vodka, I'm an alcoholic! You do the math!
SETH: I'm sorry...

ANITA: (snorts). Andrew, Lloyd and Webber. Who the hell are they anyway? Three guys trying to make a buck, they stink!

I also had Christine Ebersole, who played Stephen's narcissistic opera-singing mother who's always on tour. She got a *huge* laugh at her line-reading of the section we did together where she's talking to a 13-year-old Stephen and reveals that she and my Dad are getting divorced: "Now, I know this is a big shock for you, as it is for me, Stephen. If there's anything you want to discuss, anything at all (*she takes my hands in hers*)... Mommy will be back in two-and-a-half weeks."

Denis O'Hare was fantastic as the horrible agent, Ronald. Right now, I have a student named Sam Heldt from my alma mater, Oberlin, doing his winter term project as my intern. When I asked him to find Denis in the Barnes & Noble café and ask him to meet me for a script change, Sam went into a state of star shock (immobile and slack-jawed). It was adorable. I remember how star-struck I was when I was in college and I met the bass player from *Carrie*. I was like, "Wait a minute, wait a minute... you were actually *in* the orchestra pit when Betty Buckley sang. Oh. My. God." I'm not exaggerating!

Speaking of Sam, I took him to the *Chatterbox* and we ran into Jackie Hoffman. When she heard that Sam was my intern, she looked at him and asked, "So, Seth is taking you 'under his wing'?" Then, she lowered her glasses and voice: "Do I need to contact the authorities?"

Of course, Cheyenne was great and, after we read his chapter, I asked him to sing one of his signature audition songs. He sang "The Proposal" from *Titanic*, which he sang for his Radames understudy *Aida* audition. I love how there are so many Broadway stars that began as understudies. Did you know that Lillias White was the understudy for the gym teacher in the mega-flop *Carrie*? She told me that people would say, "We hope you get to go on!" and she'd say "Um... that's OK! Trust me."

When I got to Barnes & Noble, I bought all the participants gift cards. The man who rang me up said that he was going to leave his station and come to my reading because his idol would be there... Andrea McArdle. I love that there are people like me all over the city!

After the reading, I had dinner with David Bedella, who's in town to play the devil in *Jerry Springer: The Opera* at Carnegie Hall. We dated back in the '90s, and we both remembered how the movie *Hook* ruined our relationship. We had gone to see it with my college friend Tim, and Tim and I spent the whole time making fun of Julia Roberts' inappropriate close-ups... which culminated with her, for some reason, standing in a full evening gown ("Tinker Bell... you look beautiful."). David was raging that we were talking throughout the whole movie, and I was raging that he liked it, and that was the beginning of the end. Actually, it pretty much was the end.

I asked him to give me a full catch-up of the last decade-and-a-half. He had gone to Nashville in the mid-'90s to start a country music career (!), and right when he got there, he got a job offer to understudy on Broadway. His partner convinced him to take it since it had always been his dream. But, as the old adage says, be careful what you wish for... and by "wish," I mean dream. And by "for," I mean "of." He said it wound up being a debilitating experience because he was constantly being told by various people involved that he was an understudy because he wasn't good enough to have a role. Ouch! By the end of the run, he doubted his own talent. His partner, who had recently finished divinity school, got an offer to go to London and asked David if he would move with him. Since David had such a bad experience on Broadway, he said yes.

In England, partners of clergy get citizenship, and they give those rights to gay partners... as opposed to the U.S. David had so many negative feelings about his performing skills that he started working at a hair salon! He had always cut his friends' hair, so he knew he had a flair for it. He agreed to work as an apprentice at an upscale hair salon (making appointments, getting coffee) even though it would take four years (!) to become a full time hair cutter. Well, one day his boss started yelling at him in front of the whole salon because of a mistake he didn't even make. He decided to quit and started auditioning again.

David went to an open call for the tour of *Miss Saigon*, and while he was there, he realized that he could completely reinvent himself. No one knew who he was or any of his history. He decided he would walk into the audition like he was a star. He usually is super friendly at auditions to show how easy he would be to work with, but instead he decided not to even think about being "nice" and just knocked his performance to the back wall like he was playing Radio City Music Hall! Normally, he makes eye contact with the auditioners, but this time he decided to play his song to the "balcony." After he sang, there wasn't applause. There was silence, and then they thanked him. Ouchy wowy. He was devastated as he left the room, and while he was on the way out, someone ran out of the audition room, "Is David Bedella still here?" Yes! They told him that they were calling him back to sing for Cameron Mackintosh.

They asked him to learn a certain part in *Miss Saigon* from the CD. The role didn't have a first name and David didn't know the score to *Miss Saigon*, so he thought it was probably like the Factory Girl in *Les Miz* ("And what have we here little innocent sister..."). In other words, a great little 32-bar feature. He asked if he would be able to recognize what role it was when he listened to the CD and the casting person said, dry British-style, "Darling, it's the lead." The only thing missing was the casting person peering over a *pince-nez*. The role was the Engineer, and David immediately set out to get an agent before the callback because if he got the gig, he'd need someone to negotiate. He asked around for the newest, hungriest agent and found a young guy who had just left a big agency. The guy was working out of his apartment, but when he met David he rattled off a list of clients he had... and they were essentially all playing leading roles on the West End. David had his new "I'm a star" attitude, and the agent said that he's never signed anybody without hearing them first, but was so impressed with David that he would take a chance. David went to the callback for Cameron Mackintosh, and lo and behold, got the offer for the Engineer! *But* he was told that the man who had played the Engineer before would start out the tour in London... and then David would take over. In other words, the other guy would do the "important" cities, and then David would take on the lesser ones. David thought about what he went through on Broadway... and how he wanted to re-invent himself... and told his agent to tell the powers that be that, with all due respect, he was not an understudy or replacement, and he forced himself to wait for a role that would be his. That's right, he turned down the job!

He wound up doing a revue that toured to Australia and, when he got back, was offered an audition to play the devil in *Jerry Springer*. He was not a fan of the TV show in America, and decided to turn down the audition. Finally, his agent convinced him that the show was gonna be fabulous, and David tried out. He got offered the part, wound up starring on the West End for two years... and won the Olivier Award! So, from now on fellow actors, go into auditions acting like you're a star. And then, turn down a role after you're offered it. And eventually, you'll win an Olivier... *or* wind up getting a terrible, terrible reputation.

And finally, *Lend Me a Tenor* has been going great. When we first began performances, we had some technical difficulties and in the scene where Jim Poulos is supposed to get a wake-up phone call, the phone didn't ring. So, as he was lying there "asleep," he decided to ad lib a line to cover up. Unfortunately, he got nervous so instead of saying, "My internal clock says that it's time to wake up," he wound up saying "My *biological* clock says that it's time to wake up." Then, to continue the headachiness of the scene, while he was pretending to have a phone conversation, the phone finally rang. The good news is that the audiences are loving the show, and I think the cast and our director are so super-talented.

Peace out til next week!

Critics Are Always Right (This Time)
January 29, 2008

Well, I vowed I wouldn't look at any reviews, *but* I was reading *Newsday* (you can take the boy out of Long Island...), and as I turned a page I saw a picture from the Northport, Long Island, production of *Lend Me a Tenor* and the headline, "John W. Engeman Theater Has Its First Big Hit," so of course I had to read it. And by "read it" I mean scan to find my name.

The whole show got a great review, and my particular shout out was: "Seth Rudetsky as the bellhop delivers champagne with bubbly impertinence." Yes! I *knew* my impertinence would pay off one day. Take that, former AP English teacher, Mrs. Jaffe! Senior year in high school I somehow manipulated myself into AP English even though, as Mrs. Jaffe later publicly informed me, "they warned me not to put you in this class!" I was consistently busted for the aforementioned impertinence and things like whispering in class, using *Cliff's Notes*, etc. until finally she pointed to me in the middle of class one day and let loose with,
"Seth...
you're useless,
you're fruitless,
and what's more, I don't like you."

I was mortified... yet, impressed by her prose. First of all, the ingenious (if false) rhyme scheme (*useless* = *fruitless*) and then the shocking ending (*what's more I don't like you*). It was like a hostile haiku.

Thursday was our opening and I forgot to write that my friend Marco (who created *Caroline In The City* and is currently the showrunner for *Ugly Betty*) emailed to wish me luck. I was waiting for the flowers I assumed I'd get from him since he sent me an enormous bouquet when I opened in *The Ritz* but then I noticed there was a P.S. at the end of the letter: "For Broadway you get roses, for Long Island... a warm email." Hmm... his honesty was *not* refreshing.

James, Juli and I wanted to see *The Golden Compass* on Monday afternoon, but because it was a holiday, the afternoon showing was sold out! *P.S. 6 years later... still haven't seen it!* I'm completely obsessed with that book series, and I don't know who was more devastated; me or seven-year-old Juli. Let's just say that her crying was on the outside but mine was on the inside and much, much more intense. We were on 42nd Street, so we wound up going to *Ripley's Believe It Or Not* Museum and, "believe it or not," we all had a great time! There were so many cool things there for adults and children. Of course, Juli asked us, "What's this?" while we were walking through some exhibit about the human body as she repeatedly pushed a button that inflated a t-shirt to give it an enormous rack. James and I looked at each other, speechless, until I came up with an amazing answer: "I don't know." I'm sure that satisfied her curiosity.

This week at Sirius radio I interviewed one of my best friends, Paul Castree, who's currently playing Gerald the Herald amongst other roles in *Young Frankenstein*. I first met Paul when he was an understudy in *Forever Plaid* and I was the music director. I summed him up as a super-nerd the first day I met him because he was wearing a button-down sweater (my judgments are quick, decisive and moronic), and I wound up totally snubbing him for a week. I then realized how hilarious and talented he was and we became friends. Finally, I decided to apologize to him for completely ignoring him for the first week of rehearsal and the amazing double-triple-whammy bust on me is that he never noticed my week-long snub! I assumed he spent the beginning of his run lamenting, "Why isn't that hilarious music director honoring me with his glance?" and instead he was thinking, "What's my harmony?" and "What're my lines?" and "I notice in my peripheral vision there is a man playing the piano."

Paul has my favorite First Audition in New York Story. He was living in Rockford, IL (where he had gone to high school with Marin Mazzie, Jodi Benson *and* Joe Mantello!) and had just finished working at Opryland. Tim Schultheis (now an amazing photographer who did my 8x10!) was living in New York and told Paul that, according to *Backstage*, the *Bye Bye Birdie* tour with Tommy Tune was looking for "tenors with Midwestern looks." (Paul has a crazy high voice and bright orange hair.) New York City? Paul said it was like someone saying, "There are some great rocks on the moon. Come get them!" Nevertheless, after much pressing, Tim convinced Paul to fly to New York for the open call. Two days later, at 8 AM, Paul showed up at Equity in his "audition" outfit, which (unfortunately) consisted of jeans, high top sneakers and a multi-colored shirt he got at Kmart.

Stuart Howard was casting and asked all the non-Equity people who were auditioning to come into the room and line up. It wasn't for a firing squad, but close to it. He pointed at a few of them and asked them to stay... and the rest got a "thank you very much." Paul didn't even know there was such a thing as "typing" people and was so thankful that he dodged that bullet. It would have been really fun to fly across the country for $650 (that was a *huge* amount of money in the early '90s) to be at an audition for ten seconds and get thank-you-very-muched.

They asked the men to dance and, afterward, Paul was asked to stay and sing! He showed the pianist his song ("Magic Changes" from *Grease*), and the pianist shook his head and told him that the casting people didn't want *anything* from *Grease*. Paul was devastated because he had nothing else in his book, but decided to mask his devastation with blank-faced confidence. "That's what I've prepared, and that's what I'll be singing." He wasn't sure if he was going to get his 16 bars thrown back in his face, but apparently his fake confidence stunned the pianist into temporary silence, and Paul used that opportunity to walk center and nod politely. The pianist started playing, Paul sang and he was then asked to read! *Yes!* The only goal Paul had set for himself was to be able to sing at a real New York audition, and he'd reached it. Everything else was now delicious icing on the cake.

Stuart Howard asked him to read for the role of Hugo Peabody. Paul worked on it in the lobby and came back in and gave it the reading of his life. He was selling it to the back row. One minute into his high-energy read, Stuart put up his hand and said "Stop! Paul... this isn't children's theatre." Ouch. I guess his version of high-energy had the essence of "Milady! The moat is being crossed by a fire-breathing dragon! Everybody... clap if you're scared of dragons! *I can't hear you*!"

Anyway, Paul toned it down and was then asked to hang around. A whole bunch of other guys came in and lined up for Stuart. They were all dressed in New York dance outfits: black pants, black shirts and black dance shoes. Stuart announced that they all should come back that evening for a callback at the Uris Theatre with Tommy Tune. He then looked at the guys in their various hip audition outfits and lambasted them. "Didn't you read the breakdown? The show needs guys with *Midwestern looks*! I want you all to go home, clean yourself up, change your outfits and come back looking like *him*!" He then pointed at Paul. That's right! His Kmart shirt paid off!

Paul found his way to the Uris (now the Gershwin), which, incidentally, was where he saw his first Broadway show (*Sweeney Todd*) when he was in high school. And now he had returned, but this time he was *backstage*... auditioning for a multiple Tony Award-winner! Paul waited backstage while the ladies lined up onstage. Paul assumed that all Broadway callbacks happened on a Broadway stage. He didn't find out until later that nowadays they usually take place in a little rehearsal room, and nowadays they only happen on a Broadway stage in Lifetime movies about Broadway.

The ladies each had to do a tap combination while Tommy Tune stood in the audience at their foot level and critiqued their tapping. Wow. That's intense. He'd watch them and say "Um... you missed a sound on the second flap," and make them do it again. All the ladies danced and sang and then Paul saw a few come backstage and get their bags. Suddenly the remaining ladies onstage began screaming and hugging each other. "What's going on?" Paul asked one who was running by him in a tizzy. "We just found out we got the gig!" she screamed. "We're going on tour! I have to call my Mom!" Paul was in shock. He thought today was the first of many auditions. Turns out it was the day of the *final* callback. He realized he would find out by the end of the day whether or not he got it!

Next, a bunch of guys went out to the stage and pretty much the same thing happened. Some guys left and the others celebrated getting the gig. Soon, the only ones remaining were Paul and two other guys. They talked amongst themselves, and after weighing rumor and innuendo, decided that the two roles left open were the understudy for Hugo and Harvey Johnson. That meant that two of them were going to get a gig! Paul felt pretty good about his chances... two out of three! All three of them came out onstage and had to read for Hugo and sing, "Hello Mr. Hankle, this is Harvey Johnson..." while cracking their voice on the high note. After they sang, they awkwardly stood there while Tommy Tune, Stuart Howard, Gene Saks (director) and the Weisslers (producers) discussed them in the audience. Paul felt incredibly awkward. He tried to look pleasant and not aware that he was on display. Sort of a combination of fun-to-work-with and eager for the job, but not immature/unfocused and/or needy and desperate. In other words, more subtext went into his standing there than into his actual reading of the scene. Finally, Stuart Howard slowly approached from the back of the audience. *This is it*, Paul thought. One of them is going to be sent backstage, and the other two will get the gig. Finally, Stuart looked at them all and said... "Thank you very much." What? They had "decided" backstage that two of them would get the gig so all of them being sent home was not in the equation. Therefore, no one onstage budged. After an awkward pause, Stuart said, more pointedly, "Thank you! We'll be in touch." AKA we *won't* be in touch. All three started walking off the stage in a depression. Paul couldn't believe how close he had come only to have it all end so depressingly. They were all walking slowly and Paul was the last one to exit. Right when he got to the wings and was about to walk offstage, he heard Stuart stage whisper, "Paul!" Paul looked over his shoulder. Stuart beckoned him back onstage. Paul walked back in a state of shock. What now? Some fatherly advice? A question about the origin of his Kmart shirt? Finally, Paul got center stage. Stuart looked at him squarely and said, "Paul. We'd like to give you your Equity card and have you go out on tour with Tommy Tune to understudy Hugo Peabody and play the role of Harvey Johnson. You got the job." Paul was so overjoyed yet emotionally and physically exhausted that he immediately collapsed his body into a compact, tight ball. He said he didn't *ex*ploded... he *im*ploded.

He did the tour (with Ann Reinking as Rose, Susan Egan as Kim, Marilyn Cooper as Mae and Marc Kudisch as Birdie) and met one of his best friends, Jessica Stone, who played Ursula. Can you imagine? Flying in from the Midwest for your first New York open call and by the end of the day having your whole life changed! How thrilling is that? And, P.S., how terrifying for the ladies to have Tommy Tune watch your feet while you tap. It's like singing in front of Barbara Cook as she stares at your larynx. Paul also said that for every amazing story about getting a gig, there's the parallel story for someone else: many years later, Paul was backstage and telling his *Saturday Night Fever* co-stars his Tommy Tune audition story. He then found out that one of his fellow actors was one of the three guys in that final audition! *His* version was: "I went to callback after callback for *Bye Bye Birdie*. Finally, at the final one, this red-headed kid from the Midwest appeared out of nowhere and got the gig!" The good news, that performer has gone on to be the brilliant choreographer of *In the Heights* — Andy Blankenbuehler! *P.S. Andy won a Tony Award a few months after I wrote this!*

Also this week, I got a call from my agent who told me that I had an audition for a Sandra Bullock movie... to play a flight attendant. I've decided that I've had it with the unfunny/stereotypical gay roles and asked if the word "flamboyant" was in the character description. That's always the code word for gay and it means the character comes on, throws a few sassy quips and saunters off. I don't know why that's the majority of gay characters that are written for TV/films. Don't gay people have any personality traits besides bitchy asides? Anyhoo, she checked out the traits and "flamboyant" was nowhere to be found. I was thrilled and agreed to audition. I got the script emailed to me and boastfully told James the story about how I set a professional boundary. I opened up the email in front of him and proudly read the character description. "Listen to this, James. The role is 'Flight Attendant.' The description is, 'A middle-aged' — *What the?!?!?!?!?!!*" I went into a state of shock, and James remarked that perhaps "flamboyant" would have been preferable. Not cool.

All right everyone, my West Coast best friend Jack Plotnick is visiting all week, so I have to hightail it to delicious brunch. Go see a Broadway show!

Chip, *Jerry* and a *Late Nite Comic*
February 4, 2008

Welcome to February! I love February because, not only is it my birthday month, but also because I think of it as the transition to spring. Peace out, winter... see ya next year! Although, with the charming onslaught of global warming, that should actually read "see ya next year for a period of one, maximum two days."

My life has gotten kind of hectic with doing *Lend Me a Tenor* and my radio show, etc. While I was performing in *The Ritz* on Broadway, the performance schedule was a typical eight shows a week, but *Lend Me a Tenor* is only five shows a week, so sometimes it's hard for me to keep track of what I'm doing on the other nights. That being said, I called James on Monday night and asked if he and Juli had time for dinner. He started to say "Don't you have to do-" and I thought he was going to say that I had to do *Celebrity Autobiography*, which I'm not doing 'til next week. So I was about to do my signature interruption, cut him off and tell him that *Celebrity Autobiography* is next week, but I decided to resist my rudeness urge for once in my life and let him finish the sentence, which wound up being, "Don't you have to do a Barnes & Noble show?" *Holy you-know-what!* Not only was he right and I had totally forgotten, but it was 5:20 PM and I was supposed to be there at 5:30! Revelation: maybe I shouldn't constantly and consistently interrupt people because I "know what they're going to say."

I ran out of my apartment and got down to the Lincoln Center Barnes & Noble ASAP. I was there to celebrate the release of the *Late Nite Comic* 20th anniversary CD (whose proceeds go to The Actors Fund). Brian Gari wrote the music and lyrics to that show, and it was a devastating flop (opened and closed on Broadway in one weekend). He tells the whole story in an amazing book called *We Bombed in New London* (which they certainly did). I love backstage books because it's always fascinating to know all the ups and downs that go into bringing a show to Broadway... and this show had more than its share of downs. On Monday night, Brian recounted the story about the director trying to cut the song "Late Nite Comic," AKA the title song. Brian went to The Dramatists Guild and filed a complaint and they ruled that the song couldn't be cut. Yay! It was back in. Brian came to the show that night and found out that he'd been banned from the theatre! He forced his way past the producer and found a seat, and sure enough, even though they were told *not* to cut the song, it was missing more than Madonna's vibrato! However, in Act Two, they did keep the reprise. Reprise of what?

After Brian told the story, he performed the title song from the piano and, whether or not it worked in the show, it's beautiful. The CD is star-studded: Brian D'Arcy James, Julia Murney, Daniel Reichard, Marty Vidnovic, Mary Testa and, in a small but pivotal role, Seth Rudetsky! I play one of the comedy club owners in the song "The Best in the Business," and I performed the song on Monday night with one of the women who was originally in the show, Luba Mason. You may remember her as Linda Eder's velvet-voiced replacement in *Jekyll and Hyde*, but you probably don't remember her in *Late Nite Comic* because she used a completely different name back then. Lubitza Gregus is her original name, and when she started on Broadway, she wanted something more vanilla, so she used the stage name Kim Freshwater. Wow. That's a lo-o-o-o-o-ong way away from Lubitza Gregus. The only similarity is that it consists of a first and last name.

Jerry Stiller introduced the whole evening and said that, early in his career, he was helped tremendously by Brian's grandfather. Brian's grandfather happened to be Eddie Cantor who, incidentally, was born with the name Israel Iskowitz. Hmm... Israel Freshwater?

Tuesday I went to see *Jerry Stiller: The Opera*... I mean, *Jerry Springer*. I was very proud of David Bedella, who plays the warm-up guy and Satan, and whom I've known since the early '90s and whose voice sounded fantastic! The show was super fun, and there is something inherently funny about hearing the moronic vernacular of *Jerry Springer* in an opera. Singing "whatever" like a Valley Girl is one thing, but singing it on a high G in a covered tenor voice is hilarious.

A couple of days before the show, I got an email from a group asking me to protest the show, and I wrote back immediately. I didn't argue whether or not it was offensive to them, but I mentioned that it seemed to me there were many more devastating problems in the world (war, homeless vets, children that need fostering) and if they were going to organize something, aren't there more important things that all that energy could go to? I concluded by reiterating that it seems to me that there are more pressing issues that could use all those people's help. No response. I heard there was a group of protesters outside Carnegie Hall, but I missed them because I entered through a different door. My seat was next to a very New Yorky elderly lady who looked at me as I sat down and immediately said, "Do you wanna hear something funny?" I said, "Sure," and she said, "Well, first of all, I was in the lobby, and I approached two women and said, 'Do you wanna hear something funny?' and they both said, 'No.'"

Ouch. I guess that's why New Yorkers are known for their honesty. She continued. "The story is that I normally have bible study group tonight, and I didn't feel I could tell them I was seeing this show, so I said I was busy. I figured that they'll never know. Then, as I walked in, I saw the TV cameras filming me!" Busted. I'd love an update on next week's class.

This week I also interviewed Chip Zien on my Sirius radio show. First of all, he's so charming. Even though many of his theatre stories had a section where he admitted that he had a big, fat angry fit about something that he now realizes was not worth it, he would tell me about it with a big smile, and I would think, "That must have been *adorable*!" He grew up in the Midwest, and when he was a boy, his Mom enrolled him in dance class. Soon he got cast as one of the little kids in a professional production of *South Pacific*. She then made arrangements with a New York couple to take Chip to live with them so he could get a Broadway gig. The only problem was, she never consulted with young Chip and he said, "No way!" He didn't want to be shipped off to New York City to live with random people. It was very *Into the Arms of Strangers* (the film about parents during WWII who gave away their kids to live with families in safe countries), but instead of wanting Chip to escape the London Blitz, Mama Rose Zien wanted him to get his Equity card.

He eventually got an Ivy League education and, after spending a few years teaching, he moved to NY. He soon met an agent (who lived in the apartment above his friend) and she flat out told him that he didn't look like an actor... at all. She asked what his father did. He told her that he was a plumber, and she told him to move back to the Midwest and become a plumber. The next day, though, she passive/aggressively got him a commercial audition for Planters Peanuts... and he got it!

Speaking of peanuts, he next did a national tour of *You're a Good Man, Charlie Brown* playing Snoopy, and then he got cast in *How to Succeed in Business Without Really Trying* at The Equity Library Theater playing the lead role of Finch... or as Chip called himself in the role, Finchstein. His wife was working as a dancer for the New York City Ballet and one day she ran into a fellow ballerina when she and Chip were in a store on the East Side. As the ladies stood there chatting, a man tapped Chip on the shoulder and said, "Don't try anything with the lady... she's my wife." Turns out the man was joking... *and* he was Dustin Hoffman! Well, just the night before, Dustin's name was on the backstage list of celebs seeing *How to Succeed* so Chip was excited to hear what Dustin had to say about his performance. Well, instead of commenting about Chip's portrayal of the lead role in a play he literally just saw, he instead asked Chip what he did for a living. Zero recall. Chip was mortified and muttered that he "worked at night." They then all went back to Dustin's apartment, and Dustin asked if Chip was an actor. Finally, Chip said, "Look, you saw me last night starring in *How to Succeed*, and obviously I was so bad you don't even remember me." Dustin laughed and told him that he hadn't come. His business partner had used his name! He then asked Chip to audition for a play he was directing, and Chip got the understudy. Chip said that Dustin was a brilliant director but had no confidence. He kept saying, "If you all don't like what I'm doing, I can get Mike Nichols." Interesting... I often say sentences like that. While I was in *The Ritz*, I would tell my boyfriend at night, "If you don't like what I'm doing, I can get Ryan Idol." Unfortunately, he tried to take me up on the offer. And thus ends the Borscht Belt section of this column.

The big turning point in Chip's career was when he auditioned to play Marvin in *In Trousers* at Playwrights Horizons. He sang "Jackie" from *Jacques Brel*, and Bill Finn (who wrote *In Trousers* and was directing it at that point) told him that a) he hated that song and b) if he insisted on singing it, he should put his hands in his pockets and stand on the piano... which Chip did. Suffice it to say, Chip thought that Bill was the oddest person he had ever met, but he got the gig and they became great friends. *In Trousers* turned into a cult hit and next came *March of the Falsettos*. Michael Rupert took over the role of Marvin and Chip became Mendel, his psychiatrist, which he considered a demotion. He says he remembered that there were a lot of lunches where he was explaining his issues to William Finn, and at one of them he offered to write his own song for Mendel. The offer was not accepted.

He told me that *March of the Falsettos* was being considered a workshop so there was no official opening date. However, one random night, Frank Rich came, gave it a rave and suddenly the show was frozen. We then talked about *Falsettoland*, which is the sequel to *March of the Falsettos* and one of my favorite shows ever. He said that *Falsettoland* is the only show where he didn't care what the critics said at all. He felt that the show's message was so important that it transcended anything negative a critic could possibly say. I asked what he felt was so important, and he said that the show spoke so well to our time and what people in the theatre have gone through in terms of the losses we've suffered due to AIDS. And the message was that all of us treat each other as best we can, whatever our peculiarities... and that we're all a family. I then asked him if he was completely obsessed with the song "Unlikely Lovers" as I am. Of course, Chip-style, he said that song was a big bone of contention for him, and he was constantly arguing about it because he felt that it was missing something... him! (And Trina). Addition denied.

Finally, I brought up *Into the Woods*. He was in L.A. doing TV work when Ira Weitzman (the fabulous producer) called him and said that they were considering him for the role of the Baker *but* if anyone called and asked him to audition, he should say no! Ira felt that the creative team didn't know what they wanted and if Chip came in they would find a reason why he wasn't right. But if he didn't come in, they would just offer it to him. Well, they did ask him to audition, he said he couldn't... and they offered him the role! While they were rehearsing in La Jolla, James Lapine (the director/writer) said that he was concerned because Chip didn't look like a baker. He imagined the Baker as a big roly-poly guy and Chip is small and wiry. Chip got incredibly insecure during rehearsal until Joanna Gleason had lunch with him and told him not to freak out because she was sure he was going to keep the part. He calmed down, and they told everyone that the show was coming to Broadway — unfortunately, not for another eight months... and Chip has two kids. Hello, money? He didn't feel he could accept another job knowing he'd have to leave in eight months. Thankfully, his wife was working for the ballet and his family continued eating.

The reason the show waited eight months is that the second act was being worked on. Audiences didn't like the fact that the Baker's Wife died and they never saw her again. So the creative team decided to bring her back during Act Two... but then they couldn't decide if Jack's Mother should also come back. Apparently, the only time you can have two dead people visiting is in a dream (See: Grandma Tzeitel and Fruma-Sarah).

They worked it out, and Chip loved doing the show... and working with Sondheim. He said he remembers Sondheim coming into a rehearsal room at La Jolla and performing new music for them. He said it was so moving when Sondheim sat at the piano, got out his sheet music, laid it out so it was neat and then sang "No One Is Alone." He remembers Paul Gemignani, the music director who's a big, imposing presence, literally having tears streaming down his cheeks. And Chip remembers that when the show was rehearsing in New York, Sondheim presented him the song "No More." Chip said he couldn't believe that Sondheim was writing songs based on how Chip played the character, what his range was, etc... and that he was actually going to be able to sing that brilliance onstage!

His fondest memory is about when they filmed *Into the Woods* for PBS. The audience was filled with Sondheim fanatics who simply loved the show. Chip went back to his dressing room after the curtain call and noticed that it was dark even though he had left the light on. He opened the door and saw someone sitting there. Chip turned on the light and Sondheim looked up at him with tears in his eyes and said, "When could it ever be this good?" How sweet is that? Isn't it nice to know that it's not just the audience that's moved by a genius' work, but the genius himself can be moved by the piece, the performances and the love from the audience as well?

All right, tonight I'm hosting *Broadway Backwards* for the third time and later this week I'm seeing *Applause* at City Center Encores! (featuring Chip Zien and starring Christine Ebersole) and then I'm interviewing Nathan Lane for Sirius radio! All this Broadway makes me thirsty. Maybe I'll have a nice, cold glass of FreshWater. Gregus? Mason?

Nathan, Christine and *Broadway Backwards*
February 11, 2008

This afternoon James borrowed my laptop, so he could go to a coffee shop in the village and do some writing. In the middle of the afternoon, I suddenly began thinking about what would happen if he lost it. I'd definitely have to replace it but would feel awful asking him to pay for it. Yet I don't have any insurance on it. Later that evening I was at Sirius, and I got a call on my cell phone.

RANDOM PERSON: Is this Seth?
ME: (Distrustingly. Subtext: Aren't I on the "do-not-call" list?) Yes…
RANDOM PERSON: I have your laptop.
What the-!?! I got his address and said I'd be right over.
I called James and told him I just got a phone call from a man who had my laptop.
"How?" James asked. "I have it here."
"You do?"

That was odd. I wondered if I was being scammed. Suddenly I heard a lengthy, loud gasp. It *was* gone. James told me that he had picked up Juli from school and decided to take a cab home because he had to get her dinner and help with her homework before we saw *Applause* that night. He realized he must have left it in the cab because he was in such a rush. He was *so* apologetic. I told him not to worry since: a) That morning I forgot my sweatpants at home and had to do a full cardio workout in tight jeans, b) That afternoon I walked a block down Ninth Avenue before I realized that I left my wallet sitting on the floor of The Coffee Pot on 49th Street, and c) That evening I left my Treo cell phone in studio D at Sirius. *I don't think Treo phones exist anymore! AND there's no more Studio D at SiriusXM!*

Anyway, I advise you all to put a little card inside your computer carrying case with your name and phone number in case it's lost. It worked for me! And Christine Pedi, my co-host on Sirius, advised me to always leave a cab only after you've leaned back in and looked everywhere… something she calls the "lean and look"… which I've re-titled the "Bend and Snap" in honor of *Legally Blonde*'s Orfeh. Speaking of which, I did a full video blog deconstructing her unbelievable riffs in *The Great American Trailer Park Musical*. She riffs down and then riffs *up* the same notes! It's like a staircase of riff… you must listen! Look it up on my website!

Okay… lots of Broadway this week! First of all, I hosted *Broadway Backwards*. It's a benefit for the New York Lesbian/Gay/Bisexual/Transgender Community Center where men sing women's songs and vice versa. But what makes it special is that the director, Bob Bartley, puts the songs in a context to make it about gay relationships. Tony Yazbeck from *A Chorus Line* and Aaron Lazar from *Les Miz* sang "A Boy Like That"/"I Have a Love," and it wasn't about them pretending to be women, it was about a gay man being warned by his brother not to be in love with the wrong guy. And "I Want It All" from *Baby* was brilliantly performed by Jose Llana and Gavin Creel as men who were eagerly attending a meeting of "Wanna-be Daddies" at the Center and Brooks Ashmanskas as a guy who was only at the meeting because his partner wanted a kid. Of course, by the end of the number, Brooks was belting "I Want It All!" à la Beth Fowler. It brought ye olde house down. I commented that people are always talking about how "gay" Broadway is, but there are *so* few actual gay stories that have been told on Broadway in musicals. Off the top of my head, I can think of *Falsettos*, *La Cage* and *Rent*. There are some more, but it seems as though Broadway is behind Hollywood in terms of gay stories. What's up with that? Or as the kids say, "what" up with that?

It was so great to see all different kinds of gay characters portrayed at *Broadway Backwards*... including Michelle Blakely and Jenn Colella doing *Into the Woods'* "Hello Little Girl" (the song where the Wolf first encounters Little Red Riding Hood) as a song between an aggressive and a reticent lesbian at the downtown bar Henrietta Hudson. Keeping with the theme of this column, I just realized I left my black sweater at that bar years ago when I was doing stand-up!

Lainie Kazan sang "The Gal That Got Away," and I wouldn't let *her* get away 'til I got a *Funny Girl* story out of her. I asked her about the first time she went on as Fanny. She said that she was a Ziegfeld girl and waited more than a year before Barbra finally missed a show. Lainie got the call in the afternoon and spent the rest of the day calling everybody she had on a special list... relatives, critics, publicists, etc. Lainie showed up at the theatre... and so did Barbra! She was suddenly well enough to go on. Hmm... The next day Lainie got a call from the stage manager. "You're on today... but you can't call an-y-body on your 'list'!" Lainie asked if she could at least call her mother. "Fine." said the stage manager. Lainie told us that she called her mother... who also had a copy of the list! And a star was born!

That night, James and I went to City Center to see the final dress rehearsal for *Applause* (after the laptop debacle). First of all, what I love is that Encores! gives free tickets to big groups of students. Excellent! Please get more teenagers to see and experience live theatre, not only so they can grow to love Broadway, but also so when I finally have a lead in a Broadway show, I'll have an audience show up (I'm nervous that my following will be too infirm by that late date). Before the show, Encores! artistic director Jack Viertel announced that Christine Ebersole had the flu and had missed the last few days of rehearsals (at Encores!, you only rehearse for a few days, so essentially she missed 75 percent of rehearsal!). He said that she didn't want an announcement made, but he assured her that the Metropolitan Opera does, so Encores! can, too! He said he was worried they were going to have to transpose the songs back down to Lauren Bacall's basso profundo keys, and I was about to exchange my free ticket, but he said they didn't. Phew. Well, cut to, Christine was amazing. I told James that I was obsessed with her performance because it was obvious she was sick, but only vocally. She was so *relaxed* onstage. Not pushing anything, not nervous before she had to sing, making us completely comfortable. *And* it was the first performance in front of an audience! Where was the panic? Where was the "I hope I land this joke and if I don't, it will confirm I have no talent"? Where was the "We haven't rehearsed this section enough so I'm going to make it obvious I'm uncomfortable"? Why doesn't she have all the demons that plague me constantly? It was so inspiring. She was completely at ease. *And* she did all the dances flawlessly! Had she been rehearsing via satellite? *This was pre-Skype. Brava!*

I also have to give a big shout-out to Mario Cantone, who gave a fantastic performance as Duane, Margo's hairdresser. The role could have been played with no nuance... simply as the sassy sidekick delivering every punchline straight out front, and I'm sure people would have laughed. However, I love that Mario played Duane as a warm person who happened to also have a great sense of humor. Here's the thing, in real life, people make jokes to their friends; in bad-acting world, they make jokes to the audience. So many sitcoms have people rattling off funny quips but, for some reason, no one around them acknowledges that the comments are funny... it makes me crazy! And, P.S., Mario also looked amazing and sang up a storm!

Later in the week, I interviewed Nathan Lane for my Sirius radio show. He told me that he grew up in Jersey and, shockingly, only did one musical in high school. It was *No, No, Nanette* for a neighboring all-girls school. I assumed it was like being an Equity Guest Artist that's jobbed in... and by "Equity Guest Artist," I mean "Catholic High School closeted Senior" and by "jobbed in" I mean "driven by your mother."

Nathan went to college for literally one day (FYI, Chip Zien went to law school for one day and dropped out) and left when they told him that, although he had a scholarship, he still owed more money. He went back to New Jersey and got his Equity card doing two local shows. One was a tribute to all things New Jersey called *Jerz* (seriously) and the other was called *One for Good Measure* and, '70s style, was a tribute to the metric system. It never caught on (the show or the system).

Once he moved to New York, he enrolled in a summer program at The Stella Adler Acting Institute. Unfortunately, Stella was not the teacher. Nathan did not disguise his disappointment when his teacher asked the class to do an exercise where they were to look out the window and describe what they saw. One student said, "I saw a homeless man... crying." One said, "I saw a secretary through a window as she was drinking coffee and daydreaming." Nathan said, "I saw $400 going down the drain." Acting is honesty.

His Broadway debut was with George C. Scott in *Present Laughter*. George was a notorious drinker and told Nathan that the producers bet him that he couldn't stay sober throughout the whole preview period. Well, opening night happened, and George proudly told Nathan that he won the bet and he could finally drink again. Then he was out the whole next week!

Nathan was also in the musical *Merlin* starring Doug Henning as Merlin and Chita Rivera as the Evil Queen. Nathan played her son, and if you were in New York in the '80s, you probably remember Chita on the commercial. There was a close-up of Chita where she said, "Wonder," but she Chita-ized it by saying "Won-dah!" Anybody?

Nathan said he remembered a trick where an actual tiger was in a cage, a sheet was put over the cage, and when the sheet was removed, there sat a sexy lady. Because he was backstage, Nathan could see how the trick was done: there were two tunnels. The lady crawled through one, and the tiger was tempted out of the other with horse meat (P.S., gross). Nathan asked the trainer, "What about when the tiger gets sick of horse meat eight times a week? Is the cage going to be revealed with the tiger still sitting there but part of a Theoni Aldredge sequined red costume hanging out of his mouth?"

I asked him about *Guys and Dolls*... specifically the song "Sue Me." He and Faith Prince argued in the song and at one point would hold one of the notes forever:

FAITH: The best years of my life I was a fool to give to yo-o-o-o-o-o-o-o-ou!
NATHAN (Simultaneously) All ri-i-i-i-i-i-i-iight already!"

He couldn't remember who came up with it, but he was very proud that Liza Minnelli came backstage and told them that she'd seen the show many times, and that particular moment was very original and fresh.

While he was doing *Laughter on the 23rd Floor*, Mike Nichols came backstage and told him that he was interested in him playing Zsa Zsa in the film *The Birdcage*. Nathan had already committed to playing Pseudolus in the Broadway revival of *A Funny Thing Happened on the Way To The Forum* and asked the producer, Scott Rudin, if the dates could be changed. Scott said no, and Nathan told Mike Nichols that he felt it would be unethical to leave them in a lurch. Every once in a while Mike Nichols would call Nathan's dressing room and say, "I've been seeing other actors, and I don't like them." Finally, Nathan told him, "You're Mike Nichols! Maybe you should call Scott..." Mike did, *Forum* got postponed, and *The Birdcage*, starring Nathan Lane, was on! Originally, it was supposed to be Robin Williams in Nathan's part and Steve Martin as Georges, but Steve Martin had to drop out. Robin's wife suggested that because Robin had just played Mrs. Doubtfire, perhaps he should take a non-drag role. I asked Nathan what Robin was like and Nathan said that even though Robin told him that sometimes it was hard to be the "straight man" while Nathan got to go to town, Robin was the most saintly, sweetest, giving and supportive co-star, and the whole thing was the happiest movie experience Nathan's ever had. *Nanu!*

Onto *The Producers*. Jerry Zaks was first attached to the show and mentioned the role of Max to Nathan. Then Nathan heard nothing... 'til he was on vacation at the Paris Ritz. He went down to the pool and saw only two other people... Mel Brooks and Anne Bancroft. Mel asked him to play Max Bialystock, and Nathan readily agreed. Martin Short was slated to play Leo, but because of his family in L.A, decided he couldn't be in New York for so long. At this point, Susan Stroman was directing/choreographing, and they did a reading with most of the leads who later did it on Broadway. Nathan said that when he first watched Gary Beach during rehearsal, he commented that Gary was going to win a Tony Award. Brava on the Jeanne Dixon psychic-ness! During intermission of the reading, investors offered Mel all of the capital needed to mount the show!

During the reading, Nathan didn't have a big 11 o'clock number, and before it came to Broadway, he was presented with one. It was a sentimental song that Nathan thinks was called "Farewell to Broadway." He told everyone that he felt if you were going to stop the show after "Springtime for Hitler," you really had to stop it or go straight to the courtroom scene. He felt that a sweet song wouldn't cut it... but in the middle of the song, there was a monologue about his anger towards Leo. Nathan told Mel that the monologue had the right theme for the song. Max was bitter and felt betrayed... and a new song was written called "Betrayed." And, let me verify that I played in the pit numerous times, and it did indeed stop the show!

Stay warm, everyone and I'll see ya next week!

Henchmen Aren't Forgotten

February 19, 2008

Wah. With only two months since *The Ritz* closed, I'm now dealing with the closing of another show. Yes, *Lend Me a Tenor* played its last performance. *And* I'm still coping with the final episode of *Crowned: The Mother of All Pageants* and the imminent ending of *Project Runway*. So much loss. I feel like Sally Field in the *Steel Magnolias* cemetery scene.

Anyhoo, last Sunday night I saw the Actors Fund performance of *Young Frankenstein*. First of all, it was delicious to hear an overture with a big, fat orchestra. The Hilton Theatre has a relatively large orchestra minimum (the size of the orchestra corresponds to the size of the theatre), but Mel Brooks wanted more strings (lots of the show is underscored like those old, gothic Hollywood movies), so the orchestra is actually *over* the minimum! Brava! That whole cast is so talented, it's mind-boggling.

First, I must give a shout out to Megan Mullally's high belt. I first met Megan when she played Marty in *Grease!* I was often in the pit for that show, and I'll never forget the story that circulated around the cast for years about the performance when one of Megan's understudies went on. In the opening scene, Marty takes out a pair of glasses and Frenchie comments, "Hey, Marty! Are those new glasses?" Marty responds, "Yeah! Do they make me look smarter?" Frenchie then sasses her with, "Nah. We can still see your face." Well, Megan's understudy forgot to pre-set the glasses in her pocket and spread the word surreptitiously. *No glasses!* Jessie Stone (who was playing Frenchie) whispered not to worry, she'd handle it. The big moment came, and Jessie said, trying to save the day, "Hey, Marty! I hear you're *going to get* new glasses!" We all expected to hear, "Yeah! Do you think they'll make me look smarter?" to which Jessie would reply, "Nah! We'll still be able to see your face." Instead, the understudy replied with a terse, "No." *Silence*. And I mean a lo-o-o-ong silence. Finally, Heather Stokes, who was playing Jan, desperately tried to help and said the next line she could think of. Unfortunately, it was a line from *three pages* later, which, more unfortunately, was dangerously near the cue line for "Summer Nights." Before anyone knew it, the cue was said, "Summer Nights" began… and Sonny hadn't even made his entrance yet! Carlos Lopez (Sonny) was forced to slink on during the opening vamp. Everyone was so obsessed with what happened that we decided to turn the understudy's acting method into a whole school to counteract the "Yes, and" approach to improve:

"Hey! Do you see the six-foot monster coming towards us?"
"No!"
Curtain.

Back to *Young Frankenstein*. Andrea Martin was fan-tas-tic as Frau Blucher. Just opening the door to the castle and glaring, she got an enormous laugh. I've been obsessed with her ever since my friends and I would gather on Friday nights to watch her on *SCTV*, and I feel that she's literally a comic genius. *And* she's so great in her big number, which is all centered around a chair à la "Mein Herr." While watching *Young Frankenstein*, I was also obsessed with Sutton. Not only her brilliant singing/comedy/high kicks, but this weird comic bit she did; both times after she gave the monster a shot in the butt, she would run around blowing on the spot of the "injection." Why would that make it feel better? Is it hot? I thought it was hilarious.

And it was great to finally see Chris Fitzgerald get to play a big comic role. I remember him auditioning to play The Cat in The Hat in Broadway's *Seussical* years ago... and not getting it! If anyone can give me an answer as to why that happened, use your superior brain power to find a cure for cancer. And finally, brava to Roger Bart, whom I first realized was a great comedian when I saw him in *Triumph of Love* singing "Henchmen are Forgotten." P.S. That song is so great. Why doesn't anyone sing it? In other words, why is "Henchmen are Forgotten" forgotten?

This week on Sirius Radio I interviewed Raúl Esparza. Turns out, he first wanted to be a lawyer (!) but then got into NYU's Tisch School of the Arts and got his acting degree. He wasn't the best student (a lot of not showing up for class) and was told by his acting teacher that, with his terrible attendance, how dare he think he can do a Pinter monologue?! Raúl told me that when he was in rehearsal recently for *The Homecoming* (by Pinter), he remembered that reprimand and finally felt vindicated.

After he graduated, he got two simultaneous offers: Randy Newman's musical *Faust* (starring Sherie Rene Scott) and a play at Chicago's Steppenwolf. He chose to move to Chicago and lived there for years, doing just straight plays. Naturally, I skipped over that part of his life and segued to his stint in the national tour of *Evita*. At first, his family forbad (the past tense of forbid) him from playing Che because they actually knew him and said he was crazy. Not Mandy Patinkin, the real Che! Raúl's family is from Cuba and his grandfather had always told them that Che was a decidedly not great guy. So, Raúl decided to not play him as a hero. He said that because Che is the narrator, the audience automatically trusts him, but what if the show ends and they think that *nobody* on the stage is trustworthy? I was looking at him slightly askew, and he admitted that the text of *Evita* didn't support his interpretation, but he still loved doing the show... and it got great reviews, so I guess brava on the re-interpretation! Because of those good reviews, he felt like he could actually come to New York, which had always terrified him.

The first Broadway musical he got was *The Rocky Horror Show*, where he played Riff Raff. The audiences were always yelling and throwing things (like a movie audience), but director Chris Ashley decided that only Tom Hewitt, who played Dr. Frank N Furter, could respond. Besides the loud, rude comments, the cast also had to deal with the audience throwing rice, pieces of toast and firing water pistols! I assume it was "fun" to constantly worry about being electrocuted (body mic + non-stop water = unintentional perm/death).

While he was doing *Rocky Horror*, he auditioned for *tick, tick... BOOM!* but wasn't particularly interested in doing it. He thought it was just going to be a literal biography and he wasn't looking forward to switching his Broadway production contract money for Off-Broadway wages. When he went to the audition, he did a monologue as Jonathan Larson and, in the middle, looked up to see Jonathan's parents looking back at him with tears in their eyes. He was so moved when he realized he could be playing an actual real person. He got home that night and listened to a CD of Jonathan singing music that would be in the show. Halfway through he had to stop because he was crying and then decided that he didn't care about the money or the cache of Broadway; he knew he had to do the show because it spoke to him. He felt the theme of the show was, "it's easy to stay an artist when you get praise, but what do you do when everybody tells you that you suck?" He said *tick, tick... BOOM!* is about weathering on no matter how bad things get... and being able to say, "This is who I am and who I'm meant to be." I think a lot of people forget that when Jonathan Larson died, *Rent* was nothing but a little Off-Broadway show about to open at a relatively small theatre. He always had all that talent inside of him that allowed him to write *Rent*, but he never knew in his lifetime how successful his work would eventually become. Like in *tick, tick... BOOM!*, he really was able to weather on without ever getting recognition and praise from the public.

Raúl was then set to play Zangara in the revival of *Assassins*, which was going to play the Music Box Theatre. However, after September 11th the show was canceled because of the theme. Unfortunately, Raúl had already quit *tick, tick... BOOM!*, so he had no gig. Out of the blue, The Roundabout called and offered him the role of the Emcee in *Cabaret*. He had seen it months before and coveted the role but never thought he'd ever get it. He loved doing it and felt that whole experience was about conquering fear and constantly growing. Sam Mendes, who directed it, told him that if he gave the same performance two nights in a row, he was failing himself. He needed to keep changing and re-inventing it. The hardest and scariest part for him was that, as the Emcee, he had to constantly improv with the audience. He eventually grew to love it... especially when he got to sass audience members who put their drinks onstage.

We then spoke about him playing Philip Sallon in *Taboo*. He said that the real Philip came to see the show on Broadway and afterwards Raúl asked him what he thought. Philip said, "Hmm... do you want me to be honest?" Raúl said, "Yes." (Mind you, Philip was still dressed in his "going to the theatre outfit": A Vivienne Westwood white pantsuit, Vivienne Westwood brooch and an afro made out of shaving cream. Seriously.) Philip shook his head, and afro, and said, "Frankly, darling... I'm not that camp." Interesting.

I dared to ask Raúl about the famous fight he had with Rosie O'Donnell during *Taboo*. He said that the rehearsal period was a very stressful time: the show was in the gossip columns a lot, Rosie was being sued by her former magazine, and he felt there wasn't a strong director taking control. During one rehearsal, it was apparent that Raúl was having a hard time making a quick change. Rosie asked him to exit the scene earlier so he'd have more time to change. Raúl said that he needed to be in the scene because his character needed the information being said onstage and wanted the costume change cut. The argument escalated until Rosie said that another actor could play his role just as well, and Raúl said that she was right! He stormed off the stage and out of the theatre.

Unfortunately, for those of you that think he had an incredibly sassy exit, please now visualize the outfit that he was storming off in: Henry VIII balloon pants, a cape, a crown and orb, scepter and elf shoes (that curled up at the end). So, first of all, (this was also confirmed by Jen Cody who was standing onstage with him at the time) his "storming off" was greatly de-sassified by the incredible difficulty of walking in elf shoes. Plus, right before he got offstage, his crown fell off and rolled on the stage. Everyone in the theatre was stunned by Raúl's departure and froze in silence — silence that was only broken by his dresser scurrying onstage, picking up said crown so it wouldn't get dirty and scurrying off. Charles Busch (who wrote the script) immediately tracked Raúl down and, over lunch with Polly Bergen (!), they both convinced Raúl to get back to work ASAP. Raúl said that he and Rosie get along great now and he thinks she was an excellent producer. As a matter of fact, he wishes she'd do another show because he feels she had amazing ideas that helped bring Broadway into the twenty-first century.

Finally, we discussed *Company*, and he informed me that he gets annoyed by the people who always say Bobby can't be acted because all the action happens around him. He feels that there's a lot to be done in observation. The audience is watching a character grow by how he reacts to the situations around him. He explained it by saying that sometimes, during a conversation, the one not speaking is the more interesting one. I was about to agree, but realized that I usually speak non-stop during conversations, so I wound up feeling insulted. Not cool, Raúl. He admitted he was terrified playing the piano during "Being Alive" and was so nervous the first time that his over-sweated hands kept slipping off the piano! Sondheim saw that first nerve-wracking performance and afterwards asked Raúl if he could look up while he was singing at the piano. Raúl flat out said no. "I can act, sing, do the correct lyrics or play the piano… but I can't do it all at the same time!" Brava on the honesty! Raúl thought Sondheim would hate what they did with the show, but he loved it. When they were discussing the theme of the show, he told Raúl that the show is about accepting exactly who you are, and the moment you do that, you become an adult. Hm… I guess that's why I'm a kid at heart?

The interview ended with Raúl saying that he's going to be doing a new musical, but when I asked him for any information, he was more silent than the *Taboo* cast after he stormed offstage in his elf shoes. (P.S. He also sang a song that got cut from *Company*, "Multitude of Amys," and I played for him.)

Another time, we were *Show Boat* and during intermission, the guy playing Ravenal went next door to the ice cream place for a cone. Suddenly, Act Two began and he was still there! The ladies playing Magnolia and Parthy were stuck onstage, frantically making up lines while waiting for him to appear. Jason knew where Ravenal was, but instead of running outside and getting him, he ran to the men's dressing room and breathlessly informed everybody, "Ravenal's still getting ice cream, Magnolia and Parthy are stuck onstage waiting for him… *and they're ad-libbing!* Come on!" Everyone ran to the wings to crouch down and watch Parthy repeat over and over again, "Well! He's just a river rat, that Ravenal. Yes, he is. A river rat." While Magnolia kept up a constant and low energy, "Oh, Mother. Mother, stop." It was the one time it would have been appropriate to use the *Grease* school of improv:

"Do you see Ravenal coming?"
"*No.*"

All right. I'm off to mourn the loss of *Lend Me a Tenor* and try to get another gig… one that allows me nights off for the new season of *Top Model* and *Top Chef*. Best of both worlds. Peace out!

Buckley, Brown, *Blonde* and Martin
February 25, 2008

This week began with an interview with Jason Robert Brown for the Broadway Artists Alliance. BAA, which is the sassy abbreviation, is a great program for kids where they come and train for a few days and then present a song or a monologue for casting agents and agent/managers. Jason talked about his first big job in New York which was at the WPA Theater music directing *New York Rock*, the musical Yoko Ono wrote. The music was as great as other songs she's written and recorded. Let me repeat: It was at the same level as other music she has put out in the world. 'Nuff said... and implied. It was a "challenging" experience for Jason and, as a thank you, the WPA offered to do something for him. He asked them to produce a revue of his songs, and that's how *Songs for a New World* got a production.

He knew Andréa Burns from the summer camp they had both gone to when they were tweens-teenagers (French Woods), and then he ran into her when he moved to NY. She started doing demos for him and that segued into her getting cast in his show. He told us that he also used to accompany Brooks Ashmanskas and Billy Porter because they'd both come in and sing at Don't Tell Mama, where Jason worked in the piano bar, and that's how Billy and Brooks wound up in the show. I love how Jason met all three of them in everyday life, and I feel it's a perfect illustration of how the people you start out with can wind up working with you in the big league. And by "big league," I mean "limited Off-Broadway run," but regardless, it's cool!

Songs for a New World was directed by Daisy Prince (whose voice I'm obsessed with on the *Follies* concert CD), and then her father (Hal Prince) asked Jason if he wanted to work on a new project. Actually, what he said was "Are you interested in working on a project I'm doing... because Sondheim dropped out?" That's right, Jason was asked to replace Stephen Sondheim! That's like someone asking, "Can you run the world? God's taking a break." Jason wrote the words and music to *Parade*... and won the Tony Award (before he was 30!). But the show wasn't a hit, and the experience left him depressed. He decided to write a really small show after *Parade* so that he'd have more control and wrote the brilliant *The Last Five Years*. I loved the show so much and ditto the CD. Not only must you listen to all the brilliant orchestrations which Jason did himself, but you also need to hear Sherie Rene Scott's excellent E flat on "A Summer in Ohio" (when she sings "...and Mrs. Jamie Wellerstein...") and Norbert's amazing hard R's in "Shiksa Goddess" ("...if your motherrr and your brotherrr had relations with each otherrrr"). Love 'em! Right now, Jason's working on *13*, which is a musical featuring all 13-year-olds. *And also starred a 13-year-old pre-pop stardom Ariana Grande!* Not only are the actors 13, but so is the band! Where was this show when I was hating seventh grade!?!! I would have auditioned with the Haftorah section I did for my Bar Mitzvah which was, no surprise, entirely belted and featured full vibrato. *L'Chaim.*

Tuesday night, James and I went to see Betty Buckley at Feinstein's. After the show, James and I went up to her hotel room to hang out, and Betty said that she was doing an all-Broadway request show on Saturday. What happens is people show up, write down the name of a song that Betty has sung on Broadway, and she'll sing it. I brazenly started rifling through her music charts and began hyperventilating when I saw the music to "Writing on the Wall" from *Drood*. She knew her only options were to get me oxygen or ask me to be a guest pianist at the show, and she chose the latter. We came back for the Saturday show, and Betty was a little stressed because she had done a ton of shows at Feinstein's and then flew to Texas to do a concert the night before! Betty had gotten around three hours of sleep and, before she went on, told me that I should pray her voice holds out. Turns out, she sounded more amazing than ever! She was belting so high I wound up being incredibly impressed with my praying skills. I guess my Haftorah paid off.

Someone (thankfully) requested "Writing on the Wall," and I shot up from my seat and walked onstage. When Betty began, it felt surreal to me. I've been listening to the recording of Betty singing this song obsessively since college... and here I was, onstage, actually playing it for her. It was *thrilling*! Then I stayed onstage and we wound up duetting on "Love Song" from *Pippin*... which was also surreal for me because I saw Betty play the role of Catherine when I was seven! Every song Betty did was prefaced with a hilarious, self-effacing story (including Betty's two attempts to get the role of Genevieve in *The Baker's Wife*... both failures), and I decided that she *must* do this show in New York at a bigger venue. It's a delicious, mega-dose of Broadway with a brilliant star. *Betty asked me to do the entire show with her and we wound up doing "Broadway By Request" all over the country for the next few years... and spent an entire month at Feinstein's!* The only devastating part was one request someone shouted out from the audience. I was not devastated by the breaking of the fourth wall, but because the request was for the song "Memories." Let me be clear: *there is no Broadway song called 'Memories'!"* That makes me crazy! It's called "Mem'ry." And, by the way, so-called Barbra fans, there's no Barbra song called "Memories" either. It's called "The Way We Were." 'Memories' is the first word she sings, not the title. That's like me calling Frederik's first song in *A Little Night Music* "Now." Oh, it is called that? All right then, what about "Soon"? Huh. "Later"? And cut.

This week I also had the thrill of interviewing Andrea Martin on my Sirius radio show, and, of course, she was hilarious. She told me that her childhood inspiration to become a performer was Chita Rivera. Her parents had a condo in San Juan, and they would go see Chita perform, and Andrea (who's Armenian) thought that if Chita could make it and not be blonde and all-American looking, then so could she. Right after Andrea moved to New York in her early twenties, she got her Equity card playing Lucy in the Canadian tour of *You're a Good Man, Charlie Brown* (FYI, Judy Kaye played the role in the American tour). Andrea stayed in Canada and decided to try out for the Toronto production of *Godspell*. She thought she was right for it because, although she didn't consider herself a great singer or even actress, she knew the main requirement for the show was personality. Everyone who was auditioning was able to see everybody else because they were in a theater. Finally, Andrea was called to the stage and belted out "Somebody," a song from *Celebration* that's basically about being a sex kitten. After 20 measures she got the dreaded "thank you" and was not asked to stay for the callback. She said that perhaps she tried too hard... and by "perhaps," she admits she was pushing more than a mother whose baby has crowned.

After her humiliation, Andrea saw a young woman get onstage who wore pigtails and skipped around the stage singing "Zip A Dee Doo Dah." She was so adorable that everyone in the theater gave her a standing ovataion. Andrea left the theater devastated, feeling that if she couldn't get *Godspell*, she had no hope of ever getting a show. She started a daily depressive regimen of eating large quantities of donuts and then going to the gym to work it off and sit in the steam room. One day, while literally in the steam room, she got paged for a phone call. It was Eugene Levy, who had recently starred opposite her in the film *Cannibal Girls* (seriously... directed by Ivan Reitman). He said that the woman that was cast to sing "Day By Day" was being let go and that there was going to be a big party that night. He told Andrea to show up and be as funny as she could be. She did... and got the gig. And listen to who else was in that cast: Eugene Levy, Martin Short, Paul Shaffer as music director and Victor Garber as Jesus. And, of course, that girl with the pigtails turned out to be Gilda Radner! Can you imagine all that brilliance in one cast?

Andrea then joined Toronto Second City after a lot of the first cast left to start *Saturday Night Live*. Second City then decided to create a Canadian version of *SNL* and thus began *SCTV*. I grew up watching that show every Friday night. I, of course, asked her about the origin of some of her characters. She said that Edith Prickley was developed at the Second City improv show. Cast members would bring in old clothes to be used to create on-the-spot characters. Andrea was told by the audience to be a mother of a delinquent. She put on Catherine O'Hara's mother's leopard coat and hat, walked in and said, "Hello, Dear! I'm..." Catherine said, "Mrs. Prickley?" And Andrea said, "That's right, dear. Edith Prickley."

Andrea based Libby Wolfson on a real talk-show host in Canada who was always discussing women's issues. I'm obsessed with the episode where Libby stars in the feminist musical *I'm Getting My Own Head, Screwing It on Right, and No Guy's Gonna Tell Me That It Ain't!* Libby is completely insecure and always smelling her armpits asking, "Is there a cat in here? I'm smelling some male cat urination." Then, she'll smell her hands and say, "No. You know what, it's Tabouli. Serves me right for eating with my fingers."

Andrea didn't get to Broadway until the early '90s with *My Favorite Year* and remembers giving an *awful* audition initially and asking to come back a second time and getting the part. She said the same thing happened with the *Hedwig* movie. She really wanted to play Hedwig's agent, Phyllis Stein. She read with John Cameron Mitchell (who wrote and directed it) and told him in the middle of the audition that she knew she wasn't nailing it. She asked him if she could go back to L.A, work with her acting coach and fly back on her own dime to try one more time in a week. He said yes, and she got it! She wants actors out there to do that if they feel they're not performing at their best. Take control of the situation. But she also wanted to caution that she's asked casting people if she can come back and then been equally terrible, so it doesn't always work out!

My Favorite Year closed in the winter and, months later when she was in L.A., Andrea found out she was nominated for a Tony! She didn't really know anything about the Tony Awards and hadn't been thinking about it. Now, of course, she says she does non-stop obsessing about the word counts in her bios to make sure she can get every one of her awards listed.

Many people don't realize that she was the original Cat in the Hat during the workshops of *Seussical*. When it came time to take it to Broadway, she was incredibly torn because she had to choose between starring in a new musical or missing her son's High School senior year in California. Of course, she wanted to be the actual star of a show (instead of a sidekick) and make some delicious money, but she also knew there would only be one senior year he'd ever have and she'd miss all of his sports games, jazz ensemble concert, prom etc. She was torn until she spoke to her agent Richie Jackson who asked her, "Would you rather be remembered as a good Cat in the Hat or a good mother?" Brava! Even though she loved that show, and especially its score, she turned down the role and told us she never regretted the decision. Brava motherhood and peace out 'til next week!

Lane and Len
March 3, 2008

February 28th was my birthday so I decided to have a little get-together on Saturday night. Friday night at 11 PM, my buzzer sounded. Juli had gone to bed two hours before so I tiptoed through the dark living room to the intercom. "Hello?" I whispered. "Seth Rudetsky!" I heard from downstairs. "It's Norm Lewis! Happy Birthday!" I buzzed him and confronted him on the staircase, me in my pajamas, him covered in snow. "Uh… the party is tomorrow." Norm claimed his email said it was tonight which doesn't make much sense since I sent out the exact same one to everyone. I could have told him that he was right and invited him in to sit with me in a depressing, dark living room and talk nonsense… but I already saw Pinter's *The Homecoming* and had no intention of re-creating it in my own apartment. After Norm left, I quickly checked my email and only had one; it was from Cheyenne Jackson saying, "Sorry I missed your party last night." What is it with Broadway stars and the calendar!?

Anyhoo, the next night wound up being a great little soiree, and I felt so highfalutin' because I ordered a big plate of sushi. Around 11, James asked if I would order a pizza. He's from Texas and did not ever grow into enjoying the big city taste of sushi. I rolled my eyes and asked what I was gonna do with all the leftover pieces of pizza, and he assured me we could eat it for dinner the next night. Cut to, I ordered the pizza begrudgingly… and it was gone in two minutes flat. *And* I'm writing this column surrounded by an almost full platter of negihamachi and salmon skin rolls. Turns out, Broadway don't go for highfalutin'!

That last story brings me to last week's *Chatterbox*. Around two weeks ago, I did a performance of *Celebrity Autobiography* with Matthew Broderick and asked him to do the *Chatterbox*. He was very sweet and agreed readily. He told me to check in beforehand to double confirm. Of course, I waited 'til the night before and left a perfunctory message on his assistant's voice mail. She called me back in a panic. Turns out, Matthew had to go to L.A. at the last minute and couldn't make it back to N.Y. to do my show. Ah! It was sold out and I didn't want BC/EFA to lose out on all that money. I had to get a replacement whom the crowd would adore just as much. I thought of *The Producers* and remembered how much fun I had with Nathan Lane at my Sirius interview recently. I called his assistant, Andrea, and she told me that he's doing a reading all day long and starring in *November* at night. In other words, he's too busy/tired to do anything extracurricular. She said she'd ask him anyway, and, 20 minutes later, called me back in shock and said, "He'll do it!" How amazing is that!?! I showed up at Don't Tell Mama, and Nathan immediately said, "I don't wanna talk about the stuff we did before. Ask me other stuff." Uh-oh. I'm old school. I thought the show was frozen. I'm used to going through a celeb's career from start to finish, but he said we should do it differently… and go backwards. Didn't he know *Merrily We Roll Along* flopped? I was panicked… but it wound up being an amazing/hilarious show.

First, we talked about the Marc Shaiman/Scott Wittman/Terrence McNally musical *Catch Me If You Can*, which is the reading he's doing right now. He said he's done so many readings of it that he now feels like he's doing a revival! He's playing the Tom Hanks character from the movie and thinks the show's gonna be great. *Of course, Norbert Leo Butz wound up playing the role because when the show finally came to Broadway, Nathan was playing Gomez Addams in THE ADDAMS FAMILY. Both shows weren't loved critically, but THE ADDAMS FAMILY ran much longer than CATCH ME IF YOU CAN so Nathan certainly made the right choice financially!*

Here's where the interview got "real." At one point, I had my cell phone onstage to check the time, and I said, "Do you want to see a picture of my boyfriend James?" Well, that was enough to send Nathan on a five-minute tear about how every week in my Playbill.com column I have to mention "my boyfriend James this" and "my boyfriend James that" and how I always pepper it with "his daughter Juli." Nathan made it clear; *Yes, I got it! You have a boyfriend*! Hmph. I wanted to tell him that he was exaggerating and that no one else is bothered by it until I saw the entire audience nodding in unison. Then he had the nerve to ask if James is the first boyfriend I've ever had. *Well*! I will now explain myself and say sometimes James comes up as part of a story I'm telling, and I didn't want new readers to look at it and say, "Who is this random James person that Seth is talking about?" Hence the moniker, "my boyfriend James." But I know that when the public speaks to you (or in this case, yells at you), you must listen. So from now on I will simply write James' name without a precursor or I shall simply list him as my BF.

After his hiliarious tirade, Nathan wound up telling me a Doug Henning debacle that he hadn't told me before. They both did the musical *Merlin* back in the '80s, and one night Doug was regaling him with magic-gone-awry stories. One New Year's Eve, Doug was doing a Vegas show and the final act was turning his wife into a tiger. He finished the trick, but when he looked at the chain attached to the tiger, he noticed it was broken! Doug said that the rest happened in slow motion. The tiger started prowling towards the audience, who then began screaming. Also, since it was a New Year's Eve show, it was packed with celebrities. This took place in the '70s, so I'm imagining an audience filled with terrified Loni Andersons, Bonnie Franklins and Gabe Kaplans. Doug grabbed onto the tiger's chain and started yanking the tiger backwards. The tiger turned and started to advance on Doug. Suddenly, the tiger leapt on top of him... and licked his face. I, of course, thought that was adorable, 'til Nathan explained that tigers aren't licking to be affectionate... they use their tongue to clean their food before they eat it. The tiger then put Doug Henning's *entire* head inside his mouth!!!!! Doug was so petrified that he fainted. It could have been the end, *but* because what the tiger considered prey suddenly seemed so limp and odd, it let go of his head. Doug told Nathan that the next thing he remembers is waking up in his dressing with Bob Hope standing above him. And what did Bob say? "Doug! That's the best finale I've ever seen!"

Also this week, I interviewed Len Cariou on my Sirius radio show. Len is from Canada and in 1969 made his Broadway starring debut in Henry the Fifth (*King Henry V*)... or as he called it, show biz-style, "Hank Cinq." He said that, right before he opened in that show, he was called in to audition for *Applause* to play Lauren Bacall's love interest. He was a fan of her work... which is weird because usually actors can be competitive if they both have the same vocal range. Regardless, he got the role of Bill Sampson and remembers that, when they did the gypsy run-thru of *Applause*, a nice man with glasses perched on his head approached Len after the show and said, "I think you're one of the best leading men I've ever seen in my life." Ron Field, the choreographer, ran over to Len and told him who the pleasant gentleman was: Hal Prince!!!

That compliment would pay off later, right after *Applause*, when Len became the associate artistic director at The Guthrie Theater in Minneapolis. While he was there, that pleasant gentleman called him and asked him to audition for *A Little Night Music*. Len read the script (no music or lyrics yet), loved it and wanted the part of Frederik... but they asked him to audition for Carl-Magnus. Even though Len didn't want that part, he was dying for a chance to sing for Sondheim and Prince. He flew to New York and auditioned, but he remembers that he was so nervous he had to hold onto the upright piano that was onstage to stop from shaking! Still, it went well, and Hal gave him an updated script to take home and look over. This time, the script still didn't have any music attached, but now it had lyrics. Len thought it was now even more brilliant, and when Hal called a day later, told him so. Before Len had a chance to make a pitch to play Frederik, Hal said, "I'm glad you like it. We want you to play Frederik!" Brava! Frederik was supposed to be in his mid-fifties, and Len was only 34, but they figured that, as long as he was fairly older than his wife, it would work.

Len went back to the Guthrie and told the artistic director the good news. Unfortunately, he reminded Len that he was supposed to star as Oedipus in rep when rehearsals for *A Little Night Music* began. Len realized it wouldn't be right to leave the Guthrie for a Broadway show because he was the associate artistic director. He called Hal who was vacationing in Majorca (huh?) and told him that he had to pass. Hal was in shock. Not because he was angry, but because he couldn't believe how much integrity Len had. A month later Len's agent called, asked him if he was sitting down and said that *Night Music* had moved all of their dates later so that Len could do the show! Talk about being wanted! Len approached the head of the Guthrie and asked if he could perform his rep shows in a clump each week so he could rehearse in New York but come back to the Guthrie to do *Oedipus*, and the Guthrie said yes. So, Len would do a *Oedipus* matinee on Sunday, fly back to New York to rehearse *Night Music* Monday, Tuesday, Wednesday, fly back Wednesday night and perform, fly back to rehearse Thursday morning, rehearse again Friday, Saturday and fly back to perform Saturday night and Sunday. Sorry, Elaine Stritch, that trumps your train trips to Connecticut. Len Cariou is "at liberty"!

After *Night Music,* Len went back to Canada and became the artistic director of the Manitoba Theater Center (the original MTC, as he likes to say) and while he was there, Hal told him that Sondheim had written a show for him! Len was thrilled... 'til he read the script. He thought *Sweeney Todd* was *really* bizarre. He read it again, and although he couldn't figure out how they were going to do all the killings, etc., he knew that if the score was very romantic, it could work. It obviously did and Len wound up winning the Tony Award! I asked him if he ever missed a show when he played Sweeney Todd, and he said an emphatic "No." I asked why and he said, "It was my part." He's old school! My favorite Len story was told to me by his former voice teacher, Paul Gavert. During previews, Hal asked the sound designer to turn down Len's body mic because he sounded so much louder than the other singers onstage. Hal was told that Len was the only one *not* wearing a body mic! Brava!

All right, I have tons to tell you about the *Legally Blonde* reality show on MTV but the network told me I can't reveal anything until the episodes start airing, so my trap is now officially shut. But it's soon going to be wide open, so stay tuned!

Freeman, Burgess and Hitting the *Heights*
March 10, 2008

Ossining matters. No, literally, that's the name of the organization: "Ossining Matters." It raises money for the town of Ossining's school district and I'm here playing a fundraising concert with Kerry Butler. She's so much fun to play piano for because she's super-nice, super-funny, always sounds great *and* I get to sing a duet from *Bat Boy* with her! I love that show so much. I saw it four times... tying with *In the Heights*, which I saw for the fourth time last week. *P.S. Final IN THE HEIGHTS tally: 8 times!* I feel like that show is my child. I went to see the *In the Heights* workshop around two years ago because my good friend Andréa Burns was in it and I flipped out. Then, I saw the Off-Broadway run twice last year and finally, last Friday night, I got to see it on Broadway!

As soon as the opening song began, I literally had tears in my eyes because I was so happy and proud of everybody in it. Watching *In the Heights* made me feel like I did when I was a kid obsessed with Broadway. Lin-Manuel Miranda wrote the show and also stars in it, and I was so impressed by his performance because, two years later, it's still so natural, real and not pushed. I was also loving watching him because I knew he was living his dream. He started writing this show in college, and now it's on Broadway!! What I love about *In the Heights* is that there are lots of shows that have really talented casts, but sometimes they're doing material that doesn't fully show them off. *In the Heights* not only has an amazing cast but they're all given material that makes each one look amazing. And the ensemble is given choreography by Andy Blankenbuehler that is so creative but doesn't take me, as an audience member, out of the moment. A lot of times I see something on Broadway that's innovative, but I feel a sense of "Aren't we amazing," and I stop focusing on the stage and start thinking about the choreographer making it up thinking, "I'm so cool," and the cast learning it for the first time high-fiving each other saying, "Nobody's ever seen this before," and the stage managers giving notes about it so it remains the *amazing* moment everyone's talking about... and by the time I finish my timeline, it's intermission. But not *In the Heights*. It's joyous and thrilling and I want it to run forever. *Sadly, it didn't. But it won the Best Musical Tony Award and I got to be in the audience at the closing night years later. Still fantastic!*

This week I interviewed Jonathan Freeman on my Sirius radio show. First of all, the coolest thing is that, when he was a kid, he was obsessed with Disney villains and always wanted to be one... and he wound up originating the role of the voice of Jafar in the movie *Aladdin*! And when *I* was a kid, I always wanted to be a Broadway star, and when I became an adult I... got to meet some. *P.S. He not only originated Jafar in the movie, he got to originate the same role in the Broadway show, which opened in 2014!*

Jonathan did a lot of performing as a child when he lived in Cleveland, but never the cute kid parts because, as he told me drily, "When I was 10, I was 40." He said that the character he's playing now in *The Little Mermaid* is the exact same one he played in *Snow White* when he was ten! The only difference is the name. Now: Grimsby, then: Sir Casper Cupcake. Which reminds me of what Bebe Neuwirth told me recently in an interview. When she turned 40, she said, "Finally. I'm the age I was always meant to be."

In college Jonathan was told he wouldn't work much until he got older because he was such a character actor, but he ignored that and "starved himself" so he could stay really skinny and play juveniles. He did *George Washington Slept Here* with Jimmy Coco, Marilyn Cooper and Dodie Goodman. Talk about people who needed to turn 40! And speaking of Dodie, I remembered that she played Miss Lynch for a while when I did *Grease!* in the '90s. I just googled her and saw that she was born in 1915! Zoinks! I hope I'm sassy enough to get a gig when I'm 80... Brava, Dodie!

I asked Jonathan who else started out with him in New York and he said he became friends with Nathan Lane because they were always auditioning for commercials at the same time. Those were the days when big celebrities didn't do commercials, so Jonathan remembers auditioning for five a day. He and Nathan did a commercial together where they played soldiers and Nathan's character has Sara Lee cake sent to him from home. Yet, the last shot was Jonathan eating the cake. Jonathan asked why him and not Nathan and was told, "You have a cake-eating face." Is that a special skill? "Good with children, driver's license, cake-eating face, easily plays 40 years old."

His first Broadway musical was *Platinum*, which I saw when I was kid. First of all, I just IBDB'd it and discovered that it ran for one month. I can't believe my school happened to get tickets within that little window of time... *and* I don't understand who in my school chose it. It seems a bit mature for Long Island young'uns. Although, this *was* the late '70s when there weren't Broadway shows created specifically for school groups, so probably the choices were *Platinum*, *Oh! Calcutta!* and *The Best Little Whorehouse in Texas*. No matter what, I was bound to go home with several boundaries broken. I remembered that there was a nude hot-tub scene and Jonathan said that it was a completely see-through Lucite hot tub and while Richard Cox was in it, Jonathan and other cast members would go downstairs, stand underneath it and tap and wave at him while Richard was playing the scene. I'm not saying that Jonathan's unprofessionalism closed the show, but need I remind you again how long it ran.

The first time I remember seeing Jonathan on Broadway was in *She Loves Me*. It was a small role (the Headwaiter), so naturally he had six callbacks. What!?! The final one was a work session, which, incidentally, was the first time he had heard that phrase. Let's think about all the new annoying Broadway phrases that have cropped up since the '80s: a) "Track," as in "whose track are you covering?" Remember when they were called "roles"?; b) "Jukebox musical." Remember when they were called "revues"?; c) "American Airlines Theater," etc. Remember when it wasn't awkward to say the name of a theatre?

Anyhoo, Jonathan got the gig and during rehearsals, they wanted him to not only do the role, but to be in some group numbers later on. He felt that doing ensemble in other numbers would diminish the impact of the restaurant scene because, even if they costumed him differently, some of the audience would recognize him and wonder if it was supposed to be the waiter coming on again to shop in the parfumerie, etc. so he only wound up appearing in the one scene. Apparently his instincts were right, because his 20 minutes onstage earned him a Tony nomination! He remembered that when Marilyn Cooper won the Tony for *Woman of the Year* someone said, "Wow. Aren't you only onstage for thirteen minutes?" and she said, "Twelve." Brava!

Jonathan told me about his audition for the *Aladdin* movie. What's bizarre about animation auditions is that, when you walk in the room, everyone auditioning you has their eyes covered because they don't want the way you look in real life to influence them. He said that what helped his audition was that he asked for a drawing of Jafar before he came in, and that's how he found his voice. His initial contract only offered him around four days, so if Disney didn't like him, they could can him ASAP. Ouch. "You got the gig! And by 'getting the gig,' I mean we're offering you a contract shorter than the run of *Platinum*."

We then talked about the revival of *42nd Street* and he said that he doesn't like the term "revival" and wants to instead call it a "new production." I glared, and he reminded me that no one says that they're doing a revival of *Hamlet*. Hmph. *Hamlet* is from the 1600s. If *42nd Street* is revived in the year 2588, I'll then allow it to be called a "new production."

Jonathan was telling me about his audition for *The Little Mermaid* and I was outraged that he even had to audition. He told me a) he was, too and b) he's the oldest person involved, not only amongst the actors, but in all aspects of the production! He said he's older than the cast, the director and the producer. And Dodie Goodman.

Speaking of *The Little Mermaid*, I had Tituss Burgess (who plays the crab) on the *Chatterbox* this week. He said he first came to New York in the late '90s and stayed with a friend in Queens. Unfortunately, he got on the N train instead of the R and exited at the wrong stop in Queens. He didn't have a cell phone, was too scared to ask anybody for directions and didn't write down the address of where the person lived! I was in shock. How can you possibly find a random apartment in an entire borough? He said he decided to walk up and down different streets in Queens until he recognized the apartment building. I could walk up and down the Upper West Side and probably not recognize my own apartment building. Actually, he shockingly found it by 3 AM.

His first Broadway gig was in *Good Vibrations*. I asked him about the out-of-town tryout. He said, "Out of town? We were in Poughkeepsie." Doesn't that sound like an old Vaudeville punchline? After the Poughkeepsie run (seriously!), but before Broadway, he got cast in the La Jolla production of *Jersey Boys*. He said he was originally supposed to be Bob Crewe, but then they wanted to keep it historically accurate and keep the character white. I asked Tituss about the crazy high note he does in "Oh, What a Night," and he said that, in rehearsal for that number, he was on the side of the stage with the rest of the cast, and he was pretending to smoke a cigarette. Des McAnuff walked over, and Tituss thought he was in trouble. Des said, "Wouldn't it be funny if Tituss came onstage and offered up a joint?" The music director, Ron Melrose, asked if Tituss could sing something sassy while he did it, and that's how Tituss got his solo. Hmph. Whenever I joke around offstage, I always get a stern look from the ASM and then hear a loud "focus up" from the stage manager. Where's my high solo? Come to think of it, where's my high range? I think my money note has topped at middle C.

Tituss left *Jersey Boys* after just a few weeks in La Jolla to do *Good Vibrations*, and I asked if the producers had a fit. Turns out, they were the same producers! Speaking of *Good Vibrations*, does anyone remember the beach ball finale? The cast would hit them all over the stage as well as into the audience. I remember writing the Easter Bonnet Competition opening a few years ago, and there was a section in rhyme, talking about new shows: "*Good Vibrations* is such fun!/You'll have a ball, or be hit by one."

When he tried out for *The Little Mermaid*, Tituss sang *Under the Sea* fairly straight, but on the first day of rehearsal they had a read-thru. It was the whole cast, the producers, the music team with composer Alan Menken, etc... The cast was about to read through the script and were told that they could sing if they knew the song. Tituss decided that he wanted to use that moment to show everybody how he wanted to sing the song, AKA with some added notes and sass. In the film version, it's sung straight and there are a lot of camera cuts that sass everything up. Tituss felt that since there's no camera to cut away to shots, he could add that same excitement with his interpretation. He sang it, reworking some melodies on the spot and taking other things up the octave. When he finished, he was nervous he'd be busted for changing the way it's always been done, but everybody applauded. Yay! He got permission to sing it his way! Now, however, it's one of those "be careful what you wish for" things because every night before the number he's a nervous wreck because it's so difficult to sing. What's easy in a read-thru ain't so easy eight times a week!

I've been doing the *Legally Blonde* reality show this whole week and am still under a gag order from MTV, but I will tell you some of the devastating things that have happened during the filming. First, as a preface, James (BF) was talking to Juli about *Project Runway* and was concerned about her seeing how skinny the models were. He asked her if she wanted to grow up to be thin and she said, "No." Ah. Our work is done. Then she continued. "I want to be like you and Seth." Ouch. Our work*out* is beginning.

At the beginning of the week, I was working with the *Legally Blonde* girls who are all super-young. I made some joke about having a lot of experience on Broadway. "Believe me, a lot happens by the time you're 60." One of them looked at me and said sweetly, "Aw! You're not 60." The line reading wasn't like "You're *nowhere* near 60." It was, "Don't say you're 60 until you get there... in three years." Later on, I was talking to casting director Bernie Telsey who suddenly stared at me and said. "Hmm... have you ever been in for *Hairspray*?" I thought to myself, "Well, I'm a *little* long in the tooth for one of the teen 'nicest kids in town,' but I can still shake it." He interrupted my reverie with a cold glass of water entitled "...for the role of Wilbur." What the-! If you don't know, that's Tracy Turnblad's father. According to Wikipedia, Dick Latessa was 73 when he played the part! Well, at least Bernie doesn't think I'm 60. He thinks I have the maturity of a 73-year-old. Perhaps Dodie Goodman and I could do *The Gin Game*.

Peace out everybody, and I'll write next week... after I attend my annual AARP convention.

(Almost) Sailing On
March 18, 2008

James (BF), Juli (his daughter) and my mom (neurotic) are all on the Rosie O'Donnell R Family Vacations cruise (for gay parents, their families and friends, *rfamilyvacations.com*). I'm not there because I'm still filming the MTV *Legally Blonde* reality series 'til Tuesday. The production company is kindly flying me out that afternoon to Puerto Vallarta where I'll meet up with their Holland America ship.

The first night on the boat is always a show called *Broadway Belters* and it was a fabulous lineup. It's so weird putting it all together and then having the show happen while I wasn't there. Kevin Chamberlin sang "Solla Sollew" from *Seussical* (beautiful song), Shoshana Bean sang "The Wizard and I" into "Defying Gravity" (brava on the vocal chops), Julia Murney and Gavin Creel sang the fabulous *Baby* duet "What Could Be Better"…

I'm so sorry I missed the show! The only "good" news is that apparently the seas were rough, and I would not want a repeat of what happened in Alaska in 2006. Actually, why don't I set the record straight and tell everybody what really did happen in Alaska because, contrary to what Cyndi Lauper says, I did not throw up!

It was the week of the '06 summer cruise and the night of the comedy showcase. I was the host; there were three comics, and Julia Murney was going to end the evening singing the hilarious Andrew Lippa *Wild Party* song (first sung brilliantly by Alix Korey) "Old Fashioned (Lesbian) Love Story." Around a half hour before the show, the boat started rocking. I am easily nauseated (see my reaction to *From Justin to Kelly*) and was a nervous wreck. Julia came up to me at "places" and said that people were already leaving their seats to go back to their rooms because the rocking is making everybody sick/terrified. She said we should just cut the last song. But I said, "No, no, no (tip o' the hat to Amy Winehouse), I'm seeing this show through to the end." I did some stand-up (and by "some," I mean the same jokes I've been hauling out for ten years) and went backstage while the first comic performed. Well, if you don't know, let me tell you that a good way to not be seasick is to look at the horizon. Unfortunately, the backstage not only had no view of the horizon, it had no windows! There was no way to get a sense of where you were. The only way I could feel not disgusting was to lie completely down. So, that became my routine: intro a comic and then immediately run backstage to lie down. I would get up 30 seconds before I had to come back onstage to minimize nausea. Cut to the end of the show, I stood up because I was told that the last comic was about to end, but she wound up going on for a few more minutes. Uh-oh! No horizon. I really began to feel sick. But I decided that I had made it this far and I was determined to hear Julia belt the end of that song! I came out onstage and introduced Julia. She started making her way up from the audience, and I sat down at the piano. Suddenly, I felt my stomach start contracting. I knew I wasn't pregnant… not at my age (See: Bernie Telsey's casting idea for me in last week's column. Hint: a 73-year-old). I knew I was about to throw up. I thought to myself, "Not only am I about to throw up onstage… but the show is being *videotaped*." That recorded image is something I would find hilarious to play on a loop… if it was someone else! I didn't want anyone to have embarrassing footage of *me* to deconstruct! I knew I had to get the H offstage and lay down ASAP. I fled offstage before my stomach came up and immediately lay completely flat offstage. My stomach calmed down as I lay in an exhausted heap. Unfortunately, this all happened while Julia was approaching the stage, and she didn't see any of it. So, she essentially went center stage, adjusted her mic, nodded to the piano and suddenly saw there was no one sitting on the piano bench. It was like the ending of *Phantom*, where he's suddenly not in the seat he just sat down in... except I didn't leave a mask behind. Instead, I left behind a knocked-over microphone stand. Yes, not only wasn't I there, but I had knocked my boom microphone down in my haste to make it offstage, which I barely did. So all Julia saw was a microphone stand awkwardly clunked on its side and, off to the side, the bottom half of my legs sticking out from the wings, Wicked Witch of the East-style. AKA Nessa Rose. Hm... Seth-a Rose? Julia paused, turned out front and said simply, "That's the show," and the curtain came down. The next thing I know I'm at the breakfast buffet and everybody was telling me that Cyndi Lauper said I was a wuss for throwing up during the storm! Well! I see *her* "True Colors." I may be a wuss, Madame, but I most certainly did not throw up! I simply crawled offstage in a blind panic leaving a feed-backing microphone in my wake.

Anyhoo, I can't wait to fly to Puerto Vallarta and meet up with everybody on the cruise. I'm doing a show with my comedy partner Jack Plotnick, a cabaret with Gavin Creel, an onboard *Chatterbox* with Julia Murney and Shoshana Bean and then hosting the '70s show on the final night!

This week I had the pleasure of interviewing the majorly prolific and tuneful Alan Menken. Turns out, he didn't grow up wanting to be a theatre composer. He graduated from NYU as a musicologist major (please wake up after that last boring phrase) and wanted to either be a "serious" composer or a singer/songwriting pop star. To appease his parents and make it look like he was doing something for his career, he joined the BMI workshop where he met Maury Yeston (who later wrote *Nine* and *Titanic*). Maury recommended Alan to Howard Ashman, who was writing a musical version of *God Bless You, Mr. Rosewater*. Even though Alan was a composer/lyricist at the time, he joined up with Howard who was writing the lyrics, book and directing. The show ultimately didn't run very long. One of the problems with the show was that it had a 14-person cast and was too expensive to run Off-Broadway. Howard told Alan that he always wanted to write a musical version of the movie *The Little Shop of Horrors*, and this time they would use a smaller cast (nine people).

Alan was giving me some scoop on how the show was written and I love finding out things that seem so obvious now that didn't begin that way. For instance, when they were first writing the show, the music was very Kurt Weill/Brechtian à la *Surabya Johnny*. They played the score for people, and people said, Sura-Bye-a. Ouch! That was a headache-y pun/joke even for me! My point is, no one was interested until Howard told Alan that they should make this show the dark side of *Grease*. Alan said that Howard thought it would work if they told this macabre story through bubble gum rock 'n roll. Unfortunately, he wasn't right... he was completely correct! By the way, that's a film/advertising cliché that drives me crazy. The hacky "I don't like it... I *love* it!" I'm always yelling at my TV, "You're lying. You *do* like it. You can't love something without liking it." The phrase should be, "I don't *just* like it... I love it." That would be honest... but also would leave out the "hilarious" reveal when we find out that he/she loves it. Call me when it's funny.

Back to Menken: Alan said that Howard taught him to base his songs on specific musical models... like a Belafonte Calypso or a Phil Spector girl-group song. Alan is incredibly facile at basing something on a signature model and then making it his own.

Oh yeah, I've mentioned this before, but in case you forgot, Faith Prince was originally cast as Audrey... but couldn't get out of an industrial she was doing, so the role went to Ellen Greene who was, of course, brilliant Off-Broadway and in the film. And Lee Wilkof was cast as Seymour... and edged out the second choice based on his amazingly flexible voice (he can sound nerdy/legit/rock 'n roll). The second choice was... Nathan Lane! And more trivia: the first Mr. Mushnik was the guy who played Sam Breakstone. I love finding out that these classic commercial actors also did theatre. I'd love to see a production of *I Love My Wife* with Sam Breakstone, Mr. Whipple, Madge "you're soaking in it" and the "Where's the Beef?" lady. Wait. Those commercials are so crazily old I have no idea who's still living. How about one couple made up of those kids (now middle-agers) from the Underoos or Garanimals commercial paired with the two brats from "You sank my battleship!" Are they all still in the biz? Can they belt? Anybody else still living in the past? *P.S. Re-reading this shows me how deep my obsession with the '70s is and how it all led to me co-writing DISASTER!*

Alan said he had so many shows before *Little Shop* that didn't do very well that, when he was offered a full-time job writing jingles in an office, he *almost* took it. As a matter of fact, he told them that he just wanted to open up *Little Shop*, and if it went the way of the other shows (AKA bomb), he would take the office job. Obviously, he never worked in that office. He credits Howard Ashman with changing his whole life: Howard thought up the idea of turning the *Little Shop of Horrors* film into a musical, wrote the book and lyrics *and* directed the show. Brava!

Alan said he remembers seeing the screening of their musical *Little Shop of Horrors* in some town in California. The lights came up and he said to David Geffen, "Wow! It's great!" His comment was greeted with complete silence. Alan may have thought it was great, but he later found out that the audience was devastated that the film ended like the stage show... with all the leads being eaten and the plant taking over the world. Howard was the book writer and after he got the missive from David Geffen, he was able to change the ending of the film without having to do much extra filming! If you go to *Bluegobo.com*, you can see the original ending of the film... it's devastating! After *Little Shop*, Howard got a deal with Disney, and they gave him a choice of films to do: Tina Turner's autobiography (which became *What's Love Got to Do With It?*), the Thief of Baghdad (which later morphed into *Aladdin*) and Howard chose the third: *The Little Mermaid*. Howard had just worked with Marvin Hamlisch on *Smile* but came back to Alan to write the film. I thought *The Little Mermaid* was the return to animated musicals but Alan reminded me that there was one right before it... *Oliver & Company*. Does anybody remember it? I remember the '60s musical *Oliver!*, the '70s musical *Company* and the *Chorus Line* song "And...," but I don't remember all three of the twain meeting in one giant box-office flop.

After *Little Mermaid*, they started work on *Beauty and the Beast*, and this time Alan was told to write a song that could cross over to the pop charts. He recorded himself singing a pop version of "Beauty and the Beast" with his best Top 40 voice and various sassy riffs. Howard then recorded a version of the song using his best old lady voice and sent it to Angela Lansbury, asking her if she'd play Mrs. Potts. She said a prompt and immediate "No." She felt there was *no way* she could sing it. Alan and Howard were in shock and couldn't understand why she'd think that... until they figured out that someone sent her the pop version by mistake! Angela must have listened to it and thought, "That's *not* how young I feel." She thought that they wanted her to Celine Dion-it and panicked that the only "riff" she knew was Mickey Calin (original Riff in *West Side Story*. Anybody?). She accepted the part, and they went into the studio to record the title song. She did it once all the way through... and they kept it! Yes, the version we all know from the movie was done in one take! Go "old-school, one-take Lansbury"!

The terrible part of the Howard and Alan story is that Howard started acting very hostile during the writing of the movie. Alan couldn't understand why Howard was so difficult to be around. Finally, after they won two Oscars for *The Little Mermaid*, Howard told Alan the news... he had AIDS. Alan realized that was why Howard had been so upset and angry and hard to work with. Howard didn't want anyone to know because he was afraid he'd be discriminated against (have projects taken away from him, be blackballed, etc...), so Alan kept it mum and they continued to work on *Beauty and the Beast*. It was hard to keep it secret, though. Alan remembers going to rehearse with a singer for the film with Howard and David Friedman (the conductor, now brilliant composer/lyricist). Alan got to the singer's apartment and started walking up the five-flight walk-up. He suddenly realized how difficult this would be for Howard, and when he looked downstairs he saw Howard slowly making his way up. But Howard did it and Alan didn't tell anyone what was going on.

One of my favorite stories Alan told me was that Howard wanted to write a big song for all the objects in the castle, so Alan said he'd record a silly little melody in the style of what the song should be, Howard could write the lyrics and then Alan would write the real song. Howard wrote the lyrics, and Alan started writing the real song. Well, after listening to both versions, they realized that the dummy melody Alan thought up super quick worked the best, and thus was born "Be Our Guest"!

Sadly, Howard died six months before the movie came out. Alan is so appreciative of Howard for many reasons... one is because Howard told Alan to score *The Little Mermaid*. That means to write all the underscoring throughout the film. Howard told Alan to do it because he knew how upsetting it was during *Little Shop of Horrors* because, as Alan related, Miles Goodman wrote around nine minutes of underscoring for the film, which really just consisted of adaptations of Alan's songs. When the Golden Globes came out, the "Best Score" nomination for *Little Shop* went to Miles Goodman!

Howard and Alan wrote a lot of songs for *Aladdin*, but Disney changed the story (cutting characters, like Aladdin's mother), and suddenly all the songs didn't fit except for one. So the rest were written with Tim Rice. When Alan first wrote the song he wanted to become the pop hit from the movie, he wrote the lyrics for the hook "the world at my feet." Actually, the way it was sung was "the world at my Fe-e-e-e-e-e-t!" Feet is the word he decided should be held? Showstopper! No, literally, the show has to stop because the audience is gone. Thankfully, Tim Rice changed it to "a whole New wo-o-o-o-o-o-orld."

Alan has written so many great things that I barely had time to cover his other work: *Pocahontas*, *The Hunchback of Notre Dame*, *A Christmas Carol* and the new musical *Sister Act*. Alan's next project is a musical version of the Steve Martin film "Faith Healer" called *Leap of Faith*, and it will star Raúl Esparza in the upcoming reading! Also, for you fans of that early '90s musical film, there may soon be a stage version of *Newsies*! How cool would that be! *It would wind up winning him his first Tony Award!*

All right, the next time I write you will be after my half-cruise and after I film the final episode of the *Legally Blonde* reality show. One event I will give you tons of details about... the other I will continue to honor my "cease and desist" order from MTV. All will be revealed when the episodes start airing. As to the exact date of when that will be... I must cease and desist. Bon voyage!

Mermaid Boggess' Tales; Cruising With Creel
March 24, 2008

I'm back on dry land. The sixth R Family cruise has ended and I'm in my typical post-vacation depression. Let me cheer myself up by describing *everything*.

First of all, I need to tell you about the *Chatterbox* I did with the star of *The Little Mermaid*, Sierra Boggess, before I left. Turns out, Sierra grew up in Denver and spent her childhood training as an ice skater! It sounded so fun, and I began to regret that I didn't spend my childhood doing it until she told me that she didn't train *after* school, she trained *before*... at 5 AM. What the-? The only reason I'd have gotten up that early as a child would be if Patti LuPone had rung my doorbell. And even then I would have made her wait in the living room while I made my coffee.

Sierra said that she did competitions as an ice skater but never came in first place. I mock-judged her for not winning, and she hauled out this hilarious self-hating quote: "Second-place is the first loser." It's so negative, I love it! Sierra moved to New York after college and came very close to getting a Broadway show... *Good Vibrations*. Suffice it to say, she's not devastated she wasn't cast. Her first big break was getting the national tour of *Les Miz* as the "hair hag." I started singing, "Come here, my dear. Let's see this trinket you wear..." and she immediately corrected me by saying, "That's the locket crone." Hmm. Why does the character name Hair Hag have alliteration and the Locket Crone doesn't? Why not the Locket Lady? Or the Necklace Nag? She then gave me more insight into the *Les Miz* character track world by telling me that the Hair Hag role is known as the "Snack Track" because it has so little to sing. In "At the End of the Day" she only sings "...and in a bed." Then after her hair hag section she has no other solo 'til Act Two during "Turning" when she sings "...nothing ever will." She said one time the woman soloing before her forgot to stop and sang the first and second part: "Nothing changes... nothing ever will." Poor Sierra heard "Nothing Changes" and started to sing "Nothing e-" and watched as the last two syllables of the precious five she got to sing in Act Two were sung by another. Of course, the rest of the song was spent trying to hold in laughter. She said that "Turning" is the big church laughter song because all the women have just been off-stage chitty-chatting but suddenly they're onstage, looking each other in the eye solemnly and singing a sad song. Sierra said the juxtaposition of worlds is too much and there wasn't one performance where someone didn't have to turn upstage to suppress their laughter. Luckily, they had the turntable constantly rotating.

Besides the Hair Hag/Snack Track, she also got to understudy Cosette and the first time she went on happened to coincide with her parents seeing her in the show for the first time. She didn't tell them she was playing Cosette that night, and they found out when they opened their programs and saw "At this performance..." How exciting for them... and how terrifying for her!

While doing *Les Miz* in DC, she took a train to NYC to try out for the Vegas production of *Phantom*. After her audition, she said she got on the train back to DC with plenty of time but her train was delayed because someone had committed suicide on the tracks! I remarked that her consternation reminded me of Tracy in *Hairspray* apologizing for being late ("Stupid bus crash"). She had never called out of a show before and was mortified because she wasn't really allowed to go another city for an audition. Her friend told her she had to tell the truth and she called the stage manager and 'fessed up. He was super nice and, even though she got there *incredibly* late, she was still able to go on as a hag at the end of act one because *Les Miz* is French for "5 hour show."

She wound up getting a callback for *Phantom* and thinks of *that* as her Broadway debut because it was onstage at the Ambassador Theater. In the audience were Hal Prince, Gillian Lynne and Andrew Lloyd Webber! Her callback was at 9:30 in the morning and by 11 AM, she had gotten the call from her agent that she got Christine!

While on vacation in New York during her Vegas run, she got the audition to play the Little Mermaid. Unfortunately, the night before her audition she got food poisoning and wound up in the hospital! Still, she was determined to get the role and dragged herself to the audition that afternoon and sang the next day. She didn't hear anything until months later right after a Bikram yoga class — the kind where they heat the room to 100 degrees. I asked her why she would take something like that in Vegas, and she said she loves hothouse yoga because it's so difficult that you sometimes feel like you're going to die… but then the class ends and you get the good feeling of knowing you're still alive. That makes perfect sense. Unless you actually think about any of the words she said.

Anyhoo, right after yoga she got a call from her agent saying that they wanted to see her again for Ariel. She had to fly herself and it cost her $700! I couldn't believe she had to pay for it and told her to submit Disney the receipt (which she still has). *She still hasn't.* The callback was around five hours long and I asked her if it was all about working the Heelys they have to wear to look like they're swimming. *Remember? Those sneakers that have wheels on the heel so you can flex your foot and roll around.* Turns out, that part of the audition was only ten minutes at the very end. She had spent hours in Vegas in her garage (which was all cement) spinning around on Heelys that she borrowed from her dresser. Why a grown woman would have Heelys readily available to lend to someone is a question that remains unanswered.

Sierra had to wait a full three days, as opposed to the one hour she had to wait for *Phantom*. She was driving in her car and her agent called. When Sierra answered, her agent said, "Ariel?" Of course, Sierra began crying and then drove around with the top down, blasting "Yentl." Brava! That is *exactly* how I'd react if I got a lead in a Broadway show!

Sierra was so happy, but the more she thought about it, the more she didn't believe it because it seemed too amazing to be true. She thought she misheard so she didn't tell anybody (even her parents!) and finally, after two days, she got the guts to call her agent to make sure that she really had the part. The answer was a definite yes, and now she's playing Ariel eight times a week! I asked her what the hardest part was and she said she thinks it's the kind of role she'll look back and think, "Wow, that show was hard." She has to deal with manipulating her tail, being half-naked and working those Heelys. Then, when she first thought about the show, she figured, "Ah… I lose my voice at the end of Act One, so I can rest it all during the second act." No. Turns out, Ariel spends Act Two "singing her thoughts." *And* in the scenes where she can't sing, she has to get her point across by wildly gesticulating. So, all in all, Ariel ain't the "snack track."

All right, now the cruise. I finished filming the *Legally Blonde* reality show for MTV, which was super fun. I got so emotional during the finale seeing my girls sing with the orchestra that I totally teared up. Of course I was thinking, "I'm so proud of these girls," mixed with, "My reaction will make great TV. Those cameras better be catching this." I've watched enough *Top Model* and/or *Chef* to know what works. Right after the finale, I hightailed it to the airport to catch a plane to Puerto Vallarta to meet the Rosie cruise halfway through their trip. Well, my plane was supposed to make a stop in Dallas, but because of tornadoes down there, they cancelled the flight! Not delayed it, *cancelled it*. I was devastated (stupid bus crash) but they got me another flight that flew into Mexico City and would allow me to connect to Puerto Vallarta. It was great being back on an R Family Vacation and seeing so many people I've seen for the past six cruises. The first night, Jack Plotnick and I did our show called *Mortification Theater*, where we re-enact and reclaim devastating moments from our childhoods. I showed my signature: a video of me jazz dancing to the disco version of "I Am What I Am" wearing purple plastic jazz pants, leg warmers and white Capezios (I thought white was better to show my line).

The next night, I played for Gavin Creel, who did an act in the piano bar. As usual, his voice sounded glorious. Gavin said he's planning on playing Jesus on Broadway in *Godspell*, and he asked the audience to leave a note backstage if they're seeing the show. I sassily said that it was to remind him not to mark that night. He laughed and said he normally gives 40 percent but if he knew that a friend was in the audience he would give a full 100 percent... of 46 percent. Brava! *P.S! Scandal! That was the GODSPELL that was slated for Broadway and one week before rehearsals began the whole thing was cancelled. Nachtmare! And Gavin turned down auditioning for Tony in WEST SIDE STORY because he thought he already had a gig.*

Gavin said that one of his favorite composers was Sondheim and he proceeded to sing "What Can You Lose," which is the song from *Dick Tracy* that Madonna sang. It was very interesting to actually hear it sung with vibrato. (Madonna made the bold choice of singing it straight tone and just slightly under pitch... brava, trailblazer!) Gavin also sang Jimmy's big Act One song from *Thoroughly Modern Millie* and I mentioned to everyone that he was nominated for a Tony for Best Actor in a Musical (at 26!). What a coup!

He said that Sutton performed "Forget About the Boy" on the Tonys, but he made a delicious $2,000 for singing the end of the title song and lifting each arm once. It worked like this: (Run onstage) "Beat the drums 'cause here comes Thoroughly Mo-dern Mil-lie (one arm lifts = $1,000) No-o-o-o-ow! (Second arm lifts at button of song = another $1,000)."

The next day, I did a *Chatterbox* interview with Shoshana Bean and Julia Murney, or as I called it, "Dueling Elphabas." Julia said that she first met *Wild Party* composer Andrew Lippa when she was auditioning for the Stephen Schwartz revue called *Snapshots*. The director asked her if she could sing "Meadowlark" and she said that she could but didn't have the music. Even though Andrew was the music director and not the audition pianist, he got up and played it for her. He had just started writing *Wild Party* and put a note down about her on his audition sheet that said, "Queenie?" She got to do all the initial readings of *Wild Party* as Queenie, but then right before the big workshop of the show, they made her try out for the role. She said she walked in with a huge chip on her shoulder because she was annoyed she had to try out for a role that was pretty much written for her, and — cut to — she didn't get the gig, Marin Mazzie did. Before it came to Off-Broadway they asked Julia to try out again and she said, because the worst had already happened, she didn't have the chip anymore, and she got the gig! I then, of course, ran to the piano and made her belt all of "Raise the Roof." She's still got it!

I asked Shoshana and Julia how hard it was going to a theatre conservatory (Shoshana went to CCM and Julia to Syracuse), and they said that all the girls were made to feel neurotic about their weight. At Shoshana's first evaluation they asked her how much weight she felt she needed to lose (!), and Julia said her school would post a "weight list"... which would have the names of students who needed to lose weight. That's great for the self-esteem of any 18-year-old. We talked about Sho having to go on for Idina Menzel on her final weekend because Idina got injured. She said she went on for the last five minutes of the show, but refused to think she'd be going on for Idina's last show. She didn't want to think that was possible. But it happened. People had flown in from *around the world* to see Idina do it one final time, and instead they got the dreaded "At this performance, the role of Elphaba..." But I'm sure once they heard one of Shoshana's signature high notes/crazy flexible riffs they were like, "Bring on the Bean!"

The final night of the cruise I hosted an all-'70s show. I started with Jimmy Smagula (from *Phantom*) who sang "Love Will Keep Us Together" and sounded great... in the original Toni Tennille key! I even put that weird back-up part in at the end... remember? "Bah... bah, dah, dah, dah... Sedaka is back..." Neil Sedaka told me that by the end of the '60s, he didn't have any hit songs. Suddenly, the Captain and Tennille did "Love Will Keep Us Together," and his income went from something like $50,000 to $1,000,000! Sedaka *was* back... and rich! Then, my friend Traci Lyn Thomas, who was in the Vegas *Mamma Mia!* sang "The Winner Takes it All," and I told the audience that I was annoyed she had moved to Colorado, and after she sang, I wanted them to tell her whether they felt she should stay or come back to Broadway. After she belted that last amazing C, they were all shouting for her to "come back to Broadway." She later informed me of the irony in their shouts since she had never actually been on Broadway. Details, details. Shoshana Bean came out and sang "I Will Survive" which she should have re-titled "I Will Survive (And Interpolate Sassy High Notes in the Process)." Then, I introduced James and said that we started dating late in life, and I'm always jealous when he talks about his other boyfriends. I said that tonight I would allow him to talk about his first relationship and we'd see how jealous I get from the piano. He started singing. "Oh, What a Night... late December 1963..." when he got to the part about "Oh, I... got a funny feeling when he walked in the room..." Gavin came out in short shorts, high white gym socks and an afro. He was dancing all around James and working it, and finally near the end of the song, I got up from the piano, ripped off Gavin's wig as he scurried offstage... and James and I ended the song in a kiss. Awwww, cute!!

It wound up being the Gavin show when he came back out and sang the H-E-double hockey sticks out of "Enough is Enough" with the multi-talented Matt Zarley. Matt and I realized that we've known each other for 20 years! I met him when he was first doing *Chorus Line* on Broadway, and I was trying to sub on the piano. Then, we went on the *Chorus Line* tour of Germany, or as my mother still calls it, Nazi Germany. Matt and Gavin both sounded so great together and added a full layout to the middle of the song that had Gavin asking me for an aspirin the next day on the plane home. Seriously. Kevin Chamberlin then came onstage and sang the Barry Manilow classic (that I also sang in ninth-grade chorus) "Daybreak." In the middle of the song, all these kids filed onstage. They had been working on the song all week as part of the cruise's version of "Rosie's Broadway Kids," and they sang along with adorable choreography (no layouts.). Kevin sounded great despite the fact that he was hit with a 15-foot wave while body surfing in Puerto Vallarta. Ouch. *He had to miss the Playbill cruise I offered him years later because he was getting surgery on his shoulder because of that effing wave!* Finally, Marya Grandy got up and sang "Last Dance" and sounded phenomenal on the signature Donna Summer high F. Matt Zarley and Frankie Grande (who was voted Mr. Broadway last year) did a dance break in the middle of the song that had the moves of *Solid Gold*, the tackiness level of *The Shields and Yarnell Show* and the hotness of an old '70s Colt video. *That's the same Frankie Grande who was on BIG BROTHER and is brother to Ariana Grande!* It's so nice that so many non-gays come on the cruise... and so many non-parents! And the cruise inspires everyone. As a matter of fact, James ran into two couples who came on the last cruise just for fun, and were so inspired, they've now become parents! Brava, R Family Vacations!

My sis and I = In The Heights stalkers

Autumn Hurlbert at the final audition for the LEGALLY BLONDE long-titled reality show.

Rosie Perez, backstage at The Ritz, talking to Juli and her friend with Terrence McNally looking on.

My Mom offering to sing her role on the Audible.com recording of Broadway Nights. #OfferDenied.

After recording Broadway Nights, I made Kristin take the subway and we wanted this to be the TMZ shot of us dodging paparazzi. #NoOneWasInterested

After our performance at the Hangar Theater, Andrea Burns, Josh Henry, Julia Murney and I wanted a photo like those ads where everyone is laughing.

My LEGALLY BLONDE obsessed nieces.

What happens when you eat at an outdoor cafe on 46th street? You eventually run into Norm Lewis, Gavin Creel and Andrea Burns!

Jen Cody as a young Seth Rudetsky in Broadway 101 (PS I was never that short). Photo by Jay Brady.

With the amazing (non-winners) of the Legally Blonde reality show! Me, Lauren Zarkin, Cassie, and (future Tony Award winner) Celina Carvajal, AKA Lena Hall!

Andrea Martin, Larry Pressgrove and I backstage, going over our parts for the BROADWAY NIGHTS release party.

I ♡ U SETH!

Daphne and Priscilla
March 31, 2008

This week I interviewed Daphne Rubin-Vega for my Sirius radio show. I thought it was very cool that she was born in Panama and then moved to New York. That's probably the same way people feel when I tell them that I was born in Jamaica and then moved to Long Island. At first they think I'm an exotic island specimen 'til I clarify and tell them Jamaica, Queens. Anyhoo, the first Broadway show that changed her life was *The Me Nobody Knows*, which was the early-'70s *Spring Awakening*... as opposed to the *late* '70s *Spring Awakening*, which was *Runaways*. My sister Nancy did *The Me Nobody Knows* in high school, and there's nothing like seeing a group of 1970s Jewish Long Islanders put away their Frye boots long enough to sing about how hard it is growing up in a slum. I think Nancy wore overalls to look "poor" and left one strap hanging off her left shoulder for street cred. Daphne went to the High School of Performing Arts and majored in art. P.S. Irene Cara made the High School of Performing Arts famous and was in *The Me Nobody Knows*. Daphne, with her Latin looks, said that Irene Cara was the only role model she had because Irene was a "citizen of the world." She was one of my role models, too, but mainly because she danced on a car, which I thought was super cool. Even though Daphne was an artist, she always wanted to perform, and when she was nine years old, she bought a *Backstage* (the newspaper that lists auditions) and saw there was an audition coming up for a children's theatre. She showed up ready to book it and was devastated that children's theatre means that it's *for* children, not that it has children in it!

Daphne went to NYU's film school and wound up being six credits shy of graduating... but ended up in a girl group called "Pajama Party." Her look included braces, a nose ring and pink hair. Why didn't it catch on? Anybody? Nobody. Pajama Party opened for Menudo and Milli Vanilli... all the big "M" groups of the '80s. (AKA two.)

Speaking of the letter M, Daphne told me about getting Mimi in the workshop of *Rent* and told us what it was like right after Jonathan Larson died. They did the final dress rehearsal and he died that night. The next day was supposed to be their first public performance, and they didn't want to cancel the show, so they decided to just do a table reading. Well, Daphne said that it became really hard to do it that way. She asked me, "How do you do 'Out Tonight' sitting down?" My question is: "How do you do it standing up?" At least sitting down you can keep the top button of those signature pants mercifully open. Daphne said she got up on the table during the song (tip o' the hat to Irene Cara on the car), and by the end of Act One, the whole cast was on its feet. During intermission, director Michael Greif ran backstage and said, "Let's do the second act for real!" Everyone got into their costumes and make-up, and Daphne said it was the best way to exorcise the grief and show their love for Jonathan.

She said the hardest thing about that whole period of *Rent* was losing her anonymity, being watched when she wasn't onstage. As I get older, I also find that I've been losing my anonymity... and by "anonymity," I mean "high notes" and "hair."

I interviewed another Latina actress this week, *In the Heights*'s Priscilla Lopez. What a career! Her first audition was at the Broadway Theatre for the role of Baby Louise in the original production of *Gypsy*. She saw the girls ahead get in a line and she watched as the casting person told a few to stay. There was one girl who got typed out and started crying immediately. Priscilla vowed that she would not cry. She lined up with her group of girls... and was typed out. She remembered her vow and didn't cry... in the theatre. She was able to hold it in while exiting, but as soon as she stepped outside, she started crying like the "Leave Britney Alone" guy. *That was a very current reference when I originally wrote this.*

She then started taking dance classes because a guy from an amateur TV show came to her apartment, touched her foot to the back of her head and said "this little girl could be a star," which is a line in *A Chorus Line*... but it's not Morales who says it... it's Kristine. Priscilla also said *she's* the one who said she walked around as a kid saying "I'm gonna be a movie star," which is Bobby's line in "Hello Twelve." The script mixed and matched many lines and stories. As a matter of fact, Donna McKechnie told me that Maggie's story in "At the Ballet" is really hers. As a child, Donna would "dance around the living room" with her arms up in the air, pretending she was dancing with her father. Coincidentally, as a child, I would dance around *my* living room... pretending to be in *A Chorus Line*.

Every time I ask Priscilla about something in *A Chorus Line*, she always says, "It's all true!" The weirdest thing for her was the fact that so much of Morales was based on her, but Morales wasn't her. There's a section where Morales doesn't want to talk about herself to Zack, and he says, "Don't you want the job?" And she says, with much need, "Sure, I want the job!" One night, she didn't feel that needy and said it with a little more maturity and confidence, and Michael Bennett came backstage and told her that she was no longer playing herself. He said, "Even though you are growing as a person, Morales isn't. You have to freeze her in this moment."

Back to her childhood, she did indeed go to the High School of Performing Arts and, devil's advocate-style, I asked her why she couldn't just improv with the rest of the class! She said she remembers being on "that bobsled," and she felt the rest of the class was faking it, pretending to feel the snow and the cold. She really didn't feel anything and thought that either she could lie... or she could tell the teacher she wasn't feeling it. She hoped that by telling the truth, he would teach her how. But, alas, she became the class pariah when she admitted she felt "nothing."

As soon as she graduated, she got her first Broadway show: *Breakfast at Tiffany*'s with Mary Tyler Moore and Richard Chamberlain. It was not the *Spring Awakening* of the late '60s — more like the *In My Life*. She remembered one review that said, "Even Dr. Kildare can't save this show." Ouch! Then she did *Her First Roman* (more on that later) and *Henry, Sweet Henry*. That was her first Michael Bennett show, and she "fell in love" with him at the audition. She still doesn't know why. She admits that he was short, and he had moles all over his face, but she was mesmerized. She said that he'd put his arm around you and talk to you like it was the most important and private conversation of your life. He asked her to be the swing, and she said yes. She literally thought it meant sitting and swaying glamorously on a swing onstage. She didn't know it meant understudying all the girls in the ensemble... including future *Chorus Line* cast member Baayork Lee and Pia Zadora! Priscilla heard that Pia's last name was fake, and had based it on her mom always saying, "Look! Pia's adorable!" Say it out loud. It sounds like Pia Zadora!

Priscilla heard about a new show coming to Broadway called *Hair* and traipsed down to the Public to try out for it. She walked in and saw the whole creative staff behind the table, apparently stoned. She didn't know what the show was about, so she decided to sing her signature audition song. She nodded at the pianist... and... "Raindrops on roses and whiskers on kittens..." She did not get it.

Priscilla then did the national tour of *The Boyfriend* and inherited Sandy Duncan's costumes. Inside one of the hats someone had written, "Sandy Duncan, the Texan Grasshopper." Priscilla crossed that out and wrote "Priscilla Lopez... the Puerto Rican cockroach." When Priscilla got back to NY, she heard that they were having auditions for *Follies*, and now that she had played various leads, she wanted to show Michael Bennett that she wasn't just a chorus girl. She auditioned for *Follies* with... a song from *The Me Nobody Knows*! Shout out to Daphne Rubin-Vega! Michael wound up offering her a part in *Company*... she was the standby for Donna McKechnie and then took over the role. Priscilla got to dance that crazy '70s "Tick Tock" solo in Act Two and thinks it's the best dance Michael Bennett ever did.

While she was backstage, she saw a C-U-T-E guy. She found out he was a sub trombonist and realized she had to work fast! There was a Coke machine right outside the pit, and she kept going over to it and bending down in front of him to make her selection. One thing led to another... and 36 years later, they're still married!

After *Company*, she heard they were looking for a new Fastrada for *Pippin*. She thought she could do the part, but knew that Fosse would have a hard time believing her as John Rubinstein's mother... especially because she and John went to high school together. She didn't want to leave it to Fosse's imagination, so she had a friend who worked at NBC do some old age make-up on her, and she had another friend who worked at *Pippin* steal Leland Palmer's Fastrada wig! She literally walked into the audition in full costume, hair and make-up. She felt like an idiot standing around all of her peers and thought, "I'm either going to be the laughing stock of Broadway... or I'm going to get this gig!" She came onstage in her crazy get up, did the number, which she had choreographed in front of her mirror at home, and when she finished, Bob Fosse ran up to the front of the house, slapped his hand on the stage and said, "Now that's what I call a well-prepared audition!" She got the gig, but soon had to deal with what she called the "Nazi Dance Captain." Every time Priscilla was onstage, the dance captain would be in the wings, taking notes. Every finger move, every eye direction, every aspect of her performance was scrutinized. Priscilla used to pray for Fosse to come and free her. Finally, Fosse watched the show, and Priscilla realized why the dance captain was such a specificity ogre... because Fosse was a bigger one!

Right after that began the infamous tape sessions with Michael Bennett that eventually led to *A Chorus Line*. She was nominated as Best Featured Actress for Morales and it was a difficult time for her because she *really* wanted to win. When Kelly Bishop's (Sheila) name was called, Priscilla said it felt like a truck hit her in the stomach. *But* she was also thrilled because Kelly is her best friend. As a matter of fact, they had side-by-side dressing rooms at the Shubert Theater, and they had the wall knocked down so they could be in the same one! The good news is Priscilla won a Tony for the fantastic show (I saw it twice) *A Day in Hollywood/A Night in the Ukraine*. In Act One, she played an usherette at Grauman's Chinese Theater (listen to the fantastic Jerry Herman song "The Best in the World"... I'm obsessed!) and in Act Two, which is essentially a live Marx Brothers movie, she played Harpo Marx. Unfortunately, to this day, she's still devastated that she was so frazzled when she won the Tony, she forgot to thank Harpo Marx. She actually got hate mail about it! (Sending hate mail is what people had to do before they could just post on a theatre chat board under the name "Priscilla'sUngrateful432.")

Now it's time to get back to *Her First Roman*. It featured one of my favorite onstage mishaps and I made Priscilla save it for the end of the *Chatterbox*. In order to wear a wig, the chorus girls had to pin wig caps to their hair, and because Priscilla's hair was short, it was hard to attach the caps. She found out if she stuffed some clothes underneath the wig cap, it would give something for the cap to be attached to. She'd stuff anything she could find: underclothes, socks, whatever... it all worked. One day, she taught this trick to the other chorus girls as they were applying the leg paint to themselves that made them all look Egyptian. Well, in Act Two there was a funeral procession where all the ladies walked in a solemn line around a coffin. Priscilla happened to look up at the dancer in front of her during the procession, and saw that she had taken her advice. Unfortunately, as Priscilla marched in the solemn funeral, she saw that the dancer didn't tuck all the clothes in, and swinging freely from underneath her wig was a large white bra. Priscilla wanted to laugh, but of course, couldn't, because it was supposed to be a sad scene. She tried to suppress it, but all that did was cause incredible pressure... which resulted in her peeing onstage! She couldn't stop and was mortified that it was also causing her leg makeup to run in rivulets to the stage. Soon she was even more horrified, because the stage was raked. A raked stage means that the back is tilted up and it lays in a diagonal towards the audience. Well, what comes down must go further down, apparently, because soon the pee was running downhill and overflowing from the front of the stage to the pit! I'm obsessed thinking about those poor musicians sitting in the pit wondering what was dripping on them. Hopefully, they felt some comfort in knowing it was from a future Tony Award-winner!

Don't forget that this week is Sherie Rene Scott's concert for BC/EFA (*BroadwayCares.org*). Go see this brilliant entertainer and support a great cause! *It was called YOU MAY NOW WORSHIP ME and it went to Broadway a few years later as EVERYDAY RAPTURE.* And when you have a moment, download *The Me Nobody Knows*. It's not just for Latinas... Long Island Jews love it, too! Peace out!

Hey, Old Friends
April 7, 2008

Last Monday, I went to a concert of music by Leonard Bernstein and lyrics by Alan Jay Lerner. You may not know, but in 1976, they wrote the show *1600 Pennsylvania Avenue,* which was a musical about many of the different presidents who lived in the White House and the staff that served them. The show was a Bicentennial bomb (seven performances only... I guess seven's not always a lucky number) but then had its script thrown out and they combined a chunk of the songs to form *The White House Cantata*. The show was performed by some great soloists and the Collegiate Chorale.

Afterwards, I hosted a post-performance discussion with some original cast members and the original co-director/choreographer, George Faison. Beth Fowler recalled how she was offered an audition to be in the chorus of the original show and to understudy the First Lady. Her agent told her that she absolutely should not audition because she had already been featured as one of the Liebeslieders in *A Little Night Music,* and it would be a step back for her career. But she felt that she had to audition because (as she reenacted, all a-flutter) "Leonard Bernstein wants my voice." She said that she remembers talking to Patricia Routledge (who played The First Lady), who told her that when she first read the script, she thought it needed a lot of work but... "Leonard Bernstein wants my voice." Original cast member Jack Witham talked about meeting Beth Fowler during rehearsal, asking her out... and they've been married ever since. I guess the seven performances paid off for some people! And by "some," I mean two. *This talkback was before Beth's newfound fame as the nun on ORANGE IS THE NEW BLACK.*

I asked director George Faison the biggest problem he had with Bernstein and he said that they once had a note session at The Watergate hotel with Bernstein in a silk dressing gown eating from a sumptuous buffet of truffles and lobster... as they discussed writing for the common man. I understand what George was saying, but it's not like Bernstein came from such opulence. He certainly understood what it was like to not be rich, and as they say in *The Producers*, when ya got it, spend it.

Back to the *Cantata*, Emily Pulley gave a great rendition of "Duet for One" where she portrayed the outgoing First Lady (Julia Grant) as well as the incoming one (Lucy Hayes) at the Hayes inauguration. Beth Fowler recalled the final performance of *1600 Pennsylvania Avenue* where Patricia Routledge got such an ovation that she finally did the whole song again! After the talkback, I ran into Alice Playten and, like I always do, brought up *Henry, Sweet Henry*. She told me that on opening night, the audience wanted her to sing "Nobody Steps on Kafritz" again... but she employed ye olde adage, "Always leave 'em wanting more." If you've never seen Alice do this number (she got a Tony nom. for it), you must visit *Bluegobo.com* and watch her on the *Ed Sullivan Show*... brilliant!

On Sirius Radio, I interviewed my old friend Emily Skinner. I've known Emily ever since she graduated Carnegie Mellon and reminded her that I coached her for her audition for the '90s revival of *Grease!* She then promptly reminded me that she didn't get the part. Touché. She told me that she grew up in Virginia and was so hyper as a child they wanted to hold her back in school and not have her enter first grade, but her teacher gave her another option. Emily was told she could have ten minutes every day where she could entertain the class, and after that she had to be good in class. Emily took the option, doing mini-plays, singing songs and lip-synching Jackson Five albums, and she was able to avoid being held back! I'm jealous. I want a delicious captive audience ten minutes a day. Must I go back to kindergarten? Wait a minute, I just remembered, I started first grade at five years old... I skipped kindergarten! That's why I'm still desperately searching for the audience I never had. After 20 years of therapy, it just took one interview with Emily Skinner to pick up on the reason for my neediness. Brava!

Like me, Emily grew up listening to the *Annie* album. I asked her who she was obsessed with, assuming it was a toss-up between Andrea McArdle, Laurie Beechman and the girl who played Duffy ("Who cares what they're wearing on Main Street or Saville Row"). Turns out, it was Dorothy Loudon! I forgot that Emily's been a character actress her whole life.

Emily's first big break was doing *A Christmas Carol* at Madison Square Garden, which was her last ingénue role. The good news was she didn't have to worry about remembering her character name (it was "Emily"); the bad news was they had 15 performances a week! Wowza. In one week they more than doubled all the performances of *1600 Pennsylvania Avenue*. Then she got cast in *Jekyll and Hyde* as Linda Eder's understudy. Thus follows a story I'm totally obsessed with: during previews, Linda Eder, who normally has vocal chords of steel, lost her voice, but the understudies hadn't been rehearsed yet. Emily didn't know any of the stage fighting and didn't want a "new life" as someone with a sword stuck in her arse (British pronunciation). Plus, the stage was constantly filled with London fog, and she was terrified of falling into the pit... even with all those synthesizers there to break her fall. They told her that they understood and she would not have to go on. Hmm... sounds good so far. However, they really meant she wouldn't have to go on... stage. Instead, they asked Linda Eder to act all the scenes and when it came time to sing, Linda had to star onstage and move her mouth while Emily sang into a mic backstage! Seriously! It wasn't that devastating since, thankfully, it was only a rehearsal with a few friends in the house. Oh, I'm sorry... it was an actual performance with a full paying audience! The thing is, I've never run into anybody who actually saw that performance, and I have a terrifying suspicion that the producers wanted the story never to be told, so they had everyone killed on their way out of the theatre. Any survivors? Email me! *I've since found out that not only did the audience survive... but there's a bootleg of the performance!*

Emily got her first starring role on Broadway as Daisy Hilton in *Side Show*, the story of real-life conjoined twins, Daisy and Violet Hilton. I was the assistant music director on the first reading of *Side Show*, but then it was called *The Songs of the Siamese Twins*. By the time the title was changed, I was unceremoniously replaced. Emily kept the role through various readings and they brought her in to audition with various actresses up for Violet. Emily remembers auditioning with Alice and saying, "We sound great together!" Again I say, if you've never seen them do the show, get thee to *Bluegobo.com*... phenomenal! I literally thought they had costumes that were connected to each other. I was shocked that all they did was just stand, hip-to-hip. Emily said a man once approached her at the stage door with a knowing smile and said, "I saw the Velcro." Ah... there's nothing more annoying than a know-it-all know-nothing.

The most devastating thing that happened was at the Macy's Thanksgiving Day Parade. Do you remember the year when it was so windy that a balloon was knocked down and hit a woman on the head? Well, Emily and Alice were doing a number from *Side Show* that same year, and the wind came up in the middle of it and literally blew them apart! It was only for a few seconds, but I remember Alice telling me that it was one of the worst days of her life. Perhaps that's a little dramatic, but that's why she's an actress, folks! Emily said that she loved having Alice next to her the whole show because having someone so close to her meant she always felt supported and not vulnerable. She said that during the workshop, where they rehearsed eight hours a day for six weeks, she would have dreams at night and wake up feeling the bed next to her for Alice. I've done the same thing, but I wasn't doing *Side Show*, and I was feeling for my ex-boyfriend who dumped me in 1989.

One of my other favorite Broadway debacles (besides the Linda Eder lip-synching craziness) happened during *Side Show*. Emily and Alice were doing the show at night but also getting up crazily early to do morning shows. I was working on *The Rosie O'Donnell Show* at the time, and I remember Emily and Alice singing "Who Will Love Me As I Am?" and right after that, Emily burst a blood vessel on her vocal chords! She had to take off a few shows to repair it, and her understudy, the fabulous Lauren Kennedy, went on for her. Emily was back, and she and Alice were finishing "Leave Me Alone." Usually at the end of the song, they back up until they're behind the set, do a 20-second costume change and are then revealed inside a sarcophagus for the Vaudeville Egyptian Number. Well, this was Wednesday night and during the crazy quick change, Emily couldn't get her costume on. She thought, "Could I literally have gained this much weight in two days?" and then she saw her dresser's face go white. Turns out, Lauren had gone on that matinee and the dresser had laid out her costume... and Lauren is a size zero! The music onstage now had started doubling, and the dancing boys started to repeat their dance steps because the sarcophagus wasn't opening. The dresser went running to Emily's dressing room (three flights up!!), and Alice helped out... by laughing hysterically. Finally, the dresser came back (the boys were now on their tenth repeat), Emily got into her costume and she and Alice entered the sarcophagus. Right before it opened, they realized that when they got into the sarcophagus, they somehow wound up on the wrong side of each other! It's like they had gotten the operation to separate conjoined twins, and then got sewn back together on opposite sides. Alice screamed, "There's no way I'm reversing this choreography!" and they got out of the sarcophagus, changed sides and it opened... to reveal ten chorus boys, wildly panting with a glazed look of "What the hell happened!?!??!?!!"

The show closed in the winter after 100 performances... but months later they found out it was nominated for Best Musical! But what about them? Would they compete against each other for Best Actress? No, the Tony committee solved that and nominated them as one nomination for "Best Actress." They sang "I Will Never Leave You" and sounded amazing! That was the same year I wrote the opening number starring Rosie O'Donnell (and of course, featuring my faves: Betty Buckley, Patti LuPone and Jennifer Holliday), so I got to be in the audience at Radio City and see Emily and Alice re-create their brilliance. Thrilling! Now they tour all over the place doing concerts separately and together and, if you haven't, you must get all of their CDs and give a special listen to Emily's version of "Sleepy Man" on their newest CD (*Raw at Town Hall*) and both of them doing "Little Me" on their first one, *Duets*. "Sleepy Man" is so beautiful and romantic, and I listen to "Little Me" at the gym all the time, and it puts me in the best mood.

Okay, people. This is my final week preparing for my big Actors Fund Benefit, *Seth's Broadway 101*. And next week Matthew Broderick is at the *Chatterbox*. Stay tuned for a recap!

"Bravas" for Kristin and Matthew
April 14, 2008

Hi! This week began for me at The Zipper Theater where I saw my old stand-up comedy compatriot, Britt Swenson. Britt and I not only did stand-up together in the past, but like me, she's played in many a Broadway pit. The difference is she's a violinist and I play the piano. As a matter of fact, for a while she was my violin teacher, but then she moved to LA. I'm not saying it was my devastating violin playing that made her flee across the country, but you do the math. After she studied and performed with The Groundlings (the L.A. improv group), she moved to Colorado. She brought her one-woman show, *So Many Ladies*, to the Zipper, and the audience ate it up. One of my favorite characters was a substitute teacher that began class with, "I have a wicked hangover, so don't push me." She also angrily tells the class, "Teacher means talker." I was literally laughing more than anyone in the theatre at that sketch. I'm sure it can't be related to the fact that I haven't emotionally moved on from high school where I hated most of my teachers.

This week, Kristin Chenoweth did a benefit to help find a cure for ACD, which is a terrible fatal disease that affects babies like SIDS. NiCole Robinson, whom Kristin worked with on *The West Wing*, lost a baby to ACD and asked if Kristin would help. Of course, Kristin said yes right away and gave a solo concert (with the amazing Andrew Lippa at the piano) on Saturday. She hilariously referred to her portrayal of Marian in the film of *The Music Man* as having received "mediocre acclaim" and also said that she hasn't been singing lately, so doing the concert was like crack for her. Thankfully, James' seven-year-old daughter was there, and I've always felt that the sooner she learns about Kristin's crack addiction, the better. When I was interviewing Kristin on my Sirius radio show about the benefit, I brought up *Thoroughly Modern Millie*. Did you know that Kristin was cast as Miss Dorothy in one of the workshops of the show and then bumped up to the role of Millie?! But before it came to Broadway, she got her own TV show, so she had to drop out. Then the keys got dropped so Sutton could belt it all. Then Kristin's TV show got dropped after a few episodes. And before that all happened, I was the music director of the early *Millie* workshop and *I* got dropped.

Speaking of dropping, the good news is that Kristin's TV show *Pushing Daisies* was renewed. The bad news is, she had to drop out of doing *Candide* in London. So, if any of you were planning on flying the Concord to go see her, cancel your tickets ASAP. That's right, I'm stuck in the '70s and still think people fly the Concord, or shall I say the SST. Does anyone remember it being called that? Quick, look it up on Netscape. That's right, I'm also stuck in the late '90s.

I also interviewed the hi-larious Matthew Broderick on my *Chatterbox*. Matthew grew up in the Village, and I was immediately jealous. Listen to the difference:

PERSON # 1: I grew up on Ninth Street and Fifth Avenue.
PERSON # 2: I grew up on Rosedale Road on Long Island.

Who would you rather hang out with? The only thing that paid off for me is that it helped my supposed drag name. There's a theory that your drag name is your childhood pet plus the name of your street, so mine is Shoshana Rosedale. I love it because it indicates the high riffing of Shoshana Bean mixed with the hotness of Gwen Stefani's husband, Gavin Rossdale. That's about the only positive of where I grew up. I always wanted to be one of those cool kids who grew up in Manhattan. When I got to Oberlin College and anyone asked me where I was from, I would say with Manhattan-like attitude "New York." Which was true... New York State, that is. If someone would follow up the question with, "Where in New York?" I'd go into immediate vocal rest.

Matthew still lives in the Village, and I asked him if he ever thinks about moving to the suburbs. He said that it might be lonely out there... and he imagined himself spending his time saying, "Hey... look at that tree. It's coming in nicely... look at that tree." When he was a little kid, he got a library card and wrote his profession as "actor," but it wasn't until he was in high school that he really thought about it. Right after high school, he got the lead in a movie opposite Sally Field! It was called *No Small Affair*, and two weeks into shooting, he showed up and they told him that the director was ill and that he should stay in his trailer 'til they needed him. Hours went by, and they finally told him to go home and that they'd call the next day. A *week* later his agent called and said, "Are you sitting down? It's over." They canceled the whole movie! He said he was in a full depression having to go back to auditioning after just having a lead in a film. It also makes you sound like a crazy person:

"OK, number 53... any recent jobs?"
"I just did a film opposite Sally Field!"
"Wow! When does it come out?"
"Um... never."
"OK. And that's when we'll offer you this job."

A year passed and Matthew was finally offered his next job: the Off-Broadway version of *Torch Song Trilogy*. He played the son that Harvey Fierstein adopts in Act Three, and at that point the show lasted five hours! Wow! That's the length of three *Xanadu*s! Or one of Jackie Hoffman's ad libs. Since the show was so long, he didn't have to get to the theatre 'til Act Two began, but of course, he would wait 'til the last minute to arrive. And it was the kind of theatre where he could only get backstage by walking through the audience then across the stage. He was supposed to arrive during intermission, but he said he would often time it "dangerously," and one time the lights were literally going down to begin Act Two and Matthew flew across the stage in the dark as Harvey was getting set onstage to begin the act. Matthew remembers hearing Harvey laugh and ask, in the dark (à la Harvey), "Is that my son?" The producers, though, didn't laugh and said they were going to fine Matthew for getting there so late. But, Matthew said, since they weren't getting paid, it didn't matter!

Matthew remembered that there weren't a lot of people coming to the show at first, *but* they all stayed to the end. And then, when the show got great reviews, Harvey cut it down a tad, and people were flocking. Matthew's dressing roommate was every gay man's dream dressing roommate... Estelle Getty! How fun is that?! I would have asked her for non-stop Sicily stories. Oh, wait... she's not really Sophia in real life? Thanks for devastating me. Matthew said that Estelle wasn't friendly at first because she really liked the boy who played the part before Matthew did.

ME: How did you know?
HIM: She told me.

Ouch on the directness. She would actually haul out the old "*He* did it like this." Maybe Matthew should have threatened her with "the home," à la Bea Arthur — although he'd have to drop his voice an octave, get taller and figure out where camera three is so he can stare at it.

Matthew tried out for the Broadway production of *Brighton Beach Memoirs* and the director, Herb Ross, handed him another script at the audition. It was the film *Max Dugan Returns*. Matthew wound up trying out for both at the same time. On his way out of the theatre, the casting agent told him that he got both parts! Can you imagine? Getting a feature film and a Broadway show at the same moment? I asked Matthew if that's ever happened to anybody else and he said simply, "No." He then said he thought it would always be like that. I asked him if it was and again he said simply, "No."

I wanted Matthew to tell me about one of his most embarrassing onstage moments. He said it was going to be a gross story and, with his signature dryness, asked the audience to "turn off their ear sets," which was a reference to the ear set that hearing impaired people can get on Broadway, as opposed to my talk show at Don't Tell Mama. I informed him that my *Chatterbox* wasn't a Broadway show, and he then asked, "Then why am I here?" As usual, hilarious. He said that while he was doing *Biloxi Blues* in California, he went out between shows and ate bad Mexican food. He then got to the scene where the sergeant character says he's going to look each one of the soldiers in the eye to find out who's gay. When he looked Matthew in the eye, Matthew said, "I'm gonna throw up" and promptly left the stage. He was woozy offstage, and when he finally realized that he'd better rejoin the cast, he heard them improving onstage with such brilliant lines as "The sergeant sure seems mad" (pause), "Yeah... do you think he'll be mad tomorrow?" (pause), "Could be... because he was mad today." Where were Britt and The Groundlings?

Since Matthew can sing, I asked him why he didn't sing in *The Lion King* movie and he said he tried! He went to the recording studio and sang through the songs three times and remembers each time being told very intensely to "Loosen up!" He was repeatedly asked with more and more fervor, "Why are you so uptight? WHY?????" Needless to say, they didn't use his singing voice in the movie.

He was offered his first musical, *How to Succeed*, but asked the director, Des McAnuff, to come hear him sing at a voice lesson to make sure he could do it. Des gave him the thumbs up and he was raring to go. But when rehearsals began, Matthew had another gig so he had to miss the first three days. He said that he showed up, and it seemed like the whole cast was ready to start performing that night. He said that musical theatre people are always completely prepared, whereas he said he was like, "So... where's the coffee?" He remembers Megan Mullally, who played opposite him as Rosemary, was the most polished out of the cast. Her performance was brilliant from the first rehearsal they did together... and he was super-impressed by her singing. Actually, what he said was that her singing could "blast your head off," but he meant it in a positive way. I recalled that she got that part after being devastated by losing another big role... the lead in *Busker Alley*! That was the show that wound up never coming to Broadway because Tommy Tune broke his foot while it was still out of town. I love those stories about not getting something and then getting something better instead. I'm sure the fact that I didn't get the role of the pianist in *Master Class* lo those 15 years ago will lead to a better job. I'm patiently waiting. Still.

His then-soon-to-be wife, Sarah Jessica Parker, wound up playing the leading lady for the end of the run, and I asked if it was weird playing opposite someone that you were involved with, and he honestly said, "All anyone cares about is 'are you interfering with my laughs?'" Brava on the theatre shallowness! Speaking of which, I got an email from one of my favorite English professors whom I had at Oberlin. He wanted me to know that "Brava" is actually the feminine of "Bravo" and is not supposed to be used on a man. I had to explain that it's essentially a joke, and I've appropriated that word to mean both "Brava" *and* "Bravo." I also have no shame using it as a noun like: "His singing was a total brava." I didn't mind explaining, but I was devastated that my writing is still being evaluated by my college professors! Isn't this like that dream people always have where they're suddenly back in college, and they have a big exam? I thought I was free from that dreaded red ink, but it's still there, lurking. Every word I write is subject to his scrutinizing eye and well-worn copy of Strunk and White's *The Elements of Style*.

Matthew talked about being in the original workshop of *Parade* as Leo Frank. After the workshop, he heard the show was going to Toronto but never got any details about when he would begin. Then he got a letter from Hal Prince that had the essence of letting him go, but didn't say it. The key line was *Even if this doesn't work out, I'd love to work with you again.* He thought, "Huh... I think I'm fired." He would show the letter to Sarah and his friends and say, "I think I'm fired? Don't I seem fired to you?" He claims that he finally knew he wasn't doing it once the show opened on Broadway without him.

As for *The Producers*, Martin Short got the offer to do Leo Bloom before Matthew, but Martin didn't want to leave his family in L.A. Then Matthew started reading that he was about to be asked to play the role, but no one actually asked him. Finally, he had a meeting for a movie that Mel Brooks was going to act in, and at the end of the meeting, Mel asked Matthew to play Leo. Matthew had a meeting later that week and read through the script with Mel as Glenn Kelly played the score. Matthew said he really wanted the part, so "I was acting my heart out — which is a teeny bit more than when I'm not doing anything." As usual, dry.

All right, people... this is a busy week. Right after *Broadway 101*, I go into rehearsal for a reading of *The Road to Qatar* (*roadtoqatar.com*). This is a musical that's actually a true story about a lyricist (Stephen Cole) and a composer (David Krane) who got hired by a mega-wealthy Arabian man to write a musical in Qatar! Meaning, these two "short, Jewish musical comedy writers" had to go to Qatar to write it... and suffice it to say, it didn't work out so well. But they did turn it into a musical. I'm playing the composer and, speaking of *The Producers*, Brad Oscar is playing the lyricist. It sounds like a brava. That's right, you heard me, professor. And by "heard," I mean "read." Hmm... maybe I can convince them to change it to *The Road to Brava*. Peace out!

Broadway 101 and Roger Bart
April 21, 2008

Last Monday night was *Broadway 101* and it went GREAT! So many exciting moments. The show began with the *Gypsy* overture played by nine musicians and then, after 16 measures, I stormed onstage and told the audience not to settle for the new-style small Broadway orchestra. P.S. I wasn't joking. Some orchestras on Broadway really just have nine people! And, as I say in the show, that's the size of *The Brady Bunch* including Alice. Not including Oliver. Remember him and his bowl cut? Anyhoo, I then brought on a full orchestra that played the whole overture and it was *thrilling*! It's so delicious to hear a full string section. The hard thing about Monday is that we teched all afternoon and then did a 7 PM show... followed by a 9:30 PM show! I was getting really tired by the second show but felt that, if I complained, I'd be like those people who say, "It's so hard for me because I want to spend time relaxing at home with my handsome husband, but our tickets to Hawaii are non-refundable."

I did a section of the show on riffing and told the audience that I had once conducted a benefit where the woman singing "Don't Rain On My Parade" ended the song with this amazing riff. I then demonstrated the riff and heard crickets. I waited a minute and said, "That's odd... it always brings down the house when Lillias White does it... *trust me*!" At that moment, the "Don't Rain on my Parade" vamp began, and Lillias came out onstage... and did indeed bring down the house! She is such a fantastic performer because her riffs are so musical and from an acting choice, as opposed to certain pop singers whose subtext is either a) I'm amazing, or b) that note is too high for me so instead of sustaining it, I'll hit it for a nanosecond and then riff off it. If you wanna see some *Broadway 101*, there are tons of clips on *SethRudetsky.com*.

On Thursday, I interviewed *Young Frankenstein* star Roger Bart for the *Chatterbox*. He grew up in Princeton and then moved to Savannah, GA. His father worked for a paper company, which, Roger says, had a large part in ruining the Savannah River. Roger has a mortifying childhood memory of wearing a T-shirt that said "Trees Are Renewable." At least his is just a memory. I still have my 8x10 shot from when I was 12 sporting a pageboy haircut combined with Dorothy Hamill wings.

Roger said he loved performing in madrigal groups in high school, and when he's doing Broadway cast recordings, he can always tell who's been in a high school madrigal group because they know how to blend. I asked him if he shows up to recording sessions in ye olde madrigal outfits, and he asked me if I meant a "madri-gown." Brava on that term! Roger Bart, get thee to a Renaissance faire *stat*!

I was shocked to find out that Roger's uncle ran Paramount Pictures with Robert Evans (!) and made the films *The Godfather* and *Rosemary's Baby*. He's now the editor of *Variety*. I asked Roger if he used that connection, and he said that his uncle was able to get him an audition for Juilliard, but they told Roger he'd have to repeat his first two years of college, and he was too eager to graduate, so he stayed at Rutgers. Speaking of Rutgers, he was classmates with Kevin Chamberlin and remembers taking theatre class and spending a long time studying period bows. Of course, he figured he'd never need them. Cut to 15 years later, he was co-starring opposite Kevin in *Triumph of Love*, and every night they ended the show with Restoration bows! Hmm... perhaps Roger's next play will employ mask-work or "pass the pulse."

Roger had a manager after college who got him an audition for *Big River* and said if it didn't work out, he should go in for *Star Search*. He wound up getting the first national tour of *Big River* and was relieved he didn't have to go in for *Star Search*... but I was disappointed to hear that. Was anyone else obsessed with *Star Search*? First of all, I want to know who coined the expression "spokesmodel"? The same people who did "nanny-gate"? And remember the acting category? We'd actually sit through two different actors doing the exact same scene twice! Ah... it was a simpler time. And a more boring one.

Roger was cast as Tom Sawyer in *Big River* and got to take over the role on Broadway. He admits that he was decidedly not well-liked amongst the cast, probably because of his practical joking. He was backstage during the show one night and sat down on an extra inflated whoopee cushion that he had planted. Instead of the laugh he expected, his dresser said, "You are such an a__hole." Then he was talking with another actor who had an entrance at the same time he did, and Roger kept the conversation going until the last second and then started to go out onstage. But he was just pretending. It was way too early for their entrance! It was still the scene before their entrance, where two people are on a raft. So, the other actor saw Roger start to walk out, and wound up onstage in what was the middle of the Mississippi River. He stood there awkwardly, got glared at by the King and the Duke who were on a raft... and then fled, prompting him to a) bruise Roger's arm b) call him the same word that the dresser had first coined.

Roger became good friends with Jonathan Larson and recorded many demos for him, including all of *Superbia* and the first three songs of *Rent*. Roger played "Roger" on the demo and when Jonathan asked him to audition for the actual role, Roger declined because he felt he would never get it and didn't really want to play it. Roger felt that Jonathan was an idealist who wrote his heroes as incredibly noble, and Roger wanted to play someone with more of a sense of humor. Later on, he regretted not auditioning when Roger was doing the not well-received *King David*. That was the first show at the restored New Amsterdam Theater and Roger remembers looking across 41st Street at the crowds for *Rent* and feeling like he was literally on the "wrong side of the street."

Roger was cast as Cousin Kevin in the first national tour of *The Who's Tommy* and credits Wayne Cilento with helping him dance for the first time. He said that it was a nightmare at first.

ME: What was hard about dancing?
ROGER: (immediately) Moving. (pause) Moving my body to rhythm.

I love how he stated the literal definition of dance. On the first day of rehearsal, Wayne taught the cast the "dance vocabulary" (i.e. steps and the style that would be used throughout the show), and Roger said that he went into a fetal position. When he left rehearsal, he thought he would never go back. But the net day, Lisa Mordente (who was assisting... and is also Chita Rivera's daughter!) brought him into another studio and taught him the dances really slowly, and he was able to get it *and* sass it! That's why I constantly advise young kids studying the theatre to get thee to dance class now! I always say: fifth position now negates fetal position later.

Roger did both *Tommy* and *The Secret Garden* and grew to be not fond of child actors. He overheard a few horrible conversations between child actors and their parents: during *The*

Secret Garden, one little boy asked his mom for a dollar. She told him that she had just given him a dollar on the last break. He replied, "Mom, who makes the money in this family?" And the mother sheepishly gave him the money. Ouch!

I thought Roger was fantastic as the Harlequin in *Triumph of Love*, and he said that the rehearsal period was crazy because F. Murray Abraham would quit the show every day right around 5:50. Then, that night, he would call the director, Michael Mayer, and rejoin the show. Speaking of Michael Mayer, he pushed for Roger to get the role of Snoopy in *You're a Good Man, Charlie Brown* because it was a toss-up between Roger and another actor. That's why Roger was so thankful to him in his Tony speech. And speaking of *You're a Good Man, Charlie Brown*, whenever my friend Jack Plotnick wants to bust theatre people for abbreviating show titles, he'll say pretentiously, "That was back in '91 when I was doing *Good Man*."

Roger said that it was hard to get laughs in "*Good Man*" (*wink*) because the show was basically old-school sketches. At one point, one of the gang says "Hi, Snoopy!" and he's supposed to lament, "Nobody ever calls me sugar lips." (Silence). He said that he tried to solve it by beginning the scene by licking "down there," but that idea shockingly had the kibosh put on it ASAP. One of the ways he did get a laugh was when he would sing a really pretty phrase in the show… and immediately follow it by frantically gnawing on his arm. I remarked that the sound he made while gnawing was similar to the noises he'd make when he took over the role of Leo in *The Producers*, and he agreed. He said he always feels that you should add mouth noises for foreign audiences because, even if they don't understand the show, they'll get that. We then segued to him playing Carmen Ghia, and he said that Mario Cantone originated the role in the workshop but passed on the show because he was planning on doing *Assassins* that year… which unfortunately got cancelled because of 9/11. The scene Roger had to audition with had him opening the door and saying "Yesss?" At the audition, Roger took that idea, but expanded it and held the "S" out for 30 seconds, like he wound up doing in the show. Roger said Mel Brooks laughed so hard that he turned purple. However, when Roger first tried it in rehearsal, Nathan Lane said sassily, "I can't wait to see that bomb in Chicago." But the second time they ran it, Nathan played the "Where is that noise coming from?" bit, and the two bits combined made the moment always land.

When Roger did the workshop of *Young Frankenstein*, he played Igor, not Dr. Frankenstein. Then he got a call offering him the lead! Everyone was giddy offering him the role and expected him to scream, "Yes!" But instead, he told them that he wanted to think about it. He said that it was a tough decision because he's a major Marty Feldman fan, and he was so excited to play a role originated by him. Also, Roger loves playing the kind of role where you come onstage, get the laugh and the audience always wants more. However, he decided to challenge himself… and now he loves it.

I went to my mom's house for both Passover Seders. Everything is as it always ways. The same story of Passover, the same delicious, traditional meal and the same jokes I've been peppering the Haggadah with since time immemorial. AKA whenever the name Nahor came up, I acted offended and said, "Who you calling Na*hor*?" and whenever bitter herbs were mentioned, my sister and I would emphasize the word "bitter" and point to my mom. Ahh… tradition.

Okay, Chag Sameach everyone, and next year in Jerusalem!

Life Is a Cabaret
April 28, 2008

Bring on the bread, Passover's over! I had a few non-matzoh slips, but I was relatively good. And speaking of good, let's just say that those Starbucks breakfast sandwiches are hard to resist. 'Nuff said. *Still eating them, years later.*

The week started out at Birdland, where Wayman Wong put together another fantastic *Leading Men* show for BC/EFA. I played the piano for most of the acts and did some deconstructing! The men all sounded great, and I must give a special shout-out to Tom Andersen who performed his signature song that he also wrote, "Yard Sale." It has such a simple, beautiful melody and tells about a yard sale that Tom really went to in San Francisco. He sings of speaking with the man and as the song progresses, you realize the yard sale is happening because the man knows he's soon going to die from AIDS. It's so well-written and literally makes me cry as I play it!

The whole show ended with Norm Lewis doing a blast from both of our pasts. As I've mentioned before, when he first moved to New York, Norm wanted to do a song that guys don't normally do, so he'd audition with "Before the Parade Passes By." Back then he was non-Equity, and I had a 30-inch waist. Norm sang a phenomenal arrangement of it that completely brought the house down, and it's going to be featured on his new CD. *I cannot wait!* Even though he's a baritone, he literally hits a B flat in it... which is a full two octaves above Carol Channing's high note. *If you've not heard it, stop reading RIGHT NOW and get it from iTunes. And watch me deconstruct it at SethRudetsky.com.*

On Wednesday, I saw *Young Frankenstein* again because my mom hadn't gone yet, and she *loved* it. After the show, I was gabbing with Paul Castree backstage and Megan Mullally came out of her dressing room and said, "I thought I heard your voice." *I* have a recognizable voice? Who's the one with the high-pitched, nasal, fast-talking twang? Oh. Both of us.

On Sirius radio, I interviewed one of my childhood obsessions, Joel Grey. He told me that he grew up in Cleveland, and his father was a famous Yiddish comedian named Mickey Katz. Joel said that all of the New York Jews who moved out to Los Angeles didn't have any entertainment, so his dad moved his family to California and created the show "Borscht-capades," which was obviously later bought by WASPS and re-titled *Ice Capades*. Get it? Mary Tyler Moore's icy performance in *Ordinary People*? *The Ice Storm*? Anybody?

Joel said he was very inspired by Mickey Rooney and Judy Garland... especially the Andy Hardy movies. Eddie Cantor saw Joel singing and dancing in his father's show and, when Joel was 18, put him on TV. I watched that episode on YouTube, and Eddie says, "This kid might be the Danny Kaye of tomorrow." Joel said it's embarrassing, but I loved it! Watch Joel talk to Eddie Cantor... he's obviously so nervous and keeps his eyes totally downcast throughout the whole interview. But then he tears it up during his number and does some sassy high kicks and crazy turns.

Right after that, he performed in nightclubs (the Copa in N.Y.) *and* the London Palladium. In London, he performed with Johnnie Ray (who sang the big hit, "Cry"), and Joel said that he had to perform after Johnnie and kick away the panties that lined the stage — panties that had been thrown by girls in the audience. My question is: when girls do that, are those panties that the girls were actually wearing? What do they hope to get from throwing them? Do they stitch their phone number inside? And do they take them off during the show? Isn't that awkward? Do they bring along a dresser to help them?

Joel said that he couldn't get a job after his nightclub career because producers looked down on nightclub performers. He remembers auditioning (and being rejected from) the Broadway productions of *West Side Story*, *Irma La Douce* and *The Sound of Music*. He wanted the role of Rolf, who sings "Sixteen Going on Seventeen," and later becomes a Nazi. Hmm... perhaps the fact that his father was a famous Yiddish comedian prevented Joel from playing an effective Nazi. Speaking of Jews inappropriately trying out for *The Sound of Music*, Barbra Streisand also tried out for that show and got a big, fat rejection. *And* years later, I myself auditioned to be one of the Von Trapp kids at the Equity Library Theatre and got ixnayed faster than you can say *Sh'ma Yisroel*. Is there no place for a Jewish person on Broadway? Besides every single show but *The Sound of Music*?

Joel said that he brought along an audition pianist for *Irma La Douce*... John Kander! Joel didn't say that's why he didn't get the gig... but perhaps somebody should stick to composing classic musicals. Joel kept getting feedback that he looked too young for the roles he was trying out for, so when he went in for *Stop the World — I Want to Get Off*, he showed up in the kind of make-up Anthony Newly wore in the show, and he felt it made him look ageless. The embarrassing part was that he got into the make-up across the street and had to walk to the audition in full clown-face. It paid off! He got the lead on tour and then replaced Anthony Newley on Broadway! He then replaced Anthony in *The Roar of The Greasepaint — The Smell of the Crowd*. P.S. What's with the long-winded titles? In my day, we did shows like *Carrie* and *Rags*. We were also out of work by Sunday.

Joel did a horrible show at the Jones Beach Theater called *Mardi Gras*, which ran seven days a week (!), and he hated it so much that he was on the verge of quitting the business. Suddenly, Hal Prince (who had seen him in *Stop the World...* or as people annoyingly now call shows on message boards, STWIWTGO) called Joel and said that he was doing a musical based on the novel *I Am a Camera*, and there was a part that was being created that was right for him. It was the first role he got without an audition! I guess if he did have to audition, he would have asked John Kander to play, which would have been weird since John wrote it. But at least he would have known what the composer thought of his audition.

When Joel started working on the Emcee, he knew it was what he had waited his whole career for and had essentially given up the hope of ever getting. The Jones Beach show was his lowest career point but was then followed by what he had always wanted... so those of you struggling right now, doing some headache-y show, or doing *no* show, hold on!

When he first got cast, his role only had the four songs written ("Willkommen," "Two Ladies," "The Money Song" and "If You Could See Her") and no real character. There was someone whom Hal saw during the war that Hal wanted to base the character on, but since there was no dialogue or scenes for the Emcee, it was really up to Joel to create something to connect all those songs. He did it by writing a complete history of the Emcee, so he knew everything about him when he was onstage, and that way the character could live within the show when he was offstage. The look came from what Hal had seen, and Joel added to it. Joel decided that the Emcee would always want to look young, so he chose a base color that reads as white, but was actually called "Juvenile Pink." There were no readings or workshops like there are today. They just rehearsed and then took it out of town. Joel said that people were extremely negative when they heard about *Cabaret*, judging it as a "musical about Nazis." That actually makes me happy to hear, because I'm constantly reading things on message boards saying, "Audiences aren't interested in (fill in the blank)." Let me say that *no one* knows what audiences are interested in!! You can have the best subject matter in the world and do a bad show, or the most bizarre theme and do a brilliant show, so let's put the kibosh on pre-judging what shows will be a hit because *no one knows*!

We started talking about the song "If You Could See Her," where the Emcee is performing a comedy song with a gorilla. He sings of his love for her and about how everyone judges their relationship... and right at the end he sings, "If you could see her through my eyes... she wouldn't look Jewish at all." It's a brilliant theatrical device because the audience laughs along with the song, but at the end, you realize you're laughing at a horrifically anti-Semetic song. Audiences would gasp in shock because it's almost as though they were an actual audience in Berlin, complicit in the Anti-Semitism by laughing throughout the song. Unfortunately, B'nai B'rith didn't understand the point of it and simply saw it as Anti-Semeitc. They made Hal Prince change the ending to "she isn't a meeskite at all," which completely takes away the impact the song had. The song showed the audience how Jews were dehumanized by Germans who were then able to follow through with the Holocaust. Joel was forced to do the new lyrics on Broadway... and the film didn't want the original ending either! Joel insisted that they shoot two versions, and thankfully, the original/horrific version got in the film.

Speaking of the film, Joel almost wasn't cast. First considered was Anthony Newley and... Ruth Gordon! Joel didn't have any details except to say that she was up for it and my head reeled. Would it have been done Drag King style? Linda Hunt style? Victor/Victoria style? If so, which Victoria? Julia Andrews, Liza Minnelli or Raquel Welch? The National tour version with Toni Tennille? And what about the Captain? How would he have figured in? Would she have sung "Muskrat Love"? Okay, I'm out.

Not only was Joel one of the few people who originated a role on Broadway and got to play it in the film version, but he was also nominated for an Oscar. His competition included Al Pacino for *The Godfather*... and Joel won!!!! Brava on the Tony *and* the Oscar.

On Thursday night, I had to walk my dog late and didn't feel like getting dressed again, so I just went outside in my pajama bottoms. "Who am I going to run into?" I asked myself. Answer: Jonathan Groff. He said he was on his way to Lea Michele's apartment to watch a movie and invited me over to say hi. So, two *Spring Awakening* stars saw me in my PJs, but that's nothing compared to what I saw of them onstage. AKA an exposed arse and a boob!

I'm excited about this coming week because I'll be recording my book, *Broadway Nights*, for *Audible.com*. This week I'll be voicing all my stuff as the narrator, and then I'm going to bring in my co-stars. For now, farewell to Passover and let me say, "next year in Jerusalem"... if there's a Starbucks within walking distance.

The *Gypsy* in Their Souls
May 5, 2008

What the hell happened to global warming? Why is it May and the heat is still on in my apartment? I decided to go to the play that most described the month it feels like… *November*. It was the Sunday night Actors Fund performance and the audience loved it. Nathan Lane was hilarious, and I can't believe he did my *Chatterbox* a few weeks ago and then did the show that night… it's a mammoth role! People are always talking about roles where "he/she never leaves the stage"… and then they follow it with "…except to change costumes" or "…and except for a short time during a few scenes in Act Two, but she's getting a new wig on at that point." Okay, once the word "except" is used, it's called "He/she leaves the stage." Whereas Nathan *never* left the stage! Except during intermission. But while the play is on, he's there the whole time. It's very similar to my role in *The Ritz* in that *I* never left the stage… if all the world's a stage.

Monday afternoon, I saw the Easter Bonnet Competition, and seated behind me was one of the contestants I just worked with on the *Legally Blonde* reality show. Because we finished filming a few weeks ago, I know who won… and quite frankly I can't take the tension of keeping it a secret. It's very tense seeing anyone involved with the show because I'm always nervous that whatever I say will give away to the people around us whether or not the person got the role of Elle Woods. Example: "How are you today?" Meaning, "still giddy from getting the role of Elle Woods?" or "How are you coping with not getting the role of Elle Woods?" Even "Hi" makes me nervous to say because I can't tell whether people can tell my subtext is "Hi, winner!" or "Hi, not Elle Woods."

On Monday night, I was a judge at the second annual Broadway Beauty Pageant. Male beauty, that is. I judged alongside two of the brilliantly talented stars of *[title of show]*, Susan Blackwell and Hunter Bell. The five male contestants were from *Grease, Curtains, Xanadu, A Chorus Line* and *Hairspray*. I loved Mr. *Curtains* who sang "Show Off" from *The Drowsy Chaperone*. He went en pointe (!), played the saw, did rhythmic gymnastic scarf dancing and, during the snake-charmer section of the song, was about to pull off his underwear, but then decided he didn't want to "show off." He also put cookie dough in an "oven" and, at the end of the number, served the three judges cookies. Brava!

The winner of the evening was Marty Thomas, who was Mr. *Xanadu*. He sang an amazing version of "Proud Mary" that sounded like it was in the original Tina Turner key. I remember seeing him years ago on *Star Search* when my friend Billy Porter was on a winning streak. Marty was in the kids' category and was up against a buck-toothed brunette who sold it a little too hard. He wound up winning… and the girl who lost wound up becoming a mom with two kids. She also wound up in the Off-Broadway show *Ruthless, The New Mickey Mouse Club* and the film *Riding in the Car With Boys*. Yes, his singing won him *Star Search* over Britney Spears' performance... which incidentally may have been the last time she didn't lip synch.

I had so much fun judging with Hunter and Susan. First of all, I'm so obsessed with their "*[title of show]* Show." It's these ten-minute movies they've filmed over the last few months with amazing Broadway guest stars. I love the episode entitled "Snake Eats Tail" and Susan's seriousness when she talks of "sexperts." It's not a word and/or profession! How dare she infuse it with such gravitas? Brava on the line reading.

At the *Broadway Beauty Pageant*, Hunter asked the contestants what he called "tough questions," such as "Tyne, Bernadette or Patti?" I focused solely on the latter and asked one contestant a string of Patti questions which hit him like a machine gun: *Evita* or *Anything Goes*? *The Old Neighborhood* or *Noises Off*? *Life Goes On* or that TV movie about Lady Bird Johnson? After each option I threw out, Hunter would nod his head and mutter "tough questions..."

Speaking of Patti, on Thursday at the *Chatterbox*, I had two of *Gypsy*'s sassy strippers: Alison Fraser, who plays Tessie Tura, and Marilyn Caskey, who plays Electra. Alison grew up in Natick, MA, where Bill Finn is from. After Bill graduated college, he came back to town and saw a high school show where Alison was singing "Stormy Weather." Why do so many theatre kids perform stuff they need 30 more years of life experience to be able to perform with any understanding? Why, at 13, was I one of the 27 (!) performers in my camp's production of *Jacques Brel is Alive and Well and Living in Paris*? Did I need to know that the "old folks never die... they just put down their heads and go to sleep one day..."? Why was that my solo? Devastating.

Anyway, Alison and Bill began performing together in the town square (he'd play piano and sing with her, and they'd get tips), but then she went off to Carnegie Mellon University. She hated the way they taught there, which she thought was sort of based on the theory, "You've all been the stars of your high school, so let's tear you down completely and then build you up again." She wound up leaving and moving to New York. Bill started working on *In Trousers* with Mary Testa and Alison. Alison said that she told Bill they should do a concert of the music in his apartment and see if anyone's interested. She remembers that they borrowed chairs from the local synagogue. Borrowed? I asked if she barged in and said, "I'm Christian. I'm taking these." But she claimed Bill was a member. Ira Weitzman, who was developing projects for Playwrights Horizons, came to the apartment concert and gave them a date to do a show. I'm obsessed that their allotted time for rehearsals was 12-4... in the morning! It was in the Times Square area during the terrifying 1970s when anything went.

Alison said she remembers that Bill, at around 3 AM and exhausted, was super thirsty and walked up to an assistant, begging, "Get me some Coke!" The assistant ran out and came back an hour later. He said that he couldn't get any right then, but was promised some tomorrow. Bill said "Why'd you go outside? There's a machine right in the lobby!" Yes, that ol' chestnut about mixing up Coke/cocaine actually happened.

Alison also talked about auditioning. She absolutely hates it. She said that she's one of those actresses who really needs to delve into a role for a while to finally nail it. She thinks it takes a brave director to watch her audition and say, "Hmm... she's terrible... but might one day have it." She got cast in the original *The Secret Garden* and cut her hair super short as did Rebecca Luker, who was playing the ghostly wife. Rebecca is from the South and would hold hands with Alison when they left the theatre. One day, they were being interviewed for the radio, and the interviewer turned the tape off and asked, "So, you can tell me off the record. How long have you two been together?" It's that old equation: short hair + hand holding = hot girl-on-girl action.

Speaking of auditions, Alison didn't have to audition for *Gypsy*. Arthur Laurents saw her at the Bay Street Theatre last year, took her out to dinner and offered her Tessie Tura. And it was a perfect role considering her life now as a student. Yes, she regrets dropping out of college and has recently decided to finish her degree. She's going to John Jay and studying every night. Literally. The strippers don't enter 'til the middle of Act Two, so they have a lot of time on their hands. Alison was supposed to read *The Odyssey*, but it was hard to take in, so she started reading it out loud. Marilyn heard her and asked if she could play one of the parts. Soon they read the whole thing, as well as *The Iliad*, and Marilyn spends the beginning of the show testing Alison's knowledge of those classic snoozefests... I mean, masterpieces. Marilyn brought her notes on Thursday to the *Chatterbox* and tested my audience. For every question that the audience got before Alison did, they donated $20 to Broadway Cares/Equity Fights AIDS. Turns out the audience knew everything, and they gave a donation of $160! I was onstage the whole time and found out after that Alison was giving the audience the answers as Marilyn was reading! Pret-ty sneaky, sis.

Marilyn grew up in Utah and studied voice in college and then went to ACT in San Francisco. She played Cunegonde in a production of *Candide* at Arena Stage in DC, but had very little money when she got to New York, where she had moved. She was on a bus going uptown and saw someone she had just done *Candide* with. She was mortified because she had just come from a temp job as a secretary and saw her former castmate, who was now in *Phantom*, get on the bus. Marilyn tried to hide, but the woman came over. And it's a good thing she did, because she told Marilyn that she was gonna try to get her an audition! Marilyn said that the woman moved mountains to make it happen and it finally did. She got an audition for Carlotta and prepared the managers' scene (which goes to a high E!) and the speech that Carlotta says when something almost falls on her head in the first scene and she storms out. ("These-a things do happen? Well, until you stop these-a things from happening, this thing does *not* happen!") She inhaled to start the speech, and Hal Prince yelled, "Stop! This is not a comic monologue... She takes this very seriously. Her life was just threatened." I agree with him, but how did he know she was going to have a comic take on it from one inhale? Was her inhale hilarious? How do you inhale and make it funny? I'd ask Bill Clinton, but we all know he *didn't* inhale! That's right, now that it's election year, expect a string of numbingly unfunny jokes from me.

Marilyn said that she spent a year visualizing herself in that part: imagining how it felt coming to the theatre, seeing her name in the *Playbill*, having her picture outside. It was *The Secret* back when "Secret" just meant a deodorant strong enough for a man, but made for a woman. She had five auditions and was told that she had to go to Trump Tower to give her final audition for Sir Andrew (The Lordship came later). She had borrowed a pair of shoes for the audition that were too small, and they messed up her whole back. She remembers riding the bus home, leaning against the window and weeping because her sciatic nerve was flaring up so badly. When she got home, she got a call saying that she didn't need to do the next audition... she got it!

She also covered the role of Norma Desmond in the Toronto production of *Sunset Boulevard*. The role was being played by Diahann Carroll (who, you remember, was the first black female star of a TV series, *Julia*), and Marilyn said that there were certain performances where she (a red-headed white girl) would go on for the second act. My *Chatterbox* audience gasped, and Marilyn said, "That was pretty much the reaction of the audience up there." I remember doing *Forever Plaid* in Toronto and running into Marilyn. She made me laugh so hard because, as the standby, none of the front-of-house staff knew who she was because she was always backstage. So when she was scheduled to first go on, she heard one usher tell another, "Marilyn Caskey is playing Norma tonight." Marilyn walked up and said, "I hear she's fan-tastic! I drove from Florida to Toronto to see her." Marilyn explained to me, "Rumors are going to happen, why not start them yourself!"

The good news is that last Monday, I started recording the audio version of my novel, *Broadway Nights*, for *Audible.com*. I'm playing the lead character and I have a ton of actors coming to play all the others. Audible felt that in case an actor suddenly cancels at the last minute, I should first record the *entire* book! It's more than 350 pages!! I did the whole thing in four days and have the nodes to prove it. Now that I've recorded everything, I'm going to keep the narration parts, and I just started bringing in Broadway people to play the other roles. Last week, I had Ann Harada come out and play the cheap, nightmarish producer character, Bettina Geisenshlaag. Ann was fantastic and was joined by Kristin Chenoweth, who played Francoise, my assistant music director who is obsessed with the harpsichord... or, as she says, the "harp-see-chord," which is the way she claims it was originally pronounced. I paid for Kristin's car service there but then neglected to mention she'd be joining us on NJ Transit for the way home from Newark. We were all exhausted slash devastated.

On a side note, I did *Grease!* years ago with Marissa Jaret Winokur and I am super proud that she's on *Dancing with the Stars*. Well, cut to, she's desperate to stay on that show and just sent me an email asking me to beg my friends to vote for her! The best part is, you don't even have to watch the show! You can listen to your CD of *Hairspray* and just keep your finger on the re-dial button. *She told me a few years later that the show pays up a storm and every week you remain on the show means an even higher paycheck. Sign me up ASAP!*

All right, everyone, this week I finish recording *Broadway Nights*, see *South Pacific* and celebrate my mom's birthday. *And* I got an invite to the opening of *Glory Days*, the last show before the Tony cutoffs. I feel like such an insider — if an insider has to wait a complete theatre season to finally get an invitation to an opening night. Anybody? Nobody. *I wound up not being able to go and I so wish I had. It was one of those shows that opened and closed on the same day!*

Glory Days and Nights
May 12, 2008

I finally finished the audio version of my book *Broadway Nights*! Oy, what a headache I had... and what manipulation I had to pull. First, I had to ask all these actors to be voices on my book... then I had to drop the bomb that it was being recorded in Newark. I was walking down Amsterdam Avenue in the West 70s mulling about how I couldn't find the right actor to be the voice of the horrible, shallow agent character. I needed somebody with amazing comic chops. Suddenly, I ran into Richard Kind. The next thing he knew, he was on a New Jersey Transit train heading to Newark at ten in the morning. I also had James play one of the roles and I was talking about it in front of Juli. I thought maybe she'd want to come watch us record, but I felt bad she couldn't play anyone in the book. Hmm, I considered, maybe the ex-alcoholic star who married a Mafia Don? Then I remembered there is a role for a seven-year-old who's trying out for the role of Young Cosette! The scene in the novel takes place when the lead character is playing auditions for *Les Miz* and this girl walks in and asks him to transpose a Charlotte Church song... and then blames her clanky singing on him! As she walks out, she turns to him and passive/aggressively says, "Thanks, anyway." Juli told me before she recorded that she decided the first word should be sweet and the second one sassy. Brava on the acting beats! To make sure another female in my life wasn't jealous of a seven-year-old, I also cast my mother on the recording. She actually read *three* roles: a rude usher, a pretentious actress and an anxiety-ridden usher. I decided to cast my mom according to the theory, "act what you know."

Speaking of my mom *and* because last Tuesday was her birthday and Sunday was Mother's day, I've decided to regale you with one of her signature tales. When she and my dad split up, she decided to "treat herself" and get some ice cream. She lives on Long Island and drove to the local ice cream store to get a cone. Well, even though she was enjoying her ice cream immensely, she was obviously still feeling stressed out because of the divorce and, before she knew it, she had run through a few stop signs. She pulled into her driveway and saw a car pull in behind that had "pretty lights" on top of it. She snapped out of her daze and realized that the "pretty lights" were a siren, it was a police car, and the cop inside of it was probably going to ticket her for reckless driving. She then remembered that her license specifically states that she must wear glasses when she drives. Uh-oh! Where were they? In her bag, phew! But then she panicked because she had an enormous ice cream cone in her hands, and she thought the cop would say, "Ma'am, apparently you were so busy with your ice cream that you didn't see all those stop signs." P.S. My mom was basing the cop's personality on her own. *She's* the one who says things like, "You were so busy with your new iPod that you forgot to call Aunt Phyllis!"

Anyhoo, she began to freak out; she was torn between wanting to get rid of her ice cream and panicking because she wasn't wearing her glasses. *Ice cream, glasses, ice cream, glasses...* finally, she shoved the whole ice cream cone in her hand bag, took out her glasses (which were now covered in ice cream), put them on, and turned to the window of the car just as the cop approached. She decided to speak calmly. "May I help you?" she asked. Her face remained impassive as the ice cream dripped down her glasses. She thought if she didn't acknowledge the ice cream, maybe he wouldn't. The cop looked at her and perhaps picked up on her state of being. He inquired, "Are you okay, ma'am?" She replied mysteriously, "I will be... soon." *What*? Well, essentially, the insanity defense worked because, instead of revoking her license as he should have, he wound up walking her to her door.

Okay, I saw *A Catered Affair*, which was thrilling for me because it marked the Broadway debut of my good friend and performing partner, Kristine Zbornik. The show opens with her talking through her window with the other neighborhood ladies. I was so excited and happy for her that I started to cry... it was so cool! Also, I'm really glad I didn't see the first preview or opening night where I'd be nervous that she was nervous. I knew that she had done it before and I didn't have to worry about her not making a costume change in time or forgetting a step in a big splashy dance number. I especially didn't have to worry about the latter because it's essentially a chamber musical and has less dancing than the town of Beaumont (*Footloose* reference. Anyone?). But regardless, I was especially impressed by her role as a salesgirl. She's really just there to show the super-talented Leslie Kritzer a wedding dress, but Kristine is hilarious. What I love is that she found the humor in a tiny moment without making me think, "Oy. What a needy actor. Taking a small role and desperately trying to get a laugh out of it." (See bootleg footage of me as the pianist for *Forever Plaid*.) The whole cast was great and I'm so happy to see Harvey Fierstein on Broadway again. He's not only a pioneer/trailblazer, he's also a terrific actor and Broadway legend. And we really don't have that many Broadway legends. Thank goodness two of them are starring on Broadway right now (if you don't know who the other one is, let me just say, she lived in the Natchez Trace, moved to Buenos Aires, sold her hair, took a cruise ship at Lincoln Center, visited the old neighborhood... oy, all right already, it's Patti LuPone. I don't have the energy for more clever clues).

Monday night, I hosted a benefit for the Roundabout Theater that was a karaoke night. I didn't know what was gonna happen, but it was great. It was really fun to see a different kind of benefit. The songs were ones actors would never sing in a regular benefit (Susan Blackwell of *[title of show]* rocked "Rio" and *Xanadu*'s Kerry Butler belted "I Will Survive"). The biggest surprise was Ben Walker, who's in *Les Liaisons Dangereuses*. He was hilarious in his intro: "This is the second time I've ever done karaoke and the first time I've done it sober." Then he proceeded to belt the h-e-double hockey sticks out of "New York State of Mind." Who knew? I was miffed, though, because after Nellie McKay did a jazzy version of Cole Porter's "I Get Along Without You Very Well," I complained that the lyrics that were streaming on the karaoke screen were wrong. They read, "What's in store? Should I fall once more?" I asked the audience to back me up on the fact that the lyrics are "What's in store? Should I phone once more," and I got blank faces. Well, I went home and researched it online, and I've found *both*! On a Billie Holiday site it's "should I fall once more," and on a Frank Sinatra site it's "should I phone once more." I make you a bet someone just transliterated the lyrics from listening to Billie and her sassy diction and thought it sounded like "fall once more" because what the hell does that mean? Fall *where* once more? Fall in love once more? You already are in love... that's the point of the song. Annoying! But most bizarrely, as I was researching the Cole Porter lyric, I got taken to a website that not only a) offered Cole Porter ring tones but b) the banner on top was *Get "I Hate Men" ring tones. That's* the song they decided to advertise heavily? I'm dying to see if there's a Sondheim site with *Get "Bring Me My Bride" ring tones.* By the way, I'm not joking about the Cole Porter.

Tuesday, I recorded my audio book with the sweet and talented Jonathan Groff. We wound up taking up so much time because he's one of those people who gets the giggles and I'm one of those people who only encourages it. There was a lot of us saying to the audio engineer: "OK... Mason dialogue, page 46, here we go." There'd be a pause, Jonathan would inhale and then crazily start laughing and, of course, I would too. It was hilarious, 'til I realized we had to keep stopping so much that we went too long, and I was running out of there at 4:20 PM to catch a

4:30 PM back to Penn Station. Jonathan was telling me about his obsession with *Thoroughly Modern Millie*. When he first moved here, he auditioned for the ensemble and, after he sang, he got the ol' "Thank you." Before he left, though, he told Rob Ashford (The Tony Award-winning choreographer) that he had prepared a dance. First of all, everybody, let that sink in. He then asked if he could perform his prepared dance, and Rob said yes, perhaps simply to have an amazing story to tell his peers at the Choreographers Club. Well, Jonathan had watched the video of *Millie* on the Macy's Thanksgiving Day Parade over and over again 'til he had memorized the dance to the opening number. He did it for Rob... and got a callback! He went to the callback and was kept after numerous cuts, until he finally got ixnayed. But on his way out, he told Rob that it was his favorite show in the world and had him autograph his souvenir program. A few years later, Jonathan ran into Rob again... right after he was nominated for a Tony Award for *Spring Awakening*. He reminded Rob of the story, and the weird part is, Rob only vaguely remembered. How many people came to audition for him with a *memorized dance from the show*? Perhaps Rob's brain forgot the whole thing to protect him from remembering the trauma of watching something so awkward.

On Wednesday, I went with my mom to *South Pacific*. All I can say is brava to whomever decided to use the original size orchestra. Thirty delicious instruments! The current school-of-thought that it's too expensive for a full orchestra makes me crazy. Why does no one balk at having custom-made shoes? Ever hear of Florsheim? And the audience went crazy when the stage moved backwards, revealing the pit with all those musicians. They went even crazier when my mom's cell phone went off during a scene ("Sorry...I thought I turned it off"), but we shan't discuss that. The cast is great and I L-O-V-E-D Loretta Ables Sayre, who plays Bloody Mary. I obsessed with the vibrato she puts on the "ha" in "Happy Talk." Speaking of that song, my friend Mary Ann Hu is her understudy and actually got to go on last Saturday! Because they just opened, she hadn't had a full understudy run-through yet. She sang "Happy Talk" once when she was learning her blocking and told me that it was thrilling/terrifying to sing "Happy Talk" for the second time in her life... and this time be accompanied by a 30-piece orchestra. My friend Chris Gattelli did some great choreography, but I totally laughed when they put on the big Thanksgiving show in Act Two. Everyone is in makeshift costumes, and they announce that Nellie and the gang made their costumes out of old newspapers and stuff found on the island. I'm just wondering where they got the pointe shoes that one of the girls wears. The South Pacific island Capezio outlet store?

First of all, I announced last week that I was so excited to see the opening night of *Glory Days*, but I wound up not being able to go because I was in audio recording hell. I figured I'd catch the show this weekend. Then, I was so overwhelmed with doing my audio book that I didn't have time to book a *Chatterbox* guest. I was about to cancel when I got an email from one of the investors in the Broadway show *Glory Days* telling me that it closed right after opening night. I felt bad for everyone involved in the production and annoyed that I'd never get to see it... but then I thought... wait a minute, this could pay off for me! I called my friend Jesse Vargas, who did the musical arrangements, and he got the whole cast and creators to come to the *Chatterbox*! It was great. The swing was there, too, and of course, I asked if he had gone on. Shockingly, no. Everyone had such a great attitude, and no one was bitter. Except maybe, rightly so, Andrew Call, who showed up at the theatre for a meeting the day after opening, not knowing what it was about, and saw a box-office person through the glass of the theatre who mouthed, "Sorry, your show closed!" He was like, "It did?" Unfortunately, the same thing happened to him last year when he did *High Fidelity*. Before he heard anything from people involved in the show, someone who saw it on *Playbill.com* called him to offer their condolences for his show closing. Again, he was like, "It did?"

Alex Brightman (the swing) said that everyone gathered onstage right before the show on opening night, and Nick Blaemire (the composer) said that, no matter what happens, no one can take away the fact that they played Broadway. I thought that was very sweet and mature for his age. Speaking of mature, I was mortified to be onstage surrounded by people whose first Broadway show they listened to was *Rent*. I felt like Stephen Spinella during the curtain call of *Spring Awakening*.

James and I hightailed it to City Center on Saturday to see *No, No, Nanette*. I was very proud of Rosie (O'Donnell) who started taking tap lessons recently so she could tap in the show. Right at the end of the show, she hauled out some steps, and I was mind-boggled at how clean they sounded. And she wasn't tap-synching. Lip-tapping? I don't know the exact word to use, but you know what I mean: having someone backstage tap for her. And it was definitely her feet tapping onstage... as opposed to what I saw in the film version of *Chicago*. People involved in that movie were constantly saying that Richard Gere did all of his own tapping in "Razzle Dazzle." Hmm... I guess that's possible, but a) Why was there never a full body shot? b) Why only shots of the top half of him showing "style," and then the bottom half tapping and c) Why was it filmed completely in the dark?

Anyhoo, I also loved Michael Berresse's amazing dancing and Beth Leavel's hilarity in *Nanette*. Plus, she is the queen of hitting a high note and making you think, "Wow... she can't belt that, but it sounds amazing in head voice... good choice!" and then, one minute later, belting that same note and then belting one even higher just to show you that she can hit any note she wants, however the hell she wants. Brava!

This week I can finally relax a little (AKA pay all my overdue bills... sorry Equity) and continue the "fun" search for a new apartment. James and I are moving in together and want to stay on the Upper West Side. We decided that our ideal apartment is a ground-floor duplex in a brownstone with a backyard (for my doggie, Maggie). We saw two apartments that we loved and *both* were snatched by someone who applied before us. Not cool! Note to NYC: before you apply for an apartment, please clear it with me at *SethRudetsky.com*. Thanks! *We're now on our third apartment since then! From the 80s to the 120s and back to the 70s!*

All right, everyone, this week I'm also gonna see *Spring Awakening* one more time because Jonathan Groff and Lea Michele are both leaving, *and* I get to interview Christine Ebersole at Sirius radio and Boyd Gaines at the *Chatterbox*. It's another week of Broadway! Peace out!

Signature Tunes
May 19, 2008

All right, here we go. I began the week interviewing the lovely Christine Ebersole who, with Billy Stritch on the piano, just came out with a new CD called *Sunday in New York*. I asked her about "Around the World," which is my favorite song from *Grey Gardens*. Turns out, she saw my deconstruction of it on YouTube and told me that she gave it five stars, which she told me stood for "awesome." Brava! I asked her about the song and why she begins it sounding almost shrill, but suddenly adds vibrato on the lyric "...which is mother's way..." She said that she feels it's the voice Little Edie has inside her. Little Edie wanted to be a singer and this is the voice Little Edie thought she sounded like. I kept asking Christine what she sang at auditions for all of her classic roles and she couldn't remember. She could only remember what she wore. She is a big believer in showing up to the audition looking like the character, but not literally in costume. Speaking of which, I have a friend who had a commercial audition where they asked him to look like a pirate. He showed up with an eye patch and swashbuckling outfit and was the only who looked like that. Turns out, they told him to show up looking like a *pilot*. He did not book it.

On Thursday, James and I went to see *Spring Awakening*. Me, for the second time, him, for the first. It was Jonathan Groff and Lea Michele's final week, and I wanted James to see it before they left. Thankfully, it was still as fresh as the first time I saw it and I was particularly impressed with the sound. The band and singers sounded great, and also I love Lea's E at the end of the reprise of "Mama Who Bore Me," and I love how Jonathan does old-school focus: he's constantly looking to the balcony and box seats. I guess it's his vaudeville training, even though he was born 60 years after vaudeville died. After the show, James and I went backstage to Jonathan's dressing room. I was dying of thirst, and Jonathan offered me some Diet Coke. It was super fizzy, and he asked me if it was gross that he was putting his finger in my glass to stop the fizzing. I said it was fine because I was sure he took a shower after his exhausting, long and sweaty two-act show. There was silence... then he removed his finger.

After we all chatted for a while, Lea and Jonathan gigglingly told us they were planning on doing something not allowed. "Hmm... use vibrato during the show?" I thought. No, it turns out it was something even more scandalous. They decided to spend the night in the theatre! Apparently, they had slept over with John Gallagher, Jr. before he left the show, and now that they were leaving, they wanted to do it again. It was their way to say goodbye to "their theatre." Jonathan started scotch-taping up large tapestries underneath the shelves in his dressing room so they could hide behind it when the stage doorman did his final look before he locked up. After he taped, Jonathan asked us if we'd be accomplices. Accomplices? How dare he? To a crime no one really cared about? How could I lower my moral rectitude? But... looking into that Tony-nominated face, I had no choice but to say yes. James quickly agreed, too, and the next thing we knew we were walking down the stairs and loudly saying (so the doorman could hear us), "Boy! I guess everyone left while we were in the bathroom!" The stage doorman was very sweet and asked if Jonathan was still upstairs. I very awkwardly/loudly said (I also come from the vaudevillian school of no mics), "No! He left the building." Awkward pause while I remembered my line. "And Lea. Lea Michele has also left." The doorman looked miffed. James piped up. "Yep. They have left. Both." As we walked out of the stage door, we saw a long line of folks waiting to get autographs, and then the doorman had to tell them that Jonathan and Lea left already. James and I felt so bad for the fans as they dispersed, but we knew that Jonathan and Lea always signed autographs and tonight was a special occasion for them.

Of course, I think sleeping over in the theatre is probably one of those things that sounds like it's so much fun, but winds up with you getting a neck-ache from sleeping on an Equity cot in a cold, dark theatre and then waking up at 4 AM and realizing you forgot your toothbrush. Suffice it to say, I didn't want to be in the theatre for their "Spring Awakening" without an emergency supply of Listerine strips.

The next day, James and I caught an Amtrak train and comfortably traveled down to Washington, D.C. Maya Weil, a board member at the Signature Theatre who works at the Kennedy Center, wrote me an email saying that she loved my Sirius radio show and invited me to the Signature Theatre Gala in Arlington, VA. The theatre has been doing a Kander and Ebb salute all year (*Kiss of the Spider Woman, The Happy Time*), and the gala was for the premiere of their new show, *The Visit*, with book by Terrence McNally and direction by Frank Galati. I said *Yes*, Liza-style (AKA "Say yes." "Liza With a Z?" Anybody?). It was black tie so James borrowed a suit from Norm Lewis and I wore the tux I bought for the time I played Carnegie Hall with Audra McDonald. That was in 1999 and my waist is now in a different time zone. Hoo boy, was it tight.

I must praise Miss Chita Rivera, who is so commanding on stage and made the audience go crazy by simply doing one syncopated contraction (choreographed by Ann Reinking, sitting a few rows back). Chita just exudes theatre and it was thrilling to see her give a full Broadway performance from only a few feet away.

Before the show, I was in the lobby and ran into John Kander, who is one of the nicest men ever. I met him at my graduation from Oberlin. He had graduated years earlier and was getting a special degree. When I moved to New York, he got me some fabulous jobs playing piano for his TV film scores, and he's always been incredibly supportive and sweet to me. I got to interview him for Sirius radio and my favorite story involved the title song from the movie, *New York, New York*. He and Fred Ebb performed all the songs they had written for the film for director Martin Scorsese and the film's star, Robert De Niro. Scorsese and De Niro had a little convo after they heard everything, and Scorsese told the songwriting team that De Niro felt that one of the other songs, "The World Goes 'Round," was so good it was outshining "New York, New York," which should be the best song in the film. Kander and Ebb were totally irritated they were being given notes by the star, but because they're pros, they didn't argue. John said that they went home with big chips on their shoulders and wrote their "(expletive) you" version of the song. Cut to: *that's* the song that Minnelli and Sinatra then made world famous and John can't even remember the first version. Viva De Niro!

I sat with John at the bar and asked him what he thinks will happen with *The Visit*. Of course, he said he didn't know yet. I suddenly felt so awed to be with him at that moment. It wasn't opening night, but because it was the big gala, it had the same vibe, and I thought about all the shows he's been in the lobby of before they opened — *Cabaret, Chicago, The Rink*, etc. — and I couldn't believe I was sitting there with him. I'm used to doing one-night concerts of shows that have already worked, or limited runs of past hit shows. I can't even comprehend what it's like to be him. He's on a level very few are because he's literally created musical theatre history. After John and I chatted, I went into the theatre, and James asked me if I really take in the fact that my life is such where I can go to events and be surrounded by Broadway celebrities and actually know them well enough to say hello etc., and I thought back to the time I was nine years old, seeing *Chicago* from the balcony. Here I was in a theatre with the composer and the original star. The thought made my eyes fill with tears. Well, it was that thought plus the waist size of my pants versus my actual waist.

In conclusion, anyone in the Washington, D.C. area better hightail it to the Signature and see *The Visit* ASAP (P.S. Wear stretch pants). THE VISIT *just played again with Chita in the summer of 2014. Still waiting to come to Broadway!*

Now, let us discuss nominations. Perhaps some of you remember that I was in *The Ritz*. Perhaps you also remember that I had four lines:

1. We're busy.
2. I said we're busy.
3. Thanks a lot.
4. Careful, Googie.

Plus a tight 16-measure performance of the song "Magic to Do." Well, imagine my surprise and joy when I discovered that I was nominated for a *Broadway.com* audience award! And not for "best walk-on," but for "best featured actor in a play"! First of all, I can't believe I was actually *in* a Broadway play, let alone nominated for anything. And apparently, neither can anyone else. The always-hilarious Joe Mantello wrote me: *Not since Pia Zadora won a Golden Globe for BUTTERFLY has there been such a scandal.* Brava! I wish I could see F. Murray Abraham's face when he read the list of his competition:

F. MURRAY: Let's see here… Raúl Esparza, wonderful. David Morse, wow! Stiff competition. Brooks Ashmanskas, yes, yes… well-deserved. And finally… what the-? Seth Rudetsky? Who the hell is he?
F. MURRAY'S ASSISTANT: He was in The Ritz.
F. MURRAY: I don't remember him.
ASSISTANT: Neither did I. I looked him up on *ibdb.com* and he played "Fire drill patron" in Act One and "Sheldon" in Act Two.
F. MURRAY: I still don't remember him.
ASSISTANT: Neither do I.
 Silence.
BOTH: So….yeah.

OK, everyone, I'm signing off to go obsessively listen to my copy of the *In the Heights* CD. *I still listen at the gym. Especially CARNAVAL DEL BARRIO!* This week I'm going to see the fabulous Nina Hennessey at the Metropolitan Room and finally see *Sunday in the Park With George* — and either get a new tux or call Star Jones' doctor.

A Tale of Two Seths
May 28, 2008

Here's the deal: Thursday night, I began to feel sick. When I woke up Friday, I assumed I had gotten strep from Juli, who had it a week-and-a-half ago. I had a fever and hightailed it to the doctor. Of course, Murphy's law-style, the strep test came back negative and I had no fever. It was literally the only five-minute period in the last four days where I haven't had a fever! I don't know why it happened right at that moment, but it made me look like a crazy person. He said not to worry and whatever I had would go away. I guess it did, if by "go away," he meant get progressively worse where I'm now on Tylenol with Codeine so I can sleep... and it's not even working!

The next morning, James checked my throat with a flashlight and let me just say that the only thing in recent memory whiter than my left tonsil is Hugh Jackman's 2004 Tony Awards performance of "One Night Only." I called my doctor and said that I must have strep and since I'm allergic to penicillin, he gave me a Z-pack. He assured me, though, that I wasn't contagious anymore. But I felt terrible, so I had to cancel my afternoon tickets to *Sunday in the Park With George*. Devastating. Well, at least I could nap the whole afternoon. Really? Keep reading.

Since James' mother is in town, I forced myself to go out for a quick lunch and then they all went to the South Street Seaport. I crawled back to my apartment to discover that James had my keys! Yay! It's fun to be locked out of your apartment with a fever and a white sweater on your tonsil. I had keys to James' apartment and slept there all day. By Sunday, I was determined not to cancel any more tickets, so I forced myself onto the subway and saw the amazing *Gypsy*. I'm so glad the show came to Broadway. People are always commenting, "Why do we need another revival of *Gypsy*?" My comment is, "Why did it ever close?" It should have stayed running since 1959. It was so fantastic to see and hear a full orchestra again after having to suffer through various revivals with orchestra reductions, yet ticket inflations. And I loved that the audience was completely silent during the overture because it wasn't used as a section of music to settle the audience so the show could then begin — it *was* the beginning of the show. The cast is fantastic. How great to have Patti LuPone back in an old-school musical. I remember thinking what a long wait it was between *Evita* and then *Anything Goes*, but that was less than ten years! This has been 20! I know she did her own show on Broadway, as well as plays and *Sweeney Todd*, but I'm talking old-school, high belt, stand center stage on zero and tear-it-up musical comedy.

Side note: speaking of standing on zero, I was lecturing to some school kids about Broadway with a bunch of cast members from *Phantom* and explaining to them that Broadway shows have numbers on the edge of the stage so people know where to stand so they don't block each other/bump into each other. The cast members told me that *Phantom* doesn't use them! I was aghast and then thought that maybe they didn't need them for dance formations. But I was then informed that there are indeed formations, and the cast is told things like "Line your body up to the slight crack you'll see upstage" or "Make sure you land that jeté where the stage paint is slightly lighter." I heard it's a nightmare for the swings because they're not familiar enough with the stage to know where the cracks or fading paint is. Attention *Phantom* artistic staff: it's been twenty years! I'll paint the numbers on for you — it'll take me five minutes!

The lighting guy from *Phantom* said that Tony Walton didn't like to have literal numbers on the stage, so he'd theme them to whatever show he was doing. During *Guys and Dolls*, they all looked like playing cards, and during *Forum* they were all Roman numerals. In other words, V was actually 5, hilariously prompting Nathan Lane to have a breakdown during rehearsal and say that there was no way to find your number unless you had a classics degree.

Patti got a standing ovation after "Rose's Turn," and I think it was the first time I've been in a Broadway theatre where a standing ovation has happened in the middle of the show. Unless you count *Good Vibrations*, but the standing was then followed by walking out. *Years later, my good friend, the brilliant Andrea Martin, also got regular mid-show standing ovations in PIPPIN.*

Even though Dr. Clements said I wasn't contagious, I was too scared to go backstage afterwards, so I sent James with his mom, and he congratulated Laura Benanti for her brava-ness. James complimented her on the last scene of Act One, where she so clearly showed the devastation of June leaving with Tulsa, then the joy of finally being a family, then the horror of witnessing Rose's steely denial. James said that he learned from me to be specific in his compliments after he sees someone in a show. Let me teach you all my theory: The most annoying thing is to not say anything. I've been with so many Broadway friends who'll run into fans who'll say, "I saw you in your show last week." *Silence.* Finally my friend will have to awkwardly ask, "Did you like it?" Devastating. Then people will also say, "You were great in your show!" Hmm, you'll think, that's a nice compliment… but it'll be followed by, "and we got a parking spot right away… that was great!" I guess they're both comparable. I've found that celebs love knowing which specific moment you loved, like "Nice vibrato on the E vowel!" or "Sassy beveled leg while standing in the background!" Specifics, people, specifics! Also, I hate when someone says to me, "You were the best one in it." It implies that everyone was awful, but out of the awful people, you were the least awful. Thanks?

This week at Sirius radio, I had the ultimate pleasure of interviewing one of my idols, Harvey Fierstein! I asked him about his early Broadway experience, and he said that his mom would bring him from Brooklyn to Broadway all the time when he was a kid and he actually got to see Merman in *Gypsy*! As a kid, he wanted to be a visual artist. When he was 15, he was asked to help out a local theatre group and make posters. Then they asked him to help out by being in *Barefoot in the Park* where he got reviewed by *Backstage*. In that issue, there was a notice that said that Andy Warhol was going to do a play at La MaMa. Because Harvey was an artist, he worshipped him and decided he had to audition. It was an enormous open call. Harvey did Juliet's balcony monologue and was the only one cast… as a manic lesbian maid. He did the show at La MaMa but was too young to go with it to London. The director, Paul Morrisey, felt bad for him and said that he'd cast Harvey in his next film, *Flesh*. Harvey got so excited, went on a major diet and lost 60 pounds. He showed up for the first day of shooting, and Paul said, "What am I supposed to do with you?" Harvey asked what he meant. Paul said, "The only thing you had going for you was that you looked like a freak… a fat kid in a dress. Now you look normal." He then fired Harvey! Hmm… maybe that's why I haven't gotten any film work… I'm too skinny! Well, not to worry. Since my strep throat, I've been "treating myself" every night with a full-out chocolate malted. Stand back, Hollywood, here I come! No literally… stand back, I need room.

Speaking of Hollywood, *What Happens in Vegas* just came out, and it's the film I actually did get cast in and then had to ixnay because I couldn't take off two days from *The Ritz*. Has anyone seen it? It's too painful for me to see. That could have been me up there, saying two unimportant lines to Ashton Kutcher. Instead, I said two unimportant lines in *The Ritz* (per act). *P.S. Talk about that role being a stepping stone to stardom; I was replaced by the now totally famous Billy Eichner from BILLY ON THE STREET! THE RITZ ruined my possibility to be a star!*

Back to Harvey: I recently saw something crazy in his dressing room and found out the backstory. He recently got a New Dramatists Lifetime Achievement Award and they showed a clip of Harvey on *Sesame Street* singing "Everything's Coming up Noses." Afterwards, Arthur Laurents, who was sitting nearby, turned to him and said, "Not bad." That, of course, prompted Harvey to write a note to Patti LuPone, "Please enjoy your run. I'm next." Then Patti started sending over boxes of chocolates she'd get from fans… with her name crossed out and Harvey's written in. But she'd eat half the box first. Then Harvey sent her a bowling bag filled to the brim with *This Isn't Going to Be Pretty*, his 1990s CD of himself live at The Bottom Line called. He wrote, "Dear Patti, Would you mind hawking these in the lobby?" She wrote back, "Dear Harvey, Thank you so much for sharing your talent. I've given one to each member of the cast. As a matter of fact, we're canceling the matinee today so we can have a listening session. And if anyone shows up for the show, we'll make them listen to it." Harvey then wrote back, "Thank *you* so much. And by the way, I wasn't kidding." And he attached another whole bag of CDs! Then Patti took a cactus that she got as a gift from someone (referencing the beginning of Act Two of *Gypsy*) and sent it to Harvey with his CDs taped all over it with ugly red tape. That was what I saw when I walked in his dressing room. An enormous cactus covered in red tape and CDs. I thought it was a tasteless present from a fan, but when I found out it was from Patti, I exclaimed, "It's beautiful."

I talked to him about *A Catered Affair,* whose CD just came out, FYI! He plays the uncle of a bride who wants to have a small wedding and his character is outraged because he thinks he's being excluded because he's gay. I had heard at La Jolla that people thought his character was totally anachronistic in the 1950s and I was happy when I saw it on Broadway because it seemed so real to me. I assumed it was overhauled since the West Coast run. The family knew he was gay, but the actual word wasn't used. He had a very close male "friend," and he was a "confirmed bachelor." Turns out, that's how it was at La Jolla! So what was anachronistic?! Were people saying there weren't gay people in the '50s? Ever hear of the Mattachine Society? Morons!

Harvey told me that he feels one of the most pivotal moments of his career was when he was performing the second part of *Torch Song Trilogy*. By the way, the only reason it was in three parts is because he got the first act booked at La MaMa, and it was normally so difficult to get space there, his director told him to say it was a trilogy so he could get the next dates lined up. Brava! Anyhoo, after he performed the second part, an older woman named Mrs. Gettleman, who came to all of his stuff, approached him. She had on a turquoise suit, Brooklyn beauty parlor-styled hair, and a rose from her backyard pinned to her lapel. He turned, and she hit him on the arm. "What!?!" he exclaimed. "Write a part for a mother so I can play it!" she told him. That gave him the idea for a third part of the show, and he gave her the role. She shortened Gettleman and became… Estelle Getty! And had he not written that act, he believes the show never would have come to Broadway, and his career never would have become what it became. It made the show mainstream because everybody identified — not with the disapproving mother, but with him! Apparently, everyone's parents disapprove of something, and that allowed the audience to identify with Harvey's character. No one ever said to him after the show, "That's me and my son." They always said, "That's me and my mother." Brava Harvey and brava Mrs. Gettleman!

Finally, he told me about the celebs he met backstage at *Torch Song*. He freaked out when he heard that Merman asked for tickets to *Torch Song Trilogy*. Or, specifically, she called a press agent friend of his and asked for tickets to "that trigonometry thing." Afterwards, she came backstage and, because she hadn't read this column on how to greet a celeb backstage, Harvey was forced to ask her, "What did you think of the show?" The Merm responded with her signature candor. "Ah, I thought it was a piece of s***. But the rest of the audience laughed and cried, so what the f*** do I know?" He loved it. His other idol (and mine) also came backstage during *Torch Song*... Barbra Streisand! He said that they chatted about Broadway and Harvey feels that he and Barbra are opposites. For him, TV and movies are a great way to make money, but his heart lies in the theatre. He told me that, to him, doing a movie is like going to a job in an office. He feels you can have a great office job, but theater is where he lives. Barbra did Broadway, but it was never what she wanted. She loves to get it right and then move on to the next thing, plus she always wanted to reach as many people as possible. We should have seen the writing on the wall when she accepted her Emmy for *My Name is Barbra*. In her Emmy acceptance speech she mentions how many people saw her television special and says that after doing the math, she figured out that in order to reach that many people, she'd have to do *Funny Girl* for 63 years. My question is, why *didn't* she do *Funny Girl* for 63 years? She stopped doing it before I was even born. And whenever she does sing *Funny Girl* songs in concert, it's always the one song I'm not interested in hearing. Come on, already! Ixnay "Don't Rain on my Parade," and haul out "Private Schwartz." And, quite frankly, the last time she sang one of my other faves, "Coronet Man," she responded to the name "Mrs. Gould."

His other favorite backstage star was Richard Chamberlain. Harvey told him that he'd always had a crush on him and Richard agreed to act out a scenario Harvey had always fantasized about. Harvey left the room, waited ten seconds, Richard turned out the lights and lay on the couch. Harvey walked in, said, "Honey, I'm home," and kissed him! Hmm... I thought. That was the fantasy? I'd call that the preamble to the fantasy.

All right, I'm out. This week I'm finally gonna see *Sunday in the Park with George* and then interview Jenna Russell at my *Chatterbox*! But first, some throat-coat tea, two Halls and a delicious malted. Purely for medicinal reasons.

Jenna, Emily… and Elle Woods
June 2, 2008

After being sick last week, I am officially better. Or "So Much Better," *Legally Blonde*-style. Speaking of which, tonight is the debut of the *Legally Blonde* reality show on MTV. They came up with an amazing title: *Legally Blonde The Musical: The Search for Elle Woods*. What clever word play! It's not literal at all. Yes, it's a little lengthy, but putting the colon in the middle of the title gives me plenty of time to rest and then finish the second half.

Speaking of childhood, after I did *Broadway 101* (which, I just found out, raised $30,000 for The Actors Fund!), I got a call from a television production company. We set up a meeting and I had delicious visions of filming *Broadway 101* for network TV. Well, turns out, the woman in charge of creative development for this company saw *Broadway 101* and was very interested in the sections where I talked about my childhood. She wound up contracting me to write and develop a sitcom about my (devastating) adolescent years! Sort of *Everybody Hates Chris*, but more like "Everybody Hates Fat, Gay Seth."

There's one classic story that happened to me in English class, but I don't know if I can re-enact it in a series. My whole class was supposed to have read *The Adventures of Huckleberry Finn* but, even though it was an honors English class, essentially nobody read it. Mrs. Messner (who was always all smiles and we therefore called her "Goody" Messner à la *The Crucible*) was our teacher and first asked my friend Whitney Malin what the theme of the book was. Whitney started flipping through the book like the theme was on a certain page and she just had to find it. After some aimless flipping, she muttered, "Call on someone else." But Mrs. Messner didn't hear, so Whitney essentially had to yell, "*Call on someone else*!" Then Mrs. Messner called on Julie Einhorn who said, "Ooh… you caught me at a bad time." We were obsessed with that comment later on. Did Julie just get out of the shower and her hair was still wet? Weren't we in the middle of English class? What's a better time for a question relating to English? Finally, she called on my friend Terry Heyman by saying, "And Terry?" But because Mrs. Messner had a Midwestern accent, it sounded like "And Tirry?" Terry thought Mrs. Messner was asking about some obscure character from the book, so she looked miffed and asked, "Who the hell is Ann Tirry?" Nonetheless, we all somehow graduated.

My new favorite person is Jenna Russell, who is starring as Dot/Marie in *Sunday in the Park With George*. I interviewed her at the *Chatterbox* and she is so much fun! First of all, if you don't know, she's British. She did her first big London show when she was still a teenager and it had music by ABBA but with different lyrics. Instead of "Fernando," she sang "Back Home Now." Suffice it to say, it did not have the success of *Mamma Mia!* However, she said that because of that show, Tim Rice and Benny and Bjorn (from ABBA) decided to write *Chess*, so something good came from it. For the opening, everybody got champagne from the ABBA men, but because she was 16, she instead got an autographed album. She said there are pictures of her holding the album (*Arrival*) and glaring because she was infuriated she wasn't allowed to get drunk, but now she's so happy to have an autographed record! Also, in that show she got to work with West End theatre legend Elaine Paige. Jenna was young and didn't quite have all of her social graces. On the first day, she trotted up to Elaine and said with a big smile, "You know, I really like you." She then kept going. "I mean, everyone told me that you were a (C word), but I don't think you are!" Wow. Instead of getting her fired, Elaine told her why people were annoyed with her. Elaine started out as a chorus girl, and then she got to originate the role of

Evita. When she was still in the chorus, she'd go out after the show and hang out 'til all hours, but after she got the vocally demanding role of Evita, she had to curtail all social activity. People thought she was being a snob by not going out partying when, in actuality, she was just trying to preserve her voice so she could belt "A New Argentina" and not have her next gig be replacing Lauren Bacall in *Woman of the Year*. *Listen to "Hurry Back" on the APPLAUSE album. Lauren hits a low A!*

Jenna also did *Les Misérables* as one of the ensemble women, and then spent 13 weeks understudying Eponine. I asked her if she ever went on, and she said only once... which is 100 percent more times than I ever went on for Brooks Ashmanskas in *The Ritz*. She left the show, three years passed, and she suddenly got a call from the *Les Miz* people.

"Hey, Jenna. What are you doing tonight?"
"Um... going out to dinner."
"Oh, good. Because we *might* need you to go on for Eponine."
"Why!?!?!"
"You see, the girl playing Eponine is out, and her understudy has an abscess, and her second cover isn't prepared. Do you mind calling in at six to see if we'll need you?"

Well, Jenna had met the understudy and knew that she was the type who'd go on, abscess or not... Jenna said "sure" and called in at six, just because she promised. Turns out, she had to go on! She had only gone on once for the role... three years before... but she remembered it! She said the guy playing Marius had a great sense of humor, and when she sang her final verse of "A Little Fall of Rain" and died in his arms, she heard him say, "Take this b**** away from me, she bores me." So British!

Later on, she wound up playing Fantine. Now, a lot of you may not know this, but after Fantine dies in Act One, she then appears as a boy on the barricade in Act Two. Jenna told the people running the show that she was bored sitting backstage for so long, so they added her to the Paris scene at the end of Act One. I asked if any of the following Fantines were mad about that, and she said no but... at one point, she was talking about her dressing room being so big, and some of the ensemble women asked if she minded sharing it. She said she'd love to. And now when she meets women playing Fantine they glare and say, "Thanks for the dressing roommates."

Jenna was starring as Sarah Brown in the West End production of *Guys and Dolls* when she heard that *Sunday in the Park With George* was playing at The Chocolate Factory (which is like a small Off-Broadway house). She told Jane Krakowski (who was playing Adelaide) that they better get their a**es over there, and they went to the following Sunday matinee. They loved it. Then, the show was about to transfer to the West End, the woman playing Dot got pregnant. I asked Jenna if she hid her supply of the pill and she denied it. Not very convincingly, I might add. Regardless, Jenna was suddenly up for the role of Dot and listened to the CD in her car on the way to the audition. She said that every time she tried to sing along, she started crying because the words are so moving. I guess her puffy eyes didn't affect her audition, because she got the gig and then found out it was going to go to Broadway. But not for another year! So she took the whole year off. Delicious! I know how that feels. I've taken the last five months off from doing a Broadway show — although, not on purpose. So I don't really know how that feels. But I do need a job.

When Tony time came, she woke up early to watch the announcements, but right before they came on, Todd Haimes (who runs The Roundabout) called and congratulated her because the nominations were put online early. Unfortunately, by the time she finished gabbing with him, she missed hearing her name announced. She's not expecting to win *Patti LuPone did!*, but she's happy her show was extended. At first, it was going to close at Tony time, so she said it would have been, "Close the show, don't win any Tonys and fly home." Depressing. But now she gets to do the show til the end of June!

Sunday night, I went to Feinstein's on the East Side and saw Emily Skinner perform. She was *amazing*. First of all, she can sing anything. High soprano, belt, blues, riff (meaning many notes sung fast, not the role "Riff," although she could sing that, too). I have to also say she is absolutely one of the best actresses I've ever seen. She is so connected and real with each song. Also, her patter was so interesting... and so was the audience's. At one point she said, "I love my boyfriend, but he's not a big fan of musical theatre," and the man in front of me said, "Mine is."

I first met Emily through my friend Jack Plotnick, who went to Carnegie Mellon with her, and he told me that she's the most talented person he knows, and when I started coaching her, I soon realized why he said that! She is way too young now, but I cannot wait for the next *Gypsy* revival with her as Mama Rose. She would tear it up!

OK, everybody. I have to get ready because I'm playing an Alzheimer's benefit tonight with Jonathan Groff, and he's about to come over. Hmm... is it possible to lose 20 pounds and 15 years *and* convince my boyfriend to have an open relationship in the next ten minutes? We shall see!

Aziza, Breaker, Russell and Strouse

June 9, 2008

One week ago tonight was the premiere of the reality show *Legally Blonde the Musical: The Search for Elle Woods*. Or, as internet message boards probably refer to it, according to the new, annoying trend: LBTMTSFEW. Please stop making up show-title codes that are more complicated *and* annoying than Sudoku.

There was a little premiere party thrown for the producer, Amanda Brown Lipitz, at the W Hotel. It was great to see Amanda finally get to see her show on TV. Yes, reality shows are headaches, but I still say brava to Amanda for bringing Broadway to MTV. And unlike other musical theatre reality shows (here and in Britain), the contestants don't spend each week singing pop songs. You'll only see the Elle candidates auditioning with material from the show — plus, of course, a healthy smattering of the requisite reality-show backstage bitchery. It's hilarious how the editors take something that's not a big deal (this week one of the girls says "too many cooks in the kitchen") and make it scandalous by putting in a close-up of someone looking mildly shocked and then adding the sound of timpani. Something bland becomes an immediate nail-biter.

During the premiere, within ten minutes of the show being on, my cell phone started ringing. It was Jen Cody. I picked up. "Oh My God. I have to watch every week now. I have so much material." I guess she meant material to bust me on... and I say brava! Bring it! As a matter of fact, I did a whole deconstruction on the first episode, ending with the mortifying close up of me talking to the girls while I was standing in a pageant girl bevel. *You can watch them all on SethTV.com.*

On Wednesday, I went to a matinee with my mom. I informed her that it was the same theatre where she first took me to see *Hair* when I was a toddler. I pointed out the seats I remembered sitting in (house left) and felt so moved being in the same theatre where I saw my first show. My mom was mind-boggled that I remembered so much, but I reminded her that I've always had a flawless memory... especially for something that meant so much to me. It wasn't until around five minutes later that I realized we were sitting in the Belasco, and *Hair* played at the Biltmore. I decided to not tell my mother who was sitting with a wistful smile, tinged with yesteryear. Anyhoo, the thing I loved the most about *Passing Strange* is that my mother loved it. She's 76! Brava on reaching across the generations. As I was leaving the theatre, I heard the tail end of a conversation between the woman in back of me and her friend:

"I loved what the guy on stage said."
"Which one?"
"The black one."
(Knowingly) "O-o-o-o-oh."

Huh? All the guys in the show are black. At this point, I still can't figure out which woman is the bigger idiot.

On Thursday, I interviewed two of the *Passing Strange* stars, who I thought were fantastic: de'Adre Aziza and Daniel Breaker. Just for symmetry, he told me to call him de'Aniel Breaker. *Later on she did WOMEN ON THE VERGE and he played the donkey in*

SHREK. They are both super nice, talented and funny. De'Adre told me that after college, she was working as an intern at The Public and wanted to start auditioning for shows there, but they said she couldn't do both, so she quit. *Years later*, they finally called her in for the reading of *Passing Strange*. She told me that it was her first reading, first workshop, first out-of-town show and first Broadway show! And, I added, her first Tony nomination! Brava! They were so cute talking about their Tony nominations. Daniel said his parents didn't really know when the Tony nominations happened, so it was a lot of phone calls for days before, "Hey, it's us. Were you nominated?" Then the night before the nominations, he couldn't get to sleep 'til 5 AM... and then woke up at 7! Because the Tony nominations were released online first, he read it there... but thought it was a mistake. I thought that was very sweet. De'Adre took her son to school around 7:30 and was too tired to stay up. She got up at 11 and read on *Playbill.com* that the show got a ton of nominations. She didn't think of herself, though. Then she saw her name and, à la Daniel, kept thinking it was a mistake. She finally called her mother who broke down crying on the phone while at work. Unfortunately, her mom is a teacher, so her students were probably a little traumatized seeing their teacher sobbing on the phone... but that's what school psychiatrists are for.

Friday night, James and I saw *Sunday in the Park With George* or as cockney Dot pronounces it, *Soonday in the Park With George*. I am so obsessed with Jenna Russell. She has so many great comic moments, but they totally seem in the moment and not pre-planned. And it was so great to see my old *Ritz* friend David Turner in the role of the German servant and my buddy Anne L. Nathan as the Nurse. They still got it! Backstage, I asked Jenna to regale me and James with another *Les Miz* story, and she said that in London, the Eponine dressing room had a window that was on the exact same level as the top of a double-decker bus. Jenna said that the girl playing Eponine would put on her end-of-show death makeup early and have nothing to do. So, she'd stand at the window with her death mask on and, when a bus would go by, she'd stare blank-faced, hold out her index finger and slowly do the "come with me" motion. Can you imagine how terrifying it was to be on a fun sightseeing tour and suddenly see a specter beckoning you to the netherworld? Wearing a head mic?

This week on Sirius radio I interviewed Broadway composer Charles Strouse. As he described his childhood, I kept piping up and saying it was exactly like mine, but upon further reflection, realized they were polar opposites. He's from the cool Upper West Side, I'm from a town on Long Island I couldn't wait to get the hell out of. As a child, he went to PS 87 with Mike Nichols (although they didn't know each other... but ironically, Mike wound up being the big producer of *Annie* years later). I went to Hewlett High School with a theatre teacher who banned me from doing plays my senior year and said to my face that I'd never make it in theatre. Charles graduated high school early and went to the Eastman School of Music when he was just 15. I also graduated early, but only by one year (not impressive), and yes, I also went to a prestigious music conservatory (Oberlin) but while he was spending his time composing serious music (à la Hindemith, Bartok), I was having unrequited crushes and failing my music history midterm. Hence, his many Tony Awards, and hence my many nights watching the Tonys from home.

After he graduated, he made money by accompanying singers and dance classes. Eventually he got a gig playing rehearsals for a show called *Saratoga*, and the stage manager said that he had an idea for a musical. The idea was about a new phenomenon called... teenagers and the show became *Bye Bye Birdie*. They went through five bookwriters (!) and eventually came up with the Elvis Presley character. The first song Charles wrote was one of my favorites, "An English Teacher." I asked him about the phrase at the beginning: "Albert, Albert, A-a-a-albert!" He said that phrase stems from his classical training. He feels a straight-up pop composer wouldn't necessarily think to put four notes on the same syllable (see "The Glory of the Lord" from *The Messiah*... which has thirty notes on the first syllable of the word, "glory"). I love Chita Rivera on that song, though it turns out the role was not written for her. Rose was not supposed to be Hispanic. All of the jokes originally were about her being Polish because the role was written for Carol Haney! If you don't know, she's the original Gladys from Broadway's *The Pajama Game* and the film as well as the star who broke her leg allowing Shirley MacLaine to go on.

Unfortunately, Carol started having vocal problems before *Bye Bye Birdie* and couldn't play the role, so Charles recommended Chita, whom he had worked with on *Shoestring Revue*. They kept all the songs they wrote for Carol and added one for Chita, "Spanish Rose" (which you can see her do on the Ed Sullivan Show if you go to *Bluegobo.com*).

I asked Charles about something that's always driven me crazy. Now, you all should know that I think *Hair* is a brilliant show and every song in it is phenomenal. But... I get annoyed when people say *Hair* was the first rock musical. *Bye Bye Birdie* was the first rock musical! It was the first show to have used actual rock music ("One Last Kiss," "Sincere") and an electric guitar. Charles thinks that, because the show satirizes rock music, people don't credit it with being groundbreaking (my word). What's funny is that he said they couldn't get any backers for it because of the new-fangled score. The music was just too modern. Think about it, they started writing it in the mid-'50s when rock literally first began. It's like writing a musical in the style of (insert latest music trend here... I faded out on pop radio so long ago the last trend I know about is a young upstart named Tiffany).

Dick Van Dyke was not originally thought of for the lead role of Albert Peterson. They wanted Jack Lemmon or Steve Lawrence. It was Chita's agent again, Richard Seff, who was also Dick Van Dyke's agent, and kept pushing for them to see him again, even though the creative team thought he wasn't quite right. Then, when Dick finally got the role, his big number, "Put on a Happy Face," was bombing. Charles immediately set out to write a new song. But Marge Champion, who was married to the director (Gower), thought that the staging of the number wasn't right. It originally took place at the Ed Sullivan show while they were setting the lights, and she thought of the idea of setting it in Grand Central and making it about two young girls who were depressed. Suffice it to say, it worked!

Of course, I had to obsess about *Annie*. Martin Charnin asked Charles to write it because Charles had written *It's a Bird... It's a Plane... It's Superman*, and this was another musical based on a comic. Charles thought the idea was *awful* but liked Martin and Thomas Meehan, who was writing the book, so he went along with it. Charles told us that the original concept was for Annie to be played by... Bernadette Peters! All I can say is "what the-?" The first song he wrote was "It's a Hard Knock Life," which was also the only song in that show that had the lyrics come first. He said the fun of writing a musical is not knowing what's gonna work and what isn't. In Act One, there's a scene where Annie meets Sandy the dog for the first time and then Annie gets thrown back in the orphanage. There was a clever scene change with a sliding panel, but it needed time to get set up, so Charles wrote a song to cover it. When the change happened for the first time, the audience cheered, and Charles went to the back of the house to tell Martin that they really loved that clever scene change. He didn't realize until months later that the audience was actually loving the song he wrote to cover the change, "Tomorrow"! All these stories and more can be read in his excellent memoir, *Put on a Happy Face*.

OK, everyone, get ready for next week's Tonys!! I cannot wait to see all those performances. As Patti LuPone ad-libbed at the end of the Tony opening number I wrote in 1998, "Go, Tony!!!"

When You Got It, Flaunt It
June 16, 2008

Hello! Happy post-Tony Awards. I'm actually writing this before watching it, so I can't give you my opinion of the show. I can, however, give my *estimated* opinion of the show. Please stop with the Hollywood celebs and bring on the Broadway! I want longer performances from every musical, not four minutes and we're out. Remember *Dreamgirls* in 1982? We got to see the fight scene leading to "And I Am Telling You" *and* all of "And I Am Telling You"! These days, they'd skip the fight scene and we'd only get a truncated version of "And I Am Telling You" to make room for a headache-y TV star to present.

Ladies and gentlemen... *Dreamgirls*! "And I am telling you... you're gonna lo-o-o-o-ove me-e e-e-e-e-e!" And now... Patricia Heaton.

Since I can't (yet!) recap the Tony Awards, let me recap my week. On Tuesday I performed in a benefit that Judy Gold put together for the public school her son goes to (which is the same one Juli goes to). Andrea McArdle and her daughter Alexis performed and sounded fabulous. They're both doing *Les Miz* in the late summer with Andrea as Fantine and Alexis as Eponine. I love it! Triumph The Insult Comic Dog puppet performed and was hilarious. He talked about Judy Gold being a gay mom and said that while Andrea and Alexis are doing *Les Miz*, Judy and her sons are doing Miss Lez. He followed that with, "I'm not saying Judy is raising her sons gay, but Andrea McArdle is backstage right now singing, 'Your son'll come out... tomorrow.'" I wish I could tell you some of the jokes he said about me, but *Playbill.com* is a family site.

While leaving Caroline's on Tuesday, the weather seemed crazy — super quiet, but windy and on the verge of something terrifying. I knew *something* was about to happen, so I raced to the subway to get home before it hit. And while I was on the subway, my block was hit by a *tornado*!!!! Seriously! One of the supers was standing on the street and said he saw a swirling mass of dust at the end of the block and, when it cleared, a tree had been uprooted and was sprawled across the street! I couldn't believe it, but then Christine Pedi told me that her friend was leaving Carnegie Hall that same night and saw a twister going down 57th Street. Al Gore, please help!

At the *Chatterbox* I interviewed a young Tony nominee from *In the Heights*, Robin De Jesús. I asked him where he was from and he told me "a factory town in Connecticut." Huh? When questioned further, he admitted that just saying Connecticut sounds too middle to upper class, so he adds the "factory town" part to give him some street cred. He loved singing when he was a kid, but could not match pitch and essentially clanked, so he would pray to have a better voice. I asked who he wanted to sing like and he replied immediately, "Ariel."

Robin was working in a camp right after he graduated high school and heard about the auditions for the movie *Camp*. It was an open call and he kept getting called back. He gave his final audition on a Friday and knew he'd find out later that day. He was so excited when the casting person called him and said... he needed to come back Monday. Turns out, they had auditions in California and wanted to bring everyone in together. He went back, saw his competition and, after he auditioned, he was told they didn't need anything else from him. But the other guy was asked to stay! Robin was like, "...um... I can sing something if you want..." and they were like, "That's all we need." He thought he definitely didn't get it, but on the train ride back to Connecticut, he pulled an Oprah's secret and decided that he *did* get it. Cut to: the casting person called him later and said he was cast. Brava, Oprah!

Robin loved working with the director, Todd Graff, and after the movie wrapped (as they say in the film world), Todd paid for the cast to come to NYC, stay in hotels, and see two Broadway shows (!). Afterwards, they went to Planet Hollywood and he showed them 15 minutes of the film. I think that cost him the entire budget of the movie! One of Robin's co-stars turned to him while they were seeing the first cut and said, "Wait... it actually looks good!" They were super surprised it came out so well because the whole time they were filming they were told that the budget was non-existent and there would be *no* retakes whatsoever. After they stopped filming, Robin's friends told him that his hair was out of control (it was an enormous afro), and he needed to cut it ASAP. Right after that, Todd called and said that they got some extra money, so they were going to do a bunch of retakes. Robin had to get his courage up to say, "I, um, sort of cut off all my hair..." Todd was not fazed and immediately figured out a way to solve the problem. Let's just say that you can tell the scenes in the movie that were re-shot because they feature Robin's crazy afro wrapped up in a bandana... AKA a bandana covering Telly Savalas' head.

After *Camp*, he thought he'd be getting some delicious performing offers. Unfortunately, he got offered Priscilla Lopez's signature song ("*Nothing*"). He worked as a waiter in Connecticut and finally decided to move to New York. Unfortunately, he couldn't get *any* work in the city, so he went back to his old waitering job in Connecticut and would commute back to NYC every night. It's like Elaine Stritch's fun story about having to commute every day because she was starring on Broadway *and* in a show in New Haven... but without the "fun" part, "show" part or "starring" part. He finally got a headache-y job waitering at Bubba Gump's Shrimp Factory in Times Square and a job at FAO Schwarz. The FAO Schwarz gig was known as the "perfect" job. It was designed for actors because you were allowed to sign out whenever you had an audition, and all you had to do was play with a toy all day long. He lasted three shifts. First of all, because he was new, they gave him the most headache-y toy... *Yu-Gi-Oh* cards. Then he realized that most people coming to the store didn't want to watch him play with the cards, they wanted to ask him where certain toys were located. Because he just started working there, he didn't know where anything was, so he had to keep telling customers to ask the other "toy players," who all wound up resenting him for constantly sending people over asking for directions. That was exacerbated by the mortification of people recognizing him from *Camp*. It was very much like Boyd Gaines in the *Fame* movie. Remember? He's the hot actor at the High School of Performing Arts and, after he graduates, some students are at a restaurant and he's their waiter. He tells them what's going on career-wise and then has to awkwardly segue to, "So, today's specials are..." Devastating.

Robin said that seeing *Caroline, or Change* changed everything for him because it made him realize that theatre and performing could be art and not just a gig. He made a decision to leave his agent and not take every job that came his way. Well, when he was in high school and heard the solo in "Will I," he said to his friends, "I would love to do *Rent* just to sing that small amazing solo," and that's the solo he wound up having on Broadway when he was cast in *Rent*! He also got to play Angel on Broadway as well! One of his friends told him that he'd be perfect for the role of Sonny in the reading of *In the Heights*. He asked his agent to get him an audition, and she called him back and said he didn't have to audition, he was offered the role! The director

(Tommy Kail) and Lin-Manuel Miranda had both seen *Camp* and knew he'd be great. He did the reading, the workshop, the Off-Broadway production and now he's on Broadway!

I asked him how he found out that he was nominated for a Tony and he said that he was about to perform on *Good Morning America* when the stage manager got a sheet of paper with all the nominations. He handed it to Robin and said, "You should look at this." Robin thought that the stage manager said that because he got a nomination, and he got so excited! But then he thought that he'd better not think it because if he looks at the list, and his name isn't there, everyone's gonna see his face crack. He finally looked, saw his name and started sobbing uncontrollably, but then one second later curtailed all emotion because he had to perform and didn't want puffy red eyes. It was very *Dreamgirls*: "I got a show to do!" The most amazing part was that he knew he had a Tony nomination *and* he was performing a song from his Tony-nominated Broadway show on *Good Morning America* outdoors on the little island in Times Square, which is right across from... Bubba Gump Shrimp Company!

Finally, I asked him what he was wearing to the Tonys and the answer was a nice simple tux. He said he didn't want to pull a Todd Graff. I asked for further explanation, and he said that when Todd was nominated for playing Danny in *Baby*, he took a limo with his agent. His agent was mortified when she saw that he was wearing a tea bag as an earring (it was the '80s). She reached forward, and Todd said, "If you try to take it out, I have three more in my pocket." I wish there was a shot of him at the after party dipping his ear for three minutes in boiling water.

That's it for me. Tonight is the "music" challenge on the *Legally Blonde* reality show. I made the bold choice of wearing a tank top, and my L.A. friend Jack Plotnick left me an emergency message saying, "Never again." Hmph. I always thought, "When you got it, flaunt it." I think his point was, "When you don't, cover it." See ya next week!

Tony Thoughts
June 24, 2008

First, let's discuss the Tonys. And by "discuss," I mean have a one-sided discussion (see: my childhood with my mother). I loved how there was so much Broadway on the show! And all of it was actual performances from shows, not headache-y medleys with people I don't want to hear sing them.

A major highlight for me: Patti LuPone winning and dishing the fact that she hasn't been up there for 28 years. Regardless of whether she should have won for *Anything Goes* or *Sweeney Todd*, the issue for me is how few musicals she's been in! Patti LuPone, Bernadette Peters and Betty Buckley are three of our greatest Broadway stars; they need to be on Broadway constantly! If Will Ferrell can make ten films in the last six months, they can each do one Broadway show a year.

Secondly, I loved seeing *In The Heights* on the Tonys because, not only do I love that show, but I totally heard my friend Andréa Burns (who plays Daniela) get entrance applause!

And finally, can we please talk about Cheyenne Jackson's performance. His voice was out-of-control *perfect*! The placement, tone and vibrato was flawless. I was doing my Sirius radio show at the time and, right after he sang, my sister Nancy called me and said, "Cheyenne sounded amazing. His face is stunning and his body perfect." She, of course, had to follow it with, "And Seth, to be blunt... you'll never be him." I didn't ask her to be blunt! It reminds me of that amazing moment in the movie *Happiness* when Jane Adams is standing in a kitchen while her relatives laugh. Her sister says, "We're not laughing *at* you, we're laughing *with* you!" and Jane says, slightly bewildered, "But I'm not laughing."

Wednesday night, I went to see *Cry-Baby* with James and we thoroughly enjoyed ourselves. I thought the cast was *so* talented. Harriet Harris was hilarious as usual. I loved when her granddaughter, who becomes a bad girl, said that she kicked a policeman in the b***s and Harriet sternly corrected her with, "Scrotum." Then on Thursday, I had four ladies from the cast on the *Chatterbox*: Tory Ross, Alli Mauzey, Carly Jibson and Elizabeth Stanley. First I asked Carly how she got discovered. She was 17 and performing in her Michigan hometown, and an agent happened to be there (the opposite of *Waiting for Guffman*) and got her an audition for *One Life To Live*. Her family couldn't afford the plane fare, so her mother drove her to New York. She auditioned for the part and... Kathy Brier got the gig. *But* then she auditioned for *Hairspray* and... got a callback. And another one. And another one. Let's just say eight callbacks. She and seven other Tracys would have to do super aerobic things and sing at the same time to see if they had the stamina to sing and dance. I asked Carly if it was difficult to be so young, yet star on Broadway (she was 19). She said it was great because she didn't know anything. One night someone told her, "Ben Brantley is coming to the show," and she was like, "Cool! Who's that?"

Then I chatted with Tory Ross, who plays Hatchet Face. Her first big gig out of high school was doing the national tour of *The Producers* playing the roles Kathy Fitzgerald originated (homeless woman, ugly showgirl, lesbian techie). On her first day of rehearsal, she remembered her training at the Cincinnati Conservatory of Music and made a "bold choice," which they're always telling you to do. They didn't tell her that it could lead to being supremely yelled at. She was learning "The King of Broadway" where Max Bialystock is talking to street people about how he's gonna make a comeback. She played a homeless woman that he makes out with and, at one point, her head was in his crotch while he sang a rhythmic phrase. Every time he hit an accent, she bobbed her head in his crotch. Mel Brooks got up and started yelling at her, "Who do you think you are? This isn't your show! You're in the ensemble! No one knows who you are!" That's four ouches! She thought she was gonna get fired and didn't know anybody in the cast who could comfort her so she spent the break crying hysterically on the phone with her mother saying, "It's over before it began!" But the powers that be got her a ticket for the Broadway show so she could watch Kathy do it and, essentially, copy her. Tory said that now she and Kathy are good friends and, starting soon, they're both going to be in *9 to 5* together!

Then I got to chat with Alli Mauzey who was *brilliant* as the crazy stalker girl. I asked her about her worst audition she'd ever had, and she said that it was for *On The Town* in L.A. She was going in for the role of Lucy Shmeeler, the character who's supposed to have a cold. Alli said she really wanted to feel like she had a cold during the audition so she put some toilet paper up her nose to stuff it up and some wax in her ears to block them up. She could hardly breathe or hear, just like a real cold. Unfortunately, after she read, the director started giving her notes, and she was too mortified to take the wax out of her ears so she literally spent the whole time saying, "...What?" Shockingly, she didn't get it.

Alli was also the stand-by for Glinda in *Wicked* on Broadway, and one of the rules for a standby is that you don't have to be at the theatre every night, but in case you have to go on quickly, you can only be five blocks away. Well, turns out, she lives *four* blocks away, so she literally got to spend every night at home in her living room, watching TV. And getting a paycheck. Wow. Doing nothing but getting a Broadway paycheck. I thought that was only me in *The Ritz*.

Finally, I spoke to the gorgeous and fun-nee Elizabeth Stanley who plays the good-girl-gone-bad. She wanted to be an opera singer while she was growing up and said she was a total opera snob. Her friends would say, "I love Mariah Carey!" and she would shake her head knowingly and whisper, "She is going to ruin her voice."

While majoring in opera at Indiana University, Elizabeth switched her interest to musical theatre. Her first big gig was the non-Equity tour of *Cabaret* where she played the elderly Fraulein Schneider. Hmm… maybe I should turn non-Equity so I can finally do *The Gin Game*. I remembered loving Elizabeth's performance as April in Broadway's *Company* last year and asked her if she got to meet Sondheim. Turns out, he came to their first performance in Cincinnati, and she was totally intimidated and couldn't speak to him. They all went out to a bar afterwards, and Sondheim was sitting next to her. She whispered to her friend to make a funny face so she could take a picture of him, but in actuality, she was taking a picture of Sondheim. So now she has a picture of Sondheim in profile with her friend making a "funny" face next to him. Raúl Esparza warned her not to be devastated if Sondheim gave her notes, because he only gives you a note if he thinks you're good. Elizabeth had based a lot of the April character on the fact that she was an airline stewardess: very pert and precise. After he saw the show, Sondheim told her that April is more like someone who's perpetually stoned, even though she's not. Elizabeth tried a totally new interpretation that night, and even though she was terrified to change it so dramatically, it worked!

I asked how hard it was for the actors to play all those instruments and Elizabeth said that Rob, who played Paul, dropped the mute out of his trumpet so many times that John Doyle started charging him $5 every time it happened. ("I'd like to propose a toast" + CLUNK = $5). After *Cry-Baby* opened, Elizabeth was doing a workshop with someone who was in *Grease*, and when the Tony nominations came out, they both approached each other saying, "Oh my god! Everybody hates our shows, and we just got Tony noms. Miracles happen!" I have to say that I'm so glad I saw *Cry Baby*. I just wish there was a CD. Anybody with a cool $50,000 wanna sponsor it? A hot $50,000? Tepid $50,000?

Speaking of which, I saw *In the Heights* again ("Why is everything in this fridge warm and tepid?"). I was nervous to see it because it's my fifth time and I thought maybe I'd be a little over it by now. I literally loved it even *more*! I had full-out tears flowing down my face, which is what happens to me when I hear or see something that I think is theatrically perfect — like the ending of "At the Ballet" in *A Chorus Line* when the line forms again, or the last three "Calors" at the end of Abuela's song in *In the Heights*. As I was sitting in my box seat, I decided I want to see *In the Heights* once a week as a rejuvenating tonic. That cast is so amazing. I can't get over Mandy Gonzales' voice. She has to sing so high throughout the whole show! I know she sang just as high in *Dance of the Vampires*, but she didn't have to worry about a pesky long run during that show. She only had to sustain her vocal health through previews and then a smattering of performances. Also, special shout-out to Eliseo Roman, who plays the Piragua guy. He has one of those songs where, when the ending approaches, I think, "surely he's not going to go for the high note," and he does! It's a delicious A (track 10 on disc one of the cast album). It's the same way I felt when I saw David Carroll sing "Love Can't Happen" in *Grand Hotel*. I heard the ending note coming, and I thought he wouldn't be able to go up to it... but he did! Listen to the last track on the *Grand Hotel* CD... so thrilling! *P.S. Since then, I've deconstructed both David Carroll and Eliseo Roman. Go to my website!*

That's it for me... happy start of summer!

Andrea, Alexis and Agonizing Auditions
June 30, 2008

Greetings from Alaska! And by Alaska, I mean San Francisco. Why didn't anybody warn me that it's colder here than the reception Daisy Eagan got when she saw *Once on This Island*? (She won the Tony over LaChanze that year... remember? Anybody?)

I'm playing for beltress Andrea McArdle here in the new cabaret space called the Rrazz Room. I arrived with a pair of cool shorts and two new tank tops I wanted to work since it's gay pride and instead I've been walking around in long pants and a bulky sweatshirt. I was doing an interview on the phone for *The Dallas Voice* (more on that later), and the interviewer heard my non-stop complaining and said there's an expression that goes, "The coldest winter I ever spent was summer in San Francisco." Why didn't I hear those sage words before I boarded Jet Blue? All right, I'll get back to San Fran.

But before I do that, I also had my *Chatterbox* and I don't think I've shared my story about when *A Chorus Line* was coming back to Broadway. I desperately wanted an audition. I grew up obsessed with that show and played piano for the European tour, so I knew the choreography like the back of my hand from playing piano at rehearsals. My agent said he would have to schmooze the casting people to get me an audition because they probably thought I couldn't dance. I told him to tell them that if you watch the 1976 Tony Awards, some of those *Chorus Line* dancers look amazing and some look awful. I proudly said that I am definitely as good as one of the awful ones. My agent sounded confused and muttered, "OK... I'll tell them you're awful," and for some reason, I didn't get an audition. Well, that wasn't going to stop me. I stormed over to Equity and signed up for the EPA. I was positive the audition would consist of the opening combination and I knew I could dance it. The only thing I was nervous about was the double turn at the end of it ("turn, turn, out, in"). Well, a few weeks before the audition, the great dancer and former member of the show, Carlos Lopez, was teaching a class at Broadway Dance Center to prep for the audition! I went and told my friend, Grant Turner, to come with me because he had just gotten his green card (he's from Australia) and could finally start working on Broadway. Carlos spent a lot of time focusing on the turn, turn section, and I was actually doing it! I was psyched as I arrived at the audition. Well, I walked in with the other dancers, who all had amazing dancer bodies, and decided my trick would be to wear my shirt out. I'm sure it fooled everyone into thinking I had a six-pack that I was too humble to highlight.

Baayork Lee (the original Connie and now choreographer) was super friendly to me, but perhaps thought I was there to relieve the pianist. Instead I stood with the other dancers and prepared to do the opening. It all began well enough, until we got to the turn, turn section. I got nervous and sort of wobbled through a single turn and *right* at that moment, I heard one of the casting people say, loudly, *"He can't do it!"* Perhaps he was talking about something else entirely, but the timing was shockingly devastating. Then Baayork put us into groups. And by "groups," I mean *two people at a time*! That's not a group! How am I supposed to be able to hide and wow 'em with my personality!?! Then, because I wasn't nervous enough, I realized we had to do the opening towards a blatant *camera crew* because they were filming the auditions for a documentary! I got so panicked that my lack of technique turned my "turn, turn" into basically a "trip and saunter out of camera range." I was mortified... especially when it happened again. That's right, we were all graciously given a second chance, and I proved to everyone that my dance training ended in the '80s. I'm most thankful that I didn't do a pre-dance interview.

They were talking to people outside the audition room, and I was one inch away from saying, "Everybody in there knows me as a pianist, but they're gonna be *blown away* by my dancing." Of course, any editor in their right mind would immediately follow that set-up with a montage of my "fierce" dancing. My only consolation is that the brilliantly talented Grant *did* get the show and told me that Baayork told him if I had done the double turn, I would have gotten a callback.

On Wednesday, I flew out to San Fran and, because Juli's last day of school was Thursday, James came out that night (Juli went to visit her Gran in Texas). Andrea's show has been going great and her beautiful daughter, Alexis Kalehoff, is here with us. Alexis (now 19) made her Broadway debut as Young Cosette in *Les Miz* at age eight and loves to tell Andrea that she beat her to Broadway by five years. The Young Cosettes also have to play Young Eponine, as well as understudy Gavroche, the little boy. Alexis told me that she got to go on for Gavroche, and it was a "unique" performance. She was at the section of the show where Javert sings "Stars," and Gavroche is listening behind the barricade then steps out and sings, "That inspector thinks he's something, etc..." She said that she really had to pee and didn't know what to do... go offstage? What if she missed her cue? Finally, realizing that the show must go on, she simply peed onstage!!! She said that the stagehands who stand underneath the barricade were horrified and had to shield their heads from the onslaught. Alexis thought the story was hilarious at the time, and all Andrea thought was "Thank God we have different last names."

When Andrea was doing *Les Miz*, she wanted the kids in the cast to have an Easter egg hunt, so she hid 72 eggs all over the stage. They were the plastic kind that had money inside, so everybody in the show had a great time looking for them. Unfortunately, she hid 72 eggs... and they only found 68! The remaining eggs wound up breaking the barricade *and* the bank... Andrea had to pay $17,000 to get it fixed!

The most fun part about San Francisco is this chocolate café we discovered in Pacific Heights called Bittersweet. They make a classic hot chocolate, which reminded me of the long-ago discontinued Starbucks "Chantico" hot chocolate... AKA a melted chocolate bar in a cup... delish! What's great about the town is they have lots of zoning laws, so all these charming independent booksellers are everywhere, instead of the big conglomerates that come in and close down all the stores. I've been going into all the bookstores because I love to read (just read *Twilight*, which is a great young adult book about a 17-year-old girl in love with a vampire). *OMG! I had no idea how cutting edge I was! That's like me saying, "Just read GONE WITH THE WIND. I think people might like it."* At the first store I went into, I saw my books on the shelf, and the woman who worked there asked if I would autograph them! "With pleasure!" I said.

After that, it was downhill.

At the next store we visited, I asked where my books were and the bookseller told me they were sold out. "Excellent!" I said, with a smile. "Yep," he continued. "We sold all four." Ouch. Then I walked into another store and said to the counterman, "I see you're carrying my two books, *The Q Guide to Broadway* and *Broadway Nights*." Then I added, magnanimously, "Would you like me to autograph them?" To which I got a low energy, "If you want." Suffice it to say, if I had ever gotten a face lift, it would have fallen.

Okay, everyone, happy July and go see a show!

Hi, everyone! I just woke up from a nap. No, not the kind of rejuvenating "power nap" that corporate people take to focus their minds. I'm talking about a full night's sleep that wound up being a devastating three-and-a-half-hour disempowered nap.

James and I literally went to bed at 2 AM and woke up at 5:30! What the-?!?!?! It's because we are now on a plane headed down to Dallas and the only flight we could get left at 7:40 A.M. Our Texas jaunt is on account of I'm going to be performing with Betty Buckley at her all-Broadway request show at Lyric Stage in Dallas, as well as giving an audition master class. Oh yeah, today is also James' birthday! The good part is he gets to go to Dallas where he's from; the bad part is the lack of sleep is making us *both* look a year older.

All right, let me give you updates. First of all, last week on the *Legally Blonde* reality show, the coming attraction said that "the pressure becomes too much for Autumn," and then they showed her throwing up in the bathroom. She got sick right after she was critiqued by the judges and the coming attractions imply that the criticism overwhelmed her. Well, the real story is that it was actually the yogurt she ate that had been too long out of the fridge that overwhelmed her. That's right, she didn't realize that the parfait she had for breakfast had been sitting out since Newt Gingrich's "Contract With America." And it was just as rancid. That bit of creative editing totally annoyed me, but not as much as seeing how little I was on that episode! Rude! Then, to top it off, the only time you see me is when Autumn feebly makes her way back to the stage after being sick and I'm hunched over, ignoring her and rifling through my bag! It totally looks like I'm searching for my well-worn copy of a Jackie Collins book, but in truth, I was searching for a piece of gum for Autumn because I felt bad that she was sick and had no Listerine nearby.

Tuesday night, James and I saw *The 39 Steps* and, quite frankly, it took 39 steps to get to our seats. I've gotten really spoiled because I always can get house seats because of my Sirius radio show, and when I arrived at the theatre and was told my seats were in the balcony, I thought of hauling out the ol' "Don't you know who I am?" routine til I remembered that the most common answer when I ask that question is a firm and decisive "no." I went to the balcony ASAP. The seats were actually fine and I was impressed because that show has so much creativity in it. There are only four cast members, and they play all the characters that are in the film, but the lead (who's wonderful) stays the same character throughout, so it's really *three* people playing everybody else. Brava!

Speaking of seats, tell me if you think I was wrong in this situation: I was dying to see *In the Heights* again, and I bought one of the few seats left, which happened to be in the boxes. It was a $100 seat, but I couldn't see everything because I was over on one side of the stage. So, of course, during Act One, I eyed the orchestra seats and saw two open ones in the fourth row. They stayed that way the whole act. During intermission I came downstairs and put my bag on one of the seats. Right before Act Two began, I saw some women standing there discussing the seat. I walked over and said, "Hi! I was sitting over on the side, saw that seat and decided to snag it during intermission!" One of the women said, "Well, it wasn't yours to snag!" I was mortified. "Oh, I'm sorry!" I said, "Is it your seat?" She continued, "No. We're sitting next to it. These are *premium priced* seats." I realized she was annoyed that she paid a lot for her seat and preferred that the unsold seat next to her stay empty for the principal of it! It's not my fault nobody bought the seat next to her. I said something to the effect of, "I don't think I need your permission to sit there," sauntered past her and planted it. So, my question is: was I wrong? In *my* day of buying standing-room tickets, the ushers would always come over once Act One began and move us down if there were empty seats. Isn't that theatre protocol? It's one thing if someone else told me that they snagged the seat first or if the ticket holder showed up just for Act Two, but this woman just wanted to keep it empty... and felt she could tell me where I was allowed to sit. I wound up watching all of Act Two with an enormous smile on my face directed out front *and* an angry glare directed to my side, which took incredible facial flexibility. Hmm... maybe *I* should be in *The 39 Steps*.

This week at the *Chatterbox* I interviewed recent Tony Award-winner Laura Benanti. I've worked with her so many times and I simply adore her. She's such a great musician, such a funny performer and *so* nice! She also has a great sense of humor in real life. When she came onstage, she told everyone that, after the Tony Awards, you have to send in your Tony to get it engraved, so she happened to have it with her. Laura said she really wanted to attach a chain to it and make it into a necklace for her entrance. She thought it would be hilarious to walk out on stage casually, but with her neck jutting down from the weight of it and just be like, "Hey, everyone. What's up?"

I asked her about her first Broadway audition, and she told us that, when she was 17, she went to the open call for *The Sound of Music* Broadway revival. She wanted to play Liesl, but when the casting people looked at her résumé, they told her that she needed to update it because it only had high school credits. She told them that's because she was still *in* high school, and they were shocked. Or, as she put it, they looked at her and said, "High school? You're 40." The most devastating part of the whole day was that Laura assumed, because it was an audition, she had to get dressed up. And to her, "dressed up" literally meant... her prom dress. But she had stayed in the city the night before and forgot her shoes in Jersey, so she showed up at the audition in her prom dress... and clogs. Shockingly, she got a callback. As a matter of fact, she got four of them, and they finally made her an offer to play one of the nuns and understudy the lead role of Maria. She had just started NYU on scholarship but decided to quit (and, P.S., lose her scholarship) to take the gig. She got to go on for Maria, and contrary to Autumn, she actually *was* so nervous that she threw up right before she made her first entrance. She stayed terrified as she ran down the ramp (AKA the Alps) to sing the title song, and she remembers that as she raised her arms to start singing, "The hills are alive," they were both shaking uncontrollably. She obviously did well, though, because she was asked to audition to replace Rebecca Luker (who was leaving) and star opposite Richard Chamberlain. Unfortunately, it was raining the day of her audition *and* she was doing a reading all the way downtown that went on longer than expected, so she ran into the audition late *and* soaking wet. But instead of Richard being angry, he said, "Wow... she really *is* Maria." She got the gig and was starring on Broadway at age 18! Opposite Richard Chamberlain, who was 65. I'm sure the audience wasn't at all uncomfortable when they got together at the end of the show. Hmm...

When Laura got one of the leads in *Swing!*, she had to belt for the first time and didn't quite know how to do it. She said she thought to herself, "I think I'll sing... but yell a little bit..." and it worked! On the morning the Tony nominations were announced, she was awakened by a friend calling to tell her that she was nominated for a Tony. She thought he was crazy and explained that the *show* was nominated for a Tony. Her friend apologized and told her to go back to sleep. Then her Mom called to tell her she was nominated, and she was outraged her mom was calling so early. She was 20 years old and in that "My mom is so annoying" phase, so she said, in full brat, "I wasn't nominated, the show was... *and* you know my Broadway schedule. Don't call me before noon!" She had had it by that point and turned her phone off. When she finally woke up, she had a hundred messages congratulating her... and finally believed it.

I asked her what was up with her missed performances during *Into the Woods*. Turns out, they made her do a pratfall as Cinderella where she would leap onto a moving staircase and land in a pushup position. The show tried out in L.A. and as soon as she did the pratfall, the crew guys all said it was too dangerous. But "the powers that be" told her to keep doing it... and, of course, because she was only 20 and didn't question authority, *and* she was getting a laugh, she continued. One night, she did it and actually heard her neck snap, and by the end of the show, she couldn't move her neck at all. She went to a doctor the show set her up with, and he said that she had three herniated discs... *but* she could keep doing the pratfall. What?? Things started getting worse (her whole arm went numb for a while, and soon she'd walk around in a neck brace during her off hours). Finally, the doctor told her she couldn't do the show anymore.

She left the show and wound up getting cast in *Nine*. She started rehearsals, and one horrifying day she was lying on the floor at her mom's house and suddenly couldn't move her lower body to get herself up. Mary Stuart Masterson sent her to a different doctor, who said she had to get surgery the *next day*. Laura hemmed and hawed 'til he said that her back was in such bad shape that if she left and someone accidentally pushed her, she could be completely paralyzed! To get to the discs, the surgeon had to go through her throat first and push her vocal chords aside. Laura had to sign something saying that if it ruined her voice, she couldn't sue him. Devastating. The good news is the surgery worked and her voice is still a brava! But for those people who dish actors for missing shows, just know that most actors I've interviewed want to do all eight shows a week and are devastated whenever they have to miss. I don't know any principal people who miss performances because they don't feel like showing up. However, I do know some young ensemble people who are in their first Broadway show and are like, "I was totally out last night partying, and I'm *really* tired so I can't show up today. But we're all watching *Project Runway* later, so come over!"

Laura said that Patti LuPone broke her toe recently, but is still doing the show... however, she has to wear ugly-a** Isotoners. Boyd Gaines got everyone to make Patti a statue made out of Isotoners and then presented it to Patti... as the IsoTony. I wonder if Patti made a speech saying, "I've had to wait 29 years since my last IsoTony..."

I asked Laura about my two favorite parts of *Gypsy*: the cow and "Little Lamb." In "Dainty June and Her Farmboys," Laura's "moo moo moo moo" is so without any personality, it's hilarious. Turns out, during rehearsals, she didn't know she had to do it, so she'd watch the number and do the moos "to be nice"... as in "Okay, at this point someone will go, 'Moo moo moo moo.'" When she found out that she had to do it, she decided to keep that same lack of affect, and I can't *wait* for the CD so I can hear it every day for a laugh. I'm not the only one obsessed... Laura said she's investigating how to make the moos a ringtone because all of her relatives from Jersey are obsessed with it as well. As for "Little Lamb," the song I always avoided more than Phase One of the South Beach Diet, but I now love — she said that Sondheim told her that the words are just there to talk herself out of being sad. Even though it's not how most actors approach songs, she ignores most of the words and just focuses on the feeling. The only words she really means are "Little Cat, oh why do you look so blue? Did somebody paint you like that? Or is it your birthday, too?" The rest of the song for her is just about a girl who's been ignored her whole life, has some attention for a fleeting moment and is back to being alone again, trying to comfort herself. I, of course, brought the score with me and made her sing it for everyone, and she was *fantastic*!

Finally, I must discuss *[title of show]*. I've known Hunter Bell for years because he used to come to the comedy shows I'd do with Jack Plotnick. Then I got cast in a Rite Aid industrial and found out that he was cast as well. I thought, "Hunter Bell? That guy who's always in my audience? I didn't even know he was really in the business. Hmm... I *guess* he'll be okay." Well, we got to rehearsal and after five minutes, I was like, "*Oh my God!* He's a comic genius, and I don't deserve to be onstage with him." I couldn't believe how talented he was. Then I went to go see the first incarnation of *[title of show]* at NYMF and became completely obsessed. I saw it at Ars Nova, I saw the backers' audition at Chelsea Studios, and I saw it numerous times Off-Broadway at the Vineyard. Every time I see it, I laugh so hard, yet I'm so moved by it. When the cast found out it was going to Broadway, they asked me to come to opening night. Imagine how devastated I was to find out it's during the week I'm on the Rosie cruise. I thought maybe I could get off the ship and then fly back by helicopter, Lucy style (anybody remember when she went to Europe?), but no go. Instead, I made sure I was flying to Texas on a Sunday, so I could see the first preview of the show on Broadway Saturday night. I'm so happy I did that because there was something so incredibly moving about seeing that first performance. First of all, the theatre was *packed*. As soon as the show began and Larry, the music director, walked out onstage, the crowd went wild. So many of us had waited so long for the show to get to Broadway, we were so excited it was happening in front of us. I was there with James, who had never seen it before. I was terrified because he's told me that he doesn't usually like shows that have any kind of self-referential material. Would he like it? If he didn't, how much notice would I have to give to break up with him? Suffice it to say, I turned to him near the end of the show and he had tears in his eyes. Yes! We *can* stay together. I have to say that I get annoyed when people call the show "inside." Yes, it's about the process of writing a musical... and *A Chorus Line* is about the process of auditioning for a musical. Is *that* too inside for people to understand? *[title of show]* is really about what holds us back from true self-expression and how one measures success. Of course, people who know nothing at all about Broadway won't get 100 percent of the jokes, but so what? They'll get all the other ones. I had never seen the movie *The Red Shoes*, which is mentioned in *A Chorus Line*, but I still loved the show when I first saw it.

The most amazing part about seeing that first preview was that, after the cast sang the song near the end of the show with the brilliant lyric "I'd rather be nine people's favorite thing than 100 people's ninth favorite thing," the whole audience stood up. We were saying that we agreed and that we were so happy for them and that we welcomed their show to Broadway. I don't think I'd ever seen an ovation before the end of a show last for so long. I spoke to Kevin McCollum, one of the producers, after the show, and he said what's unique about this show is that the audience provides what the cast wants. Their "I want" song is "we want to put our art out there and have it accepted," and then we accept it, which makes the audience the protagonist of the show. Unfortunately, I didn't fully pay attention in AP English, but I essentially got what he was saying.

After the show, we went backstage with a slew of celebrities (Donna Murphy, Stephanie J. Block, Brian d'Arcy James, etc.) and got to hang out with the cast. That was fun. Leaving was not so much fun. There were so many fans at the stage door, we literally couldn't exit. It was like those photos of Beatles concerts. We had to find another way out, which we eventually did, which led to us going to bed at 2 AM... and getting up at 5:30, which is how I began this column.

All right, everyone, I'm finishing up this column looking out at Betty's beautiful Texas ranch, and I have to run to rehearsal. When you get a chance, visit and watch some of the hilarious videos at *titleofshow.com* and then come visit me in Texas!

Brava, Betty Buckley
July 14, 2008

Hello from the flight from Dallas — where I worked with Betty Buckley on three hit concert dates at Lyric Stage — to New York. The "good" news is, I'm in a middle seat. James is across the aisle from me sitting with Juli. It's been very weird for me, being in Texas the week before the cruise. Usually, this week is filled with non-stop rehearsals getting ready for the cruise. The rehearsals are still happening, but I'm not there like I usually am, supervising/getting in everyone's way.

Let me start at the beginning of last week. One of the things I forgot to mention about seeing [title of show] last Saturday night is that I stopped by the merchandising table on the way out. They have so much fun stuff... mugs and t-shirts, etc. The woman running the booth told me that the maximum she's ever sold in one night had been $500, but on the first preview of [title of show] she sold $3,000! And then I spied that they were selling my first book, The Q Guide to Broadway. I smiled humbly, held up the stack of books and magnanimously asked her if I should autograph them. I then got the amazing ego-boosting response I got in that San Francisco bookstore: a shrug and an "If you want..." Wow and ouch.

Anyhoo (P.S. I got a hostile email from a reader asking me to stop writing "anyhoo." Hmm... how about you stop writing hostile emails?), James and I flew into Dallas last Sunday (after our amazing three and a half hours of sleep), and we spent his birthday afternoon with his daughter, mom and sister at the Aquarium. Then we drove to Betty's ranch in Ft. Worth. Betty's assistant, Cathy, let us use her house the whole time we were there and cooked all of our meals for us. In exchange, I broke her garbage disposal. How was I supposed to know you're not supposed to throw cherry pits and egg shells into a disposal? One night, Betty and Cathy went to see a concert in Ft. Worth, so James and I went out to dinner at a real small-town Texas Mesquite-grill restaurant. James is excited about me on the Legally Blonde show because it's a national TV program and told me it was possible that someone in the restaurant would recognize me from watching. I bet him that no one would. Cut to, he asked the waitress if she watched the Legally Blonde reality show on MTV, and she enthusiastically said she did. He smiled triumphantly. So he was right! Then James pointed to me and said to the waitress, "Look, it's Seth!" Silence. Then I said, "Remember? I'm the vocal coach." Staring. "Um... I play the piano and teach the girls the music every week." Blinking. No recognition. So, I guess we were both right. Yay?

Betty and I had three days to put together her all-Broadway request show at Lyric Stage. For years, her fans and producers from concert venues have been asking for an all-Broadway show, but she's always included jazz as a large part of the show. She admitted that she sometimes has a contrary nature and attributed it to growing up with her mother wanting her to be Julie Andrews, yet she was wanting to be Janis Joplin. Regardless, she finally decided to give the people what they want and put together a show with songs and stories from her many years on Broadway. Betty and I spent hours each day in her music room going through songs and picking arrangements. Every time we'd get into an argument about how a song should go, Betty would laugh and say she wanted us to do that during the show. The biggest disagreement we had was which version of "Memory" to do. She wanted to do her re-arrangement of the song, which she calls "Space Memory" and begins with a few weird, mysterious chords. I wanted it Broadway-style and demanded we begin with the signature "Memory" vamp that we all know from the cast album. Finally, we agreed to compromise: I put some "Betty chords" in the middle, but got to begin it with the vamp I grew up on (Dum dum dum, dum dum). When Betty first heard me play it, she was in shock. It had been so long since she sang it with that intro.

We teched the show at the Lyric Stage on Wednesday afternoon and didn't really know how it was gonna go over. Well, first of all, we found out that all three shows were completely sold out with a long waitlist! Brava! I suggested that we seat people *Spring Awakening*-style, so the theatre brought extra chairs and put them on the stage! It was great having the audience so close — except when I started playing the intro to "As If We Never Said Goodbye," and someone's cell phone starting ringing. *Onstage*! *And* he didn't hear it! Betty finally had to gently ask him to turn it off. Oy. But even though we didn't quite know what the show was gonna be, it coalesced and was *fantastic*! Betty did a full two acts of singing for three nights and sounded *amazing*! Plus, her stories were fascinating and hilarious... *and* filled with non-stop busts on herself.

Someone asked what the funniest moment was that she ever had onstage and she proceeded to tell the following. One night during *Cats* she had a cold and a runny nose. She was crouched down at the bridge of the song ("A streetlamp dies, another night is over...") and preparing to rise up to do the final "Touch Me-e-e-e-e!" Well, when she rose up and reached towards the audience, she began the reach from her nose and, unfortunately, a long string of mucus came from her nose and reached *all the way* out towards the tip of her finger! *And* it refused to break! So, while she was singing "Touch me-e-e-e! It's so easy to leave me," it stayed right in the spotlight, glimmering. The cats crowding around Grizabella during that song are supposed to be repulsed by her, and that night, no acting was required on their part.

It was an all-Broadway request show and the only rule was it had to be from a show she'd done, and it had to be a song she sang. Nonetheless, people requested songs like "Music of the Night" and "All That Jazz." She also got a request for "I Dreamed a Dream" from *Les Miz*, which was requested as "I *Had* a Dream." Mama Fantine? Our favorite request was "Jubilation T. Cornpone" from *Li'l Abner*. Betty didn't know it, but I did, so I played the piano part while Betty made the woman who requested it sing it! Back 'atcha! All in all, Betty sang songs from *1776*, *Promises, Promises*, *Pippin*, *I'm Getting My Act Together...*, *Sunset Boulevard*, *A Little Night Music*, *Carrie*, the movie *Tender Mercies* (because she got so many requests for it) and of course, *Cats*. I had no idea that Judi Dench was the original Grizabella in London. I wondered how she sang "Memory" since I don't remember her being able to belt an E flat in "Notes on a Scandal," but turns out when Judi did the show, "Memory" didn't exist. She left *Cats* because of an injury, Elaine Paige took over, and that's when they added the song. Hm... I think if Judi had sung it, the whole show would have been a memory.

At one point in the show, I deconstructed footage of Betty performing in the Miss America Pageant. That's right, the Miss America Pageant. As a teenager, she wanted nothing to do with pageants because it went against her proud feminism (she was a charter subscriber to *Ms. Magazine*), but her parents pushed her to do it and she wanted the scholarship money. She said that all throughout her childhood, her father was vehemently opposed to her being an actress (her mother had to sneak her out of the house for dance classes) because he grew up in South Dakota and the only "actresses" he knew were dance hall hostesses who sometimes segued into becoming *ladies of the evening*. But though he was opposed to her acting, he was completely supportive of her being in pageants. I call that ironic. Betty called it hypocritical. Nonetheless, Betty was crowned Miss Ft. Worth, but did not win the role of Miss Texas. That honor went to the girl who stood next to her and was 6-foot-4-inches in her heels. For the talent portion, Betty sang, but this girl did a dramatic reading of *Gone With the Wind* as her talent. Betty knew she lost when she saw the girl end her monologue by literally eating a turnip. Nonetheless, Betty was invited to perform on the national telecast of *The Miss America Pageant*, representing all of the local pageant girls who don't get to go on to compete in Miss America. Or, as Betty put it, representing losers everywhere.

I found video footage of Betty singing on the 1972 pageant and deconstructed her terrible lack of lip-synching skills. She said that she's never been good at being able to match how she sang something. During the filming of *Tender Mercies*, they had to film the scene where she sang "Over You" over and over again because she kept clanking. In the Miss America pageant, she finally decided that if she kept her mouth wide open a lot, it would make her look like she's singing. It actually just makes her look crazy. On top of that, I showed the part of the song that featured the one time she should have kept her mouth open. Yes, on the extended last note of the song, she closed her mouth before the note ended! So you hear her high belted note ringing out, yet see her mouth clamped shut. Hi-larious!

Finally, I forgot to mention that when I was interviewing Laura Benanti last week, we were talking about audience behavior at Broadway shows. She said that she was told at *Gypsy* to constantly be on the lookout for people videotaping the show. She told me she responded, overwhelmed, with, "Really? Can't I just act?" Well, one day the whole cast noticed someone texting non-stop… *in the front row*! Patti LuPone was mind-boggled someone would pay so much for a ticket, but spend the time texting. Well, Patti demanded that the person be thrown out for Act Two! I asked Laura if the person could have insisted on staying, and she said Patti wouldn't have gone on again. Brava!

OK, people. We're getting closer to landing. Soon, I'll be writing to you from the high seas to tell you all about the Broadway-filled Rosie cruise! Peace out!

Ship of Dreams
July 21, 2008

Ahoy, mateys! I'm back on dry land. I just got off the R Family Vacations cruise. This summer's cruise had the best entertainment so far.

There's a great article that was in The New York *Times* about all the Broadway performers on the cruise. In the article I'm quoted as saying the boat has "the greatest entertainment in the world." My sister Nancy emailed me and asked if the *Times* could add a photo of me with a fat belly, smoking a fat cigar and surrounded by ladies with tassels on their tops. It's true I sound like Trump, but I was serious. Every show was amazing!

Okay, so Sunday, we got on the boat at 11... and by 11, I mean noon because I had to stop by Starbucks and get my signature iced latte with a breakfast sandwich, which I heard they're discontinuing! And I heard from a Starbucks employee that they're being discontinued *not* because they don't sell well, but because of the smell. "Do they smell bad when they cook?" I asked. "No," he replied, "but they cover up the smell of coffee." What? Who cares?! I can't believe they'd discontinue something the consumer actually wants because they think we need to smell coffee when we're there. I'll smell it when I'm drinking it! Now give me my sandwich ASAP! *They kept the sandwiches! My opinion clearly has incredible power!!*

Anyhoo, the Sunday night show was dedicated to Streisand music and it was *amahzing*. The first number was *not* a Barbra song, but had lyrics by Michael Lee Scott and Colin Sheehan and music from *La Cage*. The opening section went: *We are what we are/ And what we are/ Is on vacation*! Brava! Then Rosie came out and did a full tap dance. Those of you that saw the *Encores!* production of *No, No, Nanette* might have found it familiar for some reason. Perhaps because it was the exact same one she did in that show. To be quite honest, the steps stayed the same, and we just changed the music underneath it. I always say, if you're good at one thing, stick with it (see Carol Channing's résumé since 1964).

Rosie hosted the show and was fun-nee. She said she's been doing the "True Colors" tour for The Human Rights Campaign Fund with Cyndi Lauper and Cyndi implored the audience to vote this November. Cyndi then said if you can't make it out of your house, you can vote online. Huh? Rosie told her backstage that you can't actually vote online. Cyndi went back out and told the crowd, "Listen, everybody. Turns out, you can't vote online." Pause. "But you probably will be able to do it one day... because I'm a visionary." Good save... New Age-style!

Rosie mentioned her son, Parker, who's now 13 years old and sports a six-pack. She told us that it's proof that Parker was adopted because "...no O'Donnell ever had a six-pack on the *out*side." Then, Klea Blackhurst came out and sang the hell out of "Before the Parade Passes By," holding the last note as long as Barbra does in the *Hello, Dolly!* film, which I heard is the longest note ever held in a movie — except for the anguished wail I let out after hearing Madonna's version of "Rainbow High" in *Evita*. That was followed by James singing "Piece of Sky" from *Yentl*. He said the song is about going for something you want that's deemed impossible and equated it with growing up gay in Texas, yet wanting to be a dad, which he now is. The song went over *great* and he sounded amazing on the last A flat.

Up next was Carolee Carmello, who belted out "Woman in the Moon." She learned it only because I asked her to, and now she *must* sing it in New York. I was nervous that no one would know it was from the film *A Star is Born*, but thankfully Rosie did because she walked onstage right after and immediately launched into "Queen Bee," which is Barbra's first song in the movie. That movie is so great if you can watch it with your eyes closed just enough to block out Barbra's home perm. Next on the show were the Broadway Boys, which is a group consisting of guys whose only requirement is a) a super high voice, b) flexible riffs that would make Mariah hang up her vocal chords and c) hotness. They sounded great on "I Don't Care Much," which most people thought was a bizarre choice because they only know it from the revival of *Cabaret*, but Barbra did it first on *The Second Barbra Streisand Album*.

The genesis of that song is that Kander and Ebb were at a dinner party and someone challenged them to write a song by the end of the party... and that's what came out! How cool is that? All in the time frame of one meal. Of course, if they were having a dinner like the ones I had on the Rosie cruise, they had around five hours to write the song.

Anyhoo, the Broadway Boys tore it up and next was Christine Pedi, who came out doing her Barbra imitation. "You know... people think I'm a diva... which I'm not. But Rosie knows I am a perfectionist, and I only perform when the temperature is 68 degrees." She then licked her finger and put it in the air. "Hmm... it's 69, so I won't be singing." Instead, "Barbra" invited other strong women to come up and sing a power anthem, and Christine did her amazing "I Will Survive" where she channels Eartha Kitt, Bette Davis, Joan Rivers, Carol Channing and Ethel Merman. The audience went cra-za-zy! Finally, Andrea McArdle came onstage with her daughter Alexis, and they both belted out "Enough is Enough." My friend Mark Cortale was devastated when he saw Alexis. He assumed Andrea's daughter would be a cute little toddler, but she's literally a grown woman. AKA we're ninety.

The next night Sheena Easton gave a concert. Turns out, she's hilarious. She told the audience that if they've ever been in an elevator, then they've heard one of her tunes. She had a great attitude about all of her hit songs in the '80s, saying that by singing them today she gets to relive her youth. She sang "Morning Train," which I love not only because it's such a fun song but because I'm obsessed with the formation of it. Circa early '80s: Hmm... I can't think of anything interesting to write a song about. So let me take something completely mundane and feign that it's interesting...
Here goes: *My baby takes the morning train. He works from 9 to 5 and then...*
Ooh! Here comes the amazing part: *He takes <u>another</u> home again to find me waiting for him.*
Sheena, stop! It's called commuting. It's not interesting. I take the 1 train. And?

The next day we stopped in St. John, New Brunswick, Canada (which was beautiful), and that night was the comedy show. I hosted it and hauled out my Barbra deconstruction as well as my deconstruction of Cher singing *West Side Story*. First of all, yes, it exists. Secondly, it's not pleasing to the eye *or* ear. She not only plays the role of Maria, but thanks to an '80s split screen effect, plays Anita as well. And thanks to the drag king technology, she also embodies the roles of Tony, Riff, The Sharks *and* The Jets. When I worked on *The Rosie O'Donnell Show* as a comedy writer, I told Rosie to surprise Cher by showing this "embarrassing" clip. Rosie asked Cher if she remembered filming it and I waited for Cher to protest and beg Rosie not to show any of it. Instead, Cher calmly said it was her favorite thing she ever filmed. *Stunned silence from me.*

Then she recounted how she first filmed the role of Biff. Biff? Was it a musical version of *Death of a Salesman*?

Comic Jessica Kirson made her fourth appearance on the ship and told a joke I loved, specifically because I was traveling with my mom.

Q: What did the waiter say to the older Jewish ladies?
A: Is *anything* OK?

Brava!

Then I did a *Chatterbox* with some of the great ladies on the ship. Carolee talked about how she did all the pre-Broadway readings, workshops and recordings of *The Scarlet Pimpernel*. She loved the role of Marguerite because of the great songs she got to sing, as well as because the character was from France and French was her minor in college. Even though she had done the role numerous times in front of the powers-that-be, they still made her audition for the Broadway production and *then* they cast someone else! Ouch! She did eventually get to play the role and I had her sing "When I Look at You" to show everyone how great she was in the part. Then we talked about my *Funny Girl* concert for The Actors Fund and she recreated the 11 o'clock number she did that night: "The Music That Makes Me Dance." No surprise, the audience gave her a full standing O. Yes!

I also talked to Lillias White and asked her to recount her audition for *Dreamgirls*. She said that in the early '80s, she went in to audition as a replacement for the role of Lorrell and sang "Ain't No Party" for Michael Bennett. There's a section that has the lyrics "Now it's been seven years and it don't take a smarty to realize that even though my man throws confetti in my face, it still don't make it no party." When she got to the throwing of confetti part, she mimed throwing it from her crotch. After the move, Michael Bennett thought, "Hmm… I think she's an Effie." She came back and had to sing *every single thing* that Effie sings in the show. By the end, she had no voice. Regardless, Michael Bennett offered her the understudy to Jennifer Holliday in Los Angeles! However, Lillias didn't want it. First of all, she said, she didn't think it was right for her because she doesn't have that gravelly type of voice that people equate with Effie; secondly, she had a newborn and didn't want to go out of town; and thirdly, it was L.A., and she didn't drive! Michael assured her that she sang it great, she would definitely go on in the role and she would have everything she needed. She wasn't sure whether to trust him because, as she hilariously said, "white man speak with forked tongue," but when she got to L.A. Michael kept his word and got her childcare *and* put her in a driving school. And then there was a five-show weekend, and Jennifer couldn't do all five. Lillias went on for Effie… and Michael re-invited all the critics to see her! Of course, she got amazing reviews. I then asked her to sing "I Am Changing" because that's my favorite song on my Actors Fund CD of *Dreamgirls*. I still remember conducting it that night and hearing that crazy cheering after she sang "…nothing's gonna stop… me… now!!!!" Of course, all the R Family audience stood up immediately after her song. Brava!

All right, there's more to report… stay tuned.

Ship of Dreams—Part II
July 28, 2008

Okay, part two of the Rosie Cruise! First, let's discuss the onboard food. My version of dieting was that I would never let myself get one of the fresh baked waffles in the morning... after that small bit of self-restraint, all bets were off. I'd have delicious oatmeal with a ton of brown sugar, and thanks to a tip from Brenda Braxton, melted butter in it as well. Mmm. I was outraged, though, that the delicious chocolate chip cookies were only in the children's area of the main dining room. Rude! I had no shame about leaning my whole body over the partition that's supposed to separate the kid area from the adult area and grabbing a fistful of cookies while claiming to the shocked faces around me that they were for Juli. And no, Juli never got any from me. *Why* were they in one area and restricted from the other? Quite frankly, I wasn't acting out with food, I was standing up against discrimination!

OK, we're midway through the trip at this point. I haven't mentioned the ports we went to, so let me just say they were all beautiful, but they also all rated a ten on the melanoma-inducing scale. Is there literally no more ozone? Only after St. John in Canada did I not spend the whole night checking my moles for any changes.

Back on the boat, I did a full hour *Chatterbox* with the brilliant Christine Ebersole. She talked about what happened after she and her husband adopted their first child. Her husband was flying to China to get their second, a baby girl (they had been trying to adopt from different places) and while he was flying home with their new baby girl, Christine got a call that there was a little boy who needed a family! She couldn't call her husband because he was mid-flight, so she said yes. When she got to the airport, she met her husband, who was carrying their new daughter, and then she told him they had to go to a different terminal to pick up their new son! They went from having one child to three in literal minutes!

Christine ended the *Chatterbox* by singing "Around the World," of course. We were both a little panicked, though. Me, because it's a crazy hard piano part that I, of course, started practicing ten minutes before showtime, and she because the show closed a year ago and she was nervous about lyrics. I'm sort of fascinated by what the window is before you start forgetting what you've done in a show. And sometimes you don't just forget lyrics, you forget whole songs! Betty Buckley loves singing "Old Friend" from *I'm Getting My Act Together...* but when I suggested she do "Put in a Package," which is the opening number from the show, she stared at me blankly. Then, I started playing it for her, and the only thing she added to her staring was blinking. Of course, you have to remember, she performed that part 30 years ago, so I think that's a fair amount of time to forget something, *but* Priscilla Lopez told me something that happened when she was doing *A Day in Hollywood...* She took a one-week vacation and came back to the show refreshed. She had a *great* song in Act One called "The Best In the World." It had four choruses and pretty much each one began with "Papa said you're the best... you're the best in the world." Cut to; she stands in her spotlight, starts the song, gets to the chorus and sang, "Papa said... uh... um... *silence*." Suddenly, from the pit she heard, in a crazy stage whisper, "...You're the best!" She literally forgot the *title of the song*! I guess it's more about your brain deciding it can forget. Priscilla went on a vacation and didn't have to think about the show, and a part of her brain stayed in that mode. So, in conclusion, you can forget a song/lyrics after 30 years or after a week at a spa.

But back to the cruise. Finally, Saturday arrived, the night of the big show. Last year, we hauled out a mini-version of *Annie* starring Andrea McArdle, and this year we decided to do *Chicago*. A few weeks before the cruise, I was thinking of who should play Velma, and I remembered my friend, Brenda Braxton, whom I saw play the role twice on Broadway. I called her and said, "We're going to do *Chicago* on the Rosie cruise, and I wanted to know if you had any interest in playing Vel-," and before I could get to "-ma," she said, "Yes." Brenda had been hankering for a vacation and she told me she wasn't going to do anything on the boat besides rehearse the show... and she wasn't kidding. The cruise stopped in five different ports, and Brenda didn't get off once! She said she just sat and relaxed, ordered room service and ate it on the balcony in her room!

All right, back to casting. I had to find a Roxie. I knew Michael Lee Scott (who was the choreographer for the opening show) performed with his cousin, Sandy Duncan, so I asked him to ask her to do it. Sandy couldn't break her other commitments, so I was left Roxie-less. I was thinking, "Michael Lee is sad because he couldn't get Sandy to play Roxie." Then my mind changed the sentence to, "Michael Lee is sad, get Sandy play Roxie," then "Michael Lee is Sandy play Roxie" and suddenly: "*Michael Lee is Roxie*!" That's right, I gender-bendered that role because I knew Michael Lee was hilarious and would dance up a storm. I then asked the amazing Lillias White to reprise her Broadway performance as Mama Morton and did one more gender-bend by having Andrea McArdle play Billy (Billie?) Flynn. And, as luck would have it, David Sabella, who was the original Mary Sunshine on Broadway, happened to be on the boat vacationing as a gay dad. Well, vacation or not, I needed him onstage! We got some drag, his original music charts and the next thing he knew, he was out of the shuffleboard area and hitting high As. He was great!

Since we could only do a 45-minute version of the show, I narrated the story line between songs. I told the audience that I've been obsessed with it ever since I was a little boy. As a matter of fact, I was desperate to get the music so I could play it on the piano. While other kids were harassing their parents to get them Atari, I was begging mine for the complete piano/vocal score of *Chicago*. (I finally got it after two months of begging.) Also, my mom got me tickets to see it and I still remember they cost $15, which now just covers the newly implemented "theatre improvement" fee. I would always listen to the record in my den and try to choreograph it (never getting much past flexed hands), and one of my favorite songs was "Cell Block Tango." So, of course, I cast myself in it as "squish." It was so much fun!

Anyhoo, the last casting problem was "Class." We wanted to make it different for the boat version. Dev Janki and I decided to ask two fabulous women to do it. Actually, *four* fabulous women. My setup was: I asked the audience if anyone knew who replaced Gwen Verdon as Roxie in the '70s for a short time. A few people called out Liza. Brava. Then I said, perhaps Liza coveted the role of Velma. Then I suggested that if *Chicago* had opened in the Golden Age, perhaps Mama Morton would have been played by the premiere belter of Broadway. I then introduced "Class" as sung by Ethel Merman (Klea Blackhurst) and Liza Minnelli (Christine Pedi). Yes, it made no sense, but ending it with the "New York New York" vamp brought the house down.

Finally, Brett Macias had orchestrated "Don't Rain On My Parade" for Lillias White, but we wound up not doing it on the first night of the cruise in the Barbra show. But I didn't want to deprive the audience of her brilliance, so as an encore to *Chicago*, I kept Lillias onstage and started the vamp. Needless to say, she sounded *amazing*. All in all, the cruise was *fantastic*! Come with us to Alaska next year!

On a final note, I saw *Damn Yankees* at *Encores!* Thursday night. I'm obsessed with how funny Cheyenne is and how he can spin his vibrato. Beautiful! And I've loved Jane Krakowski ever since I saw her in *Grand Hotel* as Flaemmchen. I remember spotting her on the street a few weeks after I first saw her (in '89) and going into shock. I just stepped in front of her, stared, and said, "You're amazing." She thanked me, while stepping the hell around me ASAP. Now though, in 2008, I'm able to go backstage… and act awkward to her face in her dressing room. I love how she's such a theatre person! Jane said that she loves doing Lola because she gets to dance Fosse. And she researched the role vigorously. Apparently, Gwen Verdon complained to Fosse that she couldn't do certain steps without falling because she had to wear heels. Fosse kept telling her she could do it and Gwen finally flat-out said she couldn't. Fosse literally then showed up the next day with his own pair of heels! Once he did, he understood the problems Gwen was having, and together they fixed it.

I didn't know what to expect from Sean Hayes, since I've never seen him do theatre. Let me say: he was amazing! He had so many hilarious choices that were so original and didn't seem "I thought this up in rehearsal and now it's frozen and not fresh at all." He was fantastic in his scenes and then in his song, "Those Were The Good Old Days," he sang great *and* he had the nerve the play the piano. My jealousy meter was ticking on high. How *dare* he be so talented? Then (spoiler alert), he came out for his encore holding a violin. What? The violin is my favorite instrument. I know how to play a little, but I stink. I've always dreamed of being a concert violinist, but my terrible technique and lack of talent has prevented me. I turned to James and said, "If he sounds amazing, I've had it!" Sean lifted the violin to his chin… and promptly threw it offstage. Phew! Still, I turned to James and said, "He's so amazingly talented, I'm phenomenally jealous." James "comforted" me by reminding me that Sean is also a multi-millionaire. *Not cool!*

Okay, have a great weekend and I'll be back on Monday!

Autumn… and Bailey… and [title of show] in New York
July 29, 2008

All right, people, updates. Last Monday night, I hosted and played piano for a NYCLU benefit. At rehearsal I chatted with John Gallagher Jr. who, of course, I didn't recognize at first. He looks *nothing* like he did in *Spring Awakening*. I hate the mortification of seeing someone and having no idea who they are, so I told him from now on he has to be recognizable to me, i.e. walk around with an Eraserhead hairstyle and lederhosen and commit suicide. Anthony Rapp also performed and sported a beard rendering him unrecognizable. Stop already! Why can't people retain their signature looks? And why can't Liza ever change hers?

Right after the NYCLU benefit, I rushed to the fabulous apartment of Amanda Brown Lipitz, the executive producer of the *Legally Blonde* reality show. She had tons of people there watching the final episode. I got there late and while I was walking over, I got a text from Bernie Telsey busting me for the way I ran onto the Palace stage. When I got there, I informed him that I already dished myself in that week's video blog. I commented that my run informed the audience of two things: a) I was not popular in high school and b) I need a sports bra.

Bernie was trying to bust me because I spent so many previous vlogs busting him. On one episode he told Autumn that, at her previous audition, she "literally hit it out of the park." "Literally"? They had an audition at Shea Stadium? Then he said he was nervous about whether one of the girls could perform that well "eight days a week." Hmm… I commented that maybe Bernie was confused by the ubiquitous commercial from years ago stating that "Sunday is Funday at Carvel" and informed him that "Funday" isn't an actual day. I'm going to upload all my *Legally Blonde* vlogs to my website so everyone can see my slams, I mean, playful jabs against Bernie et al. P.S. Why do I wonder why I've never been cast by him?

Anyway, it was super fun to watch the finale with a bevy of the Elle contestants: Emma, Lindsey, Autumn, Lauren, Bailey and Celina. *Yes! Now Tony Award-winner Lena Hall from HEDWIG!*

On Wednesday, I hightailed it to the Palace Theatre to see Bailey make her debut. In "Omigod You Guys," all of the Delta Nu sorority sisters start the song. Suddenly, Autumn Hurlbert (who was the runner-up for Elle Woods) appeared, and when she sang her opening solo, she got *crazy* cheers from the audience. I felt so great for her! She's *extremely* talented and Miss Thing can *sing*! When Bailey rose up in the elevator, the place went nuts. I thought I'd be nervous for Bailey, but she was on her gig. As a matter of fact, I had spoken to Jim Sampliner (the music director of the show), and he told me that Bailey had her put-in rehearsal the previous Friday, and they went straight through the show without stopping once! That's amazing for a first-timer on Broadway… who's 20 years old… playing the *lead*! I did start to get nervous as the show progressed because the end of Act One has the song "So Much Better," and the reality show made a big deal about how hard it was to hold the last note (it's a pretty high note, and it's supposed to be held for four counts of eight). It's one thing to have to do something hard in a show, but it's a nightmare when the whole audience knows how hard it is! I always feel bad when an ice skater is doing a triple axel because I know that they know the whole audience is wondering whether they'll make it. It's like asking someone stunning out for a date while 1,000 people watch to see if you get rejected. Anyhoo, as the last note of "So Much Better" approached, I had a mini anxiety attack, but not only did Bailey hold the note the whole time, it actually didn't matter because the audience started cheering so loudly after the first four counts that you could hardly hear her voice anyway. She could have taken it down the octave, and no one would have noticed.

Speaking of noticing, I was spotted by some reality show fans in the audience and I felt like a celeb. Then, when I saw *Damn Yankees*, I went backstage and there were tons of people lined up waiting for the cast. As I passed some of them, I had several requests for autographs. I felt bad that James had to wait, but I assumed he knew I had a duty to my public. After my backstage visit, I geared myself up for my exit. I figured there'd still be people waiting for the cast and probably some of the newcomers would want my autograph... after all, I'd made nine different 5 to 10 minute appearances on *Legally Blonde: The Search for Elle Woods*. I opened up the door leading from the backstage area to the street, and as soon as I did, the crowd reaction went wild. Full out Beatles-fan screaming. "I still got it!" I thought to myself. I scanned the crowd to decide which crazed fan I should give my autograph to first, when I noticed them all looking down. That's odd, I thought. My curiosity turned to devastation when I realized that the screams were not due to my dedicated public recognizing me, but instead a direct result of the appearance of a large water bug on the sidewalk. Once it ran down the block, the screaming stopped, and I was met with a sea of blank faces. The only request I got was not for an autograph but rather for an answer to the question, "Is Jane coming out soon?" "Yes," I muttered as I shame-facedly put away my unused Sharpie and ran down the block, with James laughing behind me. I still *don't* got it.

This week my *Chatterbox* was a joy because I interviewed the two brilliant creators of *[title of show]*, Hunter Bell and Jeff Bowen. Way back in the mid-'90s, Jack Plotnick was starring in *The Boys From Syracuse* at the Alliance Theater down south. Jack suddenly got an offer to do a TV pilot with Janeane Garofalo and Bob Odenkirk right before *The Boys From Syracuse* was about to start previews. He called me and asked me what to do. He knew the show could go on because they could get a replacement for him, but he felt that it was wrong to leave a commitment. *But* he also really wanted to start doing more TV, and he thought Janeane and Bob were great people to work with who could jump-start his career. I didn't know what to tell him, so he finally called Dick Scanlan, whom we both met while working with him Off-Broadway in *Pageant*. I took over being the music director from James Raitt, Dick was hilarious as Miss Great Plains, and Jack was the swing. Most Broadway people know Dick because he wrote the book and lyrics to *Thoroughly Modern Millie. And then EVERYDAY RAPTURE and MOTOWN, and he is now working on bringing THE UNSINKABLE MOLLY BROWN back to Broadway.* Jack presented his moral dilemma to Dick, and Dick presented him with the query, "What would Madonna do?" Seriously. Well, that clinched it for Jack. He quit *The Boys From Syracuse* and hightailed it to LA, and the Alliance had to replace Jack ASAP. There was an understudy for the role in the show, but the powers-that-be thought that one of the non-Equity chorus boys would be great in the role and asked him to learn it in 24 hours. He learned it, nailed it *and* got his Equity card. That chorus boy's name was... Hunter Bell!

Jeff grew up in Florida and in *[title of show]*, the Jeff character talks about being in high school and painting a glow-in-the-dark *Aspects of Love* mural in his bedroom. Jeff confirmed that, indeed, the real-life Jeff did just that. He also 'fessed up that there is a Phantom mask thrown into the mural as well. And the delicious news is that it's still there! He also said that he went to a master class when he was a late teenager. It was taught by Terrence Mann, who had flown down from New York. Jeff got up to sing his song, opened his mouth, and out came all four verses of "Don't Cry for Me, Argentina." With no irony. He can't remember the "critique" he got from Terrence, but I'm assuming it began with "What the-?"

Jeff and Hunter met doing a production of *Good News*. The non-equity chorus was called a week early to learn the dances (Jeff), and then the leads arrived (Hunter). Hunter showed up knowing every line and every song, and Jeff *hated* him. He found out later that Hunter had just played the role, but then it just seemed like annoying over-confidence. Afterwards, they drove home to the cast house in the company van and when Hunter heard Jeff gabbing with some other ensemble member, he haughtily thought, "Hmm… they sound a little negative. I don't need that energy around me."

Around a week later, they were all rehearsing, and Hunter commented on someone in the cast wearing jazz pants ("Where did you get them? How did you get them to flair out at the bottom?"), and that's all it took for he and Jeff to become best friends. They started writing together and completed a musical version of *9 to 5*! They actually did a full reading of it and got some great people to star. How? They just left the material for them at the stage door with a letter (not unlike the blind phone call made to celebrities in *[title of show]*). However, they never got the rights to the show, and eventually found out there was another version being written. But that's what led to them writing *[title of show]*. P.S. If you don't know what I mean by the blind phone calls to celebs, I'll explain. Throughout the show, Hunter and Jeff are looking to help sell their show by having a big name attached. And throughout it, you hear phone messages from real Broadway people turning them down. They're all hilarious, and I'll tell you two that were in the Off-Broadway version but didn't make it to Broadway. One of the messages was from Amy Spanger saying very sweetly, "Hi, guys. It's Amy Spanger. I got your message, and I am very honored you thought of me for your show but, because of my schedule, I can't do it." Then you hear the sound of the phone starting to be hung up, and Amy's voice continues to someone in the background, "Stephen Oremus is giving out my f***ing number to anybody." Her line reading was amazing. There was another one where Sutton Foster called in all excited. "Hey, Hunter, I heard about your show. Of course, I'll do it! We Fosters need to stick together!" Then you hear someone say something to her and she says, "Huh? Hunter *Bell*? Who the f***is that?" and hangs up. Brava!

All right, everybody, enjoy the last gasps of July, and I'll give you an update next week!

Laura, Peter and Turkey Sheds
August 4, 2008

This was an annoying week for two reasons!

Here goes: James, Juli and I finally found an apartment that had everything we wanted (duplex on the ground floor of a brownstone with a backyard), and it was *cheap. And* we found out that there was no one else looking at it. We put in an application... and got ixnayed!!!! The realtor told us that she had no idea why the landlord rejected us. James and I both make enough money *and* have good credit. It's so hilarious because it's an apartment I've seen on Craigslist for *weeks*, and I refused to look at it because the ads seemed desperate. There was a post about it literally every day, and the price kept dropping and dropping. I essentially went to go look at it because I felt bad for it. It was like asking someone out just to make them feel better and then having *them* dump *you*. What chutzpah! I've had it.

Then I joined the throngs of blind consumers and bought an iPhone. *Holy cow! I can't believe the hurdles you had to jump through to get that annoying phone!* If you don't know, you first have to go to the Mac store and get a time to come back to actually buy the iPhone. When you do come back, they have you wait in a beautiful, air-conditioned lounge until your phone is ready. Oh, I'm sorry, they actually make you wait *outside* with no shade in crazy scorching heat for a full half hour! After that, you get the privilege of waiting on another line inside the store. *Then*, when you finally get the phone, you realize that because you're an adult male, your fingers are actually too fat to type on its little tiny screen. It's a *nightmare*! You think you're typing one thing and something crazy comes out on the screen. Right after I got it, I emailed Amanda Lipitz, the producer of the MTV *Legally Blonde* reality show, and told her I was going to have some contestants from the show on my *Chatterbox* and wondered if she wanted to come onstage and chat about the show. I got back an email from her, asking me, "What's omtahe?" That's right, "omtahe" is what came out when I typed "onstage." I've had it! I either get rid of the iPhone or put my fingers on a diet.

This week I also had an audition for the new musical version of the film *The Front*. Right after I sang and read, the director, John Caird (*Les Miz*), came up to talk to me. I was ready for some British-style direction. You know like, "I want to see 40 percent more Falstaff with a smidgeon of Lear. And then haul out ye olde Lady Macbeth." Instead, he told me that he was talking about me with someone recently, and he knew my name must be an anagram. Then when he saw it in print, he immediately realized it was an anagram for "Turkey Sheds." I was super-impressed. How can he see a name and immediately form an anagram? I then realized I have a similar talent in that I can see the name of a person and immediately know if they're Jewish. He has the British version of that skill. When I questioned what a turkey shed was, John Caird offered up, "perhaps turkey sheds are where composers go to write bad Broadway shows." I piped up with, "I guess that's where Andrew Lloyd Webber lives!" I was then mortified because I couldn't remember if they had ever done a show together (they did: *Song and Dance*), *and* I was annoyed with myself because making an ALW joke is as cheap as doing a "why do men leave the toilet seats up" routine. *And* because I love all of Andrew Lloyd Webber's musicals. And by "all of," I mean 80 percent of them. I won't qualify which ones are in the 20 percent, but let's just say that the "frequently played songs" list on my iPod doesn't include *By Jeeves*. Anyhoo, I was totally intimidated having a one-on-one with John Caird, but not as much as I was auditioning for a Coen Brothers movie! That's right! I had two high-powered auditions within two weeks. The problem was that the scene I was auditioning with began with the character crying. It's one thing to build up to crying, but it's so hard to go from chatting with the casting director: "Hi! Nice to meet you! Yes… *The Ritz* was totally fun!" to body-heaving sobs. I kept trying to think of tricks to get myself to cry. I remembered my friend Jack Plotnick told me about an actor he knew who brought a bag of cut up onions to an audition, put them in his back pocket and during the audition scene, surreptitiously put some onion juice in his eyes. Unfortunately, it didn't make him cry, but it *did* make his eyes sear with pain. We're both obsessed wondering what the casting director thought was going on when he saw this guy start acting the scene, casually bring his hand to his eyes and then start screaming in pain for no reason. *P.S. The film was A SERIOUS MAN and Richard Kind got "my" role.*

This week I also did some work with the Broadway Artist Alliance, where I interviewed Laura Benanti for the kids taking the program. Laura was, of course, beautiful and hilarious, but she noted that our dry humor was not working on some of the ten-year-olds. Keep up, kids, keep up! How dare you not get my Elaine Stritch joke? I was referring to her active alcoholism in the '50s. Anybody? Anybody under 12? Nobody? Someone asked Laura what her strangest experience was onstage and she said that when she was playing Cinderella in *Into the Woods*, someone in the audience had Tourette's syndrome. I actually have two friends with Tourette's but not with the symptoms this guy had. Apparently, he was only triggered when Laura sang. She gave us an amazing demonstration of what it was like by singing "I wish" followed by a gruff "F*** Sh** A**." She then said that during that performance, she was talking about it backstage and asking how the other actors were dealing with it, and they were like, "Laura. You're crazy. We don't hear anything." She decided she had been imagining it, re-entered with "He's a very nice prince" and was rewarded with a "Son-of-a-b**** Mother******."

At the *Chatterbox*, I interviewed three former contestants from the *Legally Blonde* reality show: Autumn Hurlbert, Celina Carvajal and Lauren Zakrin. *Again, I'm obsessed that Celina Carvajal changed her name and became Lena Hall. And won the Tony Award!* We discussed the mortifying Autumn throwing-up episode. As I stated before, the show tried to make it look like Autumn couldn't take the judges' criticism and that's what made her sick, but in reality, it was yogurt that had been left out all day, put in the fridge and then put out again. I told her that I couldn't believe they followed her into the bathroom and filmed her throwing up in the stall, but she said that the shot of her legs in the stall was actually fake! They missed filming her throw up so they had a producer crouch over a toilet in a stall and hoped the audience would think it was Autumn's gams. Tricky! Lauren said that she was actually relieved when they ixnayed her from the competition because the whole thing was such a difficult experience. So, when they did her farewell interview, she was totally at peace throughout it. Of course, that looked too boring for TV, so they began to ask her questions about missing her family, etc. (she's 18), and when she finally started crying, they re-asked her the same questions they had asked before — she gave the same answers, but this time she had tears in her eyes. Why couldn't they have tried that tactic on me before my Coen Brothers movie audition?!?! Celina "regaled" us with a horrifying story that happened to her during *Cats*. She was still a teenager on tour with the show and was promoted from swing to the role of Demeter. To celebrate, she got fake nails put on. The kind that are actually glued to your nails. While she was onstage, she had to grab the hands of another dancer but he twisted a different way than usual and she wound up pulling off two of her fake nails… *and* the real ones underneath! BUT she kept going with the show! As soon as she finished the number, she ran offstage and fainted. What is it with dancers being able to endure crazy pain!? Hmm... although the audience for *Cats* has to endure that endless opera scene on the boat... so I guess both performers *and* audience members can push their pain threshold to the limit during that show.

On Sirius, I interviewed Peter Gallagher, who is one of the nicest guys I've ever worked with (he was Nicky Arnstein in my Actors Fund version of *Funny Girl*) *and* one of the cutest! He grew up in Yonkers and his first high school musical was *The Pajama Game* with the leading lady played by his classmate... Laura Branigan! He was so intimidated by her that he couldn't get any sound out during his one little solo. The theatre teacher made someone else sing it with him because he sounded so timid. His solo became a unison duet. Then, while still in high school, he saw his first Broadway show, which was *Hello, Dolly!* starring Pearl Bailey, and in the chorus was... Morgan Freeman! Ironically, Morgan recently starred with him in *The Country Girl*! As they say, "what goes around comes around." Actually, that saying makes no sense in this case. How about a new one: "What was in the audience is then onstage... with ensemble members graduating to leads." It's sorta catchy, isn't it? *Silence.*

Peter majored in economics, but finally, after doing summer stock and loving it *and* realizing that economics is as interesting as that opera scene in *Cats*, he decided to pursue theatre and gave himself six years to make it. He remembers going to the open call for *Grease* in 1977 and his number being in the 2000s. They asked for something from the '50s, and he sang "Put Your Head on My Shoulder." The late, sweet Vinnie Liff was the casting director, and after Peter sang, he looked up and said, "That was beautiful." Peter said that his knees buckled, his eyes filled with tears and he thought, "Thank you God. That's all I need to keep going for the next six years." He wound up not having to test his resolve, because he then tried out for the *Hair* revival and got called back six times along with a bunch of newcomers: Ellen Foley, Charlayne Woodard and Annie Golden! He finally got the offer to be the understudy for Claude *and* to be a singer/dancer in the ensemble. After a few days of rehearsal, he was still the understudy for Claude, but the slash between singer/dancer was removed and he was just a singer. Peter told me that he comes from a long line of coal miners (seriously!), not dancers.

He also sang the solo in "Electric Blues"... in a sequined unitard. I was horrified at that image, but was immediately interested again when he informed me that he took it all off for the nude scene. Werk! While *Hair* was in previews, he got offered the role of Danny Zuko in the bus and truck of *Grease*. He told Vinnie Liff that he already had a job on Broadway and Vinnie asked him if he had ever seen the nation. Peter thought about how fun that would be and about how he had never played a lead. He finally approached the director, Tom O'Horgan, and asked if he could leave *Hair* to play Danny Zuko. Tom looked at him and said, "You want to go on the road? In a bus and truck? And leave a Broadway show? Before it's even opened?" Peter responded with a resounding, "Yes!" He told me that none of it would have happened if he had an agent at the time. The agent would have told him not to take *Grease*, or the agent would have asked the *Hair* people and been told no way. But because Peter asked himself, Tom listened and said he'd speak to the "guys" (Galt MacDermott, Michael Butler and Jim Rado), who all said it was fine. Tom then offered him a chance to go on for Claude, and Peter said *no way*. They had never rehearsed the understudies, and he thought he would die of a heart attack if he had to go on. He wound up doing *Grease* on the road and then did the show on Broadway.

Peter then got cast as the young lover in *A Doll's Life* (the musical version of *A Doll's House*), where, at one point, he had to play a little phrase on the violin in a scene. He practiced and practiced and, when he finally tried it out during rehearsal, he realized practice didn't make perfect. Right after Peter played, the conductor, Paul Gemignani, snatched the bow out of his hand and left the room. He returned and gave the bow back to Peter who tried the phrase again and this time produced the soothing sound of silence. Paul had put soap on the bow, so Peter could mime playing and not ruin the show. Ironically, the show wound up being one of the biggest flops on Broadway, so Peter *could* have played his screechy solo and it probably wouldn't have made the run any shorter (one weekend).

All right everyone, I'm signing off. I'm gearing up for my big Obama benefit that's coming up. *It worked!* Hopefully, I'll return next week, writing to you from my new apartment with my new slender fingers madly typing on my iPhone. If not, I'll see you *omtahe*!

Seth and the City
August 11, 2008

Last week I got an email from Lin-Manuel Miranda asking me if I'd partake in an internet film he's doing based on *Legally Blonde The Musical: The Search for Elle Woods* called *Legally Brown: The Search for the Next Piragua Guy*. I showed up at 37 Arts (where we filmed the TV show and where *In the Heights* played Off-Broadway) and filmed a "rehearsal" with each of the "contestants": Telly Leung from the upcoming *Godspell*, Derrick Baskin from *The Little Mermaid*, Noah Weisberg from *South Pacific* and Hunter Bell from *[title of show]*. It was *so much fun*, and the character I created was so horrible. My improv with Derrick was especially mean:

ME: Are you in a show now?
DERRICK: Yeah! I'm in *Little Mermaid*.
SETH: *Little Mermaid*? You are? Who do you play?
DERRICK: I'm one of the eels.
SETH: Really? Because I saw it… and… I don't really remember you…
DERRICK: I'm always next to Ursula. I'm one of the two eels.
SETH: I don't think so…
DERRICK: Maybe I was out the night you saw it.
SETH: I guess so…
DERRICK: When did you see it?
SETH: Opening night.
DERRICK: Oh… well I was definitely on that night.
SETH: You're *in* it? (pause) Huh…

Lin was planning on doing one episode for *YouTube*, but I think he got so much great material from everyone that's it's gonna be multi-episodes!

Still speaking of *In the Heights*, I interviewed Chris Jackson (who plays Benny in the show) at my *Chatterbox*. He's such a sweet guy and so fantastic in the show. He's from the Midwest and came here when he was 18 to go to AMDA (American Musical and Dramatic Academy). He had no real training, so it was super-helpful for him. He recalled going to Capezio's in the West 50s to buy dance shoes and not being able to figure out what subway to take back uptown… so he walked 30 blocks instead. I asked him why he didn't simply ask someone for directions, and he said that everyone in Times Square was a tourist, just like him. He thought he sassed me until I realized a) he was in the West 50s, which isn't Times Square and b) why couldn't he ask someone else in the ensuing 30 blocks? I still have not received a response.

He graduated AMDA and got a job as a waiter. The actor who was originally cast as Simba in *The Lion King* got a TV show, so they gave the role to his understudy, the late Jason Raize. Chris got an audition to be the understudy and showed up at 11 AM to sing for Julie Taymor and the creative team. At 11:20 AM he got the part and at 1 PM he began rehearsals! It was literally the first day of rehearsal! I asked if he got the tasty bagels, etc. that they serve on the first day, and he knew exactly what I meant and told me he's still annoyed all of that happened in the morning. Instead of a carb-laden bagel slathered in cream cheese, he arrived just in time to start learning "Endless Night." He eventually took over the role of Simba and stayed with the show for five years. He finally quit after getting surgery on his knee for the *third* time. Did you know that the stage at *The Lion King* for the first few years was made of *steel*. That feels great on your body... if you're a robot.

James and I went out with Andrea Burns from *In the Heights* for a dinner between shows on Saturday. We were sitting outside on Ninth Avenue and 46th Street at Yum Yum Thai restaurant. Suddenly we saw Gavin Creel on the corner. Then, walking down the block from the other direction we spotted Norm Lewis! They both came over to our table to chitty chat, and I felt like we should elect an Equity deputy. I complimented Norm on looking so buff. He blew off my comment and said he wanted a "chubby." I was uncomfortable *slash* intrigued, but before my mind could land in the gutter, he asked us if we liked chocolate. The next thing we knew, he had run over to delicious Amy's Bread and gotten us two Chubbys which, it turns out, are chocolate brownie cookies. Yes! It put the "Yum" in Yum Yum.

At Broadway Artists Alliance, I interviewed Tony Award-winner Norbert Leo Butz whose voice I am totally obsessed with. He said that he was embarrassed to do musicals in his high school, but he found a way to have leads all over town. He grew up in St. Louis and there were tons of all-girl Catholic high schools that were desperate for boys to be in their shows. Norbert said that he'd find out about the upcoming musicals through some crazy underground network and would shuttle from school-to-school playing Harold Hill, Sky Masterson, etc... He studied classical theatre in undergraduate and graduate school and spent most of his twenties working in regional theaters and being based in Alabama. He finally moved to New York, and one of the publicists of *Rent* heard him sing at a benefit and got him an audition. The show had just opened and Norbert tried out to be the understudy for the two male leads. After five auditions, he got it. He began rehearsals and *two days later* had to go on for Adam Pascal! I couldn't believe how little time he had, but he said that, throughout the audition process, he was learning the music, so he felt like he knew it very well. Well, turns out, there already *was* an understudy for Adam who didn't know Norbert was going on. So, of course, that guy wasn't happy. Norbert said that he began Act One and right after he sang the first big Roger song ("One Song Glory"), one of the producers went backstage and fired the other understudy! Norbert said that he left the stage and as he was walking up to his dressing room, the other understudy was walking downstairs with his stuff. Ouch! Norbert found out that the other understudy didn't come from the world of theatre and was not prepared for what it took to understudy five parts. He also said that many times, he'd do a matinee as Roger and then play Mark at the night show or vice versa.

After Norbert, I interviewed the fabulously talented Marc Shaiman. The first Broadway show Marc saw was *Fiddler on the Roof* and he remembers studying the souvenir program and being obsessed with the picture of the woman who played Tzeitel. He loved how her smile made her eyes get super-small. Then, when he was in junior high school, his chorus teacher gave him two albums to thank him for accompanying. They were Bette Midler's first two albums, and he became *obsessed*. He then realized that the woman in the Tzeitel picture and the woman on his album was the same person! He loved her so much, he used to go to the Village and wander down the street where Bette lived, hoping he'd see her. He told me he really didn't know what he was hoping he'd see — he said maybe Bette watering her flowers in the front yard? P.S. Does anyone even have a *front* yard in New York? He saw Bette's concert on Broadway and fantasized that he'd run down the aisle saying, "Oh, Miss Midler! I know how to play every song from every album you've ever recorded!" Then he'd sit onstage and play and she'd say to the audience, "This kid is good!" Well, one day when he was 16 years old (!), he wandered into Marie's Crisis in the middle of the afternoon with some friends and began playing piano. Old movie-style, the person sweeping up behind the bar said, "You're good, kid!" He told Marc that a comedy group, The High-Heeled Women, was looking for a pianist, and Marc got the gig. He stayed with one of the women in the group, and she happened to live across the hall from one of Bette's back-up singers! Marc found out that the three singers (The Harlettes) were putting together an act of their own. He auditioned to be their pianist and got it! They got great reviews, and Bette said they could open for her in Los Angeles! Suddenly, Marc was in an L.A. rehearsal studio, and there onstage was Bette Midler! He was freaking out! Bette suddenly asked the band if they could play "No Jestering" from her third album. They were just a bunch of pick-up musicians and not her actual band, so they didn't know it at all. Suddenly Marc saw The Harlettes talking to Bette and pointing at him. Bette asked him if he knew it and Marc literally got to run up to the stage saying, "Oh, Miss Midler! I know how to play every song from every album you've ever recorded!" Exactly what he dreamed! He played it and she told him to stick around for the tour in case she needed him. Instead of paying for a hotel room for him, she had him stay in her guest room! He said he went from walking down her block hoping to get a glimpse of her as well as covering his room in posters of her to literally eating breakfast with her across the table from her not wearing a bra! I told those kids that this story goes to prove that they can be obsessed with someone today and wind up hanging out with them in a few years. Hopefully with a bra on.

Marc also said that Scott Rudin first asked him to write the score for *Hairspray* and he said yes. Then, ten years passed. Margo Lion acquired the rights and asked him to do it. He said he wanted Scott Wittman to write the lyrics with him, and she was nervous because they were romantic partners and what would happen if they had a fight? She asked him to write some songs on spec, and they wrote four songs… all of which stayed in the show: "Good Morning, Baltimore," "Welcome to the '60s," "I Know Where I've Been" and "Big, Blonde, and Beautiful." He did the interview from the piano and every time he started playing one of those songs, the kids all immediately started singing and knew every lyric. At the end of the interview, he was asked by one of the kids what the most rewarding moment was in his career. Someone made a joke and said that it was today. But then Marc said it *was* amazing. He asked, "Can you imagine how thrilling it is for me to go to the piano and start playing a song I wrote… and suddenly have you all singing at me? That's as rewarding as I can ever imagine." Brava!!

All right, people. This week, my sister Nancy is coming in! She's hilarious. We're going to see *[title of show]* (I think it's my seventh time!), and I'm taking my nieces to see *Legally Blonde*. And then Wednesday and Thursday night, I'm playing for Andrea McArdle's act at the Metropolitan Room and then driving up to P-town to play for Varla Jean Merman. Peace out and put a bra on!

Working Vacation in P-Town
August 18, 2008

Greetings from Provincetown! James and I are sitting on the porch of our bed and breakfast looking out over the beautiful garden and hearing the nearby fountain splash… with our computers in our laps. That's right, this is a "working vacation." I got invited up here to play for Varla Jean Merman's annual concert called *Classical Varla*, which benefits AIDS Support Group Cape Cod. This is her fourth concert and it always raises a *ton* of money. Last night, I saw the show Varla is doing in P-town all summer and it was, as usual, hilarious. At one point, a stagehand "accidentally" left a box onstage that was filled with all of Varla's clippings, so she was "forced" to read them. She showed everyone the *New York Times* review of her Off-Broadway foray *Enough About Me* and pridefully said that they called the show "insane." She then looked closer and noticed that the *Times* "made a mistake" and left the "s" out of the word.

Anyone that does a show in Provincetown has to have a hawker who strolls up and down the street handing out flyers. One day, when I was visiting here a few years ago, Varla's hawker wasn't available so I said that I'd help out. I started walking up Commercial Street and, as Varla smiled and waved and walked in front of me, I handed flyers to anyone who passed by. Varla had many fans fawning all over her, but at one point, two guys ignored Varla and instead came up to me to say how much they loved my show on Sirius radio. As soon as they left, Varla whirled around and told me, "You're fired!"

P.S. This Wednesday, the *Project Runway* models are all guys in drag and Varla is one of them! How amazing is that?! *Her outfit wound up winning!*

Last week, I played for Andrea McArdle's show at The Metropolitan Room. Andrea belts up a storm in the show, but the "patter" is mostly her answering questions I ask. She played a young Judy Garland in the TV movie *Rainbow* and found out that it was seen by… Liberace! He liked her so much, he hired her to be his opening act and wound up designing all of her costumes. She had never seen a bugle bead, but she was suddenly covered in them. One night, she was at a party in his house. A whole group of people were in his room and Andrea wondered out loud why he had high-heeled shoes in his closet. And why were they such a large size? Remind me never to invite a 15-year-old over to my place without first locking my closet/drawers.

Monday night, I performed at an Obama Fundraiser put together by Ryan Mekenian and, when I showed up, I read the program and saw that I hardly recognized any names on the list of performers. I was thrilled to see Teri Ralston, who was the original Jenny in *Company*, listed. Of course, I've been obsessed with that cast album ever since I played Harry in tenth grade, so I was psyched to see her perform. She sang David Friedman's beautiful song "Help is on the Way," and every time she sang that refrain, she pointed to the big Obama face on her T-shirt. Regarding the rest of the performers, I sat in my seat thinking that I'd try to be supportive no matter how clanky they were. Turns out, the talent on that stage was *incredible*! I was completely intimidated starting right at the beginning when Carrie Manolakos sang "America the Beautiful." She sang phenomenally, and after the show, I approached her and decided to give this newcomer a tip on how to get her Equity card. Turns out, she's starring as Sophie in *Mamma Mia!*. Huh. Perhaps she has a tip for me. *A few years later, I cast her as one of the leads in DISASTER! What a voice!* Then, a young woman named Lindsay Mendez sang a new song Andrew Lippa wrote, and yet again, I thought, "I must give this newcomer some pointers." After Googling her, I realized she plays Jan on Broadway in *Grease*! And I've been obsessed this whole last year with how she sounds on "Mooning." What is my problem? The other person I was obsessed with was a woman named Shaina Taub who arranged the cool and creative back-up harmonies for "America the Beautiful" and then sang a great song about Halloween being scary, but election night being even scarier. She had the coolest, soulful, smoky sound, and I assumed she was a chanteuse who's been playing in all the coolest clubs in town for years. Turns out, she's 19! Why do I assume that established Broadway performers are fresh off the bus and actual newcomers are aging jazz-tresses? That reminds me… I must write and give some professional encouragement to a certain C. Rivera whom I think has potential.

My sister Nancy came to visit this week from Virginia, so we hightailed it to my long-time fave, *[title of show]*. The craziest thing happened that night. Around two-thirds of the way through the show, Hunter and Jeff exit the stage through a door, and Susan and Heidi remain onstage and sing about being the secondary characters. Well, I saw Jeff start to leave and the next thing I knew, he was flat on the floor and all that we could see onstage were his feet sticking out of the doorway. Everyone awkwardly stood there, and Jeff *did not move*! Nancy leaned over to me and asked if that was supposed to happen and I knew if I said it was an accident, her co-dependence would kick in and she'd hail an ambulance, so I muttered a combination of yes and no and kept staring at the stage. Finally, Hunter said with an odd line reading, "We'll be back," and it looked like Jeff was *dragged offstage*! What the-? I was freaking out! What was with the immobilization? Heidi and Susan sang their song and I later found out that whole time they were terrified he was a) really injured b) terribly injured or c) dead. How can you go on with a comedy scene when you're wondering if your co-star is dead?

Anyhoo, Susan and Heidi got through their scene with plenty of laughs, and normally, at the end of it, Heidi riffs up a storm until Jeff surprises her and she stops suddenly. Well, I saw someone enter in Jeff's clothes and I was sure it was the understudy. But then the lights came up fully and I saw it *was* Jeff! I was so thrilled he was able to walk (and that he was alive) and, apparently, so was Heidi, because right after she was "surprised" by him, she threw her arms around him in joy. I know she was happy, but I *have* seen the show seven times and know that it wasn't the regular blocking. As a concerned theatrical professional, I took the liberty of writing her up to Equity. I'm still awaiting a response.

After the show, Nancy and I saw Jeff, and he said he twisted his ankle super-bad. It was so bizarre to me because, when he came back onstage, he looked totally fine and was able to do all the dancing, but after the show, I saw how swollen his ankle was. He got through the show on pure adrenaline and, as my director, Peter Flynn, calls it, "Dr. Theater." That's why Andréa Burns was able to break her foot onstage yet do all the high kicks at the end of "Be Our Guest" and Kevin Chamberlin was able to do *Suessical* while *passing a kidney stone*! Seriously! Next, I wanna see Heidi from *[title of show]* sing "A Way Back to Then" while giving birth. *Sans* epidural.

I interviewed Bailey Hanks (the current Elle Woods in *Legally Blonde*) and Autumn Hurlbert (her understudy) at my Sirius radio show. I got more details on the horrors of doing a reality show. They literally confiscate your cell phones when you get there so you have no contact with the outside world. And then, after they filmed around six episodes, the girls were allowed one ten-minute phone call. Autumn called her boyfriend, but because he was performing in *South Pacific* at the time, he didn't get the call. Of course, that was great for the TV show because it made Autumn more emotionally fragile. Seriously, they would play into everybody's insecurities, so the girls would have breakdowns like, "The judges today said your dancing wasn't good. We watched the audition and your dancing really isn't good." Then they'd have her talk to the camera, hoping for "Leave Britney Alone" tears.

I asked Autumn about her first big job and it was touring the country in *Little Women*. She told me how much she loved Maureen McGovern, who played Marmee. Every Saturday, no matter what town they were in, Maureen would buy donuts for the whole cast, and every Sunday, she'd bring in a full bagel spread. They all called her "Maureen McGenerous." Generous? Generous is what my hips would be called if *I* was on that tour with Maureen McCarbLoading.

I complimented Bailey on her last note in "So Much Better" and asked her if she was happy that she got applause for it after only holding it for four counts. She said she loved the applause, but a part of her wanted the audience to hear that she actually could hold it to the end of the phrase (29 counts). She's studying with Joan Lader (Betty Buckley *and* Patti LuPone's voice teacher), and Bailey said that Joan taught her it's all about being grounded. Bailey said it's not about her vocal placement as much as it is feeling strongly planted in the ground. Hmm… maybe that's why my oak tree has such a high belt. Horticulture comedy? Anybody? Nobody.

All right, everyone. This week I'm playing the Varla benefit and then heading home to NYC just in time to turn around and do my deconstructing show in Pennsylvania! I'll be at the Fulton Theatre in Lancaster. Will they get my Barbra/Bea Arthur bit in Amish country? Will they like my show and build me a barn? Or will I be a "witness" to a slew of blank faces with beards? I'll find out at the end of this week and update you all on Monday. Peace out!

A Bloody Good Week
August 25, 2008

It's the last week of summer! That's perfect because I'm at my winter weight. I've always been ahead of the curve.

I just got back from Massachusetts and then Pennsylvania. The end of my Provincetown foray was great. The only mar was the complete lack of interest in me and my career. I was at the local gym there (Mussel Beach) and I heard them playing Sirius radio. I was so excited! Between my hosting on the Broadway *and* the dance re-mix channel (seriously!), I'm essentially on all day long. I asked the guy behind the desk if it was Sirius playing; he said "yes," and then I dropped the bombshell that would make him *freak out*. I stepped back and told him, "I'm a deejay on Sirius!" My words hung in the air as I detected a slight movement of his head. He was obviously a film actor because the nod of interest he gave me could only be read if the camera was in an *extreme* close-up. I slunk away back to the inner thigh machine. The next day, I was back at Mussel Beach and they were actually playing The Beat, which is the dance re-mix station I deejay every night! I ran up to the new guy behind the desk and asked, breathlessly...

ME: "Do you ever listen to this station at night?"
HIM: "No."
ME: (*awkward pause, then*) Oh... do they ever play it here?
HIM: (*non sequitur*) The gym closes at 9.
ME: (*silence... then*) Oh... because I'm a dee-... *fade out*

Finally, I walked into a store selling lobster rolls, and they were blasting Sirius. I decided to try my luck again... and by "try" I mean "push."

ME: Hi! Do you ever listen to the Broadway sta-
HIM: No.
Silence

The axiom I learned is: Never combine one's need for attention with a town's utter disregard for feigned interest.

Last week at the *Chatterbox*, I interviewed the Tony-nominated Loretta Ables Sayre. She has that great spirit that people from Hawaii all seem to have. But, turns out, she is originally from California and she didn't move to Hawaii 'til she was ten. If you've seen the show, you know that she has a fantastic voice. Before moving to NYC, she made her living in Hawaii as a "chick singer"... singing big band classics in beautiful resorts. I asked her if she fantasized about having a Broadway career and she said that Broadway seemed completely unattainable. Just distance-wise, it was massive. Even California is far away from Hawaii, so New York seemed impossible. However, while living there, she became friends with a transplanted Broadway actor named Randl Ask. I know Randl because I played piano for his comedy act with Amy Stiller (Jerry and Anne Meara's daughter) way back in the early '90s. He then went on to star in *Pageant* as Miss Bible Belt and was *brilliant*. After that, he was Matthew Broderick's understudy in *How To Succeed...* but then left New York for Hawaii.

Anyhoo, while he was visiting New York, he was having lunch with Ted Sperling, the music director for *South Pacific*, who told him that they were having trouble finding a Bloody Mary. Randl suggested that they actually travel to the South Pacific to find a native. Joe Langworth, a casting director from Bernie Telsey's office, was heading for a vacation in Hawaii, and they asked him if he'd use one of his vacation days to hold auditions. He said yes and notices were sent to all the theatres in Hawaii that there would be auditions for Bloody Mary. P.S. There are no professional theatres in Hawaii... they're all community theatres.

At that time, Loretta was doing very well with her band singing and her TV work. Lots of TV shows would film on the island, and she got some great gigs... including *Baywatch*! Plus, she did tons of voiceovers (she was the voice of PBS out there). However, even though she was planning on trying out for Bloody Mary, on the day of the *South Pacific* audition, she decided she wouldn't go. She knew there were some terrific singers who would show up, and she couldn't think why she'd get the job instead of them. Plus, she was nervous because she had no real training and the only big auditions she'd ever seen were on reality shows on TV. Essentially, she was scared of being humiliated. P.S. That's what makes me crazy about *American Idol* and other reality shows: they make it seem like that's the way auditions are in the real world and they're *not*. Only on reality shows do the people behind the table try to destroy the performers coming in to audition — well, reality shows *and* my high school theatre department. But that's a story better told in my one-man-show, *Rhapsody In Seth*. (Suffice it to say, I'm still in a rage over getting an F in theatre class... *in theatre class*!)

Back to Bloody Mary. Half an hour before the audition, Loretta told her husband that she wasn't going. Her husband said that whatever bad feeling she'd get about auditioning, it wouldn't be as bad as wondering for the rest of her life what would have happened if she went. She then told him that it wasn't even an option because they sent her a packet of music and scenes to prepare and she didn't work on them. He told her that he'd drive her to the audition so she could learn them on the way. She said that he drove and she belted out the songs in the car/looked at the scenes, but when she got there, she was terrified. She finally calmed herself by telling herself that she could only be who she was. She didn't have a vast amount of acting or vocal training and that was the reality. All she could be was herself. Joe, the casting director, was very nice and had her sing so he could film her for the creative staff to see. Right after she sang "Bali Ha'i," he asked her to do the ending in head voice instead of belting it. She was devastated and thought that she blew it, but he just wanted to show the creative team that she could do it. He explained that it would take several weeks for everyone to see the video, and then she'd hear whether or not she had a callback. *Two days later*, she got a call telling her that they would be flying her to New York for her callback! She had six weeks to prepare before she and her husband flew to JFK. As she was describing how momentous the trip was, she started crying and said, "What are the probabilities of a Filipino girl who grew up in Hawaii flying to New York to be seriously considered for a Broadway musical?"

Her audition was at Lincoln Center and, walking to it, she passed big posters with pictures of Yo Yo Ma and Beverly Sills, and she was so overwhelmed with feelings that people who worked in a place like this would take the time to see her. It didn't matter to her if she got the job, she was just so moved by the fact that they thought she could possibly do it. She was told that she'd have one audition for the creative team and then she would have one more for all the Lincoln Center higher-ups and the representatives from the Rodgers and Hammerstein Organization. She was incredibly nervous/panicking as she sang and read for the director,

Bartlett Sher. She said she couldn't breathe and had total dry mouth (see me running into Cheyenne Jackson). Her phrasing was a mess because she couldn't breathe. She was positive that she had blown it with the director. She spent that night sobbing through dinner but finally calmed herself down by doing what she did before the first audition. She told herself that they didn't ask if she had Juilliard acting training and they didn't ask whether she had 20 years of vocal lessons. All she could do was be herself. The next day, she had a work session with the director, where he took her in every direction dramatically and she loved it. He asked her to try the character in many different ways: angry, desperate, vulnerable. She now realizes that he was trying to see how directable she was, but at that point, she just loved it because it was like a master class.

She showed up on Monday for her final audition and sat outside the rehearsal room, terrified, holding a shrunken head (!) that someone made for her before she left. The whole cast of the last play she had done had gathered in her dressing room before she left and gave it kisses, blessed it and sent it love. Right before 4 PM, she began thinking of her father. She told us that he was a field laborer with a sixth grade education. He learned how to write by lining up grains of rice on a plate. His dream was for his children to have a better life but, unfortunately, he never heard her sing professionally. She then prayed to have all of the angels who brought her to this point in her life present with her. Suddenly at 3:55, she felt them all and said it was like the Verizon commercial where someone says, "This is my network," and they're surrounded by like 40 people. She walked in and saw that she had to audition for around 15 people. She performed all of the material and, after she was done, they asked her to wait outside. She came back and the director said, "We talked amongst each other, and we all wanted to be here to tell you this." Then he paused. She hoped he would say that she got the understudy because then it would mean that she would get to perform at Lincoln Center. He then said, "Loretta, you got the part. Will you be our Bloody Mary?" She stood there and waited for him to say understudy. Finally, he said, a little more sassily, "Darling. You got the part! What do you think?" She burst into tears and said what people in Hawaii say when they're happy, "I want to take you all home and cook for you!" He then introduced her to Mary Rodgers (daughter of Richard) and Alice Hammerstein (daughter of Oscar). As she was describing this at the *Chatterbox*, she started crying again and said that those were names she had seen on TV and on records. And to think that people connected to those two musical theatre icons thought she was qualified to perform their work overwhelmed her.

Right after the audition, she went up to see her husband, who was waiting at the fountain at Lincoln Center. She told him that she got the part, and he said that he wasn't surprised because as he was sitting at the fountain he suddenly felt angels around him... He made sure to look at his watch when that feeling happened and it was 3:55! How amazing is that?!

My final trip last week was to Lancaster, PA to do my comedy show, *Deconstructing: The Good, The Bad and the Headache-y*, at the Fulton Theater. It went over *amazingly*! I've never done the show outside of New York (let alone in Amish Country), and I'm so glad to know that it works. I've now decided to tour all religious enclaves. Next stop: Salt Lake City. *So fun reading that! It's so cool to see when I did my very first out-of-town DECONSTRUCTING show. I was so nervous it wouldn't work for a non-New York audience, but because it went so well, I felt confident being booked all over the place. I've since done it across the US, in Canada and in London!*

Weekend in the Country
September 3, 2008

Happy post–Labor Day! Labor Day has always been bittersweet for me. Sweet because it's a holiday, bitter because the next day meant I had to re-enter Hell and see those horrible people (AKA school and my peers). But now, thankfully, the only "school" I have to go to is *Grease*'s Rydell High or *Wicked*'s Shiz University, and the only horrible "People" is any version *not* sung by Barbra Streisand! Ha ha ha!!! That's right, my point is not that I work on Broadway, but that I'm a hack comic. Anybody? *Nobody*.

Last Wednesday, I finally saw *Hair* at the Delacorte! I've mentioned this before, but, if you don't know, *Hair* was the first Broadway show my parents took me to. No, I'm not in my sixties, people. It was during the final year of its run and I was barely out of diapers. But the cast sure was! To this day I remember that nude scene. And by "nude scene" I mean noticing people onstage naked for two seconds and then seeing the inside of my mother's palm that she placed over my eyes. She did the same thing during some choice scenes in *Taxi Driver*, which we went to see when I was in *second grade*! I know some of you may think, *Oh she probably thought it was a kids' movie because it had Jodie Foster from* Bugsy Malone. Perhaps, but why that same year did we see *One Flew Over the Cuckoo's Nest* and *Death Wish*? Silence. Followed by the sound of a phone dialing The Children Services Hotline.

Nonetheless, I grew up obsessed with *Hair* and I'm very thankful I got to see it as my first show. I wanted to give a link to the Tony Award performance from *Hair*, and I went to *YouTube* and put in the search word *Hair* and Tony Awards, and it led me to a clip of Laura Bell Bundy getting her hair done for the Tonys. I guess that's comparable...

Hair is one of those shows where it's fun to be a lead *and* it's fun to be in the ensemble. There are so many group numbers so, no matter who you are, you're always singing something fabulous. FYI, I thought the ensemble sounded *terrific*! It's also one of those shows where every song is fantastic. Galt MacDermott has such a brilliant gift for songwriting. Most shows have around 15 songs, but *Hair* has more than 25, and they're all amazing! I especially love the weird ones like "Don't Put It Down," "Initials" and "Going Down." (To watch me deconstruct Gavin Creel singing "Going Down," get thee to *SethRudetsky.com*.) Even though I know *Hair* really well, I was still sobbing up a storm at the end. Bring that music back to Broadway where it belongs! *And they did.*

For the last few weeks, James, Juli and I were thinking about going away for Labor Day weekend. It looked like we were going to vacation with Andréa Burns and her husband, Peter Flynn, but he's the new artistic director of the Hangar Theater in Ithaca, NY and he had to work through the weekend. I was lamenting my fate to Susan Blackwell from *[title of show]*, and she immediately volunteered her new vacation house near the Delaware Water Gap! How sweet is that? James, Juli, Maggie (my Lab/Dalmatian/Whippet mutt) and I drove down on Friday and had an amazing time. Maggie had the time of her life sniffing everywhere and going in the creek. Susan's husband, Steve, hung out with us and, on the last night, made us "campfire stew." We put carrots, potatoes, onions and fish in tin foil and he cooked it over an open fire in the forest behind their house. Delish! However, Steve gave us a lift in his car at one point, and when I got in it, I thought, *Hmm... that must be that "new car" smell*. And by "new car" I meant, "dead rat rotting in a vent." I was slightly nauseated, but kept my airways closed and appreciated the lift.

Later on, we were making ice cream in the ice cream maker that Hunter (from *[title of show]*) bought them as a housewarming gift. We were all talking about how easy it is to make ice cream now... no more rock salt and churning for two hours. Just milk, flavor and sugar. Steve said that the last time Hunter came, he thought he brought everything, but forgot the milk. A week later, Steve and Susan realized that Hunter didn't "forget the milk"... he left it under the passenger seat in their car! The carton expanded and leaked, and *that's* what that amazing smell was! Steve said that they've yet to get rid of the aroma. Hunter Bell! You owe me the oxygen I was unable to take in for the 20 minutes I spent in that car trying not to breathe!

At the *Chatterbox*, I interviewed Tony Award winner Beth Leavel. The first shocker she laid on me is that she's from North Carolina! I asked her if there was a "Lynn" involved with her name, and she admitted her full name is Elizabeth Lynn Leavel, and when she'd hear all three names from her mother, it meant she was in severe trouble. She grew up so Southern that she actually took Cotillion Class! That's where you learn social dancing like the tango and the rumba and fill out your dance card. And you wear a dress made from the drapes. The second shocker is that she didn't grow up wanting to be an actress! Not until she did her senior class play (*Brigadoon*) did she get bitten by the acting bug. She also said that she loved it because she got to kiss the cutest boy in her class. I asked her how long it took for him to come out and she said it happened around six months later.

She got her college degree in counseling, but finally decided to pursue theater for real. However, she was too scared to move to New York, so she got a masters degree in directing. She finally moved to New York and was so hilarious about the horrific-ness of her first apartment: "Remember when 45th Street was awesome in the '80s? Between Ninth and Tenth?" Oh boy. Beth got the role of Bonnie in *Applause* at the Equity Library Theater. That was the theatre where you got paid in subway tokens (seriously!), but agents and casting people would come. It was a great showcase for actors starting out. Beth got her agent then... and is still with him 25 years later!

Her agent got her an audition for the national tour of *42nd Street*, but Beth had not taken tap since she was at Betty Kovac's School of Dance back in third and fourth grade. They loved her singing and comedy at the audition, but her dancing was not up to snuff. Karin Baker (who was in charge of the tour) told her that if she could nail the dance break to "Go Into Your Dance" at her next audition, she'd have the job. Unfortunately, her next audition was four days later! Yowtch! She rented a studio and practiced every day, coached by her husband. When she went back to re-audition, her husband waited for her at a bar where he knew the bartender. He felt that Beth's tapping was still really iffy, and the bartender felt bad that Beth was about to lose out on this job, so he kept plying her husband with drink. After the audition, Beth breathlessly arrived and was met by her husband who was slobbering, "Hey, Beth! Ah love you anyway! You'll get a job shoon..." She sobered him up and told him that she got the job... right after she danced! Beth sighed and told the *Chatterbox* audience that the business was easier then. They'd tell you that you got the gig on the spot instead of nowadays when you have to wait for a "urinalysis and a pap smear."

Beth did the tour of *42nd Street*, did it on Broadway *and* did it in Japan! You can see her do her treacherous "Go Into Your Dance" tap dance from her audition in a clip on *Bluegobo.com*. They filmed it when she was in Japan and she looks amazing. If you can't recognize her at first, she's the one with the solo dance that's not Peggy Sawyer.

She talked about auditioning for the lead in *Crazy For You*. After her sixth audition (!), she got a call from William Ivey Long (a North Carolina native and the costume designer) who told her that he was going to take her shopping for her next audition. He said that she needed to look completely elegant for the role and dragged her to Macy's, where she tried on a ton of outfits. She finally got a stunning blue dress. *Then* he had someone do her hair and makeup. She showed up at the audition looking stunning... and they promptly decided they didn't want the role to be played by someone elegant, they wanted "cute as a button." Jodi Benson got the gig, but they still wanted to give Beth a job so they offered her a small role... which expanded into a delicious one. She did the show until she got pregnant and then, two weeks after her C-section, she was rehearsing *Show Boat* in Toronto! Ow!

In 2000, she auditioned for the *42nd Street* revival. She went in for the roles of Maggie or Dorothy Brock, but the director said that she fell between the cracks, so he asked her to stand-by. Christine Ebersole, who played Dorothy, had a medical emergency the first week of previews and Beth had to go on with no rehearsals! There were no costumes for her, so someone ran out to Lord & Taylor and got her what she called "some mother of the bride" outfits, and she went on. She said it was terrifying, but she learned that if she could do that, she could do anything.

She recalled auditioning for *The Drowsy Chaperone*, and afterwards, she spoke to the director, Casey Nicholaw, who said that she wasn't really right for the role. They wanted something different... maybe someone older... who knows? But he said it wasn't her. A month later, her agent called with a job offer, and she thought it was for *The Wedding Singer* because she had just auditioned for that. When her agent said it was for *The Drowsy Chaperone*, she made him call back the general manager to make sure it wasn't a mistake! Well, the possible mistake wound up leading to a Tony Award!

Right now, she's starring as Frau Blucher in *Young Frankenstein* and *loving* it. By the way, the reason I know Beth is because she directed a production of *Grease* at the Candlewood Playhouse when I was 22 and worked as the assistant music director. On the last Friday of the show, the guy playing Danny called the theatre and said that he wasn't showing up! No one really ever found out the reason, but we think it was because he got a soap opera and began filming. Anyhoo, it was 3 PM and everyone was in a panic because he didn't have an understudy. Bob Bartley, who played Kenickie, said that he could go on for Danny because he had done the role before. Ron LaRosa (now a big casting agent) was playing Doody, and he said that he would play Kenickie. That left open the role of Doody. Well, I had been watching all the rehearsals and therefore knew all the lines, songs and dance steps. I told the producer I would do the role! She said yes, and I went on without a put-in rehearsal and had *the best* time. The "funny" part is that Eric Woodall was an acting intern that summer and the understudy for Doody. And yet, somehow, *I'm* the one who went on for that role. Eric now works as a casting director for Tara Rubin. I'm not saying I devastated him by acting like a combination of Eve Harrington, *The Bad Seed* and Drew Barrymore from the film *Poison Ivy*, but here are the amount of shows I've done that Tara Rubin has cast: zero.

Hello Marvin, Goodbye Love
September 8, 2008

Greetings from Philadelphia! I'm doing a benefit to support the Andalusia House, which is a beautiful, enormous house that was built in the 1700s. And, by the way, built by the same architect who built the White House!

I'm not saying I'm the first Jew that ever set foot inside here, but suffice it to say I'm not in my comfort zone. Speaking of comfort, I planted myself in the gorgeous living room and was immediately kindly told to take my shoes off the furniture. Busted! But then I thought to myself, my feet were on a settee. Isn't that was it's for? Of course, it probably *was* for that... when it was originally upholstered by Betsy Ross. The good news is, everyone is super-nice, and the place is gorgeous and literally overlooks the Delaware River. The bad news, there was just a tornado warning. Excellent.

I got to be on NY1's *On Stage* last weekend as part of a roundtable discussion on the upcoming theatre season. They had asked me last year to do it, but we were in the middle of tech for *The Ritz*. Since this year I'm not in any Broadway show, I'm completely free. Wow. That was devastating to write. Regardless, filming it was super fun, except they didn't have a make-up person, so by the end of the segment, my forehead could have been Tony-nominated for the revival of *Grease*.

Also, this week school started for Juli, so I'm back to my early morning wake-up schedule. It's a tad devastating, but nothing has been worse than when I worked on *The Rosie O'Donnell Show*. I had to be at work by 7:30. In the morning. I know some of you people who work are thinking, "That's nothing! I have to be at my desk by 7!" But when I first got the gig, I was still playing piano for *Grease!* So, I'd work during the day and then play the show at night. Every night I got about as much sleep as I get when I go watch an opera (Three hours. Four, if there's a long intermission). We had to have three jokes ready every morning by 8 AM to "pitch" to Rosie.

a) Is it fun to try to get a laugh from someone at 8 AM?
b) Did Rosie ever use any of our jokes?

ANSWERS
a) No
b) No

The most amazing thing about working on that show was doing "stings." There were six writers and not that much to write on the show, so we'd occupy ourselves by pulling pranks on each other, AKA stings. One day, everyone was throwing a small ball around the office and, by accident, one of the writers named Linda dropped it out the window. We were located in 30 Rock (down the hall from *SNL*) on the 16th floor. Well, Alan (one of the other writers) left the room and told the security guard his scheme. Twenty minutes later, the security guard comes in the room and asked if anyone dropped a ball out of the window. Of course, Linda avoided eye contact. He then went on to say that the ball picked up velocity as it fell, hit a pedestrian and caused a serious injury. He kept up his terrifying ruse for a while before admitting it was a joke. We all *loved* it, but I think it caused Linda early onset menopause.

This week, I interviewed the unbelievably talented Marvin Hamlisch at the *Chatterbox*. He was on a path to become a classical pianist (he was a child taking lessons at Juilliard) until he saw *The Pajama Game* on Broadway. After that, bye-bye classical, hello obsession with popular music. When he was a teenager, not only did he get his first hit on the pop charts ("Sunshine, Lollipops and Rainbows"), but he became good friends with Liza Minnelli! She invited him to a Christmas party at her mother's house. If any of Juli's classmates are reading, Liza's mother was Judy Garland. If you're older than seven and don't know that, why are you reading this book? He went and accompanied Liza on some songs he had written for her. Then Judy asked him to play for *her*! He literally got to play piano for Judy Garland when he was a teenager! When *I* was a teenager, I was singing baritone in my high school chorus' medley from *Fame*. Comparable? You decide.

A few years later, he got a job as a rehearsal pianist for *Funny Girl*. *Yes!* He played for Liza Minnelli, Judy Garland *and* Barbra Streisand! I guess the next part of his story should read, "He then went back in time and had coffee with Mozart." He recalled that Barbra would change the melodies of songs, but Jule Styne didn't mind because he thought that she made them better. For instance, Marvin said that Barbra probably came up with the high note in the last verse of "People" that goes, "But first be a person who needs people... PEEEOOO-ple who need people..." At one point, Barbra's melody change in "Sadie, Sadie" didn't work with the harmony that Marvin wrote for the ensemble. He went to her dressing room and told her that her new melody clashed with his vocal arrangement. She asked him, quite clearly, "Marvin. Are people coming to hear your harmony or to hear me sing?" He promptly changed the harmony.

Speaking of Barbra, turns out, she and Marvin are both very similar. They both want things to be *perfect*, and then once they're done, they're done. He said that he would be the worst pit piano player because he'd have a breakdown having to play the same thing every night. I actually enjoy doing the same things over and over again (see my stand-up act for the last ten years. Perhaps it's time to retire those Janet Reno jokes?). Here's a perfect example: he wrote the theme to *The Way We Were* and was watching a run of the film with a test audience and was mortified to see that there was no crying from the audience in the last scene. He, being Jewish, blamed himself. He knew if the music was right, the tears would flow. Marvin had underscored the moment when Barbra brushes away the hair on the forehead of Robert Redford with the secondary music theme of the movie, not the title song. Perhaps, he thought to himself, he was wrong? He discussed it with his orchestrator. Marvin said he limited playing the main theme throughout the film, because he didn't want the audience to hear the same theme 30 times in the same movie because it could seem tacky. The orchestrator explained that it may play 30 times, but the audience would hear it around three times. Only the composer is that honed into the music in the background throughout the whole film to really notice. Marvin decided to re-record that moment and bring in the main theme from *The Way We Were*. However, the movie studio said, "No way!" They weren't going to pay for more musicians to come in and do any more playing. So... Marvin paid for it himself! That's a lot of moolah... it was a 55-piece orchestra! He re-recorded it, had it put in the movie and went back to another screening. He watched Barbra touch Redford's forehead... he heard the music play... and one woman sniffled. Then another. Then a bunch. Finally, Marvin heard the crying he was looking for! P.S. If he wanted so badly to hear crying in the mid-'70s, he needed only to visit my house every afternoon when I returned home from school.

That same year, Marvin became an international celebrity because of the Oscars. He won Best Musical Adaptation for *The Sting*, Best Score for *The Way We Were* and Best Song for *The Way We Were*. That's right, he won *three* Oscars in one night! P.S. Speaking of *The Sting*, for those of us that grew up as pianists, that was Marvin actually playing "The Entertainer" that we all listened to on that recording and tried to emulate. I asked him if he cheated and recorded each hand separately to make it easier… and he said he *did*! Aha! But not on "The Entertainer" — only on one of the rags because, he said, it was a really hard stride left hand and busy right hand and there were other musicians playing with him. Marvin knew that if he made even one mistake, everyone would have to start the whole piece over from the top, and he wanted to save them all the annoyance of having to do that.

Right after he won the three Oscars, Michael Bennett contacted him. Marvin was an incredible fan of his. When he met Michael years earlier, he told him that he wasn't going to file Michael's phone number in his address book under B for Bennett but under G for Genius. Michael called and asked him to fly to New York because he had an idea for a show. Of course, Marvin's agents were completely irritated. He was the only composer that was being booked on national talk shows… he could have any high-paying gig he wanted. But instead, Marvin wanted to work in theatre. He went to Michael's apartment and saw that it was all black. Marvin realized it was because Michael had special lights on all of his awards, and the black really made them stand out and glimmer! He met with Michael and was incredibly excited to hear the idea. Michael sat him down and told him: (pause)… "It's about chorus kids." Marvin sat and waited for the beginning, middle and end. Silence. Marvin went home, and even though it was not the way he was used to working, he knew he had to say yes. Marvin thinks that one of the reasons Bennett hired him instead of one of the Broadway greats of the time is that Marvin was a Broadway newcomer and Michael knew that he could have more control that way. Tricky! And it worked!

When they first workshopped it, the show was five hours long! After they did a run-through, Michael asked Marvin his opinion and Marvin said he could only comment on the first two hours. Brava. Marvin said that he really didn't "get" the show for a long time as he was working on it… until Michael drew the line on the floor and said it was about people "on the line." Then it became clear to him. Marvin also said that if you're composing a show, you shouldn't work very hard on the opening number. The original opening number for *A Chorus Line* was called "Résumé." The only thing that remains in the opening we all know now is the melody of "I really need this job" and the cast holding their 8x10s in front of their faces. Marvin said that composer/lyricists should essentially just write a dummy version of an opening because it's going to change later on. He said that you have to write the bulk of the show and then you'll be able to really see what the show is about. That's when you write the opening. He said that "Tradition" from *Fiddler on the Roof* and "Comedy Tonight" from *Forum* were both written *after* the bulk of the show was done. He and Ed Kleban wrote all of *A Chorus Line* and then went back and wrote the opening.

In the late '70s, he was living in California with the lyricist Carole Bayer Sager. Their next-door neighbor was Neil Simon (how amazing is that?) and Marvin was working with him on turning *The Gingerbread Lady* into a musical. While they would work, Marvin would chitty-chat with him about the ups and downs of living with a woman who was also in the songwriting business. One day, Marvin opened his front door and saw a package. It was a script from Neil Simon that he wanted to turn into a musical. Neil had taken the conversations with Marvin about living with Carole and turned them into the characters Vernon and Sonia in *They're Playing Our Song*. Hopefully, Neil won't take my private conversations with him and turn them into *The Man Who Was Co-dependent with His Mother*. Marvin said that one day, Neil wrote a scene where Vernon and Sonia are dancing at a discotheque (old-school '70s word). Marvin complained that the scene wasn't realistic because a) he doesn't dance well and b) he'd feel annoyed dancing to someone else's music! However, Marvin said, if one of *his* songs started playing he'd be like (and then he ran to the piano): "Oh ho they're playing my song/ Oh, yeah, they're playing my song!" And that's how the song was written!

Marvin told us that he adores Broadway and that's why he lives in New York. And the reason he does what he does has two answers; one day, he was going to rehearse for a Pittsburgh Symphony date with Bernadette Peters. The limo driver asked him, if Marvin originally trained at Juilliard, why did he leave classical music for popular music? Marvin gave him what he thought was a very thorough and proper answer. He talked about the freedom popular music has in form and style and how it can reach so many people, etc... He arrived at the concert and met Bernadette Peters onstage. He said that she was in a pair of tight jeans, *and* she had just showered so her hair was still wet, or as he described the whole package, "Everything I've ever wanted... and more." As he gave her a hug, saw her stunning face and felt her wet hair, he told us that he realized, "*This* is why I'm in popular music." Or as I translate it, no one wants to hug a Wagnerian soprano in a valkyrie helmet.

I'm now back in New York and I must write about the final performance of *Rent*. The cast was *amazing*. Special shout-outs to my friend Michael McElroy, who played Collins and sounded *gorgeous* on the reprise of "I'll Cover You." And Will Chase, who went to my alma mater Oberlin (as a percussion major!), had *great* star quality... and vibratoed all the top notes! And brava Eden Espinosa and Tracie Thoms for the fact that it was the eighth show of the week, yet they both added *ca-razy* high notes to "Take Me Or Leave Me." And I'm obsessed with Renée Elise Goldsberry! I saw her in *Two Gentlemen of Verona* and thought she was fantastic. She not only sounded great as Mimi, but she's beautiful and *fun-nee*! Get that lady a brilliant comedic lead ASAP!

I ran into Lin-Manuel Miranda at the after party at Chelsea Piers, and I praised him on the hilarious trailer for his parody *Legally Brown*: *The Search for the Next Piragua Guy*. Hi-la-ri-ous. Watch it at *SethRudetsky.com*. I also hung out with David Saint (artistic director of The George Street Playhouse), who was great friends with Jonathan Larson. He said that he and Jonathan would drive around with Roger Bart (whom the character Roger was named after!) and Jonathan would sing songs from the show and teach them different vocal parts so he could hear how it sounded with three parts. It was very bittersweet for David and for so many others who knew Jonathan to see this performance. It was such a tribute to Jonathan's genius, but also marked the end of this show that was his legacy. *However*, for any of you that are dying to see this brilliant cast and performance, just remember it's going to be released as a film. *And, of course, it then wound up re-opening Off-Broadway!*

On a shallow note, I'm incredibly proud of the fact that James and I are both on diets and we didn't eat any dessert at the after party! I still got it! (And by "it," I mean love handles... therefore, no dessert.) *Will my dieting ever end? And will a difference ever be made? So far the answers are no and no.*

Four *Rent*ers and a Dreamgirl
September 15, 2008

Sunday marked the beginning of the fall theatre season with *Broadway on Broadway* or, as I called it after sitting in the direct sun for two hours, "Melanoma on Broadway." What a show!
The belting: fierce.
The UVBs: fiercer.

My favorite performances were by Cheyenne Jackson who, as usual, sounded *amazing* on his big song from *Xanadu*, and the cast of *[title of show]*, who re-orchestrated their songs for the event! Normally, *[title of show]* is accompanied by Larry Pressgrove, who sits on stage with a keyboard, but for this event they utilized the orchestra that was there, and it sounded *so exciting*!

This week at the *Chatterbox*, I had some members from the final cast of *Rent*. Renèe Elise Goldsberry, who played Mimi; Tracy McDowell, who played Mark's mom; Gwen Stewart, the *original* "Seasons of Love" soloist; and Eden Espinosa, who played Maureen. I told them how excited I was to see the upcoming film version of the final performance and I asked them how terrified they were knowing that every note they sang was being filmed. Turns out, there was more than one performance filmed! They filmed a full run-through at the end of August with the cameras in total close-up (no audience), and then they did a full performance with an invited-only audience where they stopped and started to get different camera angles. So, on that final night, there was no pressure to sing perfectly for the cameras... only for my glaring/judgmental face. Actually, Renèe said she did feel pressure because both Daphne Rubin-Vega (the original Broadway Mimi) and Rosario Dawson (the film Mimi) were in the audience. Wowza! All that was missing was Maria Callas (the opera Mimi).

Renèe talked about how she never gets depressed when she doesn't get a role. She's one of those "it's meant to be" people — whereas I'm one of those "I can't let go of my past resentments" people. Try to guess who's more fun to hang out with? She said that she was doing a role on "One Life to Live" and after she'd been on for a while, her character went blind. Tip o' the hat to Mary Ingalls from *Little House On The Prairie*? You decide. Anyhoo, Renèe said that the writers got sick of her doing dialogue while "looking off in the distance," so they brought on a doctor character to restore her vision. He happened to be played by director Michael Greif's partner, and he told Renèe that Michael was a big fan of hers and would love to work with her one day. She revealed to us that she's "musical theatre illiterate," so she had no idea that Michael was the *Rent* director. All she knew was that he was a big, respected director so she hauled out the ol' "It would be such an honor," etc. A short time later, she got a call offering her Mimi! However, she couldn't do it because of schedule conflicts, and here's where the "it's meant to be" part comes: by the time she could do it, it was for the final company, so she got to be in the film!

Tracy tried out for *Rent* a lot but never got it. She finally gave up on ever doing the show. One day, Tracy's friend was going to a *Rent* open call and asked her to come along. Tracy reluctantly agreed... and got cast! And her friend didn't. Please! See all my previous warnings about bringing people along to auditions. They will always get the part over you!

Rent was the first Broadway show Eden ever saw, and she tried out for Maureen over and over again when she first got to New York, but she never got it. Her only feedback was "Stop sounding like the CD." When she had yet another callback and heard it was going to be the same casting person from Bernie Telsey's office (who no longer works there), she stopped going. Years went by, and then a few months ago, out-of-the-blue, she got an offer to play the role. And when you see the film, you'll hear that she vocally makes the role her own! And, P.S., when you see the film, don't try to copy any of her riffs unless you want to put your trachea in traction.

I asked Gwen (who was in the original company) about her initial audition and she said that she was cast after the workshop had begun rehearsals because the woman playing that part got a cold and couldn't sing it. Of course, that woman just thought she was quitting a rickety-rackety downtown workshop. I'm sure that today she's totally at peace for leaving a Tony Award- and Pulitzer Prize-winning show — as long as she takes her double dose of Paxil. Gwen said that she was allowed to do anything in her "Seasons of Love" solo and came up with the high C herself. I asked her if she's regretted having to do it eight times a week, and the other cast members piped up to say that she's never missed the note. Brava!

I asked the ladies about any particularly memorable auditions, and Renée remembered her *Lion King* audition for Nala. It was scheduled for September 12, 2001, in Los Angeles. That morning she was at home, devastated (day after 9/11), and her agent called to confirm her audition! She was like, "Surely you're joking," *and* she had no idea how the casting people got to L.A. from New York. Well, she said, even though all their planes were grounded on the way to L.A., they found other ways of getting there and were determined to have the auditions. Renèe showed up and sang "Shadowland." After she sang, they asked her to step out of her shoes (to ground herself?) and to sing it again, but this time they wanted her to really dig deep emotionally. She reminded me and the audience that the lyrics are "Shadowland, the leaves have fallen. This shadowed land that was our home. The river's dry, the ground is broken..." She remembers that she walked over to the table and said, "Are you *kidding me*? You want me to dig deeper emotionally? *Today*? I can do that, but we will all wind up on the floor, sobbing!" There was a slight pause, and they asked her to step outside. I asked her if she had to go in and sing again and she said, "No. Five minutes later, that casting director stepped into the hallway and told me I was cast. I guess I shamed them into giving me the part!"

We talked a little about her appearance in *Broadway Under the Stars*, a live concert in Central Park that was televised. They asked her to sing and she was so excited that she said she'd do anything... and then they gave her Sondheim's "The Miller's Son." She was like, "What the-!?" She couldn't believe how many words there were and how fast it was. Right before the concert she decided there was no way she could memorize it. She had a full panic attack, and (she was mortified to admit) she decided to call the producers and say she had been in a *car accident*! Before she hauled out that ol' chestnut, they told her that there would be a teleprompter. Phew! Of course, once she was up there, she didn't need it; she just wanted the security.

At Sirius, I got to interview one of the best singers on Broadway, Tony Award-winner Lillias White. What a voice, and what a spirit! We had an amazing afternoon. When she arrived, she told me that she was vocally exhausted because she was up the night before doing her gig at The Triad and singing 'til 2 AM. She needed to rest her voice so she couldn't sing on my radio show. Cut to: by the end of the hour, she tore through "Home," "Keepin' Out of Mischief" and the fight scene from *Dreamgirls*!

Lillias toured the country as the understudy for Dorothy in *The Wiz* and eventually took over the role. Then she toured the country as an understudy in *Ain't Misbehavin'*, but this time it was different... she was pregnant! However, she didn't want anyone in the cast to know because she didn't want to be replaced. She went on for the Charlayne part one day when the director was in the audience, and after the show, he told her that she did a great job... but she needed to lose 15 pounds. She agreed with a vague smile... and the costume people kept letting her costumes out. Finally, the doctor told her she had to stop doing the crazy high kicks and squats that were in the show. She told the cast she was pregnant (they were like, "We *knew* something was up") and left the show.

Then, when her daughter was a year old, she was asked to take over the role of Joice Heth, the "oldest living woman" in *Barnum*. Lillias said that when Jim Dale went on vacation, Tony Orlando was the vacation fill-in for the role of Barnum. I was waiting for some heavy-duty dishing, but Lillias said that he was amazing. He was "so saucy, so sexy and so strong!" Who knew? Attention Weisslers: Surely there's an opening for a Billy Flynn somewhere that Orlando can fill! Lillias said that the show was on closing notice for ten weeks! Every Tuesday there'd be a closing notice backstage, and then it was taken down. Finally, they knew for sure it was going to be the last week. Lillias was doing the song "Join the Circus" like she always did, but this time, her heel got caught on the stage. She fell on her face onstage and literally heard the audience gasp. She got back up immediately and didn't feel any pain. However, when she went to raise her arms above her head, one of them wouldn't lift. Turns out, she fractured her elbow, and her understudy had to go on for the last week of the show. The crazy part is, her understudy was the white Mary Testa!

In 1997, I did a benefit for the Gay/Lesbian Synagogue (Beth Simchat Torah) at Don't Tell Mama. It was a salute to gay Jewish composers, and I featured David Friedman and Henry Krieger's music. Well, at the last minute, my Effie couldn't do it, so I called Lillias, whom I didn't know very well, to see if she'd fill in. She said she'd come over right after her tech rehearsal for *The Life*. Well, she showed up and sang the end of Act One fight scene into "And I Am Telling You," and I was so *freaked out* by how amazing she sounded that I told her I had to do a concert of *Dreamgirls* with her playing Effie accompanied by a full orchestra. I knew that Audra McDonald had always wanted to be Deena, so I got her on board and shopped the idea around. After some rejection, I went to The Actors Fund and they immediately said yes. They also suggested I get Heather Headley to play Lorrell so we could have three Tony winners in the leading roles. Cut to 2001, it happened on Broadway, we made a CD, *and* the concert raised almost $1,000,000 for The Actors Fund! Go to my website to see me deconstruct the Effies of Jennifer Holliday, Jennifer Hudson and Lillias and footage from the concert!

Finally, Lillias recounted one of my favorite stories about the business. She was in rehearsal for a musical called *Rock 'N Roll! The First 5,000 Years*. The female understudy in the show decided to quit during rehearsals because she wanted to go into pop music. Lillias was mind-boggled and said, "Why would you quit a Broadway show to go into the uncertain world of pop? Stay on Broadway, make money and then later on, you can pursue pop." But Lillias' words went unheeded. Cut to: the show ran for one week and the understudy's name was... Madonna!

Heidi, Carey, Howie, Cheyenne, Bebe, Brenda, Derek and Ashley
September 22, 2008

I was working it this week in Times Square. And I mean legit work, not Donna Summer "Bad Girls"-style work.

This week was the launch of the new weekly interviews I'm doing at the Time Square Information Center for Sirius Radio and, to promote it, I did a different one every day!

Monday was the cast of *[title of show]*. I asked Heidi Blickenstaff about her Broadway debut. She did the national tour of *The Full Monty* playing Susan Hershey/understudying Vicki Nichols (played by Andréa Burns). Unfortunately, 9/11 happened, and the whole tour was canceled after just a little bit of time on the road. But then Heidi got an offer to do the show on Broadway! She was psyched that she only had three weeks to wait. A few days later, she got a call from Nancy Harrington, the stage manager, and Heidi thought it was to set up her first rehearsal. Nancy said, "How would you like to save a Broadway show?" Huh? Turns out, Emily Skinner (who was playing Vicki) was out and so were some other female cast members. There were so few women in that show that they literally ran out of people to play roles. *And* the woman who understudied Vicki was the only one who could go on for another role, so there was nobody available who could play Vicki. Heidi had gone on for the part a few times on tour but never had an actual rehearsal. Did she remember it enough to play it on Broadway? Did she have enough time to review? It was 5 PM! Of course, Heidi said yes and called her friend Ryan Perry to come see the show so she'd have a witness. It was all such a whirlwind that she didn't meet Marcus Neville, who was playing her husband, 'til she was onstage... kissing him! Heidi was used to doing the tour in *big* theatres, so her performance was geared towards that. After the show, Nancy, the stage manager, thanked her profusely for saving the show and then said, "Sister, you gotta dial it *down*." Apparently, the Eugene O'Neill Theatre isn't a 3,000-seat sports arena.

The devastating news is *[title of show]* just announced their closing date for Oct. 12. Wah! But just as I heard that announcement, I checked my mail at Sirius radio and saw this in my inbox:

Dear Seth, After hearing you obsess over [title of show], I finally stuck it in my Amazon shopping cart when I ordered my last haul. OMG — that album is so hilarious. I always enjoyed what you played on Sirius of it — love, love the straightforward 4 part harmonies and the clever lyrics. But to hear 'Die Vampire Die' and 'Filling Out the Form' for the first time was a snort-laugh out loud experience. I think 'Die Vampire Die' is just as uplifting as the Rice Krispies treats sentiment in that other song, albeit with some hysterical lyrics. (Je suis whore!). Sorry to babble - but wanted to say thanks for obsessing over good stuff like this, it makes us all better listeners and more appreciative as an audience.-Tasha in Washington State

So, *[title of show]* may be ending its Broadway run, but it will always live on! But while it's still on Broadway, see it! Don't be like me who kept waiting to see Lily Tomlin's show, never did, and was then devastated for 20 years whenever people would talk about it ('til I finally saw the revival).

I was standing online at Starbucks around a year ago and made some sassy comment, which I usually do in public to random people around me. Half the time I get an "I don't know you, crazy person" look, and the other half I get a friendly nod. Well, this time I got a friendly nod from the lady in back of me. We started talking and soon I found out she was in *Mamma Mia!*. That was how I first met Carey Anderson. Now she's starring in *Avenue Q* as Kate Monster and Lucy T. Slut, and I interviewed her and her co-star Howie Michael Smith on Tuesday at noon. Carey grew up in the Midwest and did lots of sports, totally like my childhood, just without the Midwest and sports part. She got the *Mamma Mia!* tour as the understudy for Sophie (the daughter who's getting married). After she did the tour for a while, they asked her to come audition for the Broadway show... along with the girl she was understudying! The "fun" part was they both flew to New York together on the same plane... side-by-side. They auditioned at the same time and then flew back to the tour together.

PLANE FLIGHT CONVERSATION:
POSSIBLE SOPHIE 1: How'd it go?
POSSIBLE SOPHIE 2: Really well. What about you?
POSSIBLE SOPHIE 1: Really well, too.
POSSIBLE SOPHIE 2: That's great.
POSSIBLE SOPHIE 1: Good for you!
POSSIBLE SOPHIE 1 and 2: So... yeah...
Total silence for rest of plane ride.

Cut to: Carey's agent got the news that Carey got the gig... but decided *not* to tell her before the show that night. I guess she didn't want her to be in a good mood for that performance??? Finally, at midnight, her agent called and told her she got it. Carey was thrilled... and half-awake. The crazy part is, she had her wedding planned for a Saturday, and they wanted her to begin in the show that same week! So, she literally made her Broadway debut on a Wednesday and got married that Saturday! She said she's glad she has pictures because she remembers nothing.

Carey's devastating audition story was when she tried out for a non-Equity *Grease* tour and was told her eyes were too small. Then the auditioner took out Carey's 8x10, pointed to the eyes in the photo and circled them to prove the point. Knowing how expensive 8x10s are, they kindly handed her picture back on her way out of the audition... with the eyes circled in pen. I *guess* she could use that at another audition. "Hi! Um, before I sing, I just quickly want to point out that my eyes are small. I had them both circled on the 8x10 I gave you just to give ya a heads up."

Howie Michael Smith was working as a singing waiter in New York and *hating* his job. One night, he couldn't take it and left his shift, crying. When he got home, he had a message on his machine telling him that he got *Avenue Q* on Broadway! He went in the next day and sat through the wait-staff meeting, where they were all degraded by the management, and then he got to drop the delicious bomb that this was his last shift because he was going to Broadway! I asked him for a mortifying moment, and he said the most embarrassing thing to happen onstage was right after the song "You Can Be as Loud as the Hell You Want (When You're Makin' Love)." He, as Princeton, said a line to Kate Monster, and Princeton's eye fell off. Ouch. I don't know which is more devastating; having your eye fall off, or having both of them circled.

If it's Wednesday, it must be Cheyenne Jackson. He stopped by at noon, gabbed and then sang two songs! He talked about playing Matthew in *Altar Boyz* from very early on in its inception. He did the really successful run of it at NYMF and was all set to open Off-Broadway when he got offered a Broadway gig understudying Jarrod Emick. He quit *Altar Boyz* to go to Broadway as an understudy, but then Jarrod left the show, and Cheyenne got the lead! The show was *All Shook Up*, and I'm still devastated over his lack of a Tony nomination. *And his upcoming lack of a Tony nomination for XANADU. Who do you have scr*w to get a Tony nom in this town? I'm tempted to tell Cheyenne it's me.*

Thursday was the big press conference and we had Bebe Neuwirth and Brenda Braxton. I asked Bebe about her childhood and, turns out, she started out as a ballerina. But when she was 13, she saw Ben Vereen in *Pippin* on Broadway and suddenly knew she was going to grow up and do that style of choreography... AKA Fosse. What's amazing is that her first Tony Award was for the Fosse directed/choreographed *Sweet Charity*... *and* it was presented to her by Ben Vereen! Is she a modern Cassandra with great turnout? Bebe talked about doing the national tour of *A Chorus Line* very soon after the show opened on Broadway. She understudied and then took over the role of Sheila. Sheila is the one who is "gonna be 30 real soon" and she's "real glad." And after the "kids" get a break, she asks if the adults can smoke. When Bebe played the role, she was 19! She's like Jonathan Freeman, who said, "When I was 10, I was 40." Bebe said that she had the attitude of Sheila down, but she was so young that she still had baby fat. When Michael Bennett came to see the show, he wanted her to start wearing a belt as Sheila because he couldn't see her waist! *Then*, she took over the role of Cassie! You know, the one who's been in the business forever? The one Zack doesn't want to go back to the chorus? I'm sure the audience was like, *Go back to chorus? Does he mean high school chorus*?

Brenda Braxton, the current Velma in *Chicago,* joined me after Bebe. I asked her about doing *Smokey Joe's Café*. Turns out, she didn't have an audition for it originally, but heard they were looking for a "Brenda Braxton type." What the-? Isn't she a "Brenda Braxton type?" She happened to be in the rehearsal building where they were having auditions and her friend who was working on the show got her in. She got the role and did the entire five-year-run of the show. You may ponder how someone does that without getting bored. If you're Brenda Braxton, you'd answer that query in the beautiful brownstone you own. Next question. I asked her about the morning of the Tony nominations. She said that she was sleeping but kept hearing her answering machine clicking, so she knew something was up. She decided to call her mother to find out if she was nominated, but her mom wasn't home. However, the outgoing message was "You have reached the mother of Tony-nominated Brenda Braxton." Her mom works fast!

Friday, I had Ashley Spencer and Derek Keeling, who play Sandy and Danny in *Grease*, and that night I went to go see it. That theatre was *packed*! They both sounded and looked great. Ashley began as a ballet dancer, and during the finale, she did a crazy high battement and then went right into a split! Brava!

This week, I'm doing Project Shaw for my second time. The show is *Caesar and Cleopatra* (by George Bernard Shaw), and there are some amazing actors in it, including Madeleine Martin, Brian Murray and Daphne Rubin-Vega. I'm going to try not to be intimidated by everyone around and hope that Shaw requires my signatures: bad diction and extensive mugging.

Michele Lee, Jason Danieley, Farah Alvin — and Shaw
September 30, 2008

Happy fall, everybody! I'm writing this while looking at the beautiful fall flower bouquet that AMFAR sent me after I did last week's benefit with Cheyenne Jackson in Bucks County. I forgot to mention that, in the middle of Cheyenne's show, we did an auction. Cheyenne was too shy to hawk, so I opened up my big trap. We were auctioning off four house seats to *Xanadu*, plus dinner for four at Sardi's, plus signed posters and CDs. Well, turns out, it was supposed to be one package, but I was a moron and thought they were all separate! I auctioned off the four tickets for $2,000, then the dinner for $1,000, the signed stuff for $500 and then four more tickets were offered and we got another $2,000! Turns out my idiocy paid off.

Monday, I spent all afternoon at The Players Club rehearsing for my New York debut with a British accent. David Staller, who runs Project Shaw, cast me as Theodotus, the King's tutor, in *Caesar and Cleopatra*. Project Shaw's goal is to present a reading of every single play that George Bernard Shaw ever wrote and, while I'd much prefer Project Lloyd Webber, I was still very honored to be asked to be a part of it. *And* the show was sold out! If I'd have known that George Bernard Shaw was such a draw, I would have booked him at my one of my *Chatterbox*es. I don't know how David does it, but the cast was star-studded and *amazing*. Daphne Rubin-Vega was a brava as Cleopatra's arrogant maid with the impossible to say name: Ftatateeta. And Daniel Reichard from *Jersey Boys* was hilarious as the dapper Venetian rug salesman. Then there was the great Brian Murray playing Caesar, and young Broadway star Madeleine Martin as Cleopatra. Madeleine is 15 (!) and plays the girl in *August: Osage County*. She was really quirky and funny as Cleopatra and totally nice offstage. I got a photo of the group warm-up right before the show. Daphne made everybody hold hands and throw their arms up while saying "P'shaw." It made no sense but we loved it!

Tuesday night, I saw *Equus*. During the whole show, I was obsessing about what would happen if I had been cast as one of the horses because they all wear skin tight shirts tucked into their pants. How could I keep my stomach sucked in for two acts? Can a horse wear a mumu? As soon as I walked in and saw the rows of seats on the stage, I glared and said something to James about everybody jumping on the "*Spring Awakening* sitting on stage" bandwagon. I then shook my head and muttered "how unoriginal." That night I spoke with sister Nancy on the phone, and she remembered that she saw *Equus* in the '70s while wearing a corduroy jacket and denim skirt. She said that she was lucky because she got to sit in one of the seats onstage. That's right. They had the onstage seating 30 years ago. Shockingly, I judged something without knowing all the information, something I never do. And by "never" I mean "every hour on the hour."

Wednesday, I did another Sirius *Live on Broadway* interview at the Times Square Information Center. This time it was with two of the stars of *Spring Awakening*. But first, I had a special appearance by Jason Danieley, who has a new CD called *Jason Danieley and The Frontier Heroes*. The CD is basically him recreating what he did as a child, AKA his whole family would sit around, grab an instrument and sing. Conversely, *my* whole family would sit around, grab a resentment and fight. All right, that last comment was more for comedy's sake. Actually, we also did a lot of music-making. Some of it was great (driving in the car singing Pete Seeger and The Weavers) and some of it was a terrible, terrible mistake (the duet version of "What I Did For Love" my sister and I performed at my Bar Mitzvah reception).

After we chatted, Jason sang a beautiful song from the album and made way for Emma Hunton, who plays Ilse in *Spring Awakening*, and Gerard Canonico, who plays Moritz. They were both in *Les Miz* (she was Young Cosette on tour, and he was Gavroche on Broadway). I asked him about doing Gavroche's death in Act Two, and he said that once as he got shot, a woman in the audience called out, "No! Not the boy!" Emma said that after she did *Les Miz*, she auditioned for a local show singing "On My Own." After she sang, the casting person said she sounded like Britney Spears (lip-synchy?) and that if Emma kept using that pop sound, she'd never get anywhere in the business. And by "never get anywhere in the business," she must have meant "go straight to Broadway in a show that uses a pop sound."

After the interview, I did a game show segment where people from the audience were contestants and Gerard and Emma played as a team for another audience member. Let me say that they may be on Broadway, but the fact that they are 19 and 17 has limited their knowledge of musical theatre. Ouch. They were clanking, and finally I decided to throw a question I knew they'd know. I played a phrase from *Les Miz* (when the locket crone sings, "Come here my dear... let's see this trinket you wear") and I asked, "Who sings this phrase?" Both Emma and Gerard stared blankly, and then one of the other contestants buzzed. Her answer: Anita. I thought it was so hilariously wrong that I awarded her the winner. I then gave Gerard and Emma a free copy of my book *The Q Guide to Broadway* and begged them to pass it around the cast. After that, they both sang a duet of "Suddenly Seymour" and then performed "I Don't Do Sadness/Blue Wind" from *Spring Awakening*, and I forgave them.

Every month I do a show at Cardinal Cooke Hospital that's organized by Hearts and Voices. This month I had Alison Bender, Matthew Lutz and Lindsay Lavin (my intern!). Hearts and Voices (now run by Lifebeat) is a great organization that brings music to hospitalized people with AIDS. I've been doing shows for them for around 15 years, and I love it. So many times I've brought singers with me who are in a bad mood about something and by the end of the show, they're so happy. Why? Well, a lot of times, performers lose the joy of singing because it becomes about looking for a job or keeping their job and there's something so nice about performing for people who are there just to enjoy the music. They're not there to deny you a callback because you sound too pop. And what's great is that the patients don't care what's on your résumé, they just care if you connect with them and sound great. They gave the same reaction to my sassy intern as they gave Audra McDonald.

I just realized that I had so many interviews last week, I forgot to write about the wonderful Michele Lee, whom I had at the *Chatterbox*! Her first Broadway show was *Bravo Giovanni*, and her co-star was the opera singer, Cesare Siepi. Michele said that whenever he was playing a scene with her, Cesare would look only at her forehead. Finally, Michele asked him why he said all of his lines while looking at her forehead. He said, "If I looked in your eyes... I'd forget my lines." It sounded charming 'til I remembered that he was 20 years older than her. She got to replace the role of Rosemary in *How to Succeed in Business*... because the original Rosemary got pregnant with twins. Everyone said that it was going to be difficult to play opposite Robert Morse because he was so unpredictable, but she loved it. Michele said that he'd run all around the stage and change his blocking constantly, but all she mainly had to do was sit in a chair and look on adoringly, which was easy because that's what she was feeling! She remembered filming the movie, but told us that, at the time, Europeans didn't like musicals. So they filmed one version with the songs, and then they'd film the exact same scene again but leave out the music! How the hell would the scene end?

SMITTY: Rosemary, what are you thinking about?
ROSEMARY: How happy I'd be keeping his dinner warm.
SMITTY: Oh. OK, see ya.
ROSEMARY: See ya.
Fade to black

Finally, I brought up *Seesaw*. That's the show that was out-of-town in Detroit and in trouble. They fired the director and brought in Michael Bennett who fired *many* of the cast members, including the lead, Lainie Kazan. Michele got the lead and Ken Howard kept his role as her love interest. She said it was a nightmare for him because he would rehearse an all-new version of the show during the day, but at night he'd have to do the same show, but with the old lines and songs. What a headache. As for Lainie Kazan, Michele said that it was very difficult. They had been friends since they both did *Bravo Giovanni* together and they lived down the hall from one another! After *Seesaw*, they became estranged for many years, and then, ten years ago, they were both at a New Year's Eve party at Lee Grant's house. OK, get that old-school Hollywood image in your head. Michele said that she and Lainie were standing on opposite sides of a buffet table when "Auld Lang Syne" began to play. They both burst into tears and ran to hug each other. Now, they're best friends and, she suddenly remembered, Lainie's coming over to her house this Thursday to watch the vice-presidential debate! It sounded like such a fun girls' night and I wanted to be invited... especially since Michele said they'd be joined by Donna Mills!

This week, I also saw the new Off-Broadway show called *The Marvelous Wonderettes*, which is about a close harmony girl group in the late '50s and then ten years later. I can't wait for the CD because the singing is great. One of my favorite singers, Farah Alvin, is in the show, and she goes from singing crazy high soprano to belting up a storm. A few years ago, I did a salute to Neil Sedaka with the Actors Fund and Farah sang "Solitaire." She totally brought down the house, and Neil thought she was incredible. I put the video on my website! Pay special attention to the final note (an F!), and spot how the camera view gets obscured at the end because the crowd is giving her a standing ovation.

All right, that's it for me. For you fellow Jews out there, it's the New Year... L'shana Tovah! And for you fellow Jewish Broadway lovers, L'Shoshana Bean Tovah Feldshuh!

The Sweet Smell of Success
October 6, 2008

Greetings from Amtrak train 155!

I'm on my way down to Baltimore because I was beckoned by Amanda Brown Lipitz for a fundraiser that consists of the matinee of the *Legally Blonde* national tour followed by a talk back with some of the reality TV show folk. The trip began in a totally bizarre and random way. I got on the train and, of course, immediately hightailed it to the dining car. Annoyingly, it wasn't open yet. I glared and then started walking back to my seat. I passed a man reading a newspaper and, typical of me, glanced down at what he was reading. I'm one of those people on the subway who sit next to you and not only read the page of the book you're reading, but I also completely bend and contort my body to try to see the cover. If it's a book I like, I always give the ol' "Brava! Great book!" and am usually met with a seat change.

Anyhoo, after I glanced at his paper and started to walk away, he turned and looked over his shoulder at me. I thought he was going to bust me for disturbing his reading, but I didn't scurry away. Instead, I walked back to face the reprimand and, instead of telling me how rude I was, he told me that he recognized me from a video deconstruction I did of Christine Ebersole singing *Grey Gardens* on my website! He then said he was from *Grey Gardens*. He didn't look like anybody in the cast, but he had a beard and was stocky, so I assumed he was a backstage crew member. Instead, I found out he *really* meant he was from *Grey Gardens*. He said, "I'm Jerry… the marble faun!" I couldn't believe it! Jerry is the handyman in the documentary who comes over and helps out the Beale women. He was so sweet and I was super excited to meet him. Wow! Jerry likes my corn! *And* my video! Now I'm constantly scanning all my surrounding Amtrak seats, hoping that on my way to the bathroom, someone will glance at me and say, "I enjoyed your Patti LuPone deconstruction of *Evita*. I'm Juan Perón."

Last weekend I went to the East Side and saw the York Theater's production of *Enter Laughing*. It was so well directed by my friend Stuart Ross, who created *Forever Plaid* and with whom I did countless productions as the onstage pianist/upstager of the actors. The cast was fantastic, including George S. Irving, who was in the original production of *Oklahoma*! In 1944! That's like Jonathan Groff doing a sassy musical in 2072. Josh Grisetti was so charming in the lead (and had a great voice) and, as usual, I loved Janine LaManna. She was *hilarious* in her big torch number, telling us all the requirements that the man she will love *must* have. Essentially, her list includes a nose, a chin and a working respiratory system. Janine told one of my favorite stories in my *Chatterbox* show that I recounted in my book *Broadway Nights*. She was Chita Rivera's standby on the tour of *Kiss of the Spider Woman* even though Chita was known for *never* missing performances. Well, cut to opening night. Janine is relaxing in her hotel room, and she suddenly gets a call: Chita injured herself in the middle of Act One and Janine has to take over ASAP. Janine races out of her room, hails a cab, gives the driver the theatre address and frantically starts putting on her makeup for the show. She tells the driver to step on it because it was an *emergency*! She now realizes how crazy the dichotomy must have looked to the driver as Janine applied eyeliner, lipstick and false eyelashes yet screamed, "*Please*! It's an *emergency*!"

I had three guests at my Wednesday Sirius show. The first was Josh Strickland (he was cutie Tarzan on Broadway), who sang a song from the NYMF show he's starring in called *Play It Cool*. He sounded amazing. His co-star is Sally Mayes, and I told him how Sally and I almost worked together on Broadway. She made her Broadway debut in a show by Cy Coleman called *Welcome to the Club*. David Pogue (who now writes for *The New York Times*) was the conductor and told me to come watch the piano part in the pit so I could start subbing. I hadn't yet played a Broadway show and was so excited. I showed up the very next show and felt very cool bypassing the lobby entrance and walking straight to the stage door. Unfortunately, it was locked. I jiggled the handle repeatedly and then figured out that I showed up on the show's "dark day" (the day of the week when Broadway shows are closed... in those days, Mondays). Then I remembered that it was Tuesday. Huh? Why was Tuesday a dark day? I soon realized that it was the ultimate dark day. The show had closed and nobody told me. Son of a-!

Josh talked about all of his callbacks for *Tarzan* (16!) and how they involved getting harnessed, climbing to the top of a high-ceilinged rehearsal room and jumping down a gazillion feet holding onto a vine. He said that many people would get called back, climb to the top and then say, "Forget it. I'm out!" After Josh, I had Constantine Rousouli and Marissa Perry, who play Link and Tracy in *Hairspray*. Constantine "fondly" reminisced about doing the non-equity *Hairspray* tour where they traveled by a Greyhound bus that had 45 seats and 40 cast/musician/crew members. I'm sure the bathroom was amazing. He also told me that the wigs in that production were a hazard to wear. Once, during "You Can't Stop the Beat," Penny did her line, "I am now a checkerboard chick" and hugged Tracy. Unfortunately, their wigs also hugged, got stuck together and came off — perhaps leading the Weisslers to produce a *Hairspray* tour starring Yul Brynner and Telly Savalas? We shall see.

Marissa said that she auditioned in New York and got sent to "Tracy Camp." That meant she went up to Canada to learn the role with the Toronto company, but she was told she would never play the role in that company. They just wanted her to really know the role so they could put her in a company later on. It sounds a little passive/aggressive at first; i.e., "Learn this great role in a big production debuting in a fabulous city... and make sure you know that you're *never* going on!" But after she learned it, they did put her in a company...Broadway! So it totally paid off.

On an unrelated note, James and I were walking home Tuesday night when he suddenly looked up and whispered, "Marni Nixon is walking towards us." I, of course, waited 'til she was just past us and then started singing, "I could have dahnced all night..." She stopped in her tracks and turned around. I said, "You were great in the movie," and she smiled and walked away. Some might say "scurried away." Some might even add the modifier "frantically," but my point is, we parted company.

This week, I also interviewed Kelli O'Hara, who's starring as Nellie Forbush in *South Pacific*. Kelli grew up in Oklahoma (like Kristin Chenoweth) and went to Oklahoma City University and majored in opera (like Kristin Chenoweth!). She was essentially following in Kristin's footsteps, and I thought maybe I'd get some great catfight competition story about Kelli moving to New York and confronting Kristin at an audition, but, turns out, Kristin was amazing to Kelli! Kristin got Kelli an audition with her agent, and the agent signed her! Her first big break was the tour and then the Broadway company of *Jekyll and Hyde* as the understudy for Emma, played by the sassy Andrea Rivette. Kelli used that show to learn how to change her way of singing from operatic legit to more Broadway/pop. She then became an understudy in the Broadway revival of *Follies*. She played Young Hattie (Hattie played by Betty Garrett) and then took over the role of Young Phyllis (Phyllis played by Blythe Danner). In the opening scene, Kelli was in charge of leading Joan Roberts to the stage. Joan was the original Laurey in *Oklahoma!* and Kelli played her assistant in the opening scene. But Joan also seemed to think that Kelli was her actual assistant in real life! Kelli said that Joan didn't really know her name and would call out to her at the end of rehearsal, "Hey, you! Go get me a taxi!" Kelli would rush out and hail a cab for the first two weeks of rehearsal until a stage manager told her that she didn't actually have to do that.

Kelli got an audition for *Sweet Smell of Success*, but it was while she was in tech for *Follies*. She asked if she could go in during her lunch break, but it was the same lunch break that *Sweet Smell* was taking! Still, she went to the rehearsal studio and hoped someone would be there. She knocked on the door, and there were a few people there from the creative staff (including the director) and she begged them to let her sing. Unfortunately, there was no pianist, but one of the guys there offered to play. She started singing and felt the tempo was too slow, so she did ye olde "snap at the piano player to pick up the tempo" routine. Kelli described the audition to her friend that night, including the part about the too-slow accompanist, and her friend went on the internet and pointed to a picture of a guy and asked, "Was this the pianist?" Kelli then realized that the man she snapped at was the composer… *Marvin Hamlisch*! Of course, Marvin thought it was hilarious and loves to tell the story to people. Kelli had the good fortune to get a lead in *Sweet Smell of Success* and the *bad* fortune to be doing *Follies* at the same time with the girl who did it in the workshop but didn't get the Broadway gig. Yay. It's fun to feel awkward eight times a week.

After *Sweet Smell*, she went to Sundance to work on the musical *The Light in the Piazza*, where she played Franca, the wife of the Michael Berresse character, and she was excited to know that it was coming to Broadway in February. She was then offered *Dracula* and turned it down because she was doing *Piazza* that season. However, *Dracula* said they would let her out after six months! Even though she felt a little dubious about the show, she needed the work, the exposure and the health insurance (!), so she took the gig. Kelli was told that she wasn't going to have to be naked, but the next thing she knew, it was required for her role. She recalled that right before she took off her clothes, an *enormous* group of stagehands would suddenly have a cue to prepare for stage left. She's still got it!

As she was preparing for *Piazza*, she got a call from Bartlett Sher telling her that it was decided that Celia Keenan-Bolger, who played Clara, looked too young for the role. They said that Clara has to look like a woman so that the child-like behavior she exhibits is more incongruous. They had auditions around the country and finally asked Kelli to try out for the part. She said *absolutely* not. She told Bart that everyone was happy where they were and not to change anything. But the role was definitely going to be open and Kelli boycotting the audition wouldn't have changed anything, so Kelli finally went in. She got the role and a Tony nomination, and before you're devastated for Celia, just know that she got *Spelling Bee* that same season *and* a Tony nomination as well!

Kelli said that playing Babe in the Broadway revival of *The Pajama Game* made the creative staff of *South Pacific* realize that she could do more belty-style Broadway (not just soprano), and that's why she was brought in for *South Pacific*. However, she had to wait four months (!) for a callback because they wanted to cast the Emile first. They felt that he was a more difficult part to cast, and once they had him, they could match a Nellie to whoever it was. As a matter of fact, they had three different age ranges up for the role: Kelli was in the middle, the younger actress up for Nellie was Celia Keenan-Bolger, and the older one was Victoria Clark!

This week is the "fun" holiday of Yom Kippur. Oy. Let me wish my fellow Jews an easy fast and Happy New Year!

Wright On (and Off) Fire Island
October 13, 2008

I'm back from beautiful Fire Island.

I've only been there a couple of times, and the last time was when Linda Blair was starring in *Grease*… AKA a long time ago. Suffice it to say, it's still stunning! I went out there because I was invited by Ben Hodges (one of the editors of the *Theatre World* books and the producer of the Theatre World Awards). He asked me if I would come and interview two of the writers of *Grey Gardens*. James, Juli and I stayed in a beautiful bed and breakfast (The Madison Fire Island Pines) that was all white with white flowing fabric everywhere. I felt like I was spending the weekend in one of Barbra Streisand's outfits.

On Saturday afternoon, a big crowd sat around the spacious pool and I interviewed Michael Korie, the *Grey Gardens* lyricist, and Doug Wright, the librettist. They told us that composer Scott Frankel came up with the idea of writing a musical about *Grey Gardens* and Michael quickly came on board. Doug said that they asked him to write the book and he was on the fence about the whole idea. "I'd show up every week and tell them it wouldn't work as a show. After two years we had a first draft." One of the big problems, he felt, was that the documentary is just a slice of life about these two ladies. There's no beginning, middle and end. One night, though, Michael and Scott were out to dinner when Scott suddenly took a dinner napkin and wrote Act One 1941/Act Two 1973. Those two years not only relate to Michael Douglas and Catherine Zeta-Jones' birth dates, but they gave the show a framework.

The real Little Edie passed away before the show was completed, but she did give her blessing to the show. She wrote a letter giving her consent, writing that since their whole lives were music, it was fitting that there'd be a musical about it all. Doug remembered one line in the letter that said, "With all that we didn't have, our lives were joyous." Very sweet.

If you didn't see it, let me tell you that Christine Ebersole played Big Edie (the mother) in Act One and Little Edie (the daughter) in Act Two. I asked why Sara Gettelfinger played Act One Little Edie Off-Broadway (and on the recording) but not on Broadway. Doug said that, because there were 30 years between acts, they needed a Little Edie in Act One who'd look like a young version of Christine Ebersole in Act Two. Sara is taller than Christine and has a naturally dark look, and they felt that it was confusing for the audience for the two Edies to look so different. Michael remembered being in final callbacks for the role of Little Edie on Broadway. There were two women being considered for the part, and their agents told them that one of the two of them would get it. That same day, they were having auditions for the Little Edie understudy. Cut to: Erin Davie came in to audition for the role of the understudy and later that day, her agent called and told her that she didn't get the understudy… she got the part! Michael told us that the other girls cried while they were singing the audition song ("Daddy's Girl"), but Erin had actually made *the auditioners* cry. Brava! Erin was on Fire Island with us and performed "Daddy's Girl" and "Will You?" and was fantastic.

During the interview, I mentioned that I had met Jerry (the marble faun) the week before. Doug said that Jerry is now a cab driver and while *Grey Gardens* was on Broadway, he'd drive by the Walter Kerr Theatre every night at 10:30 PM. He would always pick up a couple who had just seen the show and listen to them talk in the back seat about it. If they liked the show, he'd wait 'til he dropped them off to drop that bomb that he was Jerry, and if they didn't like, he'd keep his trap shut.

On the Long Island Railroad back from Fire Island, I asked Doug about *I Am My Own Wife*, which was the show he wrote about a transvestite who had outwitted the Nazis and the Communists. He had heard about the story when he was touring Europe to celebrate his 30th birthday with his college buddy, director Chris Ashley. He met Charlotte von Mahlsdorf, who remained physically a man but still dressed as a woman. In one of the many interviews he did, he found out that one of Charlotte's lovers was a woman! Doug said, "So, at one point, you were straight?" and Charlotte replied, "Heavens, no. I was a lesbian!"

After the show opened on Broadway to great acclaim, he was directing a reading one day and an intern kept knocking on the door of the rehearsal room. Doug didn't want to be disturbed, but the intern said that there was a very important phone call. Doug picked up and it was the publicist Don Summa, who told him that there were 100 people who wanted to interview him. Doug was shocked.
"Why?" he asked.
"You haven't heard?" asked Don.
"Um, no."
"You won the Pulitzer Prize!" Don screamed.

Doug was so excited that he immediately hung up on Don and called his parents. It was partly for them to share in his joy, partly to alleviate the dishing his mother had given him when he sold his car so he could fly to Germany for one final interview with Charlotte. It paid off. His mother was happiest, though, when he wrote *The Little Mermaid* because he "finally wrote something his nephew could see!" He said that *Mermaid* was the most fun he had writing a show. He knows that some of the reviews weren't great but has no idea specifically what they were because his boyfriend has set parental blocks on his computer. Doug said that he can go to the dirtiest porn sites out there, but he can't access any of the theatre websites or message boards!

Right now, Doug is working on a movie about Gershwin, and the movie focuses mainly on *Porgy and Bess*. He said that after Anne Brown played Bess, she couldn't get any work singing opera in America because she was black, so she went to Europe, where she had a great career. She's the last principal cast member alive from the original production, and he flew to Oslo, where she now resides in a nursing home, to interview her. She recalled auditioning for Gershwin and singing a Schubert song. He then asked her for something else and suggested a spiritual. She sassed him and said that they didn't teach spirituals at Juilliard! "Why does everyone assume I know spirituals?" she asked him. "Because I'm black?" Gershwin backed off and asked her if it would be all right if he taught her one, and she said yes. So, Jewish George Gershwin taught African-American Anne Brown "City Called Heaven," her first spiritual.

This week, I saw *13* and I'm very glad that show didn't exist when I was a kid because if I didn't get to be in it, I would have pulled a Madame Bovary. Not only is the cast all teenagers, but the band is too, so there would have been many parts for me to not get cast in. I loved lots of the voices in the show, especially Elizabeth Gillies, who plays the bee-yatchy girl and has a sassy vibrato, and Graham Phillips *later on THE GOOD WIFE as the son,* who plays the lead and whose voice is in that nether region of when your voice starts changing but isn't quite there yet. He doesn't have a boy soprano or a man's range yet. It's right in the middle, like a contralto. Essentially, he's got the looks of a Bar Mitzvah boy with the notes of Melissa Manchester.

There's an amazing benefit coming up at the Al Hirschfeld Theatre. It's called *Broadway Voices for Change*, and it's for America Votes, which is an organization that increases progressive voter registration and turnout. Now, you know that I'm not the biggest fan of sopranos, but this benefit features two sopranos that I think are a brava: Audra McDonald and Barbara Cook! I was chatting with Barbara on the phone (while holding the receiver and mouthing to James, "Can you believe I'm talking with Barbara Cook on the phone!?!?!?!"), and she told me that she loves singing with Audra. The show is going to be tons of solos for both of them and some sassy duets. I, of course, immediately began asking her questions about *Music Man*, specifically about one of my favorite Broadway songs, "My White Knight." Turns out, Meredith Willson kept changing the song because the first version was too long and by the time he came up with the final one, Barbara had sung 12 different ones! And it really was 12 versions. Barbara doesn't do my mother's style of number aggrandizing ("You spilled grape juice on me! This sweater cost me seventy fi-… eighty… ni-… a *hundred* dollars!").

One of my favorite Audra McDonald facts is that she tried out for the ensemble of *Beauty and the Beast*… and didn't get it. I'd love to see the "No Callback" pile of 8x10s from that audition with Audra's mug staring up from it. My other favorite Audra lore ties in with the sad closing of *[title of show]*. Heidi Blickenstaff and Audra grew up together in Fresno and both tried out for the local production of *Annie*. Heidi got the role of Annie, and Audra's picture yet again wound up in the reject pile. Of course, you'd think Heidi would be happy about that, but she told me that the reason Audra didn't get the part was actually because she was such a great performer that the director felt that she would outshine the rest of the cast. Poor Heidi walked around her whole life knowing that she only got *Annie* because Audra was too amazing. Well, I confronted Audra with the story, and she blatantly 'fessed up that she made up that spin just to save face. Audra said, "The truth is I tried out and didn't get it because the director said my audition was sub-par." Brava on Audra's spin doctor-technique, but no brava for making Heidi feel like a loser for getting a lead role. I finally got to tell Heidi that she got the role of Annie because she had the goods, not because Audra outshined her. And if Audra was hurt revealing the truth, she can cry all the way to where she stores her four Tony Awards. *As we all know, Audra now has six!*

Hitting New *Heights*
October 20, 2008

Ooh, mid-October!

It's finally cold out and that means that the heat is not only on in Saigon, but also in my apartment. It also means that since I can't control the radiators, it's not only 110 in the shade, but also in my bedroom. *And* just to keep the musical references going, if *I* received a "little lamb" for my birthday and sang a song to it, it would be completely roasted by the last verse.

Monday is usually benefit night in New York City and I love it! Last Monday, I did *Kickin' It*, which was put together by Lorin Latarro, who has the nerve to have done ten Broadway shows in the last ten years. She literally gets a new Broadway show every time I get my teeth cleaned. Not cool. Anyhoo, this was to help out Natasha "Nabba" Steinhagen, a Broadway dresser who's done tons of shows and is now struggling with ovarian cancer. The show was *fantastic*. Jim Newman (from *Curtains*) was the host and told people that he never likes people who host shows just to push their own agendas. He then complained it was hot, took off his jacket and revealed his boldly lettered T-shirt that read "McCain is 'Insain.'" Subtle, but blunt. Lorin directed the whole show and choreographed many of the numbers and I love that her choreography always has such humor.

On Wednesday, I did my Sirius *Live on Broadway* show where I interviewed the always funny Jackie Hoffman. She has a CD coming out called *Jackie Hoffman Live* and it's going to be hilarious. She sang one of the songs from the CD called "Please… Won't You Get Away With Your Children?" My favorite lyric: "Your double strollers on the street leaves no room for my feet. And you're leaving me no room to let me be what I wanna be. You think it makes me feel alone and makes me want one of my own… but all it's making me want… is a hysterectomy!" Jackie talked about how she would sass the onstage audience at *Xanadu* with her signature improvs and that they got longer and longer. Finally, on the last night, she did the whole ending scene from *West Side Story* (*"How many bullets are left in this gun, Chino?"*). Her co-star Mary Testa knew she was in for a long one and simply left the stage so Jackie could finish.

At the *Chatterbox*, I had Lin-Manuel Miranda, Tony-winning composer/lyricist and star of *In the Heights*. He went to Hunter (public school for smart NY kids) and, turns out, *didn't* grow up "in the heights" but rather in Inwood. I asked him why he didn't write *In the 'Wood*, and he said because Sondheim wrote it better. Quick answer! At Hunter, sixth grade pretty much just focuses on doing the big end-of-the-year musical. When he was in sixth grade, instead of one big show, they did six 20-minute musicals! He was a munchkin, an Oklahoma farmer, a son from Anatevka, Conrad Birdie, Bernardo and Capt. Hook.

One of the first shows he saw was *Les Miz* and he and his mother would listen to the cast album all the time, specifically "Bring Him Home." My mother loves that song too, but she has the Jewish gene that turns everything negative. How? Well, once I was putting on the *Les Miz* CD, and she (seriously) said, "Play my favorite song… 'He's Not Coming Home.'" It doesn't even scan lyrically! It was a wonderful childhood.

The first show that Lin-Manuel really identified with was *Phantom of the Opera*. He said, "It knocked me out. It was about an ugly songwriter who can't get girls. That was me!" I asked Lin-

Manuel who was playing the Phantom when he saw it and he didn't know! I was outraged that he didn't keep his *Playbill* and pore over it every night like I did when I was a kid. However, he countered me by saying that he *did* keep the program from when he saw *Lion King*, and he recently checked it. Turns out the Simba he saw was... Chris Jackson (!), who's now starring in *In the Heights*! P.S. Chris was first cast to play Benny because he's so light-skinned he can look Latin. At that point, the character was a Latin heartbreaker and the plot was about whether he was good enough for Nina, but producer Jeffrey Seller told Lin one day that Chris in real life is so well-spoken and charming, he's actually more interesting than the character he's playing. So, instead of Benny being a lothario, Lin changed the character to someone who's an outsider, made him black, and the character of Benny essentially became the real Chris.

When Lin-Manuel was a teenager, he got a class assignment to teach a book to his fellow students. That assignment turned into the first musical he wrote. It was not a book by Latino authors Gabriel Garcia Marquez or Laura Esquivel. It was Chaim Potok's *The Chosen*. He had the class perform it, and by "perform" I mean that he recorded himself singing all the songs and had the class lip-synch to his voice. Some sample lyrics:

(This is after a character gets hit in the eye with a baseball)
That dirty Hasidim!
I don't really need 'em!
I know I could beat 'em... if my eye weren't in pain.

What show has ever rhymed Hasidim with a triple rhyme? Actually, what show has ever rhymed Hasidim? The first draft of *Yentl*?

While he was at Wesleyan, he started writing *In the Heights*. It wasn't a school project — it was just because he felt the need to write it. The first phrase he came up with was "...in Washington Heights," and that's pretty much the only thing musically from the original production that remains in the show. The original show was about a love triangle between Benny, Nina and Nina's brother Lincoln. Lincoln was closeted and in love with Benny. That character lasted a long time until Kevin McCollum and Jeffrey Seller came on as producers. Not because they told Lin to ixnay the character, but because they invited him to see *Avenue Q*. Lin said that he sat in the audience and watched this puppet onstage (Rod) who was closeted and in love with his best friend... and he realized it was much better than the storyline in his show! And the character of Lincoln was ixnayed.

Lin met Tommy Kail at Wesleyan and he became the director of the show. Lin said that Tommy was integral in the creation of the show because of his dramaturgy. For instance, the opening of Act Two happens after Nina and Benny spend their first night together. Lin said that every song he wrote for them sounded like an '80s Pat Benatar power ballad. One day, Tommy suggested that Lin make the song a Spanish lesson with Nina teaching Benny Spanish phrases... and suddenly "Sunrise" poured out.

I asked about the song "Breathe," which I love. He said that Andrew Lippa heard the score and told him he noticed that all of the songs were in 4/4 time. Lin was very defensive and thought, "I *love* how all the songs are in 4/4." An hour later he was like, "Wah! All of the songs are in 4/4," and that's when he decided to write "Breathe" in 3/4. I'm sure after Sondheim saw it, he was like, "Why aren't any of the songs in 7/16?" but hopefully Lin will continue to ignore him. Speaking of which, when Lin-Manuel was nominated for the Tony, he wrote a sassy rap but only practiced it in the shower. He got so thrown during his speech when he mentioned Chris Jackson and got applause that he totally forgot the rest of the speech. He wound up "free-styling," as we say in the hip-hop business, and he came up with the most memorable part of his speech. He suddenly said...

Mr. Sondheim, look! I made a hat! Where there never was a hat! It's a Latin hat at that!

So great!

Speaking of Sondheim, Lin is in charge of translating the *West Side Story* songs into Spanish for the upcoming revival! Not all of the lyrics, FYI. So far, just the Sharks' part in the "Tonight" quintet, "I Feel Pretty" and "A Boy Like That." He got to go over to "Steve's" house to talk about how to do the lyrics! There are Spanish translations out there, but some parts are good and some are clanky, so they want Lin to do a new version. For instance, Sondheim said that some versions of "I Feel Pretty" translate as "I Am Pretty," which is not correct — especially if it features the Maria I saw do it in community theatre.

Finally, I saw the Barbara Cook/Audra McDonald benefit on Sunday night. It was for an organization that gets people out to vote, but just in case there was any doubt as to whom the two ladies were supporting, there was an Obama action figure doll on the piano, and Audra changed the lyrics in "Blue Skies" to "Blue States"! It was totally sold out, and they sang up a storm. At one point Barbara said about Audra, "It's not fair that she can sing like that... and *look* like that!" Then later on, Audra said, "Barbara, I'm gonna say in front of everyone what I was gonna tell you backstage. When you dance during your songs... you're so sexy." Finally, I thought, a Broadway benefit with some lesbian subtext! *And* a May/December romance angle.

Near the end, Audra announced that she wanted to sing a song about America that she's sung before and feels was prophetic when it was written by Lynn Ahrens and Stephen Flaherty. She then brought out Brian Stokes Mitchell, who joined her for a thrilling rendition of "Wheels of a Dream" from *Ragtime*. The audience went crazy, prompting my mother to ask me, "Why don't they bring back *Ragtime*?" I glared and told her to be quiet. But now I must ask, "Why don't they bring back *Ragtime*?" It's such a moving show with a fantastic score. *They did bring it back! Yet again, my words are much more powerful than I ever imagined. Or my mother is.*

OK, everyone. This coming Friday night, I'm doing a benefit for The Children of Armenia Fund (which helps bring education to Armenian children) with Andrea Martin, Bill Irwin and Cirque Du Soleil! And on Thursday at the *Chatterbox*, I'm going to have the great Karen Morrow! I've been trying to get her on my show for years, but she's always in L.A. Thankfully, she's in town because she just performed in Scott Siegel's *Broadway Originals* at Town Hall, and she'll be at my show Thursday. Whenever I have a party at my apartment, I pull out her Ed Sullivan performance of "I Had a Ball" and people become obsessed. It's one of the best-sung Broadway performances *ever*. Go to *Youtube.com* and watch her old-school, stand center stage, specific arm movements, unbelievable tone/belt/vibrato performance!!!!

High on the Morrow
October 27, 2008

It was the best of weeks, it was the worst of weeks.

Not really, but I did see *A Tale of Two Cities*. There are some *great* voices in that cast! Essentially, every song ended with someone belting a soprano high note and it was usually a guy. I hope the water backstage is infused with Throat Coat.

Monday night, I did *Celebrity Autobiography*, which is a show where people read excerpts from real celebrity autobiographies. I always read Star Jones' bio, *You Have to Stand for Something, Or You'll Fall for Anything*. Hmm... I'm sure she agrees strongly with that title and it's not just witty, meaningless word play. Anyhoo, I was backstage with everyone before the show and I was so excited to see Alan Zweibel. He was a writer on *Saturday Night Live* when it first began and wrote a book called *Bunny Bunny* — about his friendship with Gilda Radner — that I loved when I first read it. When we were backstage on Monday, Alan walked over to Matthew Broderick, gave him a pat on the shoulder and said, "By the way, belated congratulations on *Ferris Bueller*." Brava!

Speaking of which, Matthew was late because he was coming from the dentist. He told us that he was on his motorized scooter rushing through Central Park and the 72nd Street exit was closed off. He was so late that he tried to sneak through it because it leads right to the venue... and he got stopped by a cop! The cop walked over to him and Matthew took off his helmet, waiting for the, "Oh, my God, you're Matthew Broderick!" moment. Matthew said that he wished he had long flowing hair to reveal as the helmet came off, but he didn't. Regardless, the cop saw his face and had no reaction. He then asked for his license, saw Matthew's name and remained duly blank-faced. Matthew said, "I know I made a mistake, but I'm rushing to go do a play!" The cop said, "What play?" Uh-oh. Should Matthew say *Celebrity Autobiography*? Hmm... he realized that it wasn't actually a play. But then what is it? An act? Performance art? He remained silent as the cop glared. Matthew finally stammered, "Uh... I do a lot of plays." That cop asked, "Like what?" Matthew offered, "*The Producers*?" The cop shrugged and said he never heard of it. What the-? This was in New York, people! Surely, the cop heard about the Inner Circle Tickets that cost $450. If that wasn't a crime, what was? Finally, Matthew told him that he also does movies. Matthew said he wasn't trying to get out of it because he's famous, but he was trying to prove he really was rushing to do a show and not because he was totally reckless. The cop asked, "What movies?" Matthew decided to go for the big guns and said with trepidation, "Uh... *Ferris Bueller's Day Off*?" Phew! *That* he had heard of, and the cop let Matthew off without a ticket. If you reenact this story, remember that Matthew just came from dental surgery, so he said that half his face was "Novocained" and therefore immobilized, adding to him sounding desperate and crazy.

On Wednesday, I saw *All My Sons*, which, more than once, I've called *My Three Sons* by accident. I think John Lithgow is a great actor, and it was great to see him giving a sassy dramatic turn — even though he busted me the first time I met him. Kelli O'Hara got him to be a guest on my *Chatterbox* and I introduced him as John Lithgow, pronouncing it like "ow." He came onstage and told me it was Lithgow, like "oh." I immediately told him that the "w" at the end of his name should make it "ow," and he asked me how I pronounced "rainbow." Busted! I've been a fan of Patrick Wilson, who plays his son, since we first worked together on Barry Manilow's *Harmony* in the summer of 1997. I was disappointed that there was no singing in *All My Sons*. I'm always frustrated when a great musical performer does a straight acting gig. (Still annoyed about Barbra's stint in *Nuts*. Where was the belted theme song?)

I was *thrilled* at my *Chatterbox* this week because I got to interview old-school Broadway beltress Karen Morrow. She grew up in Des Moines and both of her parents were opera singers. When she was three, her parents had a party, put her on the piano bench, and she sang "God Bless America" with pretty much the same voice as Kate Smith. Even though she knew she could sing, she didn't know much about Broadway, so she decided to major in Economics. Then she heard Susan Johnson's "Ooh, My Feet" from *The Most Happy Fella* and heard how similar their voices were and Karen realized she could do Broadway. *I* grew up obsessed with Susan Johnson and *The Most Happy Fella*. I have a tape of myself singing "Ooh, My Feet" when I was three years old, and it then became my audition song when I was 12. *I put up a video on my website. Take a gander!* Karen got to work with Susan many years later in *Follies* and said that she was so thrilled and moved that she cried every day. Susan told Karen that for the opening night of *The Most Happy Fella*, Frank Loesser gave her an amethyst tiepin (the lead character, Tony, gives a waitress an amethyst tiepin instead of a tip in the first scene of the show). For the opening of *Follies*, Susan gave Karen the tiepin Frank had given her!

At the end of college, the famous choreographer Eugene Loring came to her school with his troupe of dancers. He heard Karen perform and told her that she had what it took to make it. He convinced her to move to L.A. and promised her that she could perform with his troupe as the lead singer. She got the okay from her parents and moved to the West Coast. She showed up at Eugene Loring's studio and... he didn't remember her! *Devastating!* She then hightailed it to New York. As opposed to Betty Buckley, who got a great part in *1776* within hours of arriving in New York, Karen arrived in Manhattan, went in to audition for *Subways Are for Sleeping*... and got typed out. That's when they stand you in a line and the auditioner points and says, "You, you and you stay. Everyone else, thank you very much." She got an appointment with an agent and as soon as she walked in, he asked her the existential question, "So... who are you?" Karen was dumbstruck. The agent shook his head and said, "From day one, Doris Day knew who she was." But then a friend got her another agent audition and she went in and *wasn't* asked a moronic Jean-Paul Sartre question. Instead, she sang. After her first song, the auditioner got on the phone. Rude? Hardly. He said into the receiver, "Honey, listen to this," held up the phone and had Karen sing again. Turns out, his wife was his partner, and they both signed her.

Her first big audition was as a last-minute replacement for Jo Anne Worley in the Off-Broadway show *Sing Muse*. She got hired on the spot (!) and as she left, she mentioned she was hopping on the subway. The producer stopped her and said, "Subway? Take a cab... you're gonna be a star!" He then handed her five dollars. In those days, that could have paid for a cab ride back to Des Moines. After that, she did the national tour of *The Unsinkable Molly Brown* as the standby for Tammy Grimes. She got to take over the role but didn't know how to handle doing a lead eight times a week. She thought she was supposed to go out with the cast after the show every night and par-tay. Suffice it to say, after a month of the show, her voice had the timbre of a young Joe Cocker.

After she toured, she got her voice back and decided she wanted to be thinner, so she went to a doctor to help her lose weight. She later found out that the weight loss potion he was injecting her with was speed! I guess "doctor" in the '60s was code for "pusher." Regardless, she loved her new bod and auditioned for Richard Rodgers for a revival of *The Boys From Syracuse*. He said, "I would love for you to do this role... but you're just too thin!" That's a statement that has ne'er been said to me. She still wound up getting the gig, and they had to pad her to give her some girth.

I asked her about shows she didn't get and she remembered being at the final callback for *110 in the Shade*. She was sitting backstage with Gretchen Wyler... and suddenly, in walked tall, beautiful Inga Swenson with no makeup on and a long, flowing braid. They knew they were sunk. I never realized that my main competition at auditions was the person with no make-up and the long braid. That must be why I keep losing all my gigs to Willie Nelson.

Karen had two auditions in the mid-'60s. One was for a show that there was a *ton* of buzz for, and the other one had very little advance chatter. Karen decided that the one with all the talk had nowhere to go but down, and the one no one talked about had nowhere to go but up. And that's how she wound up taking *I Had a Ball*, which gave her a signature song and a brilliant *Ed Sullivan Show* performance on film forever. The show she decided against was *Kelly*, which wound up running for 1 (one!) day! If you've not seen her brilliant rendition of the *I Had A Ball* title song on *The Ed Sullivan Show*, you must go to my website and watch the whole thing. It's the epitome of a great Broadway performance. FYI, her waist looks like it's 16 inches, yet her agent at William Morris said she was too heavy. Who was her agent? Lara Flynn Boyle? Right now, Karen lives in L.A. and teaches a wonderful musical theatre performance class. Go to her website and watch the videos *and* listen to the belting (*KarenMorrow.com*)!

On Friday night, I hightailed it to Cipriani on 42nd Street, which is a gorgeous, cavernous event room that used to be the Bowery Savings Bank. Andrea Martin asked me to help out at a benefit for the Children of Armenia Fund (*COAFkids.org*). Andrea was the host and told the audience, "I know we're going through some hard economic times, but let's forget about that tonight. And what better way to forget hard economic times than by having dinner in an abandoned bank!" Brava. The multi-talented Bill Irwin performed one of his baggy pants clown acts and Andrea opened the show with "Come on-a My House," which was originally sung by Rosemary Clooney *but* was written by two Armenians! I told Andrea that we needed a big finale to end the evening and I would be in charge of finding someone. Well, of course, just like how I did my AP English papers, I waited 'til the last minute. I emailed the fabulous Mary Bond Davis (the original Motormouth Maybelle from *Hairspray*) and spoke to her around 3 PM that afternoon. She showed up a few hours later, totally decked out, and brought the house down with Amanda McBroom's "The Dieter's Prayer" (i.e. "Lord, let me think... that tofu's a food. And not something you made up... while in a bad mood").

Tonight, I'm hosting a salon for BC/EFA. Essentially, people pay money to come to a beautiful apartment on Central Park South to eat up a storm, mingle with celebs, and watch them perform in the living room. Fun! Andrea McArdle, Chris Noth, Anthony Rapp, Bebe Neuwirth and *more* are coming! I'm, of course, obsessing about the delicious food and how I can surreptitiously do all my hosting from the buffet area.

One Day More
November 3, 2008

Finally! The election is here. It's been so much stress for so long, I can't take it! Didn't the campaigns start years ago? The lead up to this election has been longer than the endless mega-mix I had to endure at an ill-advised matinee of *Saturday Night Fever* years ago.

Okay, let me take my mind off it by talking about Broadway! This has been a busy week. I took a job as a comedy writer on the *new* Rosie O'Donnell variety show and I've been doing a reading at the same time. First the TV show: I just started, so I can't tell ya much, except that it's gonna have some fabulous guests. I was a comedy writer on the first *Rosie O'Donnell Show*, and this one has the same people I worked with ten years ago. I dreaded walking in and having everybody clandestinely count wrinkles and multiply them by my hairline (the equation for "Yowtch! You've aged."), but I was pleasantly surprised when everyone commented about how I must be working out because my chest is so big. Hopefully, I'll be sitting behind a desk for the rest of the gig or else people will start to notice that my waist gained the same amount of inches that my chest did, and not in muscle. I'm also doing a reading of *Rebecca of Sunnybrook Farm* based on the Shirley Temple movie. Yes, I'm a little long in the tooth for the role of Rebecca, but what I lack in youthful glow, I make up for in lethargy and a bad knee. Actually, there's a little girl playing Rebecca, and she's adorable. The rest of the cast is great, too. The character actor Marc Kudisch is playing a Rooster Hannigan-type, and sassy Tony winner Cady Huffman is his moll. Brooks Ashmanskas plays a shy radio engineer, and when we saw each other, we immediately started reminiscing about *The Ritz*. I was about to launch into a story about some of the inappropriate backstage behavior that the near-naked *Ritz* boys pulled when I realized that I was surrounded by a group of little, underage girls in the ensemble. I put the kibosh on my story, deciding that they don't yet need to learn what Quell is used for.

If you don't know what a reading is, it's when a play is read (and sung) by actors to give the creative team and producers insight into what's working and what's not. There's no staging — you just sit in front of a music stand and work off the script. There's a union term for it: a 29-hour reading. That means that you can use the actors for 29 hours in a week and pay them $100 each. I was talking to one of my fellow actors, who has done a ton of these types of readings, and he said that actors always jokingly complain about only getting $100, but recently he did a reading with producers who didn't use the actors for the full 29 hours (but it was very close), and therefore paid them *nothing*! How cheap is that? And who were the producers? The Ropers?

The book for *Rebecca of Sunnybrook Farm* was adapted by Daniel Goldfarb (*Modern Orthodox*), the lyrics are by Susan Birkenhead (*Jelly's Last Jam*), and Henry Krieger (*Dreamgirls*) wrote the music. I was hoping to get a big *Dreamgirls*-type ballad to bring the house down with, but then realized that it takes place in the '30s, so I wouldn't be "Steppin' to the Bad Side." However, I soon had to accept that not only would I not have the 11 o'clock number, but I wouldn't have *any* number. I will instead try to bring the house down with my baritone harmony parts in two group numbers. The best part is that my friend Christopher Gattelli is the director. We started working together on the opening number of the 1998 Easter Bonnet competition, and we've done seven numbers since then. I'm so proud of him for getting a Tony nomination this year for *South Pacific. He finally won a few years later for NEWSIES!*

Last Monday night, I hosted the Broadway Cares/Equity Fights AIDS salon. This is the one where every ten minutes, some celeb gets up and sings. Well, almost everybody sang. Chris Noth got up and chatted to the crowd… and was fun-nee. He introduced Ron Pobuda, who donated the gorgeous apartment, by saying, "Ron, like David Duchovny, just went to rehab for sexual addiction." He then said that Ron didn't finish his time because he wanted to keep his wild sex life. I found it hilarious… and so did the many ten-year-olds from the *Rebecca of Sunnybrook Farm* reading who were there. Just kidding, they were all home, probably reading *Twilight*. The other non-singing guests were the cute David Steen and TV legend Rue McClanahan. I interviewed them and they talked about their current TV show, LOGO's *Sordid Lives*, where David plays a man with no legs and Rue plays his lover. They told us that the love scene they recently filmed that a) broke the bed they were on, and b) was boycotted from LOGO because it was too graphic. Seriously. I then said, since we're talking about sexy, what's up with Bea Arthur? Rue said that they're still in touch and speak all the time, which I loved hearing because it's nice to know that the friendship on *Golden Girls* was real.

I asked Rue if it was true that her autobiography, *My First Five Husbands… And The Ones Who Got Away*, was being turned into a stage show. She said it was and I asked her if she was nervous that somebody else would get the part. She said, "Absolutely not!" I reminded her about Carol Channing/Barbra Streisand, and she said, "Carol Channing is Carol Channing… not Dolly Levi. I *am* Rue McClanahan!" She has a point.

Paul Shaffer from *David Letterman* got up and played. He offered to play a song he wrote himself, which is usually my cue to take a bathroom break, but turns out he wrote one of my favorite disco anthems: "It's Raining Men"! I *love* that song. He said that in the early '80s, Paul Jbara (who wrote "Last Dance," "The Main Event" and was the "Electric Blues" soloist in *Hair*) called him and asked him to co-write Donna Summer's comeback song. They wrote it in an afternoon and sent it to Donna. Unfortunately, he said that she rejected it because she became a born-again Christian and didn't want to say "It's raining men… hallelujah." Thankfully, they hooked up with The Weather Girls, and they let the belting begin!

At my Sirius *Live on Broadway* show I interviewed the fabulous Charlotte d'Amboise, who's starring as Roxie in *Chicago*. Turns out, she started dancing relatively late (eight years old), and even though her father was the famous dancer Jacques d'Amboise (lead dancer of NYCB), she still had to audition for the school. Rude. She always wanted to be a male ballet dancer because she would watch her dad dance and felt that he always got to do the exciting stuff and the ladies always had to do the sweet, petit allegro stuff. After she saw *A Chorus Line* and *Dancin'*, she was desperate to become a Broadway dancer because she felt the women got to be powerful when they danced. The summer she graduated high school, she was a dancer at Surflight Summer Theater on Long Beach Island in New Jersey, where I also spent many a year as a music director. It was one-week-stock, where you rehearse one show during the day and you're performing another one at night. Back then, even though they only had seven days of rehearsal, they didn't do easy little shows. They would literally do all of *Sweeney Todd* in a week! Off-book and fully staged!

Charlotte was mainly in the chorus, but the last show was *Company* and she got the dance role of Kathy. That summer, the music director was David Loud. Cut to, years later, she got the role of Kathy in the Roundabout revival of *Company* and David Loud was again the music director! When she graduated high school, she asked her parents to give her a year and if she didn't get a Broadway show, she'd go to college. Right before the year was up, she got a national tour of *Cats*. Her parents accepted that as a Broadway show even though it was a tour... and even though it was *Cats*. She got the role of Cassandra and loved doing that show. She remembers that she was constantly "working it" whether or not it was her feature. She finally had to tone it down because she hit an over-the-top cat/dancer pose (standing straight up with one paw raised) during "Memory" and held it for the entire song, and afterwards, Laurie Beechman told her to get the hell out of her light!

She was in the original cast of *Song and Dance* and got to dance with her brother, Christopher. Unfortunately, it was a romantic pas de deux, which Charlotte said had a weird incestuous subtext. People would come to the show and see that their last names were the same and, thankfully, assume they were married. It reminded me of when Hunter and Sutton Foster were both in *Grease!* on Broadway. Hunter was Roger and Sutton was Sandy, but Hunter understudied Danny. They both had a provision in their contracts that he would never go on for Danny opposite Sutton because they were horrified at the possibility of having to make-out onstage.

Charlotte tried out for the role of the mean girl in *Carrie*, but Mary Ellen Stuart was cast. However, she turned it down because, à la Donna Summer, she was a born-again Christian and didn't want to curse onstage. So, Charlotte lucked out. And by "lucked out," I mean "did one of the biggest flops Broadway has ever seen." Charlotte said that they did the show in London and it got *terrible* reviews. Then, they started rehearsing in New York... and nothing was changed! The only change was Barbara Cook left the role of the mother, and Betty Buckley took over, but the concept and direction of the scenes without Betty stayed exactly the same. Charlotte couldn't believe the show was going to open on Broadway as is. She said she remembers calling her mother after a performance and saying, "Mom... I think I got booed!" The show opened on a Thursday and closed on a Sunday, and yet she feels that if it stayed open, it would have run. Even though it was on Broadway for two weeks (including previews), there were people who saw it three times within those two weeks! She finally took it off her résumé because when she was touring, people would harass her constantly at the stage door, dying to talk about *Carrie* and begging her for a bootleg!

While she was doing *Carrie*, Charlotte auditioned for *Jerome Robbins' Broadway*. He taught her a combination and, typical dancer-style, she marked through it once to see if she knew it. She was then ready to dance it for him, but he said that he had seen enough, and she got the gig! She was hired to do a song called "Dreams Come True" from *Billion Dollar Baby* that was part dance, part comedy. However, she told him she also wanted to play Anita in "America." He didn't want her for the role because of the non-Latin way she looked, but she insisted that he let her try out. She did, and he told her she got it, but she wanted a guarantee. She knew she had to get it in her contract... and she was right. It was a six-month rehearsal process, and Charlotte said that Robbins was constantly taking parts away from people and trying them on others. Essentially, you got cast in the show and then auditioned again for the next six months.

He didn't want to put "I'm Flying" from *Peter Pan* in the show because it didn't really highlight his choreography... it was really about the flying. But the producers insisted, and it was put into the show. Charlotte auditioned for that and got it. In previews, she heard that they had to cut a number, and she was terrified that it was going be "I'm Flying." When she heard the audience reaction to the number, though, she knew that they *had* to keep it. So Robbins cut "Dreams Come True," her other big number! Busted. Be careful what you wish for!

In the '90s, *Chicago* called her to audition... for Velma! They wanted her for that role because there's more dancing in that part than Roxie. Charlotte called and said that she felt she was really right for Roxie, but they told her, "No." She had to audition for Velma. So, she prepared all the Roxie stuff and when she showed up for her audition, she launched into Roxie. They stopped her and said, "Aren't you auditioning for Velma?" and she acted confused and said, "No! Really? I don't think so. I thought it was for Roxie." They, of course, felt bad, told her not to worry about the mix up and just do what she prepared. The trick worked and she got Roxie!

At the beginning of the week, I hightailed it to Long Island to do a reading/signing of my two books, *The Q Guide to Broadway* and *Broadway Nights*. On the way home, I was waiting for a subway in Penn Station and ran into... Adam Pascal! While we were talking, I was blinded by his teeth and asked whether they were caps or if he just had them whitened... and he said neither! How dare they be so gleaming? He and Anthony Rapp are about to do the national tour of *Rent*. We talked about the *Chess* concert I put together for The Actors Fund in 2003 (directed by Peter Flynn and choreographed by Christopher Gattelli), where he played Freddie and Josh Groban played Anatoly. He recently did it in London and, turns out, the reason he got it is because someone put up a bootleg of Adam singing "Pity the Child" on *YouTube*, and the director saw it! Brava illegality!

OK, I'm out. I'll write next week... after the election and before I fly to Ithaca to launch the new season at The Hangar Theater. Peace out!

Sunnybrook Farm's Bounty
November 10, 2008

Rebecca of Sunnybrook Farm ruined my diet. There, I said it. I rehearsed *Rebecca* for a week and last Monday was the reading. Once I showed up I discovered that Kelly Gonda, one of the producers from East of Doheny, loves home cooking, so instead of the food spread at the reading being a typical cheese and fruit platter (AKA stuff I'm not interested in), it featured *everything* I love. Cakes, brownies and my personal obsession, cookies. I'm obsessed with cookies, and I ingested about eight chocolate chip ones over the course of both acts. Then, on my way out, I shoved more in my pocket, praying there wasn't an electronic tag attached that would start beeping as I left the rehearsal room.

The reading went great, and the audience loved everything... including my broad comedy moments. There's nothing more devastating than doing a bit that gets big laughs in rehearsal and then getting crickets when you finally perform it. What was stressful was that all my comedy moments came near the end of the show, so I had to be nervous the whole time, hence the eight cookies.

Henry Krieger was the composer and, as many of you know, I'm obsessed with *Dreamgirls*. Here's some fun trivia. I had heard that the first song he and Tom Eyen wrote for that show was "One Night Only." They started talking about the show at a Manhattan diner and Henry wrote stuff down on a napkin. *However*, I was listening to a bootleg someone had of the pre-New York tryout of *Dreamgirls* and it had a totally different song where "One Night Only" normally went. I asked Henry if he really had written "One Night Only" first or if he wrote it only when the show came to Broadway. Turns out, it *was* the first *Dreamgirls* song, but it was *cut* in Boston by Michael Bennett. Why? Because Michael thought it sounded too Jewish!!!! I know that sounds crazy, but if you listen to it, especially the minor introduction with the oboe, it does have the essence of my Bar Mitzvah. However, people in the cast were so devastated when the song was cut that they begged Michael Bennett to put the song back in. When the *ushers* joined in with the begging, he knew that "One Night Only" was too good to cut.

And now, some *Dreamgirls* movie trivia. I heard that certain executives didn't want the amazing through-sung fight scene (featuring the memorable "You're lyin', you're lyin', I never been so thin") that leads up to "And I Am Telling You" in the film, so Bill Condon filmed one version with the fight as dialogue, and one version with the fight totally sung. Thankfully, the belting triumphed. I listen to that fight scene almost every day at the gym. Brava!

At my Sirius *Live on Broadway* show, I interviewed the Marvelous Wonderettes. Backstage, I was talking to two of the ladies in the show and learning their names. Bets Malone pointed out that she was not related to fellow cast member *Beth* Malone. "You're not siblings?" I asked. She laughed and said, "What mother would possibly do that to her child?" My lower lip started trembling as I informed her that my name is Seth Rudetsky and my sister's name is *Beth* Rudetsky. She was mortified, and I then proceeded to tell her the many different ways it was annoying. Once, I put Beth in a benefit I was doing (she's a *great* singer), and more than one person said to me, "I saw the name Beth Rudetsky on the poster. Is that your drag name?" What the-? They think that the most creative drag name I can come up with for Seth Rudetsky is *Beth* Rudetsky? A single letter change? Come on! If anything, I'd use my favorite (and most offensive) drag name I've ever heard: Amber Alert.

One of the Wonderettes, Farah Alvin, said that she tried out for a small regional theatre a year ago and the director looked at her résumé and her four Broadway shows and asked her if she was in Actors' Equity. She laughed at his joke. He wasn't joking. She explained that since she had been on Broadway... four times... it meant that she was in the union. She didn't get the gig. What did he think the Broadway credits on her résumé were? Shows she'd been called back for?

I also interviewed three of the stars of *13*. The role of Evan, the Bar Mitzvah boy, is played by Graham Phillips. I told him that his name did not indicate "Bar Mitzvah" to me, but rather someone at a Country Club who is in charge of keeping it "restricted." He acknowledged that he is indeed *not* Jewish and I told him that the last time I was this outraged at a casting choice was when Michelle Pfeiffer got the lead in the film version of *Frankie and Johnny*... He was blank-faced and I soon realized that the film was made in 1991... two years before he was born. Yowtch. I knew then that I had to throw out the next few bits I had planned featuring riffs on Agnes Moorehead, Erin Moran and Tab. Essentially, my frame of reference had to be limited to *The Last Five Years*... and not just the show. For my next interview, I might as well get a microscopic camera and interview a triple-threat zygote.

The *13* CD is played in my apartment non-stop by Juli, so I pretty much know every song. There are some songs on the CD that aren't in the show and I asked Elizabeth Gillies (who plays Lucy and has a *great* voice) what happened to the amazing song "Opportunity." She said that it was her big song and it opened Act Two. Cut to: she showed up at the theatre and the creative staff said that there were some changes... the show is now only one act and "Opportunity" is cut. I asked her if she cried up a storm, and she said no. Then I asked if she emotionally shut down instead and informed her that it would serve well as an adult.

I went to go see *13* again last Saturday matinee and, turns out, they only let Graham do six shows a week so he can preserve his voice and perhaps star in *14*. The matinee Evan is Corey Snide, and from just watching him walk out during the opening number, I knew he was an amazing dancer. I checked his credits and saw that he starred in the West End as Billy Elliot. I still got it! I feel like *Wicked*'s Madame Morrible: "...and that's *my* talent. Recognizing talent."

Saturday night I stopped by Studio 54 because I knew *Pal Joey* would be teching and I wanted to say hi to my favorite Broadway director (AKA my only Broadway director), Joe Mantello. It was 9:30 and everybody was hard at work. I saw so many of the people whom I worked with on *The Ritz* that it was like a little reunion. Thankfully, I avoided my unitard. Joe was in the audience but didn't have the signature "God Mic" that so many directors use so they can angrily yell "CUT" when something goes wrong. Instead, he'd just hop up and walk over to the lighting designer or stage manager when something needed to be changed. I salute either his yoga regimen or his psycho-pharmacologist.

Scott Pask, who did the set for *The Ritz*, built an *amazing* set for *Pal Joey*. Wait 'til you see it! At one point during the rehearsal, a beautiful blonde came onstage and started singing "Zip." I nudged James and whispered knowingly, "That's Martha Plimpton." I had heard she has an amazing voice, but she sounded *clanky*! I put a frozen smile on my face, and after one minute, Joe leaned over and informed us, a) she's supposed to sound awful in this scene and b) that's not Martha Plimpton. Turns out, there's a moment in the show where someone else sings "Zip" and is supposed to stink. I went from a "know-it-all" to a "know-nothing" in four measures.

I asked Joe about *9 to 5* and if it's true that Dolly came up onstage during a performance. Turns out, when the show had to stop due to technical difficulties, she bounded up onstage and sang "9 to 5" *and* "I Will Always Love You." Brava! Unfortunately, the next time she did it, she sang "9 to 5" and then announced she was gonna sing "I Will Always Love You." Of course, the audience went crazy. Then, she found out that the set was fixed so she excitedly told everyone that she didn't need to sing and the show could go on. Crickets. The curtain came up and poor Stephanie J. Block had to sing her song. I'm sure it felt like when you're the understudy and the whole audience is mad they have to see you perform. The good news is, it was Stephanie J. Block, who has a phenomenal voice, so of course, she won the audience over with her brava belt.

Also at the tech rehearsal was everybody's favorite Latina dancer-turned-director/choreographer, Graciela Daniele. Every actor I've interviewed has said that they'd drop everything to work with her. I remembered one story she had told me when I interviewed her years ago. She was one half of Vincent and Vanessa, the tango couple in the original *Follies*. She told me about one night near the end of her run when she wasn't fully focusing because she was about to leave the show and her mind was on the future: she was in her dressing room and suddenly heard her entrance music! She panicked and flew down the staircase running into her dance partner in the wings. She started frantically explaining to him at what point in the music they could enter and still have their dance make sense. In the middle of her babbling, he cut her off with, "Graciela! Calm down! You're speaking in Spanish!" *Caramba*!

Thursday, I interviewed the Defarges from *Tale of Two Cities*. Natalie Toro (Madame Defarge) told us a great Broadway bitchery tale. When she graduated college, she was obsessed with *Les Miz* and desperate to get in it. She went to Japan to play Rosalia in *West Side Story* and was loving it (they would literally have a red carpet every night leading from the stage door). However, while she was there, they had auditions for the *Les Miz* national tour, back in New York. She was gonna try to fly back to audition for Eponine, but it takes so long to fly there that, by the time the plane landed, she'd be right for Madame Thenardier. Besides, she couldn't miss any *West Side Story* performances. She let it go.

When she got back, the casting director called her and asked her to audition. He told her it was for the "New York company" of *Les Miz*, and she was so naïve that she didn't know that meant Broadway! I guess she assumed there was a *Les Miz* company in Elmira. A few days before her audition, she tried out for a regional production of *Baby* and got it! She called the producer and told them that she had a big audition for Eponine coming up the next day (Saturday), and they said that she could postpone signing her contract until Monday at 5 PM. At the *Les Miz* audition, she ran into a woman who was at the *Baby* audition. Let's call her "Eve." Eve said, "I heard you got the role in *Baby*. Is that true? What are you gonna do if you get this?" Natalie explained that she had 'til Monday at 5 to sign the contract. Then they both auditioned and went home to wait. The good news is that Vinnie Liff (the casting director) called Natalie later and said those amazing words to her: "Welcome to Broadway." Natalie doesn't think she'll ever experience the thrill that went through her body during that phone call. The annoying news is that Vinnie told her that, after she and "Eve" auditioned, "Eve" went back, knocked on the door and told the creative people that they shouldn't give the role to Natalie... because she already had another job! *Sabateuse*! Months later, Natalie was on the subway going home after the show. She was wearing her *Les Miz* jacket and her Eponine hat, and when she looked up...

she saw "Eve" sitting across from her. They locked eyes and, as the poets say, *nary a word was spoken… but so much was said.*

Speaking of phone calls, Natalie also told us that she originated the role of Madame Defarge on the *Tale of Two Cities* concept album and then played the role in the workshops and the out-of-town tryout. She was therefore super-psyched when she found out that it was going to Broadway. One day, however, she was driving on the Van Wyck expressway, and the casting director called saying, "This is the part of my job that I hate." He told her that because there was a new director, she'd have to audition for her role. She literally pulled over to the side of the road because she was so overwhelmed. Natalie decided to have a good attitude and went into the audition feeling positive. She sang her big number, "Out of Sight, Out of Mind," and then read. The only sass she gave was on her way out when she called over her shoulder, "Happy hunting." She left the audition wanting to get a drink (!), but none of her friends were around. Instead, she went shopping… and bought what she decided would be her opening night shoes. A few hours later, her phone rang. She saw from the caller ID that it was the director. She didn't want to pick up because there was a big chance it was a "You're so wonderful… we can't use you" phone call. She finally answered, and he was very polite. He asked her what she did after the audition. She told him that she bought her opening night shoes. He could have said, "Wonderful. We'll definitely invite you opening night so you'll get a chance to wear them," but instead he told her that she got the part! For those of you who think that it always works out this way, you should know that many people originate roles and then get ixnayed for the Broadway production (Matthew Broderick in *Parade* and Carolee Carmello in *Scarlett Pimpernel*, for example). Just know that I want credit if *Rebecca of Sunnybrook Farm* goes to Broadway, and the guy playing Hamilton shoves eight chocolate chip cookies down his gullet backstage. I did it first!

Finally, I have to talk about election night. James and I went to turn on the news because we had a feeling there'd be a big announcement. We sat on the couch, anticipating history being made… and we couldn't get to a news channel! Why? Because DVR only lets you watch the shows you're taping and we were taping *The Daily Show* and *Clifford The Big Red Dog*. Son of a — !!!! By the time I figured out how to stop recording, Oprah had been crying for 20 minutes. I have to say that I, too, was crying during his acceptance speech. However, the elation we both felt about Obama being elected was monumentally depleted when we heard about Proposition 8 being passed outlawing marriage equality in California. *Thankfully, marriage equality is in SO many more states now… including California!*

This week, I'm off to L.A.! Details to follow!

Benefits with Friends
November 17, 2008

Hello from seat 3A. I'm on a Virgin America flight to L.A. and this plane is so cool. The design is very Jetsons looking and all I want to do is watch all of the TV shows and movies that are available on my personal screen in front of my seat. Instead, I will forgo the new *Indiana Jones* movie and write about this past week.

On Monday, I took Juli to school and then hightailed it uptown where I was meeting Josh Henry (from *In the Heights*) and Julia Murney (recently from *Wicked*). We were all going up to Ithaca to do a benefit for The Hangar Theater, which is now run by Peter Flynn (who also directed me in *Rhapsody in Seth* and *Broadway 101*). I'm one of those "don't talk to me until I've had my coffee" people and I decided to put off breakfast on Monday because I love acting out with food in airports. Right after my bag goes through the scanner, you can find me at some kiosk treating myself to a delish bagel/cappuccino and devouring it right before boarding. The only downside is that the bagel and coffee usually costs more than the AIG bailout, but it's worth it. Anyhoo, we met the van on 96th and Broadway at 9 AM and were soon on our way.

While we got comfortable in the van, Julia told me and Josh that she has a great "road trip" car and, for a while, she had thought she'd be driving us up to Ithaca. I was without my soothing caffeine, so I was extra sassy. I rolled my eyes at her and said, "Why would you think you were driving? We've gotten so many emails about this trip! Don't you read them?" I shook my head at her and then leaned forward and asked the driver if we were going to LaGuardia Airport or JFK. Julia looked at me like I was an idiot and said, "Neither." I realized that Ithaca was a small city, so we were probably going to one of those tiny airports. "MacArthur?" I offered. "Seth!" Julia yelled. "We're not going to any airport." I was totally confused. She spelled it out for me. "We're *driving*!" she said, with a subtext of "You're a moron." That's right, people... one minute after I busted Julia for not reading her emails, I was boomerang busted for never actually reading mine. I had done my version of reading the entire email. I would read the first part saying that we were being picked up by a van at 9 and ignore the rest. I kept wondering why the email told us the name of our driver. Why would I need to connect with "Randy" for a 30-minute drive? I soon found out that the 30-minute drive to the airport was actually a four-hour drive upstate. How long before my long-awaited breakfast and coffee?? Randy said we'd stop in an hour and a half. That did it. I turned on the charm (AKA tears) and begged him to find a Starbucks. He kindly pulled over and I loaded up on carbs and a smattering of protein. Ahhhh.

We got up there around 1 PM and met up with Andréa Burns (from *In the Heights* and Peter's wife) and Jeremy Webb (whom I had just seen in *The Visit* down at the Signature Theatre). For the benefit, Andréa and Julia did a section from *Broadway 101* where I explain that the biggest war on Broadway happens every night... between belters and sopranos. We showed what belting is (Julia sang the end of "All That Jazz") and what head voice is (Andréa did the Julie Andrews ending of "Do Re Mi"). Then I allowed that sometimes both head voice and chest voice join peacefully... and they performed "A Boy Like That." The audience ate it up.

Jeremy Webb is an Ithaca favorite because he did many Hangar Theater shows, including one where he was a suitor in the "Tom Dick and Harry" number in *Kiss Me, Kate*. The lady playing Bianca in that production was none other than Julia Murney in her first professional job!

Josh Henry closed the show with "Wheels of a Dream," and afterwards, all the performers decided to stay up late and eat/hang out. Josh and I were sort of full already since we had shoveled chocolate chip cookies (my fave) into our yaps before the show began, but it didn't stop us from shoveling more after the show. Then Andréa begged Josh to do what he does backstage during *In the Heights*, and we all went back to the room with the piano so he could demonstrate. Andréa explained that every night during the song "Home," she and Josh sit offstage and he sings a medley of Broadway songs while Mandy Gonzales and Chris Jackson sing onstage. Josh's mind is able to figure out what other Broadway songs can fit with the chord changes of "Home," and he changes it up every night. I sat down and played the piano, and while Andréa sang the main part, Josh was able to sing a countermelody including "I Have Dreamed," "Younger Than Springtime," "The Ladies Who Lunch," "The Life of the Party" from *The Wild Party*, "Patterns" and "The Story Goes On" from *Baby* and finish it off with "Being Alive"! Thankfully, I videotaped it and put it up on my website because Josh is brilliant, and the whole thing is amazing/hilarious!

Tuesday, I got back into town and hightailed it to another benefit. This time it was for The Hetrick-Martin Institute, which runs the Harvey Milk School, the NYC high school for Lesbian/Gay/Bisexual/Trans and Questioning Youth. I know the monikers sound like a headache, but there are many teens who are dealing with one of the those issues and drop out of school because of abuse they suffer at school or at home. I was there playing the piano for Cheyenne Jackson, who should sing at every benefit. He always sounds amazing, looks amazing and is hilarious. When he got onstage, he said, "Now, for those of you who don't know me, you probably looked in your program and when you saw the name Cheyenne Jackson, you expected a sassy little black girl. And to that I say... pretty much!" He then did an update on the Marcia Brady driving episode by saying that he was a little nervous before he went on, but he relaxed himself by picturing the audience in their Spanx. Tony Kushner delivered a great intro for Mary-Louise Parker, who was the honoree for the night. She said that she knew what it was like to be an outsider as a teen (she used to have Twinkies thrown at her), but she couldn't possibly understand what it was like for the children who have to come to the Harvey Milk School. She gestured to the table of kids from the school but got so choked up that she couldn't speak and, of course, everyone gave her a standing O. If they had a school like that when I was growing up, maybe I wouldn't have had so much unexpressed fear/sadness that came out in crazy ways, AKA crying for two hours after seeing *Flipper*. My mother was like, "What the-? It's just a dolphin!"

Tim Gunn from *Project Runway* was the host, and I cautiously approached him backstage and asked for a photo. He was so kind and I told him I was a big fan. When I said that I was gonna run the photo in my *Playbill* column, he recognized me and said that *he* was a big fan! I still got it! I begged him for a tip on where I should buy clothes and he recommended Club Monaco. I knew I wouldn't be using that info until I got a tip on how to actually have money to buy clothes and, though I scoured the mostly gay/lesbian audience, Suze Orman was nowhere to be found. However, a hilarious drag performer named Bianca Del Rio *was* at our table. Bianca was there to do the auction and I complimented her enormous sprayed/wrapped hairdo. She was hilarious and said, "I've always gone for the natural look... for a corpse." *He wound up winning Season Six of "RuPaul's Drag Race"!*

The worst part was the dinner. Not the food... quite the contrary. I got there and sat down and was psyched that the appetizer on my plate was a delicious shrimp cocktail. I was even more psyched when I saw that the person next to me wasn't showing up. Yes! I quickly ate their shrimp cocktail... and then they showed up. There was a plateful of empty shrimp shells, and I started panicking. Thankfully, only two people in their party arrived, and there were three empty seats, so I didn't have to use the excuse I quickly made up indicting Bianca.

Wednesday was a big day because Sirius and XM Radio officially merged. I used to only be on Sirius, but now I'm on both the Sirius *and* the XM Broadway channel. I'm still doing my radio interviews every Wednesday, and I recently had Nick Spangler and Margaret Ann Florence, who play Matt and Luisa in *The Fantasticks*. When I used to be a sub pianist for the show, it was at the Sullivan Street Playhouse, but now the show has moved to the Snapple Theater. The only problem with the theatre is that it's on top of a restaurant that sometimes gets smoky, and around every two weeks, an incredibly loud fire alarm goes off inside the theatre *during the show*! Unfortunately, it's always during the "Soon It's Gonna Rain" scene, i.e., the most romantic and quietest section of the show. It happened the night I saw it and I was alternately loving the sweet scene being played onstage and trying to remember the correct order of verbs in "Stop, Drop and Roll."

Nick is currently on TV's *The Amazing Race* with his sister and I asked him what filming it was like. He said that he didn't want the other contestants to know that he was an actor because he thought that they'd assume he was always putting on a façade, so he told people that he was going into his father's business as a funeral director. Unfortunately, unbeknownst to him, right after he told everybody, they went to an airport computer station and Googled him, which led right to his acting website. For the rest of the trip, he kept up the façade that he was in the funeral business, not knowing that they were keeping up the façade that they believed him. His version of not wanting to appear deceitful set him up to look ten times more deceitful.

Then I interviewed Constantine Maroulis from *Rock of Ages* and I, as usual, lamented the fact that he lost *American Idol*. Turns out, he wanted to sing a sassy song on the show for "'90s week," but they couldn't get the rights to the song for TV. So he was stuck with a headache-y one instead. Shockingly, that was the week he was voted off. He said that he loved doing *The Wedding Singer* on Broadway and, for some reason, keeps getting cast in '80s musicals. I offered the theory that probably his fabulous rock voice appealed to the producers plus the fact that they wouldn't have to pay for a lace-front wig.

Saturday night, we had "family fun night" and James, Juli and I watched *The Bad News Bears*. I never saw it back in the '70s, and let me just say that PG then is not like PG now. Those kids were cursing up a *storm*. When Juli asked what it meant when Tatum O'Neal said that some other kid had balls, I said it was a crazy '70s expression. She does not need to know any anatomical parts that are not on her own body!

This week, I spent a lot of days working on the Rosie O'Donnell variety show, and it looks like it's gonna be fun. *And/or cancelled after one episode.* Rosie has always loved the *Urinetown* Officer Lockstock sketches that appear during Gypsy of the Year, so she asked me, Eric Kornfeld and Hunter Foster to write some about her new show. Rosie said that we should bust her as much as possible, and we went to work. They were filmed last week with Jen Cody taking a break from *Shrek* to do her hilarious take on Little Sally, and the promos are up on Rosie's website (*Rosie.com*). This is my favorite thing I wrote:

LITTLE SALLY: Who's the host of this new variety show, Officer Lockstock?

OFFICER LOCKSTOCK: Rosie O'Donnell. Are you a fan?

LITTLE SALLY: Well, I liked her in "Misery."

OFFICER LOCKSTOCK: That was Kathy Bates, Little Sally.

LITTLE SALLY: I didn't mean the movie, Officer Lockstock, I meant the year she spent on *The View*.

OK, people, we're about an hour from L.A. Remember when I did *Broadway 101* last year and a cool lady from a production company hired me to write a sitcom about my childhood? Well, I finally finished the script, and we have our first network pitch on Tuesday! I've never pitched a sitcom before and I'm preparing myself for a sea of blank faces and significant flop sweat. I'm gonna go right from possibly tanking to taking the red eye home so I'm back for the SiriusXM show. I'm sure Orfeh and Laura Benanti will love being interviewed by a baggy-eyed, exhausted sleepwalker. Peace out!

On Pitch
November 24, 2008

This week began in sunny L.A. I was there to do my first sitcom pitch to a network, but I also got to see some friends. I stayed with Jack Plotnick, who's been one of my best friends since 1991! I met him because he went to Carnegie Mellon with many of my friends (Michael McElroy, Billy Porter, Natalie Venetia Belcon), and he called me to coach him for his *Pageant* audition. That was a brilliant show that featured men dressed as women doing a beauty pageant. The contestants were: Miss Texas, Miss Deep South, Miss Great Plains, Miss Bible Belt, Miss West Coast and Miss Industrial Northeast. It was one of the funniest shows I've ever worked on. Each contestant modeled an evening gown, had a talent and had to sell a product made by Glamouresse, the fake company that sponsored the pageant. I'm still obsessed with Miss Bible Belt's spiel. *Do you have an enlarged pore? Cleft, pit, or indentation in your skin? (She sassily/accusingly points at someone in the audience.) Ordinary make-up won't cover that up. That's why you need... Glamouresse's "Smooth-as-marble facial spackle."* She then demonstrated by taking out a section of dry wall and slathering spackle on it.

Jack and I had a great time and met up with our friend, Kali Rocha, who *also* went to Carnegie Mellon. Kali and I worked together on Broadway in *An Inspector Calls* and then she took over the Katie Finneran role in *Noises Off*. You probably know her as the annoying stewardess who makes Ben Stiller wait to board the plane in *Meet the Parents*. Right now she plays Dr. Sydney Heron, the perpetually peppy doctor, on *Grey's Anatomy*. She and I are the kind of friends that constantly repeat stupid jokes we made 15 years ago. Once we were eating at Josie's, which is a sort of health food restaurant on the Upper West Side, and for dessert they had non-dairy ice cream. The brand of the ice cream was "Mattus," and when I asked Kali what flavor she wanted, she shrugged and said, "It doesn't Mattus." That happened in '96, but we literally hauled out that headache-y chestnut last week in L.A. It wasn't funny the first time and it's not funny now, but we love it.

On the day of the pitch meeting, I went to Kali's house (and hung out with her adorable baby, Barlow) and she drove me to meet Amy, my writing partner. I've never done a pitch before, so I have nothing to compare it to, but Amy thinks that it went well. I got the network exec to laugh numerous times, especially when I was describing my arch-nemesis honors English teacher. (She once yelled at me, in front of the class, "They warned me not to put you in this class!" to which I retorted back, blank-faced, "Well, now you've learned your lesson.") After we pitched it, we sent the exec the pilot episode, so I guess we'll know soon whether he loved or hated it. It was a really fun experience to do, so either way, it doesn't Mattus. *I'm glad it didn't Mattus, because the network passed!*

I flew Virgin Atlantic home and, though I praised the flight out there, I must dish the return flight. It was a red-eye and when we asked for blankets, we were told that they ran out! Pretty much every person on a red eye wants to sleep, so how could they not have enough and run out? It's like going to a Patti LuPone concert and having her run out of belting. I arrived home and dragged myself to my SiriusXM *Live on Broadway* show. Laura Benanti was my main guest and was hi-larious. She felt she had to describe to the listening audience what it looked like in The Times Square Information Center where we do the interview. We're essentially in this big, cavernous room, and she talked about how on one side, there are people lined up buying tickets from the Broadway concierge, and on the other side, people are checking their email. She then held up several pamphlets available in various kiosks (including one for the Circle Line) and pointed out that, in the center of the room, we have a row of chairs filled with our audience. "But," she said, "instead of all those images, I want the listening audience to imagine me sitting on a beautiful velvet throne. I'm wearing a long, bejeweled gown... and so is Seth." And there it ended.

Thursday, I interviewed Olga Merediz, who plays Abuela in *In the Heights* and sings the H-E-double hockey sticks out of her big song, "Paciencia y Fe." She grew up in Cuba and fled the revolution with her parents when she was still a child. Her parents told the Cuban government that they were going on vacation to Jamaica, but they were actually going there to hide out. Unfortunately, her parents told Olga what the plan was, so she had the terrifying job of not revealing to anybody that they were escaping Cuba... and she was five years old! How did she do it? I *still* can't keep a secret, and I ain't five. If that were me, my whole family would still be in the Gulag... or whatever the Spanish word is for that. Olga finally moved to the U.S. and her first big theatre job was at a dinner theater in Maryland. The horrible thing was, not only were people eating during the show she was performing in, but she was also one of the waitresses! She'd wait on tables, do Act One, and then wait on tables again during intermission! After that, she felt that she paid her dues and moved to New York, where she worked at The Public Theater many times. She got the First National Tour of *Les Misérables*, where she was the hair hag ("What pretty hair... what lovely locks you got there!") and understudied a very young Victoria Clark, who was playing Madame Thenardier. She did the show for two and a half years (on Broadway as well), and after that, she didn't sing for *many* years. She felt like she was sung out. Don't forget, back then the show was three hours and fifteen minutes, and she said the whole time you were either singing, changing clothes/wigs or putting dirt on your face.

She started with *In the Heights* very early on in its inception, but she played the role of Camilla, Nina's mother, now played by Priscilla Lopez. They were auditioning people to play Abuela but couldn't find anybody the right age who could sing it with enough sass. Finally, they let Olga audition. She is way too young, but she aged herself with how she carried her body and she got the gig... and a Tony nomination! The only problem I can see is that nobody recognizes her when she leaves the stage door because she is so much younger/sassier than she looks onstage.

Last Thursday, James and I hightailed it to the stage door of *The Little Mermaid* because I asked Norm Lewis to leave me a copy of his long-awaited CD. We got to the stage door at around 8:45... and it wasn't there! We literally heard Norm talking to someone backstage because the stage door is so near the wings, but the doorman wasn't allowed to let me open it and bust him. I left the theatre and texted him, and two seconds later, he texted me back. We returned to the theatre and met up with him wearing his full costume covered by a bathrobe. He looked cra-za-zy, so, natch, I had to take a picture. My question is, how did he respond so quickly to my text? Where does he keep it? Under his beard? I just started listening to the CD, and he sounds *amazing*! I will be doing a full deconstruction on my site in the future. Until then, you must get the CD and obsessively replay "Before the Parade Passes By" and "This Is the Life" like I do.

When I was in L.A., I sent a few emails and finally got a babysitter for the following Saturday night because James and I had tix to *Road Show*. As Saturday approached, I realized that I had forgotten whom I hired. Finally, it was 5 PM on Saturday and I hadn't heard from anybody. I now have no idea whether I hired someone or dreamed it when I was in a Virgin America fitful sleep without a blanket. I started frantically trying to get someone to watch Juli and finally called Judy Gold, the hilarious comedian. I thought maybe Juli could go over there because she loves Judy, her partner Elisa and their two kids. Essentially, the situation that followed was an example of stereotypes being true: the two gay dads wanted to go see a Sondheim musical, but the two gay moms were unavailable because they were going to a football game. I would write a letter to the Anti-Defamation League if I saw that on a sitcom.

The final big news is that Broadway Cares/Equity Fights AIDS asked me to host the Gypsy of the Year Competition! It's the twentieth anniversary and I'm psyched!!!! Happy pre-Thanksgiving, everyone. See you after my signature eight-pound weight gain!

The Variety of Life
December 1, 2008

What a week! *Rosie Live*, the Rosie O'Donnell variety show, had its ups and downs... and by "downs," I mean it was universally reviled. *But* it was such an exciting experience! I will give details about the day of the broadcast, but let's start at the top of the week.

Sunday night, I got tickets for the opening of *White Christmas*. Kevin McCollum felt so guilty for not getting me opening night tickets to *In the Heights* that he vowed I'd always be invited to his openings. Of course, I immediately abused the privilege and begged for an extra ticket so James *and* my mom could come. It was a very star-studded event. As soon as I got off the escalator, I ran into Sutton Foster, whom I have not seen forever, and she told me that she's loving doing *Shrek*. Once I sat down, I saw Bobby Lopez and his writing partner/wife, Kristen Anderson-Lopez, sitting in the row in front of me. James was chatting with them, and afterwards he said that they must know me well because when he mentioned we might move to Brooklyn, they both remarked that I would be even more late than I normally am. I resent their accurate comment. During intermission, I heard a high-pitched Midwestern twang say, "I know you!" and got a gander at Christine Ebersole pointing at me, looking gorgeous in an all-white outfit. I was, of course, buying coffee at the bar and panicking I was going to trip and stain her ensemble. I asked her how she felt about her upcoming stint in *Blithe Spirit*, and she said she was thrilled to be performing with Angela Lansbury and Rupert Everett. Before she could elaborate and/or I could permanently destroy her outfit, I skedaddled holding my coffee cradled in my bosom. Then I saw beautiful, blonde Melissa Dye, who played Christine in *Phantom* when I was subbing there *and* Sandy when I did *Grease!* back in the'90s. She went from high soprano to high belting in one theatrical season and I say, Brava!

Melody Hollis plays the little girl in *White Christmas* and sings a sassy reprise of "Let Me Sing and I'm Happy." After she belted it out, I was about to yell my signature "She's still got it!" during the applause. Then I realized she was ten years old and modified it to "She *just* got it."

On Tuesday morning, I hightailed it to the Eugene O'Neill Theatre for a big press event about Broadway going green (*GreenBroadway.com*). Mayor Bloomberg has spearheaded Broadway becoming more ecologically aware and The Broadway League asked me to write a song for the event with Nell Benjamin, who co-wrote the score to *Legally Blonde* with her husband, Laurence O'Keefe. It wound up being a really fun event. There was one person from every Broadway show and I had an hour to teach all of them the song. I knew the musical theatre folk would pick it up fast, but felt bad because there *literally* was one person there from every Broadway show... including the plays! So I give a special shout out to the people from *Speed- the-Plow*, *August: Osage County*, *Equus*, etc. who were honorary gypsies for the day... and had honorary vocal damage for the night. Nell wrote great lyrics to my *Seussical/Schoolhouse Rock*-inspired tune. My favorite was *Broadway's going green/ One recycled Playbill can do so much good./ Broadway's going green!/ Can't do INTO THE WOODS if you run out of wood!*

Wednesday, I interviewed the current cast of *Altar Boyz*: Michael Kadin Craig, Travis Nesbitt, Neil Haskell, Mauricio Perez and Ravi Roth. Ravi (who plays Abraham) told me that, right before the end of a recent performance, a big fat fire alarm went off à la what happened at *The Fantasticks*. But the cast of *The Fantasticks* just kept going, whereas everyone evacuated at

Altar Boyz. (P.S. It was caused by something at *Rock of Ages*, which is next door). Ravi said everyone (including the audience) went to Starbucks for a half-hour and then came back for the end of the show. It was supposed to be a devastating story, but it sounded *fabulous*! I have done many shows where I've desperately craved coffee halfway through and had no relief.

Michael (who plays Matthew) talked about what it's like bringing up a woman from the audience every show and sings "Something About You" to her. He revealed that, around two weeks ago, a woman out of the blue literally put her hands down his pants! Maybe the woman thought she was at *Naked Boys Singing*, which is at the same theatre complex? Or maybe she was trying to set off the fire alarm with some hot action. Regardless, I'm glad Michael mistook me for a woman that night.

And now to *Rosie Live*. Right after I interviewed the Altar Boyz, I hightailed it to the Little Shubert Theatre where the *Rosie Live* show was rehearsing for the last time. I watched a run-through of the show and afterwards met with the creative team to talk about the show. The Clay Aiken appearance was basically Clay coming onstage in *Spamalot* drag while he and Rosie talked about how much they have in common: they both love Broadway, they both began on reality shows, and they both have a son named Parker. Then they would say that there was one more thing they have in common but they can't remember what it is. They'd rack their brains for a bit, not think of it, and then Clay would leave for his show. We felt that the sketch had no ending. I finally suggested that Rosie say: "I've got it, Clay! It's so obvious what we have in common. We're both Gay... briel Byrne fans!" Then Clay would gush about how much he loved *The Usual Suspects* and exit. Well, I thought it was a funny double-talk ending to the sketch... and was mortified to see it busted in every review of the show! *The Hollywood Reporter* called it "lame" and the *L.A. Times* called it "the world's most painfully long gay joke." Ouch! Um... any publicity is good publicity?

Hunter Foster wrote the *Urinetown*-inspired sketch with Jen Cody as Little Sally and Rosie as Officer Lockstock. Rosie wasn't at the Tuesday run-through so the other writer, Eric Kornfeld, and I played the roles, which was super fun. I *loved* the jokes in that sketch. When referencing the performance of Anti-Gravity, a gymnastic group that at one point was spinning rugs frantically, Little Sally said, "I haven't seen rugs spin that fast since Donald Trump auditioned for *Dancing With the Stars*." Hilarious!

On the day of the show, I watched Liza Minnelli and Rosie rehearse "City Lights," and it was *so* exciting. The orchestra (conducted by Kevin Stites) sounded great, and even though Liza wasn't singing out, she still has such a unique, powerful way of dancing that was thrilling to see from the first row. Then came the rehearsal with Alec Baldwin. Alec had wanted to come on the show delivering Rosie's door that would open to reveal the visiting stars (First one: Conan O'Brien). He'd hit Conan in the face with a pie when he appeared and then have Rosie hit him in the face with a pie as a follow-up. But while rehearsing it with two stand-ins, Rosie felt the pies were way too messy and should be cut because the cream was all over her hands/outfit *and* all over the floor. We finally figured out that there could be less cream in the pie so it didn't get all over the floor and that only Conan should be hit with the pie by Alec. Well, right before the show, Alec Baldwin was backstage ready to put on the plastic smock he was going to wear in the scene so he wouldn't get pie all over his clothes. But since we were ixnaying him getting a pie in the face, it wouldn't have made any sense for him to wear the plastic coat, and he wasn't dressed well enough for TV. We frantically looked for a suit jacket, and one of the producers (ironically, also named Liza) asked her boyfriend, who was in the audience, for his jacket. Alec put it on and looked sassy, and we were all relieved. Cut to the next day, one of the reviews mentioned that Alec appeared in a "jacket two sizes too small." Ouchy wowy!

Before the show began, backstage was *crammed* with people and I heard Rachael Ray rehearse the one line she had in the holiday song Gloria Estefan wrote. After she sang, Rachael laughed and commented: "I sound that way because I'm pre-op." I gave her a brava because I thought she was joking about having a low voice because she's transitioning to a man... but turns out she was talking about getting surgery over the holidays for a benign cyst that's affecting her voice. I hope it doesn't change her voice too much... I love her raspy/Andrea McArdle quality!

At around 7:50 PM, I hightailed it to the "truck." That's where all the technical stuff was happening. I was there so the executive producer could tell me if the show was running long or short ('cause it was live) and, if so, I would get on my headset and talk to Eric (the other writer) backstage who would tell the teleprompter person what to cut or add. It was very exciting/nerve-wracking being in the truck. There were around 15 different TV screens on the wall representing all of the different cameras, and the director was constantly yelling which one he wanted. ("One! Go! Go to five! GO! Back to One, one one!!!!! Pull out!!") Right next to me was the lighting designer, who was also yelling cues the whole time. I was incredibly anxious and realized it wasn't just because of the frantic activity all around me, but because I had two big jokes in Rosie's opening monologue. She told us that she wanted to talk about wearing Spanx and asked for some "hits," as we call it in the biz. I was so excited when she picked mine but then terrified that they would elicit crickets. It would be an awful way to start the show. She came out, looking glam and asked the crowd:

"How do I look? I haven't had surgery, I just got Spanx. Do you know what that is? It's an industrial strength girdle... super-sized. It's essentially a onesie for chubby 40-somethings."

That got a really big laugh and I felt relief flood through me. Then she talked about how it doesn't actually get rid of fat, it just pushes and smushes all of it upwards. She then pointed to her boobs and said, "These are actually my thighs." When that joke got a big laugh and then applause, I literally started crying. I was so nervous it was going to tank, I literally wept tears of joy. Cut to the next day, the reviews talked about her tired Spanx jokes. What the-? Tears of sadness?

It was one of the times where you have no idea what the reaction is. After the show, the audience was in a great mood, and so was everybody at the after-party. It wasn't until I started reading the reviews that I realized the pilot was going to be it, and there'd be no series.

All in all, it was a great experience and the reason I'm not that devastated the pilot failed is because it tanked for the right reason. A lot of times, Broadway shows bomb because there's a big committee that decides everything and all the decisions are diluted. No one takes responsibility for anything. Rosie really was the head of the show and every decision was approved through her. She wrote on her blog that it was the show she wanted to do, and even though she's disappointed it didn't work out, she had a great time doing it... and I agree! It's much better to fail with your own vision than to fail with the regret of having your vision compromised.

Peace out, and enjoy your leftover turkey... or for my fellow vegetarians, left-over Tofurkey... which actually sounds less gross than it actually is.

Charles Strouse, *Road Show* and *Gypsy of the Year*
December 8, 2008

Today and tomorrow is *Gypsy of the Year* and I'm *so* excited to be hosting. I went to my first *Gypsy of the Year* back in 1992 when I was conducting *Pageant* and James Raitt (the vocal arranger and original music director of *Pageant* and *Forever Plaid*) wrote an amazing version of "Memory" featuring the guys from *Plaid* and the "ladies" from *Pageant*. I loved how Grizabella was spoken of in the third person during the arrangement and how James added all these amazing asides ("Mem'ry... She can smile at the old days... she was beautiful then... *pretty kitty*").

Gypsy of the Year is such a fun variety show, but the main purpose of it is to celebrate all the fundraising that's happened over the last six weeks for Broadway Cares/Equity Fights AIDS. It's appropriate that I started this column talking about James Raitt because he's one of *many* incredible people we've lost to AIDS. James was 41 when he died and besides the world losing a very giving man (who I can never fully repay for giving me my start in the NY theatre scene), I'm overwhelmed when I think how much amazing music we'll never hear because he never got a chance to create it. The fundraising period may be over, but if you want to keep helping BC/EFA, hightail it to their website, where they have phenomenal gifts for your theatre-loving friends. Tons of DVDs, ornaments, CDs and autobiographies signed by Broadway stars and both *The Q Guide to Broadway* and *Broadway Nights* signed by me.

I interviewed Charles Strouse, Freddie Gershon and Andrea McArdle at my SiriusXM *Live on Broadway* show. Charles was there talking about his new book, *Put on a Happy Face*, which I am *loving*. There are so many great stories about Broadway! And I love that he worked as a jingle writer in the '70s. He was supposed to produce a jingle for a new drink called Razzle Root Beer. After they recorded the jingle, the advertising agency found out that they couldn't use the word "Razzle" because it infringed upon a copyright. There was an awkward silence in the recording studio... and suddenly Charles suggested they change the name of the drink to *Ramblin'* root beer. They gave him the OK, he re-recorded the jingle with the singers who were still there, substituting "ramblin'" for "razzle," and the root beer became a *big* seller. I totally remember that root beer, and I just looked up one of the commercials on *YouTube* and it features all different New York scenes... including a shot of Sarah Jessica Parker as Annie, which he also wrote. Subliminal advertising??? Brava!

Freddie Gershon is the CEO of Music Theatre International, which licenses *Annie*, and was at my show to present Charles with a book filled with letters from little girls around the world who've written about how important *Annie* is to them. I did a casual flip through the book to see if *I* was one of the little girls, but didn't see my bad handwriting. Freddie talked about one instance when a school down South licensed the show but then sent all the material back in the mail a week later. Freddie called the principal of the school to see why it was returned. The principal said that *Annie* was satanic. Huh? Freddie asked what was satanic about it (besides the E flat that Star-to-Be has to sustain, which obviously requires a deal with the devil), and the principal says that the script mentions... Hell's Kitchen!!! Freddie explained the misunderstanding:

FREDDIE: Hell's Kitchen? Satanic? Hell's Kitchen is the name of a neighborhood in New York City.

PRINCIPAL: I rest my case.

After the interview, I met my Mom and my friend Tim and we saw the matinee of *Forbidden Broadway*. This has to be the best one I've ever seen. *Hilarious.* The cast was fantastic. I don't know how Michael West is able to do Harvey Fierstein's voice without inflicting permanent vocal damage, and Gina Kreiezmar does the best Patti LuPone imitation I've ever seen. Christina Bianco does so many imitations perfectly, and I'm mind-boggled that during her spot-on Chenoweth imitation, she sings the end of "Glitter and Be Gay" and hits the high E flat full-out! *She's now become a YouTube sensation for her amazing imitations of pop stars!* The very last part of the show is a takeoff on *Sunday in the Park with George*, but instead of it being about George as a painter, it's about Sondheim as a composer. Cutie James Donegan did a great Sondheim. In the last moment, he stands onstage, surrounded by classic Sondheim characters. It was such a theatrical moment and it made me realize all of the great roles Sondheim has given to theatre. I got so moved thinking about all the possibilities theatre has to offer that I literally started crying in the audience. Right after the show, I saw James Donegan coming out of the theatre and I told him how great I thought he was. He smiled... and then looked at me strangely like I was acting weird. I didn't know what was up and finally asked if I knew him, because I'm notorious for not recognizing people. Well, typical for me; not only do I know him, but turns out, he's dating Marc Tumminelli, a good friend of mine, *They're now married!* and was literally at my last birthday party!

Let me just say for the record, it's not because I meet so many people that I forget what they look like; I literally have a hard time recognizing people's faces. It's not quite at the level of the guy who had a profile in *The New York Times Magazine* because he couldn't recognize himself in the mirror, but it's close! Here are two examples of my issue: when I was first watching *Friends*, I was outraged that Matt LeBlanc and Matthew Perry were on the show. Why? Because I thought they looked exactly like twins. Complete lookalikes. Then when I saw *L.A. Confidential*, I couldn't understand why one character was really nice and then he'd suddenly turn mean. I had no idea how I was supposed to feel about him. Was he a horrible person? An amazing person? It wasn't until near the end of the movie did I realize that I thought Guy Pearce and Russell Crowe were the same person!!!! So, if I meet you for the twentieth time, don't be mad if I introduce myself like you're a stranger. It's because I *do not* recognize you. And if I re-tell a story you've heard me tell a million times, it's not because I don't recognize you, it's because I only have a dozen stories, and I refuse to get new material.

P.S. On a Sondheim tangent, I was on the phone with my Mom while I was walking my dog, and she told me that the only song she likes from *Sunday in the Park with George* is "Tell Me on a Sunday." I explained that "Tell Me on a Sunday" is by Andrew Lloyd Webber and from *Song and Dance*. She paused... and then asked what show "Never on a Sunday" is from. And I'm out.

Still speaking of Sondheim, James and I went to see *Road Show* on Saturday night. A few hours before the show, I took Juli ice-skating in Bryant Park, and her babysitter met us there. I told her how long Juli could continue to ice skate for, where to get Juli dinner, and what time her bedtime was, and then I went downtown to meet James. At 7:59, James and I sat in our seats in The Public Theater and he casually asked me if I gave the babysitter the keys to the apartment. I had not. Immediate lights down and the show began. During the first Sondheim-ian chord, I hid my phone underneath my *Playbill* and awkwardly texted the babysitter and told her get the keys from my friend Jack Plotnick, who was visiting. Thus followed the most uncomfortable hour and 40 minutes where we were watching the show but inwardly panicking that the babysitter and Juli would be locked out of the apartment when we returned. Well, not to worry, it all worked out... if by "worked out" you mean James and I having a huge fight in the subway on the way home, me shutting down emotionally, and Juli having a major tantrum with the babysitter, leading me to pay her double for the night. *But* it was great to see my friends Aisha deHaas, Anne Nathan and Kristine Zbornik in the show. They all had great featured parts. Especially in the song "Tell Me on a Sunday." "Never on a Sunday"? "Sunday is Funday at Carvel"?

Finally, I saw *Speed-the-Plow* and thought the actors were all great. Elisabeth Moss was a great foil to both men and I'm obsessed with Jeremy Piven's vaudevillian physicality. Plus Raúl Esparza had so many sassy, dry zingers that I want to see him do *Company* again but this time play Joanne.

OK, I have to go get ready for *Gypsy of the Year*, and by "get ready," I mean not prepare and instead obsessively watch the *In the Heights* video Lin-Manuel Miranda made where he made a dream come true for Nicholas Dayton, a ten-year-old boy. The kid was a super-fan of the show, and his Mom told Lin-Manuel that they were coming on a Saturday. The whole cast stayed after the matinee and performed the entire finale onstage... and Lin had the kid play and sing his part! *And* he was amazing! I can't help but weep when I watch it... it's so moving! Google "Dreams Come True In The Heights" and pass the tissues. Peace out!!!!

Laughter Is the Best Medicine
December 15, 2008

OK. Let me first talk about the fun stuff from last week. Monday and Tuesday was the 20th annual *Gypsy of the Year* competition and I had an amazing time hosting it. Right before the show began, I saw Harvey Evans. Every time I see him, he tells me that he's retired, and then I see him kickin' up his heels at another gig. Last year, after I lamented the fact that he stopped his sassy singing/dancing, I then saw him featured dancing around Central Park in the film *Enchanted* as well as doing the same number on the Oscars. Of course, his recent version of retiring was standing backstage, waiting to star in the opening number. Essentially, he's had more farewell tours than Cher. At this point, he needs to acknowledge that he is the perpetual Gypsy of the Year... he'll never stop gigging!

After the opening, Tyne Daly and Jonathan Hadary took the stage and told the audience that they were the first hosts of *Gypsy of the Year* 20 years ago... right after they opened in *Gypsy*. They remembered someone from the *Phantom* company doing an anatomically correct "Dance of the Seven Veils" and, as Tyne put it, "every time you thought it was over, off came another veil." After that, Jonathan said, BC/EFA started to screen the acts before they went onstage. They then introduced me and I came out and chitty-chatted with them. I asked Jonathan why he was bald in a recent photo I saw but now sported a full head of hair. Is he the Ted Danson of Broadway? He said that he played a role a few months ago where the character was supposed to be bald, and Tyne advised him to shave his head because she felt he would hate wearing a wig cap all summer. Tyne was advising from her own experience because when she turned 50, she wanted to begin what she called the second half of life the way she began the first half... completely hairless. And so, she shaved every hair on her body... except her eyebrows. Jonathan took her advice, but it backfired because he got a review saying that he was wearing the worst bald cap ever made! I then mentioned to Tyne that since the musical *Gypsy* is constantly revived, we should probably assume that it will come back again in a few years and, by the law of averages, someone sitting in the audience will probably be playing Mama Rose. Any tips? She turned out, glared and advised, "She is *not a monster*!" and stormed off. She's still got it.

Daniel Radcliffe (Harry Potter!) was there and is *such* a fan of musical theatre. *Foreshadowing his triumphant performance in HOW TO SUCCEED!* He was watching the opening number rehearse and stood there with his eyes wide in awe, mouth hanging open. Before he went on for the *Equus* sketch, he was standing backstage, shirtless, next to me. This time, *I* was standing with my eyes wide in awe, mouth hanging open.

Onstage, I did my signature deconstructing bit where I compare Patti LuPone's amazing modulation in "Rainbow High" to Madonna singing the same thing in the film version, and Daniel told me that his father saw me on Monday and went home that night and kept playing each version back and forth. Yes! I appeal across the pond! I also deconstructed how Friedrich in the original production of *Sound of Music* sang the "la" in "Do Re Mi" and couldn't belt it, so he did it in a headache-y head voice. Later on, Christine Baranski passed me backstage and muttered, "You're right, you know. About that 'la.' It always bothered me." Yes! I appeal to Tony winners!

All in all, the show was thrilling and the whole thing raised $3.5 million. Yay, Broadway!!!!

On Wednesday, I interviewed Greg Jbara from *Billy Elliot—The Musical* at my SiriusXM *Live on Broadway* show. We've known each other since we did *Forever Plaid* together on a national tour… and by "national tour," I mean Baltimore and San Diego. Anyhoo, he's playing the dad now in *Billy Elliot* and loving it. He had moved to L.A. and said he wouldn't be doing New York theatre because his kids go to school there and it's too hard to take them out… but then the writers' strike happened. He was living off his savings and they asked him to audition for *Billy Elliot*. He *loved* auditioning for Stephen Daldry because Stephen spent so much time with him, having him try scenes all different ways. At one point, he's supposed to discover Billy in a ballet class and pull him out of it, and Stephen asked him to imagine himself showing up at the class, and all the little ballet girls were holding Uzis. That image was to help Greg feel that the girls were actually dangerous. Smart! Greg is loving the show, except that recently the giant puppet of Maggie Thatcher that flies in during the opening of Act Two got stuck on the stage. So, during his big, dramatic number that followed, he was totally upstaged by an oversized Maggie Thatcher being slowly lowered and hauled off the stage by the crew. He said he can usually see audience members wiping tears from their eyes during that song, but instead he saw rows of them pointing and laughing.

Also at my SiriusXM show was my Saturday radio co-host, Christine Pedi, who's currently doing her show, *Christine Pedi's Holly Jolly Christmas Folly* at the Laurie Beechman Theatre (see *ChristinePedi.com* for deets). I asked her about the amazing imitation of Elaine Stritch sung to "Zip" from *Pal Joey* she did in *Forbidden Broadway*: "*Stritch! / Nothing riles you up or makes you turn red. / Stritch! / You're so deadpan people think that you're dead!*"

Christine did that song in a performance of *Nothin' Like a Dame*, and Elaine was going to appear onstage at the very end and bust her. Christine was called to Stritch's dressing room before the show to discuss how it should be done. (In Stritch's voice:) "Christine! After the number, I want you to take a long bow to the right, a long bow to the center and long bow to the left. Then turn to exit and I'll be there. I'll back you into the wing." Well, Chris did the number, did the bows and went to exit… but Stritch wasn't there. What to do? She just decided to keep exiting. She kept walking and Stritch didn't appear! When Christine was one inch from walking into the wing, Stritch appeared. She and Christine stood nose-to-nose. So now instead of backing her across half the stage, Stritch set it up so she was able to back Christine across the *whole* entire stage. Christine was walking backwards and nervous she'd back into the pit. Christine demonstrated for us how Stritch helped her by muttering *sotto voce* (in Stritch voice), "That's it… a little to the left… that's right… don't veer…" all under her breath while maintaining a glaring face. Hilarious juxtaposition. Christine just got a great NY *Times* review, so get thee to her show!

On Thursday, I interviewed Haydn Gywnne, who plays the dance teacher in *Billy Elliot*. Turns out, she didn't think she'd ever pursue acting and worked as a teacher in Italy. Finally, she acknowledged she wanted to be a performer and moved back to England to give it a try. She got into a theatre school, but right before she began, got cast by Alan Ayckbourn in his company. She then made her musical theatre debut in *Ziegfeld*, one of the West End's notorious flops, directed by Joe Layton. I asked for a scandalous story and she said I'd have to take her out and get her drunk for details. Since I'm not in the habit of forcing ladies to drink spirits in order to get my way, I segued to her first hit musical, *City of Angels*. She was the sassy secretary in the

London debut and got to sing "You Can Always Count on Me." The show got amazing reviews but didn't hit it off with the public and therefore closed very quickly. What's annoying is that it won the Best Musical Olivier Award, which would have helped ticket sales tremendously, but it opened right after the deadline for that year's awards, so it didn't win until almost a year after it closed. That and a nickel will get you on the subway. Or should I say, that and a ha'penny will get you on the tube. She got a lot of work on television (or "telly" as she called it), and I didn't understand how that was possible since I thought there's only one channel in England. I asked and didn't get a straight answer. Regardless, she tried out for *Billy Elliot* using her song from *City of Angels*. Then they asked her if she could dance. She told us she couldn't decide whether to act British and say she couldn't dance at all or be what she called American and claim she was an amazing dancer. She finally told them that she didn't have training but picked up steps very well. The choreographer took her out of the room and she mentally prepared herself for a vigorous dance call. He asked her to do something like "Walk, walk, touch" and then took her back to the audition room and told the rest of the creative team that she passed. Wow. Maybe the original concept for the dance teacher was more along the *Whatever Happened to Baby Jane?* type, AKA sitting in a wheelchair.

Anyhoo, she got the gig and loved doing it. She heard that it might move to Broadway and was interested in doing it but didn't want to appear too eager. "I finally asked Stephen… but I was incredibly British about it, so I said something along the lines of, 'If this goes to Broadway, would I be wrong in assuming I might be considered for the role or would I not?'" He gave her a firm but friendly, "No"… but because of the British double talk in her question, she didn't know if he was saying she was wrong in assuming she *would* go or wrong in assuming that she would *not* go. She didn't find out she was going to Broadway until a few weeks before rehearsals began!

At one point during the interview, I was showing some video from the show that featured one of the young Billy Elliots doing some crazy ballet steps, and I coyly asked her if I was too old to play Billy. She gave me a firm but *un*-friendly, "Yes"… and then followed it with "But you're not too tall." Brava on the sass!

Okay, here's the depressing part of this week. James said I should call this column "A Very Special Episode." I'm writing this from Houston because, a couple of days ago, James' mom discovered that she has uterine cancer. It was completely unexpected. She had been getting all of her regular check-ups, but something was missed and it got very advanced. As hard as this has been for all of us throughout this ordeal, lots of hilarious things have happened. The day we heard the diagnosis, we were on our way to see an apartment. I quickly called the realtor and had this conversation:

SETH: Hi. I'm sorry about the last-minute notice, but we can't come today. James' mom just discovered that she has cancer (now crying), and we're both trying to figure out what to do. We just got the call a few minutes ago.
REALTOR: What?
SETH: Oh. Um… well, we can't come today because James' mom found out that she has cancer (crying again). We have to cancel and…
REALTOR: What?
SETH: Did you hear what I said?
REALTOR: Most of it.

SETH: OK. So, like I said, we're going home to figure out what to do.
REALTOR: So... do you wanna see it tomorrow?
SETH: Um... I don't know.
REALTOR: Because it's really a great space.
SETH: We'll get back to you!

I assumed he didn't hear the cancer part and just the canceling part, but then I got an email saying he was sorry she had cancer, but we should definitely look at the apartment.

Okay, that was craziness number one. Next. When his mom was visiting for Thanksgiving, she saw a hat on my wall that my high school friend Kevin Gerber made for his store. Kevin has his own hat line (Kevin Todd), and one day, Liza Minnelli came into the store and bought one. He had her autograph one of the ones in his store and then gave it to me because he knew I'd appreciate it more than he. James' mom saw it hanging on my wall and admired it, so I decided to bring it to Houston to give to her, but because I didn't want it to get crushed, I decided to wear it to the airport... even though I looked crazy. I figured I wouldn't run into anybody on my way to pick up Juli from school to catch our flight. Of course, a half block from my apartment, I hear, "Seth!" That's right... It was David Hyde Pierce running across the street to tell me how much he enjoyed *Gypsy of the Year*. He saw the hat and said, "I didn't know you were orthodox." Oy. I then ran to the school and immediately told Juli how great she'd look in the hat and promptly put it on her. When I arrived in the hospital bearing my gift, Elizabeth (James' mom) was shocked I would give it away and asked me, "Are you just giving this to me because you know I'm dying and you'll get it back soon?" Still sassy. She has to get radiation and chemo, so we're now going to jumpstart our apartment search so she can move in with us and get her treatment at Sloan Kettering.

The next crazy thing that happened was James and I got a hotel to stay in for the night and when we approached our room, it looked like the light was on. Did the maid clean it and forget to turn it off? James opened the door... to a room already occupied. Yay. Thankfully, the occupants weren't in bed with a shotgun aimed towards us (it is Houston, after all). We got the key to another room, and at 5 AM, I heard loud running right outside our room and then "Don't Move!!!" followed by a weak, "I'm not moving." It sounded like a woman was being arrested outside our door. Then for 20 minutes I heard "Ow! I can't breathe! Too tight!" I suddenly thought, what if she's not being arrested but being kidnapped? Of course, selfish-style, I fell back to sleep. Then, at 7 AM, someone banged on our door. "Who is it?" we called. More banging... then silence. We called James' mom, who said that our hotel was a notorious "cat house." What's happening? We literally checked into *The Best Little Whorehouse in Texas*? The front desk told us that the woman arrested was roaming through the parking lot, trying all the car door handles and was finally caught by the police. That info was followed with, "She must have been on some good stuff because they had to hog tie her to get her into the car." And cut! We got our money back.

I'm on my way back to New York to do my Sirius Wednesday talk show with *Forbidden Broadway* cast and Raúl Esparza, and then I'm gonna meet up with James in Dallas to do my workshop and then come back to Houston for the holidays. I will keep everybody updated next week. And, not to end with an old chestnut, but... hug someone you love today! *P.S. It turned out to be stage 3 uterine/ovarian cancer. And she just had her five year all-clear check-up! You can survive that kind of cancer!*

Leaving On a Jet Plane — Maybe
December 22, 2008

Traveling, thy name is headache.

I must write about my airport experience, but let's first start on Broadway.

On Tuesday, I flew back from Houston and hightailed it to the endodontist. Why? Well, after you lose your wallet (last Thursday) and find out that your partner's mom has cancer, one of the fun things to do is get a root canal. That's right, two hours after my plane landed, I was in a chair getting three Novocain shots. FYI: here's a little tip. My tooth was crazily sensitive to heat, and I knew that heat sensitivity was much worse than being sensitive to cold. But then the heat stopped bothering me. Ah... perhaps I was cured? The endodontist put something crazily hot next to my tooth, and I proudly said, "It doesn't hurt at all... I guess I'm all better!" He then informed me that the reason it didn't hurt is because the nerve that reacts to heat had *died*! He told me that patients often have sensitive teeth, and then they feel better and think they're cured. They relax and then come staggering in, weeks later, with a *crazy* abscess! So, if you have pain, get thee to the dentist!

After my root canal, Juli and I went to see *Hairspray* for the fourth time. Seeing Harvey Fierstein play Edna is like seeing Barbra Streisand play Fanny Brice. It's the perfect melding of actor and role. Every line he says/look he gives is perfect. And it was *so* fun to see Marissa Jaret Winokur back in her Tony Award-winning role. I hung out with her after the show in her dressing room and she kept busting herself for being short and old. Example A: I asked her about the beautiful pink coat hanging up. She explained that she was neurotic about getting sick when she was first doing the show and told the producers she was scared she'd get a cold from performing outside on the Macy's Thanksgiving Day Parade. To keep her snug, they made her an amazing pink coat to wear. After the parade, they told her she could keep it. Marissa told Juli to try it on for fun. Juli put it on and it fit... perfectly. Juli is eight years old and not fully grown. Marissa is. Ouch.

Also, Marissa is playing opposite Constantine Rousouli, who is adorable as Link, her love interest. She told me that she asked him what year he was born and, when she found out, became emotionally plunged because she realized that while she was playing Jan in the '90s revival of *Grease!* and I was the pianist, Constantine was seven years old. Not cool. Essentially, after hearing that news, she feels like Michael Douglas to his Catherine Zeta-Jones, and I feel like Eubie Blake.

I interviewed Raúl Esparza at my SiriusXM *Live on Broadway* show. I told the audience that he was starring in the wordy *Speed-the-Plow* and, as a joke, I asked him, "How'd you memorize all those lines?" He gave me a sassy look and asked me if I really just posed that question... and I then decided I actually *was* interested in knowing how he memorized all those lines. After I did *Torch Song Trilogy* at The Gallery Players, people asked me that question all the time, and I always would tell them about the hour-long train ride to Brooklyn (and back) that gave me plenty of time to drill my lines. Raúl had no such interesting answer. After appropriately rolling his eyes, he finally informed us that he just said his lines a lot in rehearsal and eventually they were memorized. Boring! Where's the "I say them into a tape recorder and play them back"? Or the "I hired someone to play the other two parts and run lines with me every night"? In the '80s, my friend Charlie Schwartz was hired to run lines with Sally Struthers when she was doing the female *Odd Couple*. And when I was studying piano as a child, there was a whole technique I had to use for memorizing classical pieces. My teacher would make me play the measure while looking at the music, play it on my lap without looking, and then play it again on the piano by heart. How come I have so many interesting memorizing techniques and I'm not even being interviewed? How come all Raúl has is "say them a lot 'til they're memorized"? How come I ask a question as a joke and am then outraged when I don't get a serious answer? It's called passive/aggressive.

I texted Raúl before the interview and asked him if he'd sing. When he got to the show, he had a stack of music from his piano that he had grabbed on his way out of his apartment. I searched through everything and demanded he first sing "Being Alive" (he's still got it!) and then end the show with a song he just did for a Marvin Hamlisch concert: "Soliloquy" from *Carousel*. He's always so willing to sing anything whenever we do stuff together. There's a great video of him on my *Chatterbox* show where he kept singing songs from his audition book... ending with "Defying Gravity"! Check it out (especially his ending on my piano bench) at my website.

Thursday, I interviewed John Tartaglia, the original Princeton/Rod in *Avenue Q*. He told us that he's been equally obsessed with Broadway and puppets since he was a kid. When he was six years old, he remembers being in his backyard and mapping out where people would stand for his staging of "Tradition." He then realized that the only people he had to use were himself and his two parents. What about the other citizens of Anatevka? He convinced his mother to drive him around town where he hung up signs giving the date and time of auditions for his production of *Fiddler*, AKA the song "Tradition." Unfortunately, he was then devastated when no one showed up. I couldn't believe his mom actually went with him to hang up signs and he said that she's an actress and has always encouraged him. When he was a little older, he saw that PBS was having a pledge drive, and if you donated a certain amount of money, you would get Bert and Ernie stickers. He begged and begged his mother to donate and finally, after much harassment, she made the call. As he stood there, she dialed quickly, said she was donating and gave her name and address. For months, John kept asking when the stickers were coming, and she explained to him that it took time. It wasn't until a few years ago, as he was walking down the street, that he realized, "Wait a minute! I don't think there was anybody on the other end of the that phone call!!" Like I said, she always encouraged him. And by "encouraged," I mean "tricked."

As a teen, he wrote letters to Jim Henson all the time and finally got to intern at *Sesame Street*, which mostly consisted of doing "right hand work." That's what Jen Barnhart does during *Avenue Q*. As one person holds the puppet and does the voice, another is right next to the main person and controls the right hand. John said it's the hardest thing to do because you're not in control. You have to estimate what the other person is going to do and follow along. *And* when it's on TV, you're in back of the set, reaching your hands over and watching everything on a TV screen. So every time you have to use a prop, you have to reverse your perspective because what's on the screen is backwards. Ow, my head hurts.

Right when he was about to begin college, he got hired by *Sesame Street*, so he moved into a studio apartment when he was 18 and did puppeteering while pursuing acting. I asked him about his first audition, and wow, what a story... He read that *The Lion King* was coming to Broadway and looking for actors and puppeteers. Perfect! But he didn't have a headshot. *No problem*, he thought, *there's a place that does headshots down the block*. It was the same store that did family portraits and passport photos. He made an appointment (for an hour later), got his haircut and showed up wearing a perfect headshot outfit: a vest and a bow tie. 'Nuff said. He went to the audition site (890 Broadway) and sat in the waiting room with around 20 other people. Twenty other black people. Who were also women. Finally, one of them tapped him and asked, "Sweetheart... do you know that this is a *Lion King* audition?" "Yes, I do!" he said with a proud grin and looked down at his music. *Pause*. She tapped him again. "Sweetheart, do you know it's an audition for the role of Rafiki?" *Pause*. Then with sudden feigned confidence ,"Yes, I do." He actually had read the date wrong and hadn't been planning on auditioning for the role of the black female belting baboon, but he decided to go through with it anyway. *Pause*. Tap, tap, tap again. "You're gonna be just fine," she said and walked away.

The casting person came out and read his name with a questioning lilt. *Jo-ohn Tartaglia?* Could it be a sassy woman's name à la Michael Learned? No, she saw as he stood up, it's an 18-year-old white Italian boy. John said he walked in and two people in the room looked horrified, and one had a look that said, "Uh-oh... did I schedule this by accident?" John stood center and launched into his 16-bar version of "Can You Feel the Love Tonight?" He got through around 7 measures of his 16 bars before getting an enormous "Thank you!" with a full "circle hand." He said the hand that cut him off started off high above the head of the person saying "thank you" and wrapped around in a full 360-degree-circle so as to prevent any possible extra singing. Of course, he thought that they cut him off early because he was so amazing. He walked out with chin held high, waiting for the phone to ring. I asked him if, à la the Bert and Ernie stickers, he was walking down the street years later and suddenly thought, "Wait a minute! That 'thank you' *wasn't* because I was amazing!" P.S. To this day, he's been trying to find out who was in the audition room, but no one "remembers" being there. Note to the Jay Binder Casting office: therapy can help people recall traumas they've blocked out.

I told John that I was *so* impressed with his performance as Pinocchio in *Shrek*. He took a role that didn't necessarily have funny line after funny line and found *such* comedic takes on them. I thought he was hi-larious and I asked him how he thought of adding a southern twang. Apparently, during rehearsal, all of the fairy tale characters in the show had to stand up and talk about their history and their relationships to the other characters. He decided that the wood that made Pinocchio was from trees in Georgia, and that's why he speaks like a combo of Clay Aiken and Jackée from *227*. And if you need a Xmas present for a puppet/Broadway loving kid, get the DVD of his TV show, *Johnny and The Sprites*. The puppets are adorable and it's so Broadway: music by people like Stephen Schwartz or Bobby Lopez and appearances by Chita Rivera and Sutton Foster!

All right, here's my amazing traveling experience. I had a ticket to fly to Dallas on Friday morning, where I was gonna meet James and then teach a musical theatre audition workshop the next day. I knew there was gonna be a storm but was so relieved to wake up and see that there was no snow. My plane was scheduled to leave at 6:45 AM (!) from Newark, but I didn't care about the early hour because it meant I was gonna miss the snow. I got to the airport and looked up at the big board with flight information, and instead of seeing the gate listed next to my flight, I saw the word CANCELED. The plane we were gonna fly out on must have been coming from somewhere that was snowed in. I stood on many lines and finally got a stand-by ticket on an 8:30 AM flight. I waited and couldn't get on the flight. I then went back to the line, and the guy ahead of me turned to me and said, "Make it stop, Seth." Huh? Was my passport around my neck and hanging open with my Jewish name for all to see? Turns out, he just got back from playing Mark in the national tour of *A Chorus Line* and recognized me from "the biz." I still got it! I finally got to the head of the line and the agent I spoke to told me I could get on a flight... four days later!! What the-?! I *had* to make that workshop. Finally, a nice agent got me a flight leaving in two hours... to Houston... from LaGuardia! Inconvenient, considering I wanted to go to Dallas, *and* I was in Newark Airport, but he put me in first class and didn't charge me extra, so I didn't mind the $90 cab ride. I *did* mind the cab driver not checking what terminal Continental Airlines was in. He kept insisting it was C. As we drove around, he told me, "C should be for Continental and A should be for American. All the other small airlines should be B." Maybe... but *that's not how it is*! We sat in the backseat while he meandered around LaGuardia forever trying to find my terminal, and he finally dropped me off at a baggage area. I ran upstairs, went through security and settled into delicious first class. The "fun" part was when the guy next to me got up and spilled water *all* over my seat, which completely soaked one side of my pants and seeped through to my underwear. There was no way I could dry it all off, so I just accepted I'd have one side of my pants dripping wet. I got up to go to the bathroom, and as I got out, I saw a guy in the front row look at my pants and widen his eyes in shock. It's always fun for someone in the first class section of a plane to look at you and think you've soiled yourself in the bathroom. Mortifying. Regardless, I landed in Houston, got a flight to Dallas and had a great time teaching my workshop.

This week, I'm in Houston with James, his sister, Juli and his mom. I head back right after Christmas and, hopefully, we'll finally get a new apartment. Hanukkah just began, so make sure you enjoy plenty of latkes and all the other signature deep fried Jewish foods that have prevented most members of my family from wearing two-piece bathing suits since the mid-'70s. And don't forget to see the Broadway shows that are closing!

Home for the Holiday
December 29, 2008

Hello, everyone! This year is coming to an end. Wah! Sad face. COL (crying out loud).

Anyhoo, I just got back from Houston and here's my update. Let's see: Before I left, I went to see *Shrek* and must give a shout out to the terrific cast. Chris Sieber had so many fun-nee moments as Lord Farquaad that I have briefly forgiven him for appearing on the Olsen twin sitcom *Two of a Kind*. Let me follow that with a) I don't have a sitcom credit for anyone to forgive me for and b) I'm sure Chris is accepting my forgiveness as he rows to his stunning accessible-only-by-boat manse he bought with his sitcom money. Seriously. He owns an island. I spoke to him afterwards about the moment in Act Two when he pulls up on his horse and says, "Whoa, *Xanadu*." Apparently, he changes the name of his horse nightly (recent names: Beyoncé and Condoleeza). Hmm… perhaps "Rudetsky" could one day be an option? Are there Jewish horses? Holsteins? Are they just cows?

Speaking of Jewish cows, my sister (no, not her… wait for it) was visiting from Norfolk, and went to a Jewish Steakhouse (AKA Jewish cow) on Saturday with another couple and their rabbi (and his wife) from her shul. I told Nancy I would stop by "for drinks" (Manischewitz?), and as soon as I sat down, Nancy commented on my inappropriate outfit. Not only was I wearing a T-shirt in a fancy restaurant, but the restaurant itself was Glatt Kosher, and my shirt boasted an enormous lobster. She made me block the non-kosherness by holding a menu in front of me while we were at the table.

I spent all day Saturday with her adorable daughters and need to write about one of my classic calamities. Both girls (Rachel Sarah and Eliana) go to Yeshiva and are constantly talking about things that they think I understand but have *no idea* about since I went to public school. A few years ago, I was talking to Rachel Sarah and asked her if she was excited about going into fourth grade. Rachel Sarah said that she was, but this year was different because they have to "learn *Neesach*." I had a vague idea that *neesach* was maybe something to do with a prayer on Saturdays, so I decided to give her some confidence and said, "You're so smart! You can do it!" Then Rachel Sarah randomly said, "My neighbor gave me a pear," and I thought, "That's so sweet! It's like those children from the 1920s who would get an orange for Christmas and think it was an amazing gift." I stayed on the fruit theme and replied, "You know, when I lived in Brooklyn, I used to have a peach tree!" She mumbled goodbye and handed the phone to my sister. Nancy heard the whole conversation and asked me what the H I was talking about. Huh? I haughtily said that I was being a supportive/fascinating uncle. No. Turns out, Rachel Sarah didn't say that this year she had to learn *neesach*, she said that this year she had to "wear knee socks"! To which my incongruous reply was "You're smart! You can do it!" Huh? Rachel Sarah didn't then tell me about the new pear she got but instead continued talking about socks and said, "My neighbor gave me a *pair*." My non-sequitur reply was, "When I lived in Brooklyn, I used to have a peach tree." WHAT? I'm sure she was wracking her nine-year-old brain trying to find a connection 'til she finally threw the phone in horror towards her mother.

Back to *Shrek*. I must declare: Sutton Foster is a gift to Broadway. She literally can do *anything*. She's such a great actress, such a great comedian and a brilliant belt-ress. *Plus*, she's an actual dancer, not just a moves-well-er. (She was one of the dancers in the national tour of *The Will Rogers Follies* when she was a senior in high school.) Her career is like one of those

Broadway stars from the '50s: a new leading role every two years. And I love how she remains on Broadway and hasn't done the annoying "I'm moving to L.A. to do film and television." *um... 'til BUNHEADS. But then she came back!* One of my favorite Sutton stories involves her famous family. Her actor/writer brother Hunter is married to dancer/comedienne Jen Cody (also in *Shrek*). When Sutton first came to visit Hunter in New York, Hunter and Jen (and I) were doing *Grease!* on Broadway. There was an open call, and Sutton told Jen and Hunter that she was going to give it a shot, got her 16 bars in her hands and breezed out of the apartment. Jen remembers shaking her head and commenting to Hunter, with a know-it-all Broadway attitude, "Sutton needs to learn that you don't just show up at your first New York open call and immediately get cast" — and, essentially, before she was finished talking, Sutton ran back into the apartment screaming, "I got it!" Busted!

More lauding. Brian d'Arcy James was great as Shrek and sang up a storm on all of his songs. Speaking of singing up a storm, Brian told me that he was once at an audition, belting out his audition song. He hit a high note at the end, and as soon as he did, he was mortified at how booming he sounded and how inappropriate it was for such a small room. So instead of holding the note for the full 16 counts, he cut himself off after 13 beats and sang (on the same pitch), "*Too loud!*" to make a joke and acknowledge that he was aware of how crazy he sounded. He finished with a big smile and was met by a sea of blank faces. He did not get the gig. *A few years later, I filmed him recreating the audition for an OBSESSED video. Watch it! He's hi-lar.*

After *Shrek*, I went backstage with Juli and, as we were walking into Brian's dressing room, I heard someone on a speakerphone. We entered the room and I realized that the person speaking was Brian and saw that the reason it sounded like he was on a speakerphone was because his head was underneath a towel! As he gets his mask/make-up off every night, a warm towel is put over his head every few minutes to help steam off the green make-up. It's annoying, but his skin looks amazing!

I gained a massive amount of weight while in Houston and, upon returning, scheduled an emergency training session at my gym. I went two days after Christmas day, and right next to me was Donna McKechnie. Wow, I thought. It *is* "Turkey Lurkey Time"! She said that I was looking very built (I still got it!), and then she said that I was "ruining my image." I loved her comment 'til I began to think about what image I was ruining. Hmm... apparently, someone out of shape. She, of course, looked great and is about to star in *Steppin' Out* in Naples, Florida. I'm always asking her for *Chorus Line* info, and I loved finding out that while most of the dancers in that original cast were acting out their lives, her story was mostly given to the character of Maggie. Donna is the one who used to "dance around the living room with my arms up." Donna's family thought she was putting her arms up above her head to look like a ballet dancer (in high 5th position), but she told me that her arms were like that because she was imagining putting them all the way up on her partner's shoulders. Speaking of *A Chorus Line*, I just remembered a hilarious story that Kelly Bishop told me during a *Chatterbox*. She won the Tony Award for playing Sheila and if you've ever listened to the cast album, you'd know that she's not what you'd call a "high belter." A few years after *A Chorus Line*, she had an audition and was very nervous about hitting the high notes in the song. She finally got her nerve up, walked into the audition room and sang. She finished the song, they thanked her and after she walked out of the room, she turned to her pianist and beamed saying, "Wow! That wasn't so difficult to sing after all! I hardly had any trouble hitting the high notes." He looked at her and said, "Kelly. You sang the whole song down an octave." I love how, even one full octave down, she "hardly" had any trouble hitting the high notes.

And, finally, here's the update on James' mom. She began chemo last week… and had no side effects! She literally danced a jig when we came to pick her up. Juli is still down in Texas visiting with her, so James and I are going to see lots of shows this week because we don't have to hire a babysitter. Delicious! New Year's Eve will be a game night at my place, and then New Year's Day will be the traditional pancakes at Julia Murney's. Okay, everyone, as we said in elementary school and thought was hilarious: See you next year!

Keep an eye out for Seth's Broadway Diary, Volume 2 in 2015...

Acknowledgements

Thank you to…

David Friedman who told me after a performance in the late '90's that it was great to watch me interact with celebs onstage because I'm such a fan. It inspired me to do my own talk show.

Richie Jackson who told me to do said talk show live every week, hence *Seth's Broadway Chatterbox*.

Sidney Meyer and everyone at Don't Tell Mama for letting me do the *Chatterbox* there since 1999.

Mike Peters for hiring me at Sirius.

Seth Bisen-Hirsch for filming so many *Chatterboxes*.

Frank Conway for coming to Don't Tell Mama on so many Thursday nights.

Christie Ford for being the *Chatterbox* DVD and website maven.

Rob Johnston for being my photographer so many times.

Phil Birsh for hiring me at Playbill.com and Andrew Gans for editing my column every week and coming up with those sassy titles.

Tiffany Grant for re-editing the columns.

Joey Monda for foisting this idea on me.

Ross Cohen, Ben Lerner and Travis Amiel… my dream team of interns in the summer of '14.

Proof readers extraordinaire Sierra Fox, Jen Hoguet, Ann Harada and Hannah Ehrenberg

Brisa Trinchero and Roberta Pereira for saying yes to this book and working so hard to make it good.

ALL the Broadway folk who told me amazing/hilarious/inspiring/mortifying stories.

And, finally, this book would not have happened without the guidance, ideas and harrassment of my sweet husband James. Truly.

Also From Dress Circle Publishing

By Jennifer Ashley Tepper
Untold Stories of Broadway Volume 1
Untold Stories of Broadway Volume 2

By Ruby Preston:
Showbiz
Staged
Broadway Academy

By Jeremy Scott Blaustein
The Home For Wayward Ladies

By Joanna Parson
Emily's Tour Diary: And Other Tragedies of the Stage (2014 Release)

Founded in 2011 by Brisa Trinchero and Roberta Pereira, Dress Circle Publishing is commited to taking readers "behind the curtain" through our catalog of books about Broadway written by members of the Broadway community.

Dress Circle Publising
www.dresscirclepublishing.com

Made in the USA
Middletown, DE
06 January 2017